The Polar Bear's Fake M
Sophie Stern

Shifters of Rawr County: Books 1-3

Sophie Stern

Published by Sophie Stern, 2023.

This is a work of fiction. Similarities to real people, places, or events are entirely coincidental.

SHIFTERS OF RAWR COUNTY: BOOKS 1-3

First edition. January 27, 2023.

Written by Sophie Stern.

Also by Sophie Stern

Alien Chaos
Destroyed
Guarded
Saved
Christmas on Chaos
Alien Chaos: A Sci-Fi Alien Romance Bundle

Aliens of Malum
Deceived: An Alien Brides Romance
Betrayed: An Alien Brides Romance
Fallen: An Alien Brides Romance
Captured: An Alien Brides Romance
Regret
Crazed
For Keeps
Rotten: An Alien Brides Romance

Anchored
Starboard
Battleship

All Aboard
Abandon Ship
Below Deck
Crossing the Line
Anchored: Books 1-3
Anchored: Books 4-6

Ashton Sweets
Christmas Sugar Rush
Valentine's Sugar Rush
St. Patty's Sugar Rush
Halloween Sugar Rush

Bullies of Crescent Academy
You Suck
Troublemaker
Jaded

Club Kitten Dancers
Move
Pose
Climb

Dragon Enchanted
Hidden Mage
Hidden Captive

Hidden Curse

Fate High School
You Wish: A High School Reverse Harem Romance
Freak: A Reverse Harem High School Romance
Get Lost: A Reverse Harem Romance

Good Boys and Millionaires
Good Boys and Millionaires 1
Good Boys and Millionaires 2

Grimalkin Needs Brides
Ekpen (Intergalactic Dating Agency)
Torao (Intergalactic Dating Agency)
Leo (Intergalactic Dating Agency)

Honeypot Babies
The Polar Bear's Baby
The Jaguar's Baby
The Tiger's Baby

Honeypot Darlings
The Bear's Virgin Darling
The Bear's Virgin Mate
The Bear's Virgin Bride

Office Gentlemen
Ben From Accounting

Polar Bears of the Air Force
Staff Sergeant Polar Bear
Master Sergeant Polar Bear
Airman Polar Bear
Senior Airman Polar Bear

Return to Dragon Isle
Dragons Are Forever
Dragon Crushed: An Enemies-to-Lovers Paranormal Romance
Dragon's Hex
Dragon's Gain
Dragon's Rush

Rose Valley Vampires
Vampire Librarian

Shifters at Law
Wolf Case
Bearly Legal
Tiger Clause
Sergeant Bear

Dragon Law

Shifters of Rawr County
The Polar Bear's Fake Mate
The Lion's Fake Wife
The Tiger's Fake Date
The Wolf's Pretend Mate
The Tiger's Pretend Husband
The Dragon's Fake Fiancée
The Red Panda's Fake Mate

Stormy Mountain Bears
The Lumberjack's Baby Bear
The Writer's Baby Bear
The Mountain Man's Baby Bears

Sweet Nightmares
Sweet Nightmares: The Vampire's Melody
Sweet Nightmares 2: The Sound of Roses

Team Shifter
Bears VS Wolves
No Fox Given

The Fablestone Clan

Dragon's Oath
Dragon's Breath
Dragon's Darling
Dragon's Whisper
Dragon's Magic

The Feisty Dragons
Untamed Dragon
Naughty Dragon
Monster Dragon

The Hidden Planet
Vanquished
Outlaw
Conquered

The Wolfe City Pack
The Wolf's Darling
The Wolf's Mate
The Wolf's Bride

Standalone
Saucy Devil
Billionaire on Top
Jurassic Submissive
The Editor

Alien Beast

Snow White and the Wolves

Kissing the Billionaire

Wild

Alien Dragon

The Royal Her

Be My Tiger

Alien Monster

The Luck of the Wolves

Honeypot Babies Omnibus Edition

Honeypot Darlings: Omnibus Edition

The Swan's Mate

The Feisty Librarian

Polar Bears of the Air Force

Wild Goose Chase

Star Princess

The Virgin and the Lumberjacks

Resting Bear Face

By Hook or by Wolf

I Dare You, King

Shifters at Law

Pretty Little Fairies

Seized by the Dragon

The Fablestone Clan: A Paranormal Dragon-Shifter Romance
Collection

Star Kissed

Big Bad Academy

Club Kitten Omnibus

Stormy Mountain Bears: The Complete Collection

Bitten by the Vampires

Beautiful Villain

Dark Favors

Savored

Vampire Kiss

Chaotic Wild: A Vampire Romance

Bitten

Heartless

The Dragon's Christmas Treasure

Out of the Woods

Bullies of Crescent Academy

Craving You: A Contemporary Romance Collection

Chasing Whiskey

The Hidden Planet Trilogy

The Bratty Dom

Tokyo Wolf

The Single Dad Who Stole My Heart

Free For Him

The Feline Gaze

Fate High School

Dragon Beast: A Beauty and the Beast Retelling

Boulder Bear

Megan Slays Vampires

Vampire Professor

Once Upon a Shift

The Feisty Dragons

The Vampire Who Saved Christmas

Dragon Enchanted (Books 1-3)

Grimalkin Needs Brides (Intergalactic Dating Agency): Books 1-3

Nerd Alert

Red: Into the Dark

Alien Darlings

Shifters of Rawr County: Books 4-7

Shifters of Rawr County: Books 1-3

Table of Contents

Justin

You'd think that with a backstory like mine, the idea of taking a mate is unbelievable.

You'd be right.

The only reason I'm agreeing to this entire "mates" thing is so that my mother gets off my back, my shareholders are happy, and I continue moving forward in my career. I'm the face of a multi-billion dollar company. I don't need any scandals in my midst.

REBECCA

The offer is for one year. One year of pretending to be this guy's mate, and then we can have a quiet divorce. He just needs his shareholders off of his back, and me? Well, I'd like to not starve to death.

Only, there's more than meets the eye when it comes to Justin. He might have money and brains and incredibly good looks, but there's a secret that lurks behind those beautiful eyes.

And I intend to find out what it is.

THE POLAR BEAR'S FAKE MATE is the first book in SHIFTERS OF RAWR COUNTY: a new shifter series from Sophie Stern. There is no cheating and a guaranteed HEA for our happy couple.

1

For my Jack Cat

Author's note: this story takes place in Rawr County, Colorado. While this is sadly a fictional location, my love of the mountains is anything but fictional. I had the incredible chance to live in Colorado for a few years with my husband and we spent many hours driving through the mountains, listening to music, and just enjoying ourselves. It's my hope that this story will make you laugh, make you gasp, and hopefully, make you forget about life's troubles for a little while. Now, put on some music and turn the page so we can begin our adventure...

1

Justin

"This sounds like an ultimatum," I said to my mother.

"That's because it is," she spoke quietly, pushing the paper in my general direction. She didn't need to. I could read it perfectly well from my seat at the conference room table. I didn't need her finely painted nails shoving the paper even closer to me. I stared at the stupid thing with disdain. Surely, she couldn't be serious.

Only, I knew even as I looked at the document and then back up at my mother that this was going to happen. Whether I wanted to deal with it or not was irrelevant. My mother's wishes were crystal clear.

"Why now?" I asked quietly, but I didn't need to. I already knew the answer, after all. Our company's shareholders were displeased. They didn't like the idea that the man in charge of the company – the face of the company, if you will – was a bit of a playboy.

Okay, a lot of a playboy.

The problem I had with the entire situation was that I wasn't. I didn't have a lot of time for dating, partying, or fun in general. While I may have been extroverted and wild in my youth, I wasn't that way anymore. Now, I was almost hyper-focused on work, which meant that the shareholders didn't need to worry. Only, they did.

"You know why," she said. Mother looked at me like she pitied me, and I kind of hated that. I was 32. I was old enough to decide whether I wanted to get married or not, yet she was looking at me like I was some sad, lost puppy who had just gotten kicked.

"The shareholders meeting," I muttered, frowning.

Of course, that was it. Our shareholders were older, conservative adults who liked the traditional things in life. They couldn't bear the thought of someone wanting to unwind a little or have a little fun. They also couldn't accept the idea that a young, professional adult might want to go get laid from time to time.

"They saw the pictures," she said. "It doesn't look good for business."

Of course, there were pictures.

Weren't there always?

The problem was that I hadn't done anything wrong. I was never the person in the pictures, but nobody seemed to believe that. The entire "once a playboy, always a playboy" idea was something nobody was ready to give up.

"The pictures were faked," I told my mother for what felt like the thousandth time. They were always faked. Someone who looked very much like me had gone on a wild partying spree. We both knew the pictures in question this time weren't even remotely accurate because the person in them had been drinking cherry vodka, and as my mother knew, I was violently allergic to cherries.

"I know that," she said, "but they don't."

Of course, the shareholders didn't know about my severe allergy. No one did.

For some reason, my mother had felt it necessary to hide my allergies from the world. As a child, she'd been worried about me being treated differently. As an adult, she worried that revealing my secret would mean someone could hurt me or the company.

She'd been doing this dance of secrecy for so long that it now felt almost impossible to reveal the truth. The problem was that if anyone happened to discover my inability to consume cherries or cherry flavoring, they could potentially use that against me. My mother was rightfully worried about someone poisoning me and trying to take over the business.

I understood that, logically, but in a case like this, I felt like revealing the truth could be beneficial. Explaining to the people invested in the company that I took the future of my father's legacy seriously could alter their perception of me for the better.

"Look, Rawr County needs you," my mother told me. "This company needs you."

"I think this is bullshit," I pointed out. "We can just release my medical records," I said. "We can release them and let the world know. There's not much of a reason to keep them secret anymore."

"Please," she shook her head. She was never going to budge. Not on this, anyway, and I knew why.

My mother didn't want me to be seen as weak. Even though humans knew about shifters and we didn't exactly live off in the woods, the reality was that humans were very, very scared of shifters. A CEO shifter was a scary thing. A shifter with allergies was even worse.

"Mom, don't you think it's time?" I raised an eyebrow, staring at her. This was something we'd kept secret for years, after all. In my opinion, it was time to just let people know who – and what – I was. Most of the shifters in Rawr County knew that I was able to transform myself into a polar bear, but somehow, sharing the fact that I had allergies seemed much more personal.

My mother looked at me sadly, and that was when I realized there was something else, something that she hadn't told me. I realized that this entire meeting with her was about more than the shareholders. There was something else that had her worked up.

"Mom?" I reached my hand out to hers, ignoring the paper that sat on the table between us. For the first time since my father passed away, my mother didn't seem completely put-together. In fact, she seemed a little scared.

"It's the cancer," she said quietly. "It's back."

There were very few moments in my life where I felt like everything stood still, but that was one of those moments. It was like my entire world paused, everything went silent, and I couldn't move or breathe. I must have heard her incorrectly because this couldn't be right. There was absolutely no chance that this could be right.

"No," I whispered. "It's gone. It's gone. They said it wasn't going to come back."

She shrugged and pulled her hand away. Digging around in her tiny Coach purse, she pulled out an actual handkerchief and dabbed at her eyes. Ever a lady, she somehow managed to do this without smearing her makeup even slightly.

"I don't have a lot of time," she said, placing her hands down in her lap. I was stunned with how normal she looked all of a sudden, how frail. My mother was many things, but never weak. "Please, Justin. Please do this for me."

I stared at her. So, this was it, was it? I had quite a decision to make, and it wasn't exactly going to be an easy one. She wasn't just asking me to keep my allergy a secret, but do some damage control for the company. She was asking me to take a bride to prove that I could be responsible and contained.

Would I do this for my mother?

Would I marry some random woman if it meant giving the company new life?

Would I marry someone so that my mother could see my wedding – albeit a fake one – before she passed away?

When I looked at the woman who had given birth to me, the woman who had always been there for me my entire life, I realized that there was only one possible answer. She had looked after me, guarding me, for what seemed like an eternity. After my father passed away, she'd worked even harder to make sure that the company ran smoothly until I was able to take it over. We'd had plenty of help along the way. My assistant, Phil, had been incredible. Our marketing director, Heather, had been a huge support. My mom, however, had been the rock we all stood on throughout that entire time.

So, could I do it?

Yeah.

I'd do it.

I'd do anything for my mom.

"Of course," I whispered, nodding. "Of course."

My mother let out a huge sigh of relief. I could instantly see her entire body relax. She'd been worried, apparently, but she didn't need to be. I wasn't always the best son. I knew that. I also wasn't the type of person who was going to slack out of responsibilities just because I didn't feel like I needed to obey some set of unwritten rules.

"Thank you," she whispered.

I nodded. I reached for my mom's hand and gripped it. I didn't get up and walk around to hug her. We were in a conference room that had clear glass walls, and anyone could see. If I were to get up and hug my mom, someone would know there was a problem, and this entire situation was all about resolving problems – not making bigger ones.

"Anything for you," I told her.

"We need to make a plan," she said, and I was slightly surprised she didn't already have something in mind.

"A plan?"

"For finding you a mate."

"Ah."

So, it was happening now. It was happening like, right now. My mother had decided that I needed to find someone to marry ASAP, and it was literally going to happen right now. All of a sudden, I was going from being a bachelor to getting ready to plan a wedding, and I didn't even have a girl in mind.

"What do we need to do?" I asked. The sooner we got started, the better. I wasn't sure how long it would take whoever was faking pictures of me to stop, but hopefully, once the board of directors and the shareholders alike began to see me being calm and directed with a fiancé on my arm, they'd calm down immensely. At the very least, it was going to help my mother feel like she could depend on me to do anything for the company.

"You aren't going to fight me on this?"

"No, I am not going to fight you on this."

"I'm surprised," she eyed me suspiciously. I deserved that, I supposed. I was generally much feistier when it came to stating my demands and opinions. Rarely did I ever give in like I was today. My inability to change my mind seemed to cause me problems in my personal life, but in the business world, it meant I was determined and dependable: a man of my word.

"Mom, let's just get this started. I'm sure you've thought of everything."

She always did. That was one of the best things about her. Rita Honey wasn't afraid to go all out when it came to planning. That was probably the biggest reason our company had succeeded for as long as it had. She and my father started the Honey Bear Software company when I was just a baby. Neither one of them could have possibly imagined that it would grow to be as big as it was.

After my dad passed away, my mom took over the company, and after college, I joined her. She stepped back a few years ago when she was diagnosed with cancer for the first time, and I was pretty much the face of the company now. Only, I couldn't imagine life without her. I couldn't imagine a world that didn't have my mom in it.

"I may have considered a few options," she said quietly. I was sure that she had. Most people don't just wake up one day and propose that their child go pretend to love someone. In general, parents tended to discourage lying. My parent was trying to convince me that it was the only thing to do.

"So, I'm not sure how to do this discreetly," I told her. "I assume that discretion is going to be key here." When I dated, I always kept things low-key and simple. My mom was now trying to arrange an entire *marriage*, though, and while I would obviously be seen in public and go to special events with the woman I chose, I didn't need people suspecting that our relationship was anything less than totally committed.

"Absolutely," she nodded. "We don't want anyone to suspect, even for a moment, that this marriage is a sham."

"Of course not," I said drily.

If that happened, the entire thing would fall apart, wouldn't it? The goal was for the world to see me and my bride together, view us as a happy couple, and stop paying attention to any sensationalized media coverage regarding us. They needed to know we were "real," so they couldn't believe, even for a second, that we had met under less than favorable circumstances.

"I made a list of ways we can vet potential women," my mother told me. She handed me another piece of paper, and I fought to keep from rolling my eyes. The initial "get married or get out of the company" document she'd given me was one thing, but this felt like something else entirely.

"Is it really *secure* to be writing this down?"

"It'll do for now. We'll shred this before we leave," she said, nodding her head toward a shredder that sat in the corner of the room. Most of the time, I used it for getting rid of silly documents that weren't needed after a discussion amongst other employees.

"Fine," I nodded, and I started reading over the ideas.

It seemed as though my mother had thought of everything. She was well aware that the woman we selected would need to be someone who could be discreet. The person would have to agree to date me for a very, very brief amount of time, attend events with me during our engagement, have a highly publicized wedding, and then stay married – albeit quietly – for at least one year.

After a year had passed, we could quietly separate, and then after another year, we could legally divorce. She would receive a hefty payment at the time of our divorce, as well as a very generous allowance each month that would provide for her clothing, makeup, hair, and personal needs.

It all seemed really straightforward and almost cold in its raw exchange.

It also kind of felt strange.

In some ways, it seemed as though I was nothing more than a viewer, a watcher. It seemed like I was looking in on my own life as choices and decisions were made for me. I understood why, and I had agreed to them, but it still felt strange.

"You'll run...an ad?" I finally looked up from the paper in front of me. Was that really how she wanted me to find someone? An ad? Like, a personal ad?

"Yes."

"And it won't be local," I continued.

"Absolutely not. We'll vet the women who apply over the phone and online. If they pass the background check and the phone interview, we'll fly in our favorites to a city of your choosing.

That will enable you to meet them in person and you'll have total say over the woman you choose."

"I like the idea of it being a remote location," I agreed. "That way, there won't even be an inkling as to who I am or what this is really about."

"Absolutely," my mother nodded. "Despite your publicity and moderate amount of fame, I don't think most of these women will recognize you, especially if you wear a hat or something like that."

I rolled my eyes.

A hat.

Okay, Mom.

I wasn't sure that something like wearing a hat would mean people wouldn't recognize me, but I did agree that the only people who cared significantly about my behavior tended to be local citizens and then people in the business world. Wherever I ended up going to meet this potential mate of mine, I couldn't imagine we'd be followed significantly or harassed at the meeting point.

"All right," I told my mom. "Let's run the ad. Let's find me a wife."

2

Rebecca

"WANTED: ONE BRIDE."

I read the line three different times before I realized that it wasn't some sort of weird, sick joke. Someone really did want a bride, and from the looks of it, it sounded like they were going to pay for the privilege.

Glancing over my shoulder to make sure nobody noticed me looking at the newspaper ad, I read it one more time for good measure. Despite the three cups of coffee I'd already consumed that day, I still couldn't really get over the ad. It seemed fake, but it looked real.

WANTED: ONE BRIDE
FOR A CONTRACT PERIOD OF ONE YEAR.
PAY: NEGOTIATBLE
HANDSOME MAN IN NEED OF LEGAL BRIDE
FOR THE PERIOD OF ONE YEAR. SEX NOT
REQUIRED. EMAIL
MARRYMEFORONEYEAR@MORTLEGAL.COM

I looked it over again, and then again, and then again. How could something like this be legal? Wasn't this illegal? You couldn't like, pay someone to marry you...could you? It sure as hell felt illegal. If that was the case, though, then why was I so drawn to this particular ad? Out of everything that was happening in the world around me today, I'd chosen the personal ads to hone in on.

The waitress approached my table, and I closed the newspaper quickly. Word spread fast in this town, and I didn't need anyone to know I'd been reading weird ads. Besides, I was a little embarrassed about the fact that I was so interested in it.

"More coffee, honey?" The woman's nametag read SUSIE which seemed about right. She was petite with soft curly hair pulled back in a ponytail, and her uniform was strangely clean and crisp for working in a diner. I was blown away that Susie was able to keep everything so put together. I knew for a fact that if I was the one waitressing, I would have spilled about seven pots of coffee on myself by now.

"Yes, please," I murmured, pushing my mug a little closer to her.

She grabbed the mug, poured the coffee, and glanced at the newspaper. She couldn't possibly know what I was looking at before she walked over, yet she was definitely curious about it. I didn't blame her. I wasn't a regular at this place, and I was basically drinking a week's wages worth of coffee. It was pretty weird, and even for me, that was saying something.

"Job hunting?" Susie looked at me with something resembling pity on her face, and I simply nodded. I was, technically. I needed a job. I needed anything.

"Something like that," I said.

"Good luck," she patted me on the shoulder. "It's cutthroat out there."

She didn't know the half of it.

The truth was that I had exactly one month to get my shit together. Earl, my roommate, was getting married. He and his new husband wanted to leave the country and go teach English abroad for a few years, so they were packing up all of their stuff and shoving it in storage. They'd offered to let me store my stuff with theirs, but I didn't really have much.

I had collected books during my undergrad, but I'd sold them to help pay for my graduate tuition. I'd also needed to save on space. The apartment I shared with Early was neat and tidy, but unfortunately, there wasn't a lot of room for books. I tried to make it a habit to buy all future books digitally, but I still sometimes bought the occasional paperback.

"You aren't wrong," I told Susie. "Finding something feels impossible sometimes."

"My daughter has been looking for three months," Susie shook her head. She sounded frustrated and sad about this, and I couldn't really blame her. "I told her that if she can't find anything, she can come work here, but you know how it goes. Shifts are unpredictable and the hours aren't regular."

"I'm sorry to hear that," I told Susie. I made a mental note to leave a good tip. After all, I was basically subsisting on free coffee refills at this point. The two slices of toast I'd ordered had been good, but I wasn't exactly running up a huge ticket for the amount of time I'd been sitting in the booth.

"Well, I'm sure she'll figure it all out," Susie shrugged. "Good luck to you, sugar."

She turned and left, heading back behind the counter to work on her other orders, and I turned back to the newspaper. Was it crazy for me to even be thinking about responding to this ad? Earl had offered to let me come abroad with him and Gabe, but that felt a little weird and slightly invasive.

Their lives should be their own, I thought, and that was okay.

I'd recently graduated with my master's degree and even though I'd been planning to get a job in my field – English Literature – it was proving to be harder than I thought. Apparently, all of the other recent English graduates also wanted to teach composition at the high school level, which meant finding a position was proving to be...

Well, not easy.

In a month, my lease would be up. Before that happened, I needed a job, a home, and something to live for. I'd been toying with the idea of getting a cat, but this seemed much more interesting, albeit slightly crazier.

I took a deep breath.

Was I seriously considering this?

Who the hell put an ad like this in the paper?

And who the hell considered accepting it?

On a whim, I pulled out my phone and typed out an email.

Hello! Are you still accepting applications for a wife?
I'm interested in this opportunity. What information do you need?

I hit "send" before I could talk myself out of it.

It was a stupid idea, really. Stupid. Only, as I paid my bill, left a tip, and headed out of the diner where I'd been enjoying far too many cups of coffee, I wondered whether or not it really was as crazy as I thought.

I didn't have anywhere else to be, after all. I needed money. I needed something to do. I wasn't dating anyone, so it wasn't like I needed to break up with anyone in order to make this work. The only thing I needed, it seemed, was a willingness to be weird.

I could do that, I thought.

I could do that.

"THEY WANT ME," I SAID, staring at my phone. It was a week after that first email to the strange, scammy bridal ad. I'd sent in my resume, participated in a really boring run-of-the-mill phone interview, and then I'd tried to just forget about the entire thing because it was nuts.

Only, maybe it wasn't so nuts after all.

They'd called me. It wasn't the guy. I still hadn't talked to him yet. Apparently, there was some sort of screening process. Whoever was arranging the marriage had performed a background check, gone over my personal history, and asked me a lot of seemingly random questions to make sure I was good at keeping a secret. I wasn't sure who this person was, but I had the feeling he was either very famous or very rich to need a non-crazy wife for a year.

"What do you mean?" Earl asked, looking over at me.

"Who wants you?" Gabe, his soon-to-be-husband, was sitting on his lap.

The three of us had been hanging out, enjoying a chilly afternoon, when the email arrived. I was currently sprawled out on my belly on the living room floor on our worn-out apartment rug. When I saw what the email said, I jumped up to a sitting position and stared at it. I really just couldn't believe it.

"The guy," I said. "The bridal ads guy."

"The murderer?" Gabe shrieked, gawking at me. He was staring at me like I just told him I'd accidentally eaten shellfish – which I was deathly allergic to – or like I was telling him that *I* was a murderer. Neither of those things had happened. It was *just* an email.

"I'm sure it won't be so bad," Earl said, casually smiling at Gabe. Earl reached out and tousled Gabe's hair playfully. "Maybe he's a nice murderer."

"He's not a murderer," I told them both, but it wasn't really like I could know that for sure. This was happening pretty fast, actually, and even though I'd kind of tried to push it to the back of my mind, the realization that I had been invited to an "in person" interview was a bit overwhelming. I had a good feeling. I didn't think the groom-to-be was going to be a total creeper or anything, but I was still nervous. I was just some book nerd from the Midwest. What the hell did I know about being a wife?

"What did the email say?" Gabe pressed, trying to get me to share more details. That was really typical of Gabe. He was always the careful planner. He liked analyzing things and pondering them carefully. Earl was the one who was wild and playful and spontaneous. There was a reason Earl and I had been such great roommates during my graduate studies. We were both a little reckless from time to time.

"It says that I passed the phone interview," I said. "That wasn't really a shock, though. I thought I did okay on that part."

"Didn't you say it was boring, anyway?" Earl piped up, cocking his head. "That it was mostly really basic stuff?"

"Yeah," I nodded. "So boring. They probably wanted to make sure that *I'm* not a murderer." During the phone interview, they mostly asked me questions about my job, whether I owned any property or real estate, and what my personal relationships were like. "I think they mostly wanted to know whether I secretly had any kids or a current spouse who might be upset if I up and married someone new."

"So what happens now?" Gabe looked over at Earl, and then back at me. "What? You just fly off and meet the guy? How does this work? I'm not supporting the idea, by the way," he clarified. "I still think this is crazy."

"It might be a little crazy," I agreed. "But it's something weird and unusual and new. Who knows? It could be fun."

"Fun?" Earl laughed.

"Planning a wedding?" Gabe shook his head.

"What are you talking about? You're eloping!"

"Yeah, because wedding planning sucks," Gabe told me.

"Sucks," Earl echoed.

"Okay," I shrugged. "Well, what do I have to lose?"

"Your life, if he's truly a murderer," Earl pointed out.

"They want me to come to this resort," I said. "It's for a weekend. It's all-inclusive, and there are going to be two other applicants there."

"Sounds like some sort of bad dating show," Earl rolled his eyes.

"A little bit," I nodded. "But it'll let me meet the guy before I agree and sign any papers. I mean, if I get there and he's a total freak, I don't have to go through with it, but what if he's really nice? I've never heard of anything like this happening before. It could be my chance to have an adventure."

I didn't add *because you two are leaving without me.*

Not that I wanted to go with Earl and Gabe. They deserved to find their own happiness. It was just that I wanted something special of my own, too. I wanted to have an adventure that was just for me. So much of my life had been carefully planned and meticulously cultivated. This was going to be an opportunity for me to do something totally unexpected and wonderful.

Earl stared at me for a minute, considering everything I'd said. "You really want to do this, don't you?"

"A little," I nodded. I couldn't really explain why. It was like I finally felt like I had something weird and special and cool that I got to try. It seemed like I finally had something a little unusual and a little strange that nobody else could take from me.

"Why?"

"Because it's something new and different."

Earl laughed and shook his head.

"You're crazy," Gabe pointed out.

"Maybe," I agreed.

Maybe I was crazy, but I was going to do it.

I was.

I was going to go.

"I'm going," I said firmly. "But don't worry. If you guys haven't gone too far by the time the wedding bells toll, I'll invite you to the wedding."

Earl laughed. "I can't wait."

3

Justin

WITHIN A WEEK OF MY mother telling me I had to find a bride or she'd transfer control of the company to someone who could do a better job, I was getting ready to meet three potential mates. It was a strange sort of situation, to be sure. I still wasn't sure if it was crazy or not, but it was happening whether I liked it or not, so I realized I should probably make the most of it.

On Friday afternoon, I was busy finalizing a couple of business meetings for the next week when Phil, one of my assistants, came into my office.

"Did you see the pictures from last weekend?" Phil held his phone out to me.

"I'm not looking at your phone, Phil."

"There are a couple of new photos out that show you partying with Basil Dixon. Isn't he your best friend?" Phil looked at me, blinking innocently, as though I didn't know what he was doing.

Basil Dixon was one of my favorite people in the world, yet we almost never talked anymore. While I had really buckled down and started taking the company seriously after my father passed away, Basil had partied more than me. He'd also had a lot more fun than me.

"Did you need something, Phil? Or did you just come to gossip?" I started arranging papers on my desk. I looked away from Phil as I did.

"No, I guess not," he muttered. He turned and left the room, walking sullenly out of it. I knew I probably shouldn't have flipped him quite so much shit, but I was tired, and I was already unhappy having to deal with this many meetings after coming back from a weekend of bridal shopping...literally.

"Knock-knock," Mike Parsons, one of my programmers, knocked on my open office door.

"You don't have to say knock-knock," I called out, still focused on one of the sheets of paper on my desk. It had a suggested schedule for Monday. I wasn't sure why it had been printed out and hand-delivered to me instead of emailed.

"Sorry," he said. "Busy?"

"Never too busy for you, Mike," I looked up. "What can I do you for?"

Mike Parsons was a nice guy. He was a shifter, too, like me, although we never talked about that at work. Shifters had incredible senses of scent, and I could tell. My guess would be that he was a lion, like my old buddy Basil, or perhaps some sort of big cat.

"Just got word that the next distribution for Cougar Data is all set to go," he told me. "We'll start sending them their product codes first thing Monday morning."

"Fantastic," I said. "Thanks for handling all of that. Everything went seamlessly at the meeting today?"

"Absolutely. Best as could be expected."

We chatted for a few minutes about our families. Our mothers were still casual acquaintances who met for coffee or tea a few times each month. They loved to gossip as much as any other shifters did. Then I bid him farewell and headed home for the night.

It was time to start getting packed and preparing myself for a long weekend of dating different women. We were going to meet at a resort, which was a fairly neutral location, I thought. It was a place where nobody could really recognize me. Even the women I would end up regretfully rejecting wouldn't be able to figure out who I really was or where I actually worked. That meant they couldn't "out" me if they got pissed.

The resort I chose was nestled in the heart of the Dragon Mountains. Rawr County could get pretty damn cold in the winter, and I loved that about this place. I wanted to make sure that the woman I was marrying would be comfortable with cold weather. Even though it was only the first part of October, it was already cold in the Dragon Mountains, so this weekend would be a fun time of playing outdoors. We'd have time to explore some hot springs or maybe even build a snowman. I wasn't sure.

I just needed to make sure that the person I chose was going to be someone I could hang out with. When we weren't attending corporate events, and when I wasn't at work, we'd probably want to spend time together. Maybe we could watch movies or go on walks. I wasn't sure. Hopefully, I'd also be able to find someone who was a cat person. If I didn't my sweet pet, Hector, was going to flip.

To be honest, whether I wanted this marriage or not, it was going to happen. I'd never been married, but I had the feeling that if I was married to someone, we'd end up spending some time together. We'd probably end up spending a *lot* of time together.

One of the things that concerned me about this entire arrangement was the fact that there were so many girls to choose from and I knew almost nothing about any of them. Some of them had these huge, impressive resumes, while others had only cover letters and a few words about themselves.

Somehow, my attorney had managed to conduct all of the phone interviews. Despite my mother's interest in being included,

I'd politely pushed her aside for the interviews. It was bad enough that I was allowing her to pressure me into getting married. The idea that she might help choose my bride felt childish. Working with my attorney was more than satisfactory.

It had also been effective. Out of the 50 or so applicants, the two of us had managed to narrow it down to three. We'd done that by being wildly choosy. If I was on the fence about a girl, that was an automatic "no." If there was something I wasn't quite sure about, it was a "no." If she had never had a job or didn't list any hobbies, that was a "no."

I wanted someone who could be independent, after all. I worked a lot. I was gone a lot. I had a lot of things that I had to do. I needed to make sure that the person I was with could take care of themselves if they needed to. That included entertaining themselves when I wasn't around.

Now, it was go time.

I'd arrive at the resort, have lunch with one girl, have dinner with another, and then breakfast with the last girl. I'd give each person approximately three hours of my time, and I'd have to hope that was enough time to make a decision.

Somehow, I wasn't sure whether it was or not.

WHEN MY PLANE LANDED, I headed out of the airport and found my driver. Every time I went to the Dragon Mountains to visit this resort, I always used the same driver. He was an old panda shifter named Peter, and he was a kind man. He was fast, too, and most of the time, that was what I cared about.

Today, Peter had me at the resort in no time at all. Unfortunately for me, today was one day that I wasn't in such a hurry to arrive. I still felt a bit nervous and uncomfortable with the entire situation, so I felt my body dragging as we pulled up. Instead of getting out of the car right away, I stared out of the window, wondering for the millionth time what I was getting into.

"What's wrong?" Peter looked over his shoulder at me, obviously able to sense my dissatisfaction. When I visited a resort in general, I was peppy and excited. Today was probably the first time that Peter had seen me at less than my best.

"Nothing's wrong." A lie. It was a lie.

"Looks like something is wrong," he said.

"Nothing is wrong." If I repeated a lie over and over again, would it start to feel like the truth?

Peter laughed and shook his head. I knew he could tell that there was a problem. I didn't really know how he did it, but somehow, this guy always managed to figure out what an issue was. He worked his ass off day in and day out, but he didn't miss a beat.

I wasn't sure how he managed to do that. Maybe it was because he was older and wiser than me, or perhaps years of driving travelers around had given him unique insight into the world of CEOs. I didn't know.

"Okay, maybe I'm a little nervous," I said quietly, choking on the words as I spoke them. It wasn't really like me to easily admit weaknesses. In the business world, you weren't allowed to be weak. If anyone thought there was even the slightest chance of you being an easy target, you were done.

"What do you have to be nervous about?" Peter looked at me thoughtfully, as though he really couldn't understand why someone like me might be slightly nervous.

It was a valid question, perhaps. After all, what *did* I have to be nervous about? On the outside, it probably looked like I had it all. I was a shifter in my prime. If I wanted to date, I could have anyone I wanted. Money was not an issue for me, nor had it ever been. I was reasonably attractive, somewhat funny, and I felt like I had a pretty good personality.

All of that seemed to fade away, however, when I thought about the next several hours. I was about to go meet three women who were kind, compassionate, and smart. Any one of them could be my future bride. One of them definitely would be. I wasn't sure who it would be yet, but one of the women I met with was going to walk down the aisle and promise to love me for all of time.

The two of us would know that "forever" has an expiration date, but nobody else, save my mother and my attorney, would know that. I couldn't tell Peter that now. He was a kind man, and if I told him I was about to lie to the world to appease my parent, I knew he would be disappointed in me. Somehow, upsetting Peter felt about as horrible as upsetting my late father.

"I'm meeting someone special," I finally said, choosing to keep things as simple as possible. Besides, I didn't want to lie to Peter. If I only shared vague information, it would be easy not to lie. Right?

Peter let out a low breath. He said nothing, though. He just nodded.

"What?" I needed to know what he was thinking. He wasn't giving me a read, and it was driving me crazy.

"It's just that I'm happy for you," he told me, finally.

"You are?"

"I love being married," Peter smiled at me in the rearview mirror. Peter had been married to the same woman for what seemed like a million years. I'd never met his wife, but from all of the stories he'd told me over the years, she was a sweet woman who baked a mean blueberry pie. She was always packing Peter treats to take with him on the road, and he often brought extras to share with his passengers.

"I didn't say I was getting married," I pointed out. "I just said I was meeting someone special."

"Oh, I know what you said, but you have that look about you," he chuckled quietly, almost to himself.

"That look?" What exactly did he think I looked like? In my opinion, I probably looked slightly tired from the flight and a little worse for wear because I'd skipped my morning coffee, but I was willing to listen to his opinion of my appearance. Chances were that I'd heard worse, anyway.

"The kind of look a man gets before he proposes," Peter told me. "It's a little bit of nervousness mixed with excitement and a whole lot of passion."

I guessed he was probably right. Whether I wanted to or not, I was going to be proposing to one of these women quite soon. I had to meet them first, sure. I had to determine whether they were the right one for me, but yeah, then I'd be proposing.

It was a *lot* of pressure, and it was different from what I was used to. In the business world, pressure was how you got things done. If you didn't apply pressure to yourself and to the people around you, your company would quickly grow stale. Pressure kept the world moving. In my personal life, though, pressure was what seemed to make me feel like I was going to fall apart. I just wasn't ready for this.

I understood that in some ways, I was putting more of a strain on myself than I needed to. After all, this wasn't a real marriage. It wasn't going to be a "real" wedding. I could pretend all I wanted to, but at the end of the day, this entire thing was a sham. It was a fake relationship set up to fail, and it was designed to do so.

My mother had sworn me to secrecy on every level, including from my cousins. That felt a bit difficult for me. My cousins always knew everything about me, but I'd gone along with my mom and I'd promised her. I felt like it was the least I could do.

The reality was that I was probably going to have to say goodbye to my mom for the last time this year. The cancer was back, and it was killing her. It didn't have the courtesy to kill her slowly, either. Nope. This disease was ravaging my mom's body, taking whatever it wanted.

The problem with cancer was that it was like a dreadful pirate who left no survivors.

This was basically the last thing my mother was asking of me before she died. I could do this for her. She was going to have a great time doing mother-in-law things like picking out a wedding dress and choosing floral arrangements. She was going to have the best time ever. It was now or never for dear ol' mom, and I knew that I had to do this. I could do this. For her. For the company.

"I'm nervous," I told Peter.

I didn't tell him whether he was correct or not about the upcoming proposal. Even though I actually trusted him, it still wasn't a good idea to go around blabbing the truth about my arrangement with this woman. Whoever I chose was going to have to be very patient, very wonderful, and very kind. There was going to be a lot to deal with.

Once again, I knew that I was overthinking things. The woman I married didn't actually have to *be* any of these things. She just had to be able to fake it for the shareholders and any potential photographers. She could actually be a cold-hearted bitch. She could be cruel and uncaring. She could be mean. As long as she didn't act like that in public, it would be fine.

Still...

"You shouldn't be nervous," Peter told me.

"No?"

"Not at all," he shook his head. "Whoever this woman is, she's special. I can already tell."

He could, could he?

"How do you know?"

"Because you're a good man, Justin. Whoever you choose is going to be a good person."

Coming from Peter, that was probably the best compliment I'd ever gotten in my life. I pressed my lips together and nodded. His words were just the motivation I needed to finally get out of the car and go. It was time for me to do this. I had to face the music of my life. I had to get out of the vehicle and head up to the resort.

It was time.

I tipped Peter and climbed out of the car with my bag. Bidding him farewell, I waved and watched as he drove away off into the distance. I hoped he was heading home to eat some fresh blueberry pie with that mate of his.

Turning back to the resort, I looked up at the huge building in front of me. Luckily, I didn't bring a large suitcase with me, so I didn't have much to carry as I made my way up the steps to the glass doors. Instead, I had only packed an overnight bag. It was really more of a small duffel than anything else. It wasn't very businessman-like, but that was the entire point.

When I came to the Dragon Mountains, I wanted to feel like I was normal.

I wanted to feel ordinary.

I wanted to feel like I was just some guy coming in for a good time.

That's what this was going to be after all. It was just going to be a good time. Only, the bear deep inside of my growled at me as I marched up to the doors. We both knew the truth. We both knew this was going to be the hardest thing we'd ever had to do.

4

Rebecca

I STOOD AT THE FRONT desk, smiling at the receptionist like some sort of socially awkward shark. I was so nervous that I was practically shaking, but the woman helping me check in to the hotel didn't seem to mind my behavior. If anything, she seemed amused by me.

"Don't worry," the receptionist told me, looking up. "We'll get this all sorted out, okay?"

"I'm not worried," I lied. Only, I was worried. I was wildly worried. What if Earl and Gabe were right? What if I was walking right into the arms of a serial killer? What if this was some sort of rich man's elaborate game to find people to kill? It was a stupid idea to come here.

"I'm sure it's here. Could it be under another name?" She couldn't find my reservation. I had flown on Mr. Murder's dime to the Dragon Mountains, which were in the middle of *nowhere*, and I'd arrived only to discover that I didn't actually have a room waiting for me. I didn't actually have anything waiting for me.

I wasn't just worried.

I was terrified.

What the hell had gotten into my head? Why did I ever think it was a good idea to come out to a place like this? I should have listened to my friends. Hell, I should have gotten a ticket to fly overseas and teach English with them. At least I'd be using my degree instead of trying to pretend to be some rich guy's fancy wife.

My blood pressure was starting to rise and I could feel my muscles tensing. If I didn't get myself under control *fast*, I was going to need to single-handedly down a bottle of wine just to be able to sleep tonight. I took a couple of deep breaths and tried to keep smiling. Everything was going to be fine. Everything had to be fine.

"Found it," the receptionist broke into my thoughts with a smile and a chirpy sigh of relief. "Looks like you're in one of the honeymoon suites," she explained. "And it's under the name of your fiancé. I'm so sorry about that. I was checking our general reservations list first."

"Of course," I said slowly. "My fiancé."

"Mr. Ryan Reynolds and Mrs. Rebecca Reynolds? That's it, isn't it?"

Funny.

My name was Rebecca Reynolds, but I'd bet anything that wasn't the name of the guy I was meeting. Still, I was apparently dealing with a jokester, so I'd deal with it. If he'd booked the honeymoon suite, I at least knew that he actually did have money. At least *that* part of the situation wasn't a scam.

"Yeah," I said drily, trying to roll with the punches. "My fiancé's name is Ryan."

"He sounds nice," she said politely. "Congratulations to you both!"

"Thanks," I said, pressing my lips together. I hadn't said anything about my mystery man, so how could he sound nice? That wasn't important, I guessed.

I pushed my shoulders back and held my head up tall. I tried to look like a bride. What did brides look like? People always said they were "regal" or "beautiful," but never "glowing." Glowing was a word reserved for pregnancies. I definitely didn't want to look glowing today.

The receptionist handed me the key and I accepted it, relieved the entire check-in experience was about to be over. A bellhop appeared and offered to help me carry my bag, but I politely declined. I only had the one bag. It was an overnight visit: not a soiree.

"Elevators are right there," the bellhop offered. "If you change your mind about assistance, please let me know."

"Thanks," I said. "I'm sure I can manage, but I appreciate the offer." Turning toward the elevators, I pressed a button and waited for a moment. The lobby was the main floor, but the receptionist had explained that I could go downstairs to some of the restaurants if I wanted to or upstairs to the rooms. There were a ton of other amenities located on various floors, as well, but unfortunately, I wasn't really here to explore the resort.

I was only here to lock down a groom, apparently. The elevator doors slid open, and I stepped inside. There was already one passenger riding up: a man who moved politely aside as I made my way in.

Despite the fact that I was on my way to meet someone – someone I might marry – I couldn't help but notice Elevator Guy. He was dangerous, wasn't he? He seemed to take up all of the space in the elevator. The reality was that he was a normal-sized person. He wasn't especially tall or especially wide, but there was this energy about him that seemed to suck the life out of...everything.

Out of me.

"Which floor?" The man asked politely, letting me know that I hadn't pushed a button. Instead, I'd been caught gawking. Cool.

"Oh, um..." I started fumbling with my key, trying to figure out where I was supposed to go. "I'm not actually sure," I muttered, embarrassed. I could feel my cheeks flame a little as I looked at the little card. Which floor had the clerk said?

"Honeymoon Suite?"

I looked over sharply. The man was eyeing my key. He considered it for a second, and then he nodded.

"That must be the Honeymoon Suite," he said again. "That's on the 9th floor." He pressed the button and then looked back toward the door.

"How do you know that?"

"I'd recognize that keycard anywhere," he chuckled darkly.

I wasn't really sure what to make of it. Apparently, this was the kind of guy who spent a lot of time at resorts. At least, he spent a lot of time at this one.

"So, you come here often?" I asked. I knew even as I asked the question that it was definitely the stupidest thing I could say in that moment. Of course, he came here often. Of course. Of course, this guy knew all about the honeymoon suites here.

He knew all sorts of stuff.

"Often enough."

"What floor are you staying on?"

"Excuse me?"

My question seemed to surprise him, which was good. I shouldn't be the only person thrown off my game. Should I?

"You heard me."

"That's kind of a personal question."

"You didn't press a button, either," I pointed out, nodding toward the panel of little round buttons. "Isn't it only fair?"

We were already almost at the 9th floor, and the man looked at me curiously.

"Isn't what fair?"

"You know where I'm staying. Where are you going to be?"

He smiled, as though my comment intrigued him, but said nothing. When the doors opened to the 9th floor, I got out of the elevator. I turned around and looked back at the man. He waved at me and smiled, but then he pressed the button for the door to close, so I couldn't see where he was going to go. I stood there for a few minutes, watching as the elevator went up to the very top floor of the hotel. Then it went all the way back down to the lobby.

Okay, so he was a penthouse kind of guy.

Weird.

He didn't look overly wealthy. He looked...

Well, to be honest, he looked pretty ordinary.

There didn't seem to be anything crazy or wild about him. There wasn't anything about him that screamed "money" or "wealth" to me. I shrugged as I turned away from the elevator. I didn't need to worry about him, I knew. The only thing I needed to worry about was getting into my room, taking a shower, and getting ready for my date.

From the very brief amount of information that had been provided to me, this guy was going to interview the potential wives at different times. One of us was going to be the lunchtime girl, one of us was going to be the dinnertime girl, and one of us would dine with him at breakfast. I peered around for a minute before I went toward my door. I didn't see anyone else. Maybe the other girls hadn't arrived yet, or perhaps they were already in their rooms.

I headed inside and instantly, I stopped. There had to be some sort of mistake. This couldn't be happening. Not to me.

Seriously, what the hell?

This place was *gorgeous*.

Like, it was over-the-top pretty.

I stepped farther into the honeymoon suite, but it didn't feel like a normal hotel suite. It was more like a not-so-tiny apartment. In fact, it was *bigger* than the apartment I shared with Earl.

How?

I stepped into the room and started looking at *everything*. There was a huge kitchen with a dining room, and then there was a little living room. It had two couches and a fireplace and a balcony. There was another set of doors that I was certain led into a bedroom, but I was fascinated by the balcony, and I scurried over to it.

I stepped outside and the fresh air washed over me like a tidal wave of happiness. I closed my eyes for a moment, just glad to *be*. Just glad to be present.

"Wow," I whispered.

This was it.

This was where I was supposed to be.

I could feel it.

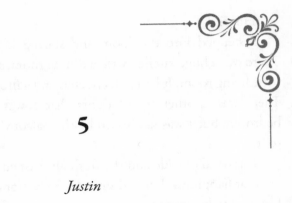

5

Justin

IT WAS HER.

She was the one.

My inner-bear started growling, clawing at me from the inside, as soon as she stepped onto the elevator. It took every ounce of my self-control not to throw myself at her right then and there. She was *everything*.

When I saw that she had one of the keys to a honeymoon suite in the resort, I knew it was going to be her. It had to be her. I didn't even need to see the other girls to know that this was the girl I wanted to be my wife.

My bear wanted her to be our mate, but I wasn't going to go that far. Not just yet. First things first. I could take things slowly.

I had to.

Rushing into a marriage was one thing but rushing into love was something else entirely. I'd never been the kind of person who just fell in love. I'd dated plenty of people, but never in the history of my love life had my bear reacted in such a way.

As soon as I got to the penthouse suite, I pulled out my phone and called my attorney, Liz. My mother and I realized quickly we'd need to bring her in on this thing, and even though Liz thought the entire arrangement was a horrible idea, she was the person who was going to help protect me and my assets during this time. She understood why my mother was urging me to do this. I'd left out the part about my mother blackmailing me into this. She was a dying woman, and I'd forgive her for that even though I probably shouldn't have.

"It's me," I told her.

"I know," she said drily. "I have caller ID, Justin. What's going on?"

Why was I calling her so soon? I'd only just arrived at the resort, after all. That was what she meant.

"I've found the person," I said. "I've found the girl."

"Already? That didn't take long."

"I'm scheduled to have lunch with her in an hour," I told Liz. It was going to be a late lunch, but that was fine. I'd paid extra for early check-in so she'd have time to get ready and do anything she needed to do before we met in person. I still had plenty of time before I was going to meet with her, but I was confident that she was the woman I wanted.

"Go to the meeting," Liz said. "If you still feel that she's the one, we'll start moving forward."

"I know it's her," I said. "Cancel the other meetings."

"Justin..."

She was speaking in that lawyer-y tone that meant she thought I was making a horrible mistake. I understood that perfectly well. It was definitely brash, but I knew it was what I wanted.

More importantly, my inner-bear knew it.

I'd been a bear shifter long enough to know that I shouldn't – and couldn't – argue with that side of myself. Even though I was a man, I was also a beast. I had to change into my animal form regularly in order to feel fully myself. My inner-bear and I could share thoughts with each other, but that side of myself was a lot more wild and wicked than my human side.

When I was in my bear form, I tended to be a little more reckless. As a human, I was self-controlled to a fault, but right now, I was acting more like a bear than a man. As a shifter herself, Liz likely recognized this, but she wasn't going to call me out on it. I paid her far too much for her to question my choices. Still, I knew that she was going to want more of an explanation than just "I don't want to meet any other new people," and we'd worked together long enough for me to be willing to admit it.

"She's my mate, Liz," I said. "I can feel it."

The words hung in the air between us. Every bear shifter wanted to believe there was one true mate out there for them. The legends surrounding true mates were vast and wide. Some people believed that when you found the person you were supposed to be with, you'd both experience this wild attraction that was unstoppable. Other people thought there would be bolts of lightning falling from the sky to let you know. Me? I had always thought the idea of mates was silly and childish.

Until today.

"You're sure?" Liz asked quietly.

"I'm certain."

"All right, then," she said. "Who am I to argue with fate? I'll go ahead and cancel the other attendees," she told me, "but Justin?"

"Yes?"

"Don't tell your mother about the mates thing."

I understood why. My mom was going through a lot. She didn't need the pressure of thinking that Rebecca and I were going to fall madly in love. After all, I still didn't feel ready for any of this, and it wasn't like I had confided in Rebecca that I was a polar bear shifter, either.

Even if a shifter found their one, true mate, falling in love wasn't always a seamless experience. My bear *wanted* Rebecca. I could tell that I was going to need to shift soon and go running around. I wanted to swim, to hunt, and to race around in the mountains. I wanted to feel the cold against my fur. That was how I coped with stress on a good day. Today, it was going to be even more important because even though I felt like Rebecca was the one, I still had to convince her that I was worth getting to know.

I still had to convince her to marry me.

She'd come to the resort with the understanding that the two of us were going to spend time getting to know each other and then, if we were both amenable, to pursue the contract of dating and marriage. What if I started to get to know her and she didn't like me? That was always a strong possibility, after all. I couldn't exactly force her to fall in love with me. I didn't even know if I *wanted* that. All I knew was that the woman I was going to marry to save my company was going to be her. It had to be her.

"I won't tell her," I agreed.

"She talked to me about the cancer," Liz continued, "and I'm under the impression that this marriage is really important to her."

"I think she wants to know that I'm taken care of," I explained gently. "Mom has always worried about me, especially since dad died."

"Your father's death was hard on all of us," she agreed. "He was so loved by all of his employees. Losing him was unexpected and even though we all adore you, I think it's fair to say he's very missed."

"I agree with you. He left big shoes to fill."

"Listen, I don't know if you and your father talked a lot about mates, Justin, but when one of them is a human, it can be complicated. I'm not saying that this woman isn't your mate. She very well may be. I'm just saying that sometimes, trying to mate with a human when you *aren't* one can be...well, it can get messy, okay?"

I understood. Even though I wanted to argue with Liz, I wasn't going to. She was right, after all. Not only did Rebecca *not* know she was my mate, but she didn't know I was a shifter. I hoped that once we were "dating" and then officially married, it would be easier to tell her how I really felt.

Then again, maybe it would only complicate things more.

"I know you're rushing into marriage," Liz continued calmly.

"It's for the company," I said hastily, reminding her.

"I understand that. Just don't rush into the emotional side of things, Justin. Love can hurt. When you're in a precarious situation like you are right now, it can hurt a lot. As your attorney, I'm advising you to be careful, okay?"

I knew that she was right. Of course, she was. Liz was a genius.

"Okay," I promised her. "I'll be careful."

6

Rebecca

I FINALLY WANDERED into the bedroom of the honeymoon suite, where I was surprised to find a cute little letter that had been set out just for me. It was beginning to feel more and more like Earl and Gabe's idea of this being a bad television show were right. I skimmed the letter to see that it contained a warm greeting from the hotel, as well as instructions for how to find the restaurant for my date.

This was it.

It was finally happening.

I was more than ready to wash the smell of airplane off myself, so I took a quick shower, styled my hair, and got dressed quickly. I hadn't packed too many items. Instead, I chose to keep things simple. I'd found when traveling that if I brought too many clothes, it was impossible to make decisions. By only bringing two or three outfits, my choices were much easier.

I rode the elevator down to the restaurant. Even though I arrived right on time, I was surprised to find that it was entirely empty. There were no patrons lurking around. There wasn't a line near the door. There was nothing. Um, was I in the wrong place?

I walked up to the hostess stand, confused. Hopefully, someone who worked at the restaurant would be able to help me out. After less than a minute, a friendly-looking woman appeared with a big smile. Hopefully, she'd know where I was supposed to go.

"Excuse me," I started to say, but the woman just smiled even brighter.

"You must be Rebecca," she said.

"I, um, yes?"

"You'll be right this way," she said, and started guiding me through the empty restaurant. She didn't seem to mind the fact that every single table was empty or that there was no one sitting around the giant fountain in the center of the restaurant. If I wasn't mistaken, there was even a little koi pond in here, but that, too, was absent of guests.

"You aren't closed?"

"No," she laughed, shaking her head. "As soon as you're seated, I'm going to put up a sign that says we are, though. Your, uh, date bought out the entire restaurant for lunch. Apparently, he wanted privacy. A lot of it." The woman smiled at me, but it didn't seem like she was judging me. Apparently, money really could buy anything. I had never even *thought* of buying out an entire restaurant so I could be alone with someone.

Seriously, who did that?

She stopped in front of an ornate looking door and gestured at it.

"Here we go. Your table is right through there."

"You aren't coming with me?" I asked, turning to her suddenly.

"Nope," she laughed. "I think you can take it from here."

She turned and walked away briskly, obviously eager to put out her CLOSED sign, and then I was alone in the restaurant. I stood there for a minute, staring at the door. I had to make a choice, I realized. This was the moment. This really was my last chance to walk away from this entire thing. It was my last chance to leave, and to go somewhere else, and to pretend that this entire little "adventure" never happened.

Was that what I wanted, though?

Did I want to fly back home and tell Gabe and Earl I'd chickened out at the last second?

Did I want them to think I was giving up because I'd gotten cold feet about meeting someone new?

No.

I didn't.

I knew even as the thoughts crossed my mind that flying home wasn't what I wanted. I didn't want to leave. If I walked away now, I'd always wonder what could have happened. I would always wonder what might have occurred if I'd only been a little bit braver.

"This is it," I whispered to myself, and I pushed open the door. Stepping inside, it took my eyes a moment to adjust to the dim light, and then I saw him.

He was there.

Standing in the center of the room, looking every bit as intimidating as he had in the elevator, the man turned toward me.

"You," I whispered.

"And you," he said, raising a wine glass.

"Why are you here?"

"Probably for the same reason you are," he said, cocking his head. "I'm in the market to get married."

"The market...to get married..."

"Yes," he nodded. "It's wonderful to finally meet you," he said, stepping forward. He held out a hand and I took it, shaking it.

"What's...what's your name?"

Suddenly, even speaking seemed difficult. Was this real? Was I really being interviewed by Elevator Man? *He* was the guy I might be fake-marrying?

The idea of being his fake wife was suddenly very, very appealing to me. Every part of my body suddenly felt like it was alive and on fire. Even my lady bits seemed to ignite, turning on at full force.

Yikes.

The ad had said that sex wasn't required in this deal, but if that were to change, then I wouldn't complain. Not with him.

"Ah," he said, nodding. "First things first." The man nodded toward the only table in this little room. I could see a single sheet of paper on it, along with a pen.

"Let me guess. It's a nondisclosure agreement?"

"Yes," he nodded.

"Your lawyer made you bring this, huh?"

"Again, yes," he smiled. "You know how pesky those attorneys can be."

"Yeah, well," I walked over to the table and sat down. I didn't finish my sentence. Instead, I started looking over the NDA. I focused on the contract as the man sat down across from me. At first glance, the NDA seemed pretty standard. It basically said that if I was selected, I couldn't tell anyone the truth. It also said that if I wasn't selected, and I later discovered this guy's true identity, I couldn't tell anyone. There were a bunch of fees listed, as well as information on all of the different ways he would sue me, and I shook my head, but I signed it.

"Now that you've signed," he started to say, but I held up a hand.

"Full disclosure," I said, "my best friend and his future husband know about this."

"What?"

"I told them," I explained. "So, I signed your NDA, but two people in my life know the true story. That's not something I can take back."

He frowned, furrowing his brow.

"Why would you tell them?"

"Because they're my family," I explained. "They're everything to me."

I kind of felt like that was obvious. I didn't want to think that was going to be a deal-breaker, but I wasn't going to spend a year lying to this dude or not being able to see Earl or Gabe. They would *definitely* think I was being abused or that I'd been abducted. Besides, I was still hoping they'd make it to the wedding.

The man considered this for a moment, and then he nodded slowly.

"We can work with that," he said. "No one else knows?"

"No."

"Okay, sit down."

I sat down at the table and glanced around the little room for a moment. It seemed like the kind of space that could be used for a party room, but there was only the one table with the two chairs. One wall housed a beautiful brick fireplace. The other walls were empty aside from several paintings of fruit. The lights were low, which was either supposed to be ominous or romantic. I still couldn't really tell.

Finally, I swung my head back to the guy in front of me. He was watching me curiously. He didn't seem to care that I wanted to soak in everything about this moment. That was good. He was patient. That was important in a fake husband, I thought.

"Do I get to know your name?" I asked.

"Justin," he said. He reached for his wine and sipped it as he looked at me. I had the feeling he hadn't been planning on telling me that just yet, but he kind of seemed to like me. That was a good thing, right? It meant he was at least a little bit interested in me.

"Justin," I said, rolling the word around on my tongue.

Good name.

Strong name.

Good man.

Strong man?

I looked at his arms. He was wearing a tight t-shirt that showed off his muscles, and I could tell that this was the kind of guy that worked out a lot. I was a little bit...fluffier...than what a guy like him might be used to. Was that going to be a problem?

"I'm a lot fatter than you," I pointed out bluntly, and Justin seemed to choke on his wine.

"Excuse me?"

"Is that an issue?" I asked.

Justin cocked his head and set the wine glass down. Then he stood up swiftly, walked over to me, reached for my hands, and tugged me to my feet. I was standing there, right in front of him, and he leaned down and kissed me like this wasn't our first day meeting each other.

Okay, that *so* wasn't what I'd been expecting when I walked in.

I felt like I was melting into the floor in one mushy pile of goo as he kissed me over and over again. My arms moved of their own accord and wrapped around his neck, pulling him closer. A girl could get used to treatment like this.

Justin reached for my ass, grabbing it and tugging me closer to his body. If I wasn't mistaken, he was enjoying this kiss just as much as I was. I was pressed right against his front, and he felt hard. Excited.

All nervousness seemed to vanish as the kiss went on and on. If we didn't stop this thing soon, I was going to forget about not having sex on a first date and just start tearing off my clothes. What kind of impression would that give my soon-to-be-fake-lover?

I slowed the kiss down, and he followed suit, teasing my lips softly. Slowly. He moved his hands so they were cupping my face tenderly. It was probably the single most romantic moment of my entire life. I didn't want it to end.

"Does that answer your question?" Justin finally whispered against my lips.

"I didn't know kissing was part of this deal," I whispered back.

He pulled back and looked at me. He stroked my cheek softly and then pressed his lips to mine once more. When he pulled back, he was all business.

"Have a seat, Rebecca. We have a lot to talk about."

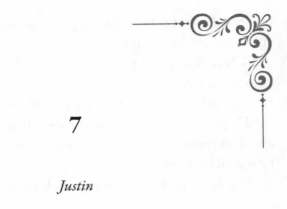

7

Justin

WHEN I KISSED HER, I kind of felt like my entire world was exploding. My inner-bear roared to life. Yeah, he thought this was our mate: our true mate. Although I'd told Liz that I believed she was *the one*, the businessman in me still wanted to be completely certain before I offered up anymore of myself.

Rebecca was soft and sweet. She was excitable. She tasted like honey on a warm summer day. Everything about her was perfect. She'd make an ideal fake partner for the next year while I showed my shareholders just how responsible I really was, but I still wasn't sure whether I was ready for something like *love*.

Besides, I didn't have time to think about the reality of mates or not. Some people didn't believe in the idea of fated mates. Others thought it was just too good to be true. I'd never really given it much thought at all until today, but that didn't matter because my bear seemed to know with certainty that she was the one we were supposed to claim.

It was crazy, but then again, this entire thing was crazy.

I sat across from her at the little table. She looked wildly comfortable. I already knew she was the person I was going to choose. I wasn't even going to go on the dates with the other women. They'd already flown in, so Liz had called them each before this meeting and let them know that unfortunately, I'd gone another way; however, their rooms were theirs until the next day. They could do as they liked and charge whatever they wanted to the room. They could consider it a miniature vacation, and I'd foot the bill as an apology for the inconvenience.

Now, looking at Rebecca, I was certain that my choice, however spontaneous and impulsive, was the right one.

"So, you want to get married," she said, picking up a glass of wine. She took a sip. "Why?"

"Is that important?"

"Yes."

"It'll be good for my image," I told her simply.

She laughed and shook her head. When she realized I wasn't joking, her expression grew sober. She stared at me for a moment, looking at me with those piercing bright eyes. She licked her lips, and then she shook her head slightly, as though it didn't make sense to her.

"What?" Rebecca finally asked. "What do you mean?"

"I run a company," I told her simply. I'd tell her more about it later. She was going to be living with me, after all, so she'd quickly learn the ins and outs of Honey Bear Software.

"Let me guess," she smirked. "You're a billionaire playboy but you secretly have a heart of gold? You have a soft side that nobody gets to know? You want people to see the real you?" She raised an eyebrow, but I frowned, not sure whether she was being serious or teasing me.

"Um, basically."

Rebecca rolled her eyes.

"Hey, it's not easy running a company."

"I'm sure it's not."

"Someone has been forging pictures with me at the center," I told her. "Competing companies do this frequently. They leak pictures to the tabloids of people that look like me and they try to discredit my company."

"Why don't you just tell people they're fake?" Rebecca asked, raising an eyebrow. "Seems like an easy solution to me. It also sounds a lot cheaper than flying out a potential bride, hosting a wedding, and giving me a monthly allowance."

"It's not really that simple."

"Try me."

I wasn't ready to reveal that I was a bear. I hadn't decided if I was going to do that at all, really. Humans knew shifters existed, sure, but not everyone truly believed we were real. I was concerned that if I told Rebecca who I was – *what* I was – that she would either run the other way or laugh in my face. I didn't know her well enough yet to properly gauge her reaction.

I also hadn't revealed that I had a severe food allergy to cherries. I'd probably have to share that with her at some point, but I wasn't ready to just yet. Even though I had planned to spill my guts regarding my allergies in particular, my mother's words were sticking with me. She was *so* certain that telling people about my secrets would make me vulnerable that I was now uncomfortable with the idea of revealing anything at all about myself.

"Okay," she said, accepting my silence. "Well, do you have any questions for me?"

"What is your quest?" I asked, trying to lighten the mood.

"Monty Python?" She raised an eyebrow. "Seriously?"

"Does that surprise you? I'm a bit of a nerd."

"It does surprise me," she told me. "I would have taken you for Mr. Serious."

"Nope. Not when I'm not working."

"So, how will this work?" Rebecca asked. "You know, if you choose me, or whatever."

"How will it work?" I wasn't quite sure what she meant.

"Yeah, I mean, will we date for a year and then be married for a year, or what?"

"No," I said. "The sooner we get married, the better."

"So, what happens next?"

"If we both leave this meeting feeling happy with the arrangement, you'll fly to my city next week. Seven days will give you enough time to pack and get your affairs in order."

"Okay..."

"You'll move in with me right away, and we'll start casually making public appearances. I'll propose to you next month at Thanksgiving in front of my family and then at Christmas, we'll get married."

Her jaw dropped and then she shook her head.

"Are you being serious right now?"

"Yeah."

"Okay," she said. "Well, I'm game."

"This year will include a lot of meetings," I told her.

"For me?"

"For both of us. I'm in the public eye a lot, and you will be, too. You'll have a ton of free time, of course, but you'll be expected to accompany me to art gallery openings and special parties...that sort of thing."

"Oh no," she said sarcastically, "free booze and parties. How ever will I live?"

I cocked my head, looking at her.

"You aren't afraid of me," I said, realizing what the situation was.

"Should I be?"

"Most people are uncomfortable in my presence, yes," I realized.

"Well, most people aren't me."

"I can see that."

Our food arrived just then. The server entered, set two plates in front of us, left another bottle of wine, and then disappeared. I'd ordered before Rebecca arrived because I didn't want us to be interrupted at all. This particular restaurant was well versed in just about any type of cuisine imaginable, and I'd had a nice time choosing a couple of my favorite dishes.

Instead of diving right into the meal, however, Rebecca stared blankly at the food. Then she looked right up at me.

"Is something wrong?" I asked.

"Yeah," she looked up at me. Then she pointed to it. "Shrimp."

"You don't like shrimp?"

"I don't like being dead," she said, pushing the plate away. "I'm allergic. Like, deathly allergic. Like, even the smell is starting to make me a little sick."

"What?"

"I told this to the person who interviewed me," she said. She didn't seem pleased to have to tell me now. I didn't blame her, either. If she'd mentioned this during her interview, I felt like it should have been at the forefront and center of the interview notes I'd gotten from Liz. I hadn't personally interviewed Rebecca, so I hadn't been aware of her allergy.

"They didn't tell me," I said.

"I'm not trying to be rude, but can we substitute this for something else?"

I stood up, grabbed our plates, and headed toward the door.

"Don't go anywhere," I told her. "I'll get us something else."

I dropped the food off in the kitchen, explained the situation, tipped the cooks, ordered two chicken dishes, and came back into the little room. Rebecca had made herself comfortable with the wine, and I sat down across from her.

Well, well, well.

Someone else with food allergies.

It probably shouldn't have put me at ease, but it did. It wasn't easy living life with such specific limitations. I wasn't personally scared or worried when it came to my own allergies anymore. I'd gotten used to avoiding cherries. Once you knew how, it became pretty simple.

Other people, however, tended to have a hard time coping when someone had an allergy. They would label you as a picky eater or a sourpuss, and then they wouldn't want to hang out anymore. It had happened to me many times in the past when I had been bold enough to tell people why I wasn't eating cherry-flavored popsicles as a kid or red Kool-Aid. Following my mom's "don't tell anyone" rule as an adult had been much simpler, if only for the social aspect of dealing with my allergy.

"So, an allergy?" I asked her, reaching for my own glass of wine. We were almost done with the entire bottle. We'd probably need another one to make it through lunch.

"Yeah," she shook her head. "I should have reminded you before you ordered. I'm sorry."

"I mean, I ordered before you arrived, so it didn't matter."

"It's annoying," she said, looking at me. "I know. Is it a dealbreaker for you?" Rebecca looked sad and a little nervous when she asked, and my heart tightened. Was that what this little human thought? She thought I'd give up on this thing between us because of allergies?

"Are you asking if I want to stop this luncheon because you're allergic to something I enjoy eating?"

"Yeah."

It was my turn to laugh.

"No, it's not a dealbreaker."

"You don't mind having a wife who can't eat shrimp?"

"I don't mind having a wife who can't eat shrimp. If you'd been allergic to sweet potatoes, though, it would be an entirely different story," I teased. She blushed.

"I'm not allergic to sweet potatoes."

"Good," I smiled. "Because they're my favorite."

"I like them a lot, too."

A few minutes later, two chicken dishes, side salads, and an assortment of garden vegetables arrived. Rebecca and I thanked the server before he left, and then we dug in. We were both starving by that point.

We finished our food in record time and got back to drinking. Soon the second bottle of wine was gone, and we were both a little tipsy. We were also a lot more relaxed than when we'd first arrived. If I had to judge the date at that moment, I would say it was going really, really well. It was going far better than I would have ever thought possible, in fact.

"Let's go for a walk," I said, tugging her to her feet.

"A walk?"

"There's a little path outside," I told her. "It goes around the lake. It'll be pretty."

She agreed, and the two of us left the restaurant and headed out to the little walking trails.

The Dragon Mountains were beautiful year-round, but October was an especially wonderful time. I liked them a lot. I liked everything about them. I wasn't sure whether it was my bear side or something else, but being in nature like that just made me feel free. It made me feel comfortable and whole and just...

Myself.

I took her hand and we walked in silence for a long time. I was surprised at just how comfortable I felt around her, and I realized that this crazy thing we'd gotten into just might work.

It just might actually work.

8

Rebecca

JUSTIN'S LAWYER FLEW to the resort and the three of us signed a bunch of legal documents saying I wouldn't do anything crazy during my time with him. The entire thing was very cold and clinical, but probably more than a little bit necessary. The attorney assured me that the contract wouldn't just protect Justin, but me, as well. It outlined what I'd be paid, how I'd receive the money, and all of those important details. The next morning, I returned home to my roommate, who was still completely blown away that I was going through with it.

Then, as promised, Justin gave me a week to "sort my affairs."

I didn't own property or have tenants or any real responsibilities, so I just decluttered a little bit, made sure I had my IDs and banking information, and then just tried to stay calm as much as possible. Justin arranged movers and he covered the cost, of course. I offered to put my measly collection of personal items in storage, but he said that was silly. He also said that he wanted me to be as comfortable as possible.

Justin said that if we were going to pull this thing off, we needed to have everything look as authentic as possible. Apparently, he had always kept a fairly private life, so the idea of him having a secret girlfriend wasn't totally unwarranted. He wanted things to look good, though, he said, so he had me move into his place ASAP.

"Are you sure about this?" Earl asked as the movers finished loading up the last of my belongings. "You really want to do this?"

"Yeah," I nodded, leaning against the thin walls of our shared apartment. It was almost entirely empty. Earl had already moved most of his own belongings to storage in order to prepare for his adventure with Gabe. Once the movers left, the two of us would have to clean the apartment and turn in our keys to try to get our deposit money back.

Neither one of us was holding out much hope for *that*.

"Promise me something, Bec?"

"Anything," I looked over at Earl. He was a good guy. Even though I wasn't going to be at his own wedding because he was eloping, we both knew I'd be there in spirit. He and Gabe were going to have some incredible adventures together.

"Make sure he's good to you."

"It's a fake relationship, Earl. He'll be picture perfect. I'm sure of it." Even though I didn't know Justin very well, he'd called me every night since our meeting to make sure that things were going well with the move. It was nice. He'd even said hello to Earl and Gabe on a video chat a couple of times.

"I know that it's a fake relationship *now*," Earl chose his words carefully, "but what if you fall in love?"

"With Justin?"

"With Justin."

"I'm not going to fall in love," I promised. It was a lie. I was certain. Justin was freaking gorgeous. He was funny and understanding. When he'd seen me freak out about the shrimp, he hadn't panicked. He'd just helped me find a solution. Most importantly, he hadn't judged me. Justin was definitely the type of guy I liked to go for, and Earl knew that.

"You might," Earl shrugged. "It's okay if you do, Bec. I won't judge you."

"I know you won't."

"Just don't let him hurt you, okay?"

"I promise," I said.

That time, I wasn't sure whether it was a lie or not. There was a chance that I would fall for Justin. After all, I'd be living with the guy for a long time: a year and some change. It was approximately two months until our wedding. I didn't even know how I was going to make it until then.

If he kissed me again and it was anything like the kiss he'd given me at the resort, I was going to be melted butter in his hands. It was kind of a gross visual, sure, but it was simply a fact. He could have me twelve ways to Sunday and I wouldn't protest. I didn't really consider myself the kind of person to just jump into bed, but with him? Anything was possible.

"Call me all the time," Earl added.

"I'll call you all the time," I laughed.

The next few hours were a blur as we cleaned and checked out of our apartment, said our goodbyes, and went our separate ways. Gabe and Earl were going to spend a couple of days visiting their respective families, get married, and then go travel around. They were going to do some sightseeing in America and then hopefully find jobs overseas. They both wanted to help people, so their plan was to teach English in at least two or three different countries over the course of the next few years.

They hugged me goodbye tearfully, and then a car arrived to take me to the airport, where I'd head to Rawr County, Colorado, which was Justin's home. If it was half as beautiful as the Dragon Mountains, I was going to be in heaven. That resort we'd met at had been absolutely unbelievable.

Somehow, I couldn't believe everything was happening so fast.

Somehow, it all just felt like a dream.

ALTHOUGH JUSTIN WAS a pretty wealthy guy, I was surprised to see that his home was honestly kind of modest. He still had five bedrooms and three stories, but he lived alone without any servants or anything crazy like that. He had a housekeeper and a chef come by once a week, and he had a personal trainer who came to exercise with him, but that was it.

When I arrived, I stood in front of the house and just sort of stared. Justin got out of the car and walked around. He'd picked me up at the airport and brought me right here. My personal belongings were all set to arrive tomorrow.

"What do you think?" Justin asked.

"That's a loaded question."

"Give me the condensed version."

"It's big."

"Not too big."

"Not too big," I agreed.

"I had it built," he explained.

"Is that why it sort of looks like a dollhouse?"

"Does it?"

"White shutters, pointy roofs, and a weird little attic window up top," I pointed. "The only thing you're missing is a ghost or a creepy doll up there."

He laughed and shook his head.

"I can get you a creepy doll," he told me. "A ghost might be more of a problem."

"It's interesting, though," I said. I reached back into the car and grabbed my backpack. It was the only thing I'd brought. All of my crap would be arriving the next day, so I hadn't bothered packing a ton of luggage. I had a feeling that Justin was probably going to be replacing a lot of my stuff, anyway. I was a skirts and t-shirts kind of girl, which probably didn't suit his style or aesthetic. I didn't care much.

We'd talked about pay, and I understood how this entire thing worked.

First, I'd stay with him free for the next fourteen months at least. There would be two months of fake dating and romance before we signed the marriage papers. During that time, I wouldn't pay for anything. Food would be covered. Board would be covered. Tickets to events would be covered.

I'd get a monthly allowance to cover anything personal I might need. Things like dresses and hair appointments and stuff like that could come out of the allowance. I didn't have to spend it all, but I could.

Then, at the end of the year, I'd receive the rest of the money.

All of the money.

I'd get it all, and then I could do anything.

I still hadn't decided what I wanted to do. Maybe I'd go traveling the world with Earl and Gabe, after all. Maybe I'd buy a little cabin in the woods and live there and paint. Maybe I'd do something totally random, like go be a librarian.

I could do anything.

Right now, though, I was hungry, and I was tired, and I was ready to get inside.

"I'll take interesting," Justin said, approving of my assessment of his house. "Let's go inside."

We headed up the steps to the porch. I hadn't had a chance to see much of Rawr County yet, but so far, I knew it was a bustling suburban area made up of several towns. There were a few areas that were more country and less city. Justin worked in a downtown area about twenty minutes from his house, which was on the outskirts of the county. I could see the mountains that surrounded Rawr County, and like the Dragon Mountains, these were beautiful.

"You must have a thing for mountains," I pointed out.

"I like nature."

"I can tell."

"How can you tell?"

"Everywhere we go together, nature is all around us," I laughed, shaking my head.

"I'm glad you like it."

"I do."

We stepped into the house. There was a lovely entryway with a bench for sitting, a table for placing your keys or bags, and it opened to a lengthy hallway. There was something else that was strange, though, I thought. What was that smell? I sniffed the air for a moment before I could place the scent. Finally, I realized that it was honey.

"Woah, are you a beekeeper?" I asked.

"Beekeeper?"

I gestured around the hall, looking for the source of the smell. I peered around, trying to see more of the house. To the left was a living room, to the right was a dining room, and if I had to guess, toward the back I'd find a kitchen and a staircase. There might be an office and sitting room back there, too, depending on how fancy he'd chosen to go for his first floor. He'd told me that he built it, after all.

I didn't see any honey, though.

"What is that smell?"

"Honey."

"Why, though? Are you burning candles?"

He pointed to a little wall outlet, where he was melting wax in one of those little warmers.

"What the hell is that?"

"It makes the house smell nice."

"Not as nice as candles," I said. "Why don't you use the real thing?"

"Because I have a cat," he said. "I don't want him to get hurt by a candle flame."

"You?"

"Me."

"You have a cat?"

"I have a cat."

I looked at him suspiciously. Handsome Mr. Justin had a cat? I didn't believe it for a second. There was no way.

"Nope," I shook my head. "No way."

"Way."

"You don't have a cat."

He crossed his arms over his chest and looked at me carefully.

"Why are you so certain that I don't have a cat?" Justin asked. "Really, at this point, you're kind of hurting my feelings a bit."

"I am not!"

"You are," he nodded, blinking innocently.

I stared at him, trying to figure out if he was messing with me or not. I was starting to think that maybe I sounded kind of like a dick. Still, the idea that someone like him might actually have a pet in this house was a bit surprising to me.

Probably, it shouldn't have been, yet it was.

"If you have a cat," I said, "then what's his name?"

"My cat?"

"Yeah."

"Hector."

"Liar," I rolled my eyes.

"What?" Justin blinked innocently, looking at me like I was the crazy one.

"Nobody has a cat named Hector," I pointed out.

Justin just laughed.

"All right, let's go upstairs."

"I don't want to go upstairs," I said, glancing around.

"Let's get your stuff put away, and then you can explore."

"Promise?" I asked.

"Pinky promise," he agreed, and we started walking toward the back of the house. I peeked into the different rooms as we made our way back. Sure enough, to the back right of the house was the kitchen. To the back left was a room that only had a staircase. Straight ahead was the backdoor, which led to what looked like a sunroom.

"You have an entire room for this staircase?" I asked, looking around.

"Yes."

"That's weird."

"Is it?"

"A little."

"Why?"

"Because a room shouldn't be empty," I said, glancing around. "And this is a weird place for a staircase."

"I designed this," he said, frowning.

"Without any architectural training?" I faux-gasped, pressing my hand to my chest.

"Nobody knows where the staircase is unless I show them," he pointed out.

I just laughed and shook my head. It was the weirdest home design I'd ever seen, but that was fine. So far, I'd learned that he had designed his own house, he had a pet cat, and he didn't like doing what people expected.

Maybe that was part of the reason he'd gone along with this "fake bride" thing.

Maybe he'd just wanted to do something a little strange and different.

If that was his goal, well, then he'd accomplished it.

We went upstairs to the second floor. There were several rooms, but he ignored all of them aside from one. He walked directly toward a door and pushed it open.

"The master?" I asked.

"Yes."

"You're giving me the master?" I turned around, looking at him.

"What?"

"I figured you'd put me in a guest room or something," I shook my head. Maybe this wasn't going to be so bad after all.

Justin stared at me for a moment, and then he laughed, shaking his head.

"I'm not giving you the master bedroom," he said.

"You aren't? But you just said..."

"We're going to share it, Rebecca. We're to be married, after all."

9

Justin

SHE WASN'T EXPECTING that.

She wasn't expecting for us to share a bedroom.

I wasn't sure whether that should be exciting or upsetting to me. What had she thought? Had I not explained things well enough to her? Rebecca seemed genuinely shocked when I said we'd be sharing a room and a bed.

"We need people to believe we love each other," I said. "I don't think it's going to work if we're sleeping in different rooms."

"Lots of couples sleep in different rooms," she whispered.

"Yeah, but not when they're newlyweds," I pointed out.

"Maybe you snore. Maybe I need the silence in order to sleep well. What about that?"

"Rebecca," I took a step toward her and placed my hands on her shoulders. "I'm not going to do anything to you, okay? It's just for sleeping."

She looked up at me, and she bit her lip. For a second, I could *scent* her arousal, but then it was gone just as fast as it appeared. Interesting. It seemed as though sweet Rebecca wasn't nearly as innocent as she might have me believe. If I had to guess, I'd say she'd even thought about me naked before.

"Unless you want something else," I murmured, raising an eyebrow.

"Sleeping is fine," she whispered quickly, and then she darted into the room. I watched from the doorway as she scurried over to the bed and set her bag down.

Curious, wasn't it?

Rebecca had chosen to accept my offer of marriage. She'd decided to be my fake mate for the year, but she was interested in me on more than a platonic level. She was curious about me. She was even aroused by me.

That excited me.

Who knew?

Maybe this year was going to be more incredible than I'd thought it was going to be.

Perhaps it wouldn't be nearly as bad as I was imagining.

My inner-bear was starting to claw at me from the inside, begging to get out. I needed to run. I'd noticed that since meeting Rebecca, I'd been spending a lot more time in my bear form. I hadn't told her I was a shifter, and if it was up to me, she'd never know. I didn't need anyone knowing that I wasn't exactly human.

The problem with information like this was that people could use it to hurt you. They could use this information to blackmail you, seduce you, or injure you. I didn't need any of those things, so I'd keep this to myself for now.

"I'm going to go for a run," I said, clearing my throat.

Rebecca looked over at me, surprised.

"A run?"

"Yeah," I nodded.

"Do you, um, want company?"

I couldn't tell whether she actually wanted to come along or not, but I did know that I didn't want her to. I needed to be alone.

I wasn't trying to be cruel or rude, but this moment called for ultimate solitude. I didn't want to have anyone with me.

I needed to change into my bear form and just be free. There were plenty of places in the mountains where I could walk around, explore, and growl to my heart's content. I could go fishing or swimming or do anything I wanted to, but I couldn't do *any* of that if she came with me.

"No thanks," I said. "Make yourself at home, okay? You can take a bubble bath or raid the kitchen. I'll be back later."

I wasn't sure whether I should hug her before I left. We weren't lovers, as much as I wanted us to be, so I just sort of nodded in her general direction, turned, and headed downstairs. I headed toward the backdoor, walked out into the sunroom, and then exited the house through the exterior sunroom door. I closed my eyes for a second, enjoying the warm feeling of sunshine on my face.

This was it, I thought.

This was the life.

This was how things were supposed to be.

I realized as I walked away from the house that I was still wearing jeans and a snug-fitting tee. Maybe Rebecca was too tired to even notice what I was wearing. If she questioned me about it, I'd have to come up with a quick lie. I could tell her that I kept a change of clothes in the sunroom, maybe, and that I hadn't wanted to change in front of her.

That would have to do.

I was already out of the house and walking toward the woods. There was no turning back now. I headed toward the cover of the trees, and then I paused and stripped down. I was certain she couldn't see me from the house, and as soon as I was naked, I took a deep breath.

Freedom.

I changed into my bear form quickly. Years of practice meant I had perfected this shift. It was no longer tricky or difficult at all. In fact, changing to my polar bear form was quite a simple task for me. It didn't take a lot of effort to be able to change into my furry alter-ego.

As soon as I was in my bear form, the wild side of my heart kind of took over. It was hard to explain to other people what it was like to be a bear shifter. Not that I spent a lot of time talking about my bear abilities with non-shifters. I didn't.

The few times I'd brought it up with people, back when I was a younger bear, it had been hard to explain, though. How could I share that I was completely a bear, but also completely a man? We had two minds, but at the same time, we had one. It didn't make a lot of sense to other people, but it made perfect sense to me.

Now that I was in my bear form – now that I had *become* my bear – I was ready to run.

Let's do this thing, I thought to my bear. I was ready to get moving. I needed to race. My body had been on fire since Rebecca and I had met for the first time. Now it was like someone had poured gasoline on that fire and the flames were going *everywhere*.

I ran.

I didn't start slowly, and I didn't take my time.

I just ran.

I knew these woods inside and out. They were where I'd grown up. Even now, as a fully-grown adult, I still loved spending time out here. There was something special about being lost in the woods. I loved the way the forest made me feel. It was like nothing else really mattered when I was out here. The entire world made sense to me when I got to run.

And all of the stress faded away.

Being a businessman was something I loved, but it was also really hard. It hadn't been easy for me, just as I was certain it hadn't been easy for my dad. Still, I did everything I could to make it work. I did everything in my power to make sure that the world I helped forge was going to be great.

I wanted to live up to my dad's legacy.

I wanted to make the world a better place.

It was nice to think that for the next year, I'd get to do that with Rebecca.

Mine.

My inner-bear loved when I thought about Rebecca. He seemed quite certain that she was my mate. Our mate. I still hadn't brought up the topic with my mom, although I probably should. She'd be giddy to know that her little plan had resulted in me finding my mate, but I still wasn't convinced. I was still planning to heed Liz's warning not to tell my mother. After all, there was no use putting pressure on the situation.

I liked Rebecca.

She was nice enough.

Cool, collected, kind.

Was she someone I could see myself mated to?

Absolutely.

Was I ready for the kind of responsibility that came from a *real* marriage, though?

I wasn't so sure.

10

Rebecca

WHERE WAS HE GOING running in jeans and a t-shirt?

As soon as Justin left the room, I waited a minute before following him. He seemed distracted because he didn't notice me following him, and I definitely stepped on at least one creaky old stair. He went outside, and I went to the back window, peering out.

He looked over his shoulder before disappearing into the woods, and then he didn't come back.

What the hell?

He'd said he was going for a jog, and that was strange enough on its own. Now I could clearly see that he was not only sneaking out in regular, ordinary clothing, but that he also wasn't jogging. So what was he doing?

Apparently, my future husband had some secrets.

That was to be expected, right?

Only, I couldn't help but feel curious about what Justin was hiding. What was in the woods that was so important? What was he hiding out there?

I watched for a little while, but soon I grew bored and decided to explore the house. The rest of Justin's space was pretty neat and tidy, just like him. It was decorated very simply, and I was beginning to detect a bit of a pattern. He might have been a rich guy, but he was definitely not comfortable showing off his money.

That told me that he wasn't always wealthy.

He hadn't shared a ton of information with me yet about his company. We were supposed to go over that at some point over the next few days, though. Apparently, if I was going to get by with tricking the world into thinking that we were a couple, I was going to have to actually know what it was that he did for work.

I explored the kitchen, the living room, and the classic dining room. Everything seemed pretty straightforward and simple. The house was decorated really simply in cool, classic colors. The furniture was nice and pretty.

The second floor was much of the same. He had a couple of guest rooms and an office. Yeah, he definitely could have given me my own bedroom. I understood why he hadn't, but I was still a little rattled by that decision.

"Meow," Hector appeared, walking around a corner. He sat down and looked at me.

"Hey," I squatted down and held my hand out to the little cat. "How's it going, Mr. Kitty-Cat?"

Hector stared at me suspiciously, as though he wasn't quite sure who I was or what I was doing in his space. I waited a couple of moments, but it soon became clear that he wouldn't be warming up to me anytime soon, so I finally gave up. I stood and headed to the third floor.

Hector followed closely behind.

"Oh, hell yeah!" I couldn't believe my eyes when I reached the top of the stairs. The entire third floor was a library. It was literally one big, open space that was full of books. Hector immediately disappeared between some of the bookshelves. I gave him some space and didn't follow him right away even though part of me wanted to. I knew it would take some time for him to warm up to me. In the meantime...there were books.

There were so many books.

It was the craziest thing I'd ever seen, and my English major heart was happy.

I walked around, impressed at how neatly Justin had organized his stories. Any good librarian would have been impressed with this. He had such an incredible collection that I could have easily lost myself up there if I wasn't careful. I explored old copies of Nancy Drew, ran my hands over Justin's first edition copy of *The Boxcar Children*, and then finally landed on some classics from the 1800s.

"Lady of the Lake," I whispered, picking up a story.

I had always loved that book. I read it originally because a book character I liked from *Anne of Green Gables* was slightly obsessed with the story. I read it as a teenager and then did several papers on it during my graduate program. Talk about passion. Talk about love and romance.

I took the book to a cozy little nook. The library floor of the house, as I was officially naming it, had a lot of nooks. There were window seats and lovely spots to sit on the floor. There were chairs and beanbags and just...

Well, there was everything.

"All right, Justin," I muttered. "Looks like you put your money to good use."

I curled up with the book and opened it, suddenly glad to have something familiar around me. I was being thrust into a world I knew nothing about. Rawr County was the kind of place where it seemed like everyone knew everyone. That might not have been true, but it sure felt true, and I was nervous about being there. I was nervous about meeting Justin's family. I was nervous about pulling off this big, huge lie.

When I read *Lady of the Lake,* though, suddenly my nervousness just flitted away, and I was very quickly immersed into a fairy tale all of my own.

"REBECCA," A GENTLE voice was speaking to me, and someone's hand was on my shoulder. My eyes flew open, and I looked up to see Justin standing there.

"Oh," I whispered, sitting up. I must have fallen asleep in the library. The book I'd been reading was still in my lap, and my cheek was wet from where I'd been drooling. Gross. Hopefully, this guy was invested enough in what we were about to do that he wouldn't freak out that I wasn't exactly a tidy napper. Still, I could feel my cheeks flush with slight embarrassment. This wasn't exactly how I wanted my future husband to see me on our first day together.

"Sleepy?" Justin smiled. He didn't seem to mind that I'd fallen asleep. If he noticed the drooling, he was polite enough not to say anything.

"Apparently," I admitted. "How was your run?"

"Not bad," he said. His hair was damp, I realized. Apparently, he'd already showered. I slightly regretted the fact that I'd passed out, so I hadn't gotten the chance to try to catch him not-running when he came out of the woods.

"Do you run in your backyard?" I asked, hoping I sounded casual.

"Usually on the road," he said. "There are some trails throughout the woods, though."

"Sounds nice," I said. "Did you watch out for big, scary monsters?"

"Always," he laughed.

"Did you go running in your jeans?"

"I changed in the sunroom," he smiled, looking like he was prepared for the question. Hmm. I knew that was a lie, but I couldn't really complain about it, could I? After all, we weren't *really* in a relationship. He was allowed to lie if he wanted to. He was allowed to keep secrets and to make shit up. He could do whatever he wanted, and I couldn't do a damn thing to stop him.

Irritation washed over me, but I tamped that down. It wasn't my problem. It wasn't like this was a real relationship where we had to find a balance of give and take. The truth was that I only had to deal with Justin for a year. After that, we'd be able to go our separate ways and do what we liked. We could date whoever we wanted...

"Ah," I said. "Smart."

I wasn't going to get into it.

Justin looked at me curiously. I couldn't tell whether he was surprised I was going to drop the issue. Did he expect me to call him out? Nope. I wasn't going to spend the emotional energy on that. Not when I could use this time to just relax and enjoy myself.

"What?" I asked when he didn't stop watching me.

"Are you hungry?"

My stomach growled immediately. I blushed, hoping Justin hadn't heard, yet the sly grin that spread across his face let me know he definitely *had* heard.

"Let's go get food," he said, offering me his hand. I accepted and allowed myself to be pulled to my feet.

"Together?"

"Yep."

"In public."

"Yep."

"So, is this our first official date?" I asked carefully. I knew that he wanted people to see us together so they would realize he was no longer single. I just didn't realize it was going to be like, right now.

"Absolutely. It's not going to be anything fancy," he added quickly, "but it's a good idea for us to start being seen together."

"Right," I nodded. "Because Thanksgiving isn't too far away."

"Exactly," Justin agreed easily. "We're going to see my entire family at that point, and I want rumors to already be circling about us. We don't have a ton of time to make that happen."

"You're right." He was right. The sooner we got started with this entire relationship thing, the better. "So, let's get going."

11

Justin

AFTER A DELICIOUS DINNER at a local restaurant, Rebecca and I went on a walk downtown. She seemed happy to just hang out and window shop, and I was, too. It was a cool, comfortable night, and even though the downtown area was bustling with activity, nobody really crowded us. In many ways, it felt like we were wrapped up in our own little world.

"Do you like shopping?" I asked her. Most of the women I dated loved to shop, especially once they realized I'd foot the bill. Somehow, I had a feeling that Rebecca wasn't that way. Even though we were looking at different items we spotted in the many boutique windows, she didn't seem particularly attached to anything we saw.

"Nope," she looked over at me. "Is that a requirement for this relationship to work?"

"Not at all."

"Good," she breathed a sigh of relief. "Shopping is just not my thing. I mean, I assume I'll need new clothes for the special events and everything."

"That would probably be best," I agreed. "Unless you secretly have a stash of gowns in that backpack of yours."

"I do not," she told me. "Unfortunately for you, I'm more of a casual kind of girl."

"Jeans?"

"Yep."

"What else do you like to wear?"

"Not ballgowns," she pointed toward a nearby window that had an assortment of poofy gowns in the window. "I mean, I studied English Lit in grad school. I feel like I kind of hit the English major stereotypes."

"What are those?"

"Plaid skirts, t-shirts, jeans, pinup girl clothing...the whole nine yards."

"Those are many different styles," I pointed out.

"I know. For me, dressing depends on my mood."

"So, what would you normally wear on a first date?" I asked her, curious. I wanted to get to know her better. There wasn't going to be any sort of quiz on how well Rebecca and I knew each other. Nobody was going to make me prove that I loved her or that I thought she was wonderful. That simply wouldn't happen; however, I still thought it was important that I get to know her.

She was about to be my wife, after all.

"On a first date?"

"Yep."

"Depends on what we were doing, I suppose."

"Well, let's say, just for the sake of conversation," I winked, "that the first date was dinner and a walk downtown."

"Hmm," she smiled. "Well, I can't say I've ever found myself in that situation," she winked sarcastically, "but I'd probably choose a skirt and a low-cut top."

"Not a t-shirt?" I asked, feigning surprise.

"Nope. On a first date, I'd want to make a good impression. That means it would have to be low-cut all the way."

"Interesting," I murmured, trying not to envision her wearing something that showed off her breasts. I wasn't under any sort of impression that Rebecca and I would be sleeping together, but still, I wanted to know what she was like when she was dating for real. Since she'd just arrived and hadn't brought too much with her on the plane, she was wearing a pair of comfy jeans and a long-sleeved top, but it wasn't low-cut.

"You know, because I'd want to show off my breasts," she said bluntly, looking over at me. Rebecca blinked innocently, as though she was quite certain I didn't realize why she'd choose a low-cut shirt. The look on her face was so adorable that I couldn't help but laugh.

"Yeah, I got that bit."

"Well, you didn't say anything, so..."

I reached for her chin and tilted it up toward me. I hadn't forgotten the kiss we'd shared. I hadn't forgotten the way she'd tasted. She was wildly gorgeous and delightfully sassy. If it was my choice, I'd be tumbling around in bed with Rebecca right now, but it wasn't my choice.

It was hers.

I'd promised to marry her – for the sake of the company, of course – but I wasn't going to make this any harder than it needed to be. I knew perfectly well that sex would only complicate things. It would make our interactions messy and strange. Awkward. That's what would happen.

Neither one of us needed that, so I didn't kiss her. I'd save that for when I was certain people were watching us. Instead, I just smiled. I wondered what kind of things were running through that pretty head of hers.

"I understood," I finally said.

Her tongue flicked out, licking her lips. Her eyes darted to my mouth. I knew what she was thinking, all of a sudden. She was thinking about kissing me, and I was thinking about kissing her.

Well, we were going to be married, weren't we?

And tonight was all about getting attention, wasn't it?

I realized, suddenly, that maybe kissing her wasn't such a bad idea after all. So what if we got emotionally entangled? Would it really be so horrible? We were both adults. We both wanted to touch each other. We had both enjoyed the last kiss. On a whim, I cupped her face in my hands and I brought my lips to hers.

For all of my faults and all of my mistakes, I could say with truthfulness that I'd never kissed anyone like Rebecca before. She was sweet and wonderful and kind, and she was delicious. She tasted like magic and wonder, and I wanted to do this over and over and over.

Even if things between us never went further than a little kissing, I was delighted that we at least had this.

I saw the flash of a camera and I stopped kissing her. I turned to see who had snapped the picture.

"It seems we've drawn a crowd," she murmured. "I guess that's a good thing?"

She looked up at me. I knew this was a question, not an outright comment. That had been the entire point of the evening, I knew, but somehow, the idea of kissing her like that and having someone take a picture felt invasive. I had lost myself in that kiss, I knew. I'd lost myself in her for a little while.

"Let's get out of here," I said, avoiding the question.

I took her hand, and I led her away from the people who were watching. Apparently, the kiss had looked as good as it felt, because people were murmuring and talking.

"Do you always draw such a crowd?" Rebecca whispered as we scurried back towards the restaurant where my car was parked.

"No."

"Are you upset?"

"No."

I hauled her along, guiding her down the sidewalk and turning down one street and then another. I didn't slow down. I just kept walking faster and faster.

"You seem upset."

"I'm fine."

"Justin..."

"I'm fine."

"Justin!"

"What?!"

I stopped, turning to her. Rebecca's eyes were big. Okay, so I hadn't meant to yell, but I had. I hadn't meant to interrupt her, but I had. I hadn't meant for any of this to happen, but it had, and I didn't know what to do.

She wasn't supposed to be this perfect.

I wasn't supposed to like her.

When my mother suggested – no, *insisted* - that I marry a stranger just to save the image of the company, I should have laughed in her face, but she was sick, and I didn't have it in me. I couldn't do that. I couldn't just tell her no.

Only now, Rebecca was standing in front of me, and she was looking at me like I was the most important guy in the world. How did she manage to look at me like that? When she smiled at me, I felt like I was floating.

Floating.

"Why are you upset? They took pictures. That was the point."

"No," I growl, backing her up against the wall. "This is the point."

Then I kissed her.

And I kissed her.

And I kissed her.

12

Rebecca

NOBODY IN THE DAMN world could kiss the way he could.

By the time I came up for breath, I felt like he had somehow managed to touch my very soul. This wasn't something I was going to be able to just bounce back from when it was all over, I realized suddenly. Justin wasn't going to be the kind of guy I could just walk away from. One day in and I was already starting to fall for him. He was funny, and he was quippy, and hot damn, the guy could kiss.

"That was..."

"Wow," he agreed.

Wow indeed.

Justin was a surprise.

Pretty much everything about him was a surprise. I had taken this "position," this gig, as a way to make money while I figured out what I was going to do with my life, but Justin had kind of taken my heart by storm. That was such a problem. He was really funny and handsome, friendly, and smart, and I...

Well, I was his fake girlfriend, soon to be fake wife.

He took my hand and led me away. Somehow, we made it back to the car, and then back to the house, and then upstairs in the bedroom. I looked over at him, wondering what was going to happen next. The car ride itself had been decidedly quiet. Neither one of us wanted to break the mood, apparently.

I was well aware of the fact that something between us had changed. There had been a second there when we were kissing that everything seemed to just *shift*. It was like all of a sudden, this thing that was supposed to be fake suddenly felt real.

I was suddenly very aware of the fact that I needed to be careful.

Until that moment, I'd been quite certain I was going to have an easy go of it. Now I wondered if I was going to actually have to be careful about getting hurt. Was I going to get wildly attached to this guy? Because that would be very, very bad.

"Are you okay?" Justin's voice was gentle, but I was suddenly jolted back to the moment.

"Sorry, I kind of spaced off a little."

"Nothing wrong with that," he chuckled, slipping off his suit jacket. He draped it over a chair that was in the corner of the room. "It just looks like you're deep in thought. Anything I can help with?"

"I was just thinking is all," I said.

"No worries," he told me. "I'm going to go take a shower."

He headed into the bathroom and I was suddenly glad for the reprieve. I understood we were going to be living together and we'd be sleeping together, but tonight, I just wasn't ready. While he was in the shower, I slipped into a t-shirt and shorts, grabbed a pillow and blanket, and headed down to the living room on the first floor.

The couch in that room was so damn soft and cozy that it felt like I was lying on a cloud. I closed my eyes and instantly felt my entire body relax. I was almost asleep when I heard a soft purring sound and felt something heavy on my tummy. I looked down to see two little eyes blinking up at me.

"We meet again, Mr. Hector," I said to the cat.

Little Hector was so quiet I almost didn't hear the tiny meowing sound he made. I started petting the kitty's head, and immediately, he stopped meowing and started purring again.

"Such a good kitty," I whispered, touching the little guy. I closed my eyes and wiggled a little bit, getting comfortable on the couch, and then I sighed.

This was it.

This was what I had gotten myself into.

I'd gotten myself into cats and handsome men who had weird secrets and took strange walks. I'd gotten myself into romantic dates and huge houses. I didn't really know what to do with all of that. My heart was pounding, and I had so many thoughts running through my head that I almost didn't hear him approach.

Somehow, though, I knew he was close.

Justin moved with absolute silence. I had no idea how a guy like him managed to walk through the house undetected. He moved with such grace and stealth that I wondered if he'd been a spy in a former life. Either that or some sort of sleek, silent animal, like a tiger or a lion.

I was perfectly still, not moving, but he cleared his throat.

"I know you're awake."

I didn't say anything.

"Your breathing changed when I came into the room," he continued.

Silence.

"We had an agreement, Rebecca."

He wasn't wrong, but I didn't want to talk about that. I just wanted a little bit of space. I wanted some time to cope with everything that was happening. Maybe that was the problem, though. Maybe I wasn't going to be allowed to cope with these changes. Maybe I really did need to just suck it up and let everything happen as it was supposed to.

"Rebecca, you're coming back to bed," he said. His voice lowered. It got deeper and a little bit sultry. "You aren't a child, but I'll carry you upstairs to bed like you're a little brat if you make me."

Something was happening to me. His words struck a chord I didn't even know I had in me. He sounded more than just mean. He sounded decisive. Dominating. Strong. I'd never really been into kink, but the idea of him calling me a brat just turned me on so much. Images of him flipping me over his shoulder, hauling me up to the bedroom, and fucking me deep and hard flashed in my mind.

That was so, so wrong.

This thing between me and Justin was *fake*.

It was *not* real.

Everything about our relationship was made up, and besides, we'd agreed not to have sex.

So why did I love the idea of him carrying me upstairs so damn much?

He sighed audibly and stepped closer. I could smell the body wash he'd just used in the shower. His hair dripped on me just the slightest bit as he reached down and lifted me up. The cat meowed and ran away, but I didn't move. I was perfectly still as he lifted me, pulling me into his arms, and then he started walking away.

"You're a bit naughty," he murmured.

I still didn't say anything. It was probably pretty weird that I wasn't speaking, but I'd gone so long at that point that I didn't quite know what to say if I suddenly decided to rejoin the conversation. All I knew was that Justin was hot, fierce, and wonderful. Was he full of secrets? Yeah. Yeah, this guy was full of secrets. Taking on a fake wife was a pretty big secret, after all, but still, I couldn't help but like the fact that I was the one he'd chosen.

I knew there wasn't a real attraction on his part. Oh, we'd kissed a couple of times, but it was all for show, right? It had to be. I was the one who was attracted to him, and I'd have to learn to keep that under wraps.

We reached his room and somehow, he managed to make his way to the bed. He didn't bop my head on any doorframes or walls or anything like that. He just set me down carefully on the bed and covered me with a blanket.

"Goodnight," he whispered. Then he pressed his lips to my forehead, and I let out the tiniest groan. He chuckled darkly and moved his lips to my ear. "I knew you weren't asleep," he said.

Then he went to his side of the bed, climbed in, and shut off the night light.

"Sweet dreams, Rebecca," he murmured. "Sleep tight."

13

Justin

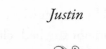

IT WAS A PITY THAT I had to go to work the next day, but I did. The problem with running a company was that business didn't care if you wanted to spend time with your new girlfriend. The only thing business cared about was cash, and if I wasn't in the office, we weren't going to make any.

My mother came over early in the morning to spend time with Rebecca and start the wedding planning. Even though our engagement wouldn't officially happen until Thanksgiving dinner with my family, my mom wanted to have things as carefully arranged as possible.

She showed up right on time just as Rebecca and I were finishing up our morning coffee. I was a little surprised at just how comfortable and relaxed the morning had been. Rebecca had been strangely cheery and perky, greeting me with a soft hug when she woke up. She'd brought a bunch of books on her Kindle, apparently, so she planned to mostly hang out and read while I was at work.

That was fine. It was great she had a hobby she enjoyed and something that would keep her busy. That relieved a little bit of the guilt I felt for leaving her at home. I needed to sit down with her at some point and talk about the company and what we did, but that couldn't be today. Today was full of meetings and stupid appointments. I'd much rather have stayed home with her.

"Good morning," my mother called out in a sing-song voice as she walked into the kitchen.

"Oh," Rebecca said, jumping to her feet. "I'm so sorry. I didn't hear you knock. Otherwise, I would have run over."

"It's nothing," my mother waved her off. "I have a key and I always let myself in."

"Okay," Rebecca nodded. I was glad that didn't bother her.

"There will often be people coming and going," I told her. "The housekeeper, the personal trainer, and the chef."

"Really?"

"Even my personal shopper has a key," I told her. "It can be annoying at times, but I'm usually not around when they come over, so it's easiest this way. Just make sure you aren't walking around naked, and you'll be fine."

She blushed, shaking her head. Then she bit her lip, and I about fell apart right there. Rebecca was so much better than I could have possibly hoped. I probably shouldn't have teased her so much, but I couldn't really help myself.

My mother just rolled her eyes. She set her purse on the counter and started rifling through it. She pulled out a couple of brochures and catalogs and set them down.

"Anyway," she said, looking at Rebecca. "I'm Justin's mother."

"I figured that," Rebecca said, but not unkindly. "It's really nice to meet you."

"And you," my mother said. She looked at Rebecca and smiled, and I was surprised to see that it was actually a pretty genuine smile. Interesting, my mother was a lot of things, but few people had ever accused her of being friendly.

My mom turned to me. Before she could say anything, I set my coffee mug down and held my hands up.

"I'm leaving."

"Good," she said. "Rebecca and I have a lot to do today."

"We do?"

I'd only slightly filled her in on what to expect. My mother could be intense, and I probably should have clarified that a little bit for her. It wasn't that my mother was bossy, but that she was so wildly organized it could actually end up being slightly stressful.

"We do," my mother said. "Don't worry, dear," she patted Rebecca's shoulder.

"I'm not worried."

"Good. I have a binder, and I have money, and I have everything we need to start planning your wedding."

"Wow," Rebecca whispered, shaking her head. "It's crazy that this is all happening so fast."

I felt a little bad for her all of a sudden. She looked a little overwhelmed. Even though she'd agreed to this, it was definitely true that there was a lot on her plate. Suddenly, she had to learn so many different things, and even though she was being paid to be here, it was probably going to be hard in many ways.

"Hey," I said, reaching for her. I tugged her close and gave her a tight hug. When she pulled back, I cupped her face. "It's going to be totally fine."

"Promise?"

"I promise," I said. "Just remember to take deep breaths, okay?"

"Okay," she nodded.

"My mom lives for this stuff, so she can practically do it in her sleep. You have to make the final decisions because it's our wedding and we don't want any of the caterers or location people to know that something fishy is afoot, but if you ever aren't sure what to choose, just ask my mom her opinion, okay?"

"Okay," Rebecca nodded.

"And Mom?"

"Yes, dear?"

"Don't scare her."

"Me?" My mother pressed her hand to her chest in mock surprise.

"Yes, you."

"I would never."

I just laughed.

"Maybe not on purpose," I said. I gave her a quick hug and then I headed to the door. They both followed me and waved from the porch as I got into my car and drove off. It was going to be a big, wild day at the office, but I had a feeling that I wasn't actually going to get a lot done.

That feeling was totally affirmed when I walked into my office and one of my assistants scurried in without knocking.

"Phil?" I was surprised to see him standing here so early in the morning. I was even more surprised to see him looking so shocked.

"Is it true?"

"Is what true?"

"You know..."

I sighed, shaking my head. I leaned back in my chair, propped my feet up on the desk, and folded my hands behind my head.

"There are a lot of true things in the world," I said. "You're going to have to be more specific than that."

He sighed and walked into the office. He came behind the desk, totally invading my space, and logged onto my computer.

"What are you doing? And how do you know my password?"

"We all know your password, Sir. It's not really a secret on this floor," he typed a few more things and then nodded. "There."

I dropped my feet to the floor and sat up straight, looking at the screen in front of me. Sure enough, there were photos from my date last night with Rebecca. No one knew her name, which was pretty good. Nobody knew where she'd come from or what she was doing in Rawr County, but there was a lot of talk about her.

"Website after website," Phil told me. "Everyone is talking about you and your date."

"So, what was your question?"

"Is it true that you went on a date?"

"Yes."

"Is it true that you like her?"

"I don't know, Phil," I said, clicking through a couple of the websites. I landed on a picture of me and Rebecca making out against one of the buildings last night. She looked lovely even in the poor quality of the cell phone camera photo. Then I turned to him and raised an eyebrow. "Does it look like I like her?"

Phil was decent enough not to say anything. He just took that as his cue to leave, and he scurried out of the room. I waited until the door was closed, and then I turned back to the gossip websites to see what people were saying.

Most of the headlines were a bit sensational, but they all made one thing very clear: Justin Honey was off the market, and his mystery woman was something special. There was a lot that Rebecca and I had to learn about each other, but luckily, we'd have an entire year to do it. Right now, at least, everything was going according to plan. Rawr County now knew that I had a girlfriend, which meant that hopefully, the fake pictures of me getting into trouble would stop and people would finally start to view me as the responsible CEO my father had always wanted me to be.

This had to work.

It just had to.

14

Rebecca

AS IT TURNED OUT, JUSTIN'S mom was perfectly lovely. She was also the only person, save for their attorney, who knew about our little secret. Apparently, the arrangement had been her idea. We sat together at the large kitchen table and drank coffee while we looked through wedding magazines, brochures, and catering menus.

"The idea is to have a smaller wedding that's intimate, but lovely," she explained to me.

"Intimate but lovely," I rolled the words around on my tongue for a moment. "I like that."

"Me too," she smiled. I had the feeling that Justin's mother liked me more than she was letting on. She could definitely come across as controlling and harsh. That was easy to see. I could understand how people might be intimidated by her; however, once she started talking about wedding planning and cakes and dresses, she really seemed to relax.

"So," I said, leaning forward. I propped my head in my hands. It was time to change the subject a little bit. I still didn't know a lot about what I was getting into. Maybe she could shed some light on my future. "Honey Bear Software."

"Justin's company."

"Your company, too," I pointed out.

"Someone's been doing her reading," Rita said, leaning back in her seat.

"A little," I nodded. "What I read is that you stepped back from the company after a cancer diagnosis. Is that true?"

"It's true," she said. "My cancer is back, and that's part of the reason I wanted to help Justin find a wife."

Her words chilled me. Cancer was probably the scariest word in the English dictionary. I couldn't quite put a finger on why I hated it so much. Maybe it was just that it was so mysterious and quiet. It was the kind of thing that could catch you off-guard and then just claim your life. Just like that. There was nothing you could do about it. No amount of fighting could save you.

I didn't say anything right away because I didn't know *what* to say, but Rita didn't seem to mind my silence. Once again, she showed how patient she was. She also showed me a lot of grace in that moment.

"Justin knows I'm going to die," she said. "Not many other people do."

"I...I'm so sorry," I whispered. "I really don't really know what to say."

"Nobody ever does, dear," she smiled softly. "That's okay, though. When I was young, I didn't know what to say to dying people, either."

"It's weird, huh?"

"Dying? Or talking to dying people?"

"Both?"

"Both," she nodded, smiling. "Well, Justin's a good man. I'm happy with the way he turned out. Every parent worries they're going to end up accidentally raising an asshole."

I burst out laughing. I couldn't help it.

"I'm sorry," I said, holding up a hand, but Rita didn't seem to mind.

"It's perfectly okay," she said. "Maybe one day you'll have little cubs of your own, and then you'll know what I mean."

"Cubs?"

A look of surprise crossed her face, but then it disappeared almost instantly.

"You know, little children. They always look like animal cubs."

"I've just never heard that phrase," I said, explaining myself. Somehow, I felt like I wasn't supposed to ask about her wording, so I tried to change the subject. "Anyway, what do you think about this place for catering?"

I handed her one of the menus in front of us. It was for a cute barbeque restaurant in town. The pictures made the food look delicious, and I felt like it would give us that small-town feel Justin and his mom both seemed to like.

I didn't mind that she was helping with the wedding. I didn't mind like, at all. I didn't get the impression that Justin was a "mama's boy," and I didn't feel like Rita needed to cut the apron strings. It seemed more like they worked well together, and they were close, and she was kind of just an overseer.

"It's good," she said. "All of the places here are allergy-friendly," she explained. "No shellfish for you. No cherries for Justin. He talked with you about his allergy?" Rita raised an eyebrow.

"No," I said, cocking my head. "No, he hasn't said anything about that."

"Right," she nodded. "Well, it's kind of a private thing, I suppose."

"He's private about a lot of things," I pointed out.

"He has to be, you know," she explained. "As the face of the company, he can't ever look weak."

"Nobody knows about his allergy?" That seemed almost dangerous to me. When I met new people, I practically introduced myself as, "Hey, I'm Rebecca and I have a huge list of allergies. Wanna see?"

"Nobody," she said, nodding. "Well, very few people, anyway."

"Why? I mean, I know you said he doesn't want to seem weak, but if it's a severe allergy, shouldn't he tell people, so he doesn't accidentally eat cherries?"

It seemed a bit risky to me. What if someone baked something that had cherry flavoring in it? What if someone brought a special item to a potluck or something with cherries in the chocolate drizzle? It just seemed dangerous.

"Justin has a very good sense of smell," Rita said solemnly.

"Smell?"

"Yes. He can smell anything. It's unnerving. You'll see."

"Okay," I nodded, feeling suddenly uncomfortable. She seemed to sense my unease, and Rita reached for my hand. She squeezed it softly.

"Hey," she told me. "Everything's going to be okay, all right?"

"I know," I said. "It seems like you and Justin really have thought of everything. It seems like you've got this all figured out, so I think it's going to be just fine."

"I appreciate your trust," she told me. "That means a lot."

I nodded, looking at her.

"There's a lot to know," I finally said. "Like, this entire situation is so weird. I feel like I should know more about Justin than I do. Can you tell me more about him?"

Rita smiled and reached for a glass of water that was sitting in front of her. She brought it to her lips, taking a long sip, and then she set it back down. Finally, she laughed.

"Yes, dear, I can help you with that. What do you want to know?"

"Well, what did he like to do when he was little?"

"What did he do? He did the same thing all little ones do."

"All little cubs, right?" I winked at her, hoping she'd think it was funny that I used her word, but her smile fell. She recovered quickly, and then nodded hastily. Weird. What was with her and that word?

"Right. Well, he liked hockey. He liked running around. He dated some in high school."

"College?"

"He dated in college. He played hockey for a semester, but then he decided to focus on schoolwork."

"Sounds like he was dedicated."

"He was. He is."

"Did he have a college girlfriend?" I asked. Rita's eyes shot up to mine, and I shook my head. "It's not a jealousy question," I explained. "But I should probably know about his dating history if I'm supposed to pass as his girlfriend. It doesn't seem like the press is a very reliable source of information."

"I see that you saw the pictures from last night."

"I did," I nodded. "I opened up my phone when I first woke up this morning."

"I don't think Justin has seen them yet."

"I'm sure someone at work will show him. That's a good thing, though, right? Isn't that how this is supposed to go?"

"Yes," she said carefully. "I suppose that it is."

15

Justin

A WEEK WENT BY, AND then another, and Rebecca and I managed to settle into a sort of quiet, comfortable routine. When I wasn't working, I was helping her and my mother with wedding plans. Thanksgiving Day finally arrived, which was the day we were going to have our faux proposal. I would get down on one knee, she would cry, and everyone would clap and cheer. At least, that was how I pictured the event going.

"Does your mother's family know?" Rebecca asked me as she tied her shoes. She'd chosen comfortable attire for the dinner: a sweater, jeans, and Converse.

"About her cancer?"

"Yeah."

"Nope," I told her.

"She doesn't want to tell them?"

"She's worried they'll act differently around her," I explained.

"What do you think?"

"It's her choice," I shrugged.

"I understand why she's doing that," Rebecca told me. "Years ago, I probably wouldn't have, but it seems like people really do get weird when they know you're sick or having a hard time."

"Absolutely. It's hard for people to deal with death." Shifter or not, it was a hard thing to face.

"Yeah, I think that if your mom doesn't tell people, they'll probably treat her as normally as possible," she said. She finished tying her shoes and stood up. Then she looked at me, confused. "What are you wearing?"

"What do you think?" I spun around in a circle, showing off my outfit.

Rebecca looked from herself to me and back again, and then she burst out laughing.

"Did you dress to match me?"

"I did, actually," I smiled. "I didn't even own Converse until you moved in."

"Lucky me," she chuckled. "It's literally all I wear."

"I noticed," I smiled. "Are you going to wear them to the wedding?"

"No," she laughed. "Your mom vetoed that idea really quickly. Believe me."

"It's nice that you get along," I said.

"Me and your mom?"

"Yeah."

"Were you worried about that?"

"A little," I admitted. "Even though this whole fake wife thing was her idea, I still feel like it would have been hard if you didn't like each other."

"I mean, it's going to be hard either way," she said.

"You know what I mean."

"I do, actually," she stood up and smiled, placing her hands on my chest. "Because I'm your soon-to-be-wife, remember? It's my job to know about you."

I laughed and shook my head. I didn't kiss her, but I wanted to. Every part of me wanted to. I'd never spent so much time fantasizing about one person, and the horrible part was that every single person who knew we were dating probably thought we were having sex.

We weren't.

It wasn't something I was going to demand from her. I wasn't going to ask her to do that for me. If we ended up sleeping together, it would only complicate things. I knew that perfectly well, and I'd spent far too much time trying to convince my inner-bear of that.

My bear wanted her, though.

I did, too.

We'd kissed a few times, but I tried to hold it together for both of our sakes. Today I was going to kiss her, obviously, when I proposed, and I was wildly looking forward to it. There was a part of me that wondered whether we were actually going to be able to make it through the year without going any farther. Then there was another part of me, a darker part, that wanted to just forget the entire "being a good person" thing and just claim her as my own.

I wanted her in a way I'd never wanted anyone before. I wanted to slide deep inside of her, filling her with my seed. I wanted to make love to her for hours in every room of the house. I wanted all of that. Still, there was a part of me that kept reminding me not to take advantage of the situation. Just because I thought Rebecca might be my mate – and it was an eternal struggle as to whether I was convinced or not – didn't mean she wanted any part of that.

A reasonable bear might just ask her.

Unfortunately, when it came to her, all of my senses seemed to flee.

I spent a lot of free time running around outside, trying to burn off the sexual energy that had been coursing through my veins. Nothing worked, though. Jerking off didn't help. Jogging didn't help. Hunting in my bear form didn't help.

Somehow, I knew without a doubt that the only thing that would make me feel any sense of relief or reprieve would be the real thing.

The only thing that would clear my head was her.

As if reading my mind, Rebecca reached for her purse and casually glanced over her shoulder at me.

"How was your jog this morning?"

"What?"

"Your jog," she said. "I thought I heard you go outside this morning...around six?"

Her tone was light and casual, but I was a shifter. I could smell her. One of the perks – and sometimes, one of the drawbacks – of being a bear shifter was that I could practically smell emotions. If someone was trying to be sly or sneaky, it was pretty easy for me to figure that out.

In Rebecca's case, she was fishing for information.

Had I left that morning?

Yep.

Had it been to run?

Nope.

I'd gone out again to change into my bear form and go swimming. The water had been crisp and cooling, and it had relaxed me. In some ways, wandering into the mountains to go swimming beneath a waterfall was the shifter equivalent of taking a cold shower.

"It was fine," I told her. The less information I offered, the better. Rebecca wasn't dumb. She had her graduate degree, after all. She was pretty damn clever, and she was the kind of person who might actually be able to figure out my secret if I wasn't careful.

I had to be careful, though.

I didn't want her to know I was a bear shifter. I didn't want her to know about our people. It was too dangerous.

Only, that wasn't quite true.

There was a part of me, deep down, that wanted to just spill my guts. There was something deep inside of me that was begging to just share the truth with her. She was going to be my wife, after all, and I suspected that we were going to be having a lot of deeply personal conversations over the next year.

Maybe I should have just told her.

I'd promised my mom that I wouldn't, so I would stick with that. I wasn't about to betray a dying woman's confidence. My mother honestly didn't ask for much, so there wasn't really a reason that I couldn't do this one thing for her.

"Did you run very far?" Rebecca asked.

She was trying so damn hard to sound casual, but she didn't sound casual. It sounded like she was digging for information, and that rattled me a little bit. I shouldn't have to defend myself for taking a stroll in the morning before she was even awake. It wasn't like I'd abandoned her. I'd just needed some time to myself.

"What's with the third degree?" I asked a little more sharply than I had intended to.

"What?"

"The questions. What's with all of the questions?"

"I'm not asking that many questions."

"Kind of feels like it," I muttered.

She bristled, frustrated, and I instantly felt bad. Only, I was at war with myself. I didn't have to tell her about my jogs. We weren't really in a relationship. I didn't have to tell her anything.

If that was true, though, then why was she so annoyed?

"Whatever. Let's just go."

She grabbed her jacket off of the coat rack by the front door and headed outside. I followed behind, locking up the house as I did. When I got into the car, she was pouting. I took one look at her and shook my head.

"No."

"What?"

"This," I gestured to her.

"Me?"

"You," I agreed.

"Can you speak in complete sentences, please? I don't know what you're trying to say."

"You can't be like this at the dinner," I told her.

"I think I can be however I want."

"You're not my real girlfriend," I pointed out. Again, the bristling. Shit. I just wasn't doing a good job with this entire fake boyfriend thing today. "Look, I'm not trying to sound mean, but it needs to seem like we're in love. You can be irritated with me all you want when we get home, but you can't be upset with me at the event."

Why not?

Because I was a polar bear shifter and so was everyone else.

I knew that nobody was going to talk about the shifter side of things. We rarely did when we were around outsiders or newcomers. One of my cousins was bringing a boyfriend who was human, so that made it easy to bring Rebecca, too. Nobody was going to talk about the shifter stuff today.

Still, they'd be able to scent her. If she had any sort of strong emotions, whether those be directed at me or anyone else, the entire family would know. If she was upset with me, yet acting happy, they would see right through it. Basically, she needed to lie her ass off if this was going to work.

Maybe I should have hired her an acting coach.

I suddenly wondered if it would be helpful.

"Why not?" Rebecca asked, glancing over at me as I started to drive. "Wouldn't it be more believable for a couple to have the occasional argument?"

"Not in my family. They're going to want us to be happy and cuddly and sweet with each other."

"Really?"

"Really and truly," I said.

She sighed and then leaned back on the seat.

"Yeah, okay."

"I'm sorry," I told her gently. "I know this is hard."

"It shouldn't be. I mean, you're paying me, right? That's what the money is for."

It was *my* turn to bristle. So, it was just about the money, was it? I should have suspected that before. I really was an idiot. Every time Rebecca and I started to have fun together or laugh or anything like that, I let myself believe, just the tiniest bit, that it was real. I let myself believe that something real could happen for us.

That wasn't the case, though.

The two of us weren't fated mates.

We weren't destined to be together.

We weren't anything but two people in a business arrangement.

I'd do well to remember that.

"Yeah," I said through gritted teeth. "Yeah, I guess that's right."

"Well," she settled back against the chair and closed her eyes. "Then I guess that's right."

We drove the rest of the way in silence. I was suddenly dreading the event even though Thanksgiving had traditionally been my favorite holiday. It was always a nice chance to see my cousins, spend time with my aunts and uncles, and to just relax and unwind.

This year would be a little different since there were two humans in attendance. We wouldn't be casually talking about shifter things, but that was fine. All of us could go a little while without having to talk about all of the cool shifter stuff we wanted to do.

When I pulled into the driveway in front of my mother's huge home, I looked over at Rebecca.

"I'm going to need you to calm down," I told her.

"What?" Rebecca turned to me, glaring. "Just because a woman has an opinion doesn't mean she needs to calm down. I'm not even doing anything. I'm literally just sitting here."

"I know," I said. How could I explain that my family would be able to sense her agitation? They'd be able to smell her irritation. It was pretty messed up, really. They'd be able to take one look at her and know that something was wrong, and that would kind of destroy everything.

"Then why did you tell me to calm down?"

Her voice sounded sad, like she was frustrated and agitated. The truth was that I was irritated, too. We both knew this was a business exchange, but we were only a couple of weeks in, and we'd both already started to get attached to each other.

In some ways, that was good. It meant our relationship would look realistic. In other ways, it meant that when the entire relationship ended, we were both going to get hurt. My inner-bear growled at the thought. Yeah, he felt it, too.

"Because they can be a little intense."

"If they're anything like you, I think I'll be okay."

"I'm not sure whether that's an insult or a compliment."

"I'm not sure, either."

"Look, it's just that my aunts and uncles are...sensitive...to peoples' emotions."

"Like, they're psychic?"

"They like to think they are," I rolled my eyes. "It's just that if we walk into this event and we're obviously upset with each other, they aren't going to believe that I'm proposing to you. Okay?"

"Okay," she nodded, looking over at me. "I can calm down. You know, for the story."

"That's it?"

"That's it," she agreed.

Then, to my surprise, she leaned across the center console and pressed her lips to mine. She kissed me quickly, sweetly, and succinctly. It wasn't an overly sexual kiss, but it relaxed me, calming me.

"There we go," she chuckled, pulling back.

"What?"

"That's how you calm someone down, dumbass. You don't yell at them to calm down. You make them forget they were even mad in the first place."

She got out of the car and closed the door, and then she started walking toward the front door. She looked over her shoulder at me.

"Coming?"

Rebecca didn't wait for an answer, though. She just kept walking.

Okay, cool. I could get on board with this. I could get on board with the idea of calming her down with kisses. If that was what she wanted and needed, then yeah, I could do that. Kissing Rebecca was no hardship for me. It wasn't difficult or tricky. It wasn't a secret to me that I was attracted to her. I figured that it wasn't a secret to her, either.

I saw my mother step out onto the big, wraparound porch to say hello to Rebecca. They both turned to look at me, and I realized I was still sitting in the car. Hurriedly, I hopped out and jaunted up to the front porch.

"Mother," I said, hugging my mom. "Great to see you."

"You, as well," she said, looking back and forth from me to Rebecca. "Is everything all right?"

"It's fine," Rebecca said. "I thought I felt a little sick in the car, but I think it was just motion sickness. I'm okay now."

Smooth.

I liked the fact that she could think on her feet. It probably wasn't a good idea to be marrying someone who was good at lying. Well, aside from the fact that this was exactly what I needed. I needed someone who could bend the truth without any planning. If we were going to pull this thing off, then everyone needed to believe that Rebecca really was the person I loved.

There would be no room for doubting.

"Oh, you poor thing," my mother said, patting Rebecca's shoulder. "Let's get you inside, shall we? I'll get you some Sprite to calm your tummy." To me, she said, "Come on, now. Your Aunt Judy is here, and you know how she gets."

Yeah.

Yeah, I knew how Aunt Judy could get.

I sighed as I followed my future bride and my mother into the large house. Although my mom could have chosen a penthouse in one of the nearby cities or an apartment close to our company headquarters, she'd chosen a place on the edge of Rawr County that was nestled sweetly in the countryside.

She liked her space, apparently, and she liked having room to roam. Just like with my own home, there were plenty of trees and places to wander around. When my mother wanted to be in her polar bear form, she could easily shift and go swimming, exploring, or running. She owned over 200 acres of land, so she had plenty of space to be alone.

Unfortunately, this meant it took me a good half an hour to drive to her house if I wanted to visit. Mom didn't seem to mind driving, though, so it worked out just fine.

When I stepped into the house, I was overwhelmed by the sounds and smells. Everyone was there. Everyone. My aunts and uncles and cousins I didn't even know I had. They were all there, and they were all ready to see me.

Well, me and Rebecca.

I wasn't really sure how things were going to go, but I had to trust that they'd be smooth as silk. If we were going to pull any of this off, then we had to get really, really lucky, and it had to be really, really fast.

16

Rebecca

"So, you're the girlfriend, eh?"

"I'm the girlfriend," I agreed.

Justin's Aunt Judy was staring at me like I was the biggest gold-digging whore she'd ever seen in her life, and to be honest, in that moment, I kind of felt like one.

I mean, he *was* paying me to be his girlfriend and soon, his wife. That was true. If we wanted to get technical, I was doing this for the money. That was kind of how it had started, anyway, but spending time with Justin was actually kind of...

Well, it was kind of wonderful.

I liked getting to hang out with him and spend time with him one-on-one. We'd done a lot of cool things lately, like going on walks together and watching movies. We'd kind of gotten into a nice little flow of how we liked to behave with each other.

Now I was meeting his family, and I was already getting the feeling that this was going to be much, much harder than I thought.

"What are your intentions with my nephew?" Judy asked, glaring at me.

"Excuse me?"

"You heard me," she said. Judy crossed her arms over her chest. The two of us were standing in the kitchen. I'd only gone in to get a glass of water. I didn't expect to be cornered so soon in the game. I definitely didn't expect to have her coming at me like this.

And I didn't really have a good answer.

Lie.

I knew that I had to lie, and I knew that today was sort of a test. It was a preamble. If I did well today, then the engagement would happen, and then the wedding, and then Justin and I would have an entire year to hang out together. If I displeased his family, though, Justin might get cold feet. He might back out of the entire ordeal and find someone better suited to his needs.

Then where would I be?

"I love him," I said firmly, setting my glass down on the counter. I crossed my own arms over my chest, mirroring her stance. Judy might be one of the older relatives in this family, but she didn't scare me at all. If she wanted to be a cranky sourpuss, then she could be one. It didn't mean that I had to tolerate it.

"Love," Judy said, practically spitting out the word. "What does a human like you know about love?"

"Human?" I raised an eyebrow. "Aren't we all human?"

Judy's eyes widened and she snapped her mouth shut. Then she turned and left the room, marching out into the living room.

Okay, so that was really weird.

Why did she call me a human?

There were a lot of weird things that had happened since I'd come to Rawr County. Of course, the entire premise of my arrival had been strange, but human? Why was she calling me that?

I suddenly wondered if Judy was the type of crazy that believed she was secretly – or not so secretly – an alien or something like that. I made a mental note to ask Justin about it later, but I didn't have a lot of time to ponder because his mom came in.

"Doing okay?" Rita asked nervously. "Judy just kind of flew out in a huff."

"She cornered me," I told Rita.

"Cornered you?"

"Yeah. She asked me what my intentions were with her nephew."

"What did you tell her?"

"The truth," I said.

Rita's eyes widened.

"I told her that I love Justin," I smiled innocently.

Rita seemed to calm, and she nodded.

"Good girl," she said, patting my shoulder. "Now, let's get back out there, okay? I know everyone's going to be a little nervous today, but they're all going to do their best to be kind and welcoming to you."

"Thanks," I said.

It didn't calm me down, though. I'd never exactly been good at dealing with my date's families. Somehow, that had always been the part of the relationship I'd been worst at. Trying to impress someone I cared about was one thing, but a family?

That was something else entirely.

We left the kitchen and headed into the nearby living room where several relatives were sitting on different pieces of furniture and telling silly stories. Justin was nowhere to be found, but nobody seemed to notice his absence. They were all caught up in reminiscing.

"Remember that one time up at Bear Creek? Oh, that was fun!"

"I remember because it was the first time that-"

As soon as everyone saw me, they fell silent. Awesome. I wasn't really sure why I was having that effect on people today. It seemed like as soon as people noticed I was there, they became tiny, quiet versions of their former selves, and I didn't really know why.

"Uh, hey," I said, waving nervously.

"Hey."

"Hi."

"Sup."

"For those of you who haven't met Justin's girlfriend yet, this is Rebecca."

"Hello."

"Nice to meet you."

"Pleasure."

Somehow, despite the nice and welcoming words, I didn't really get the idea that any of them really meant it. Yikes.

"Nice to meet you," I said, pasting a smile on my face.

Was it just me, or did it seem like people were sniffing the air a little bit?

Fuck.

Had I forgotten deodorant? I needed to check. If I was going to pull off this engagement with Justin, then I needed to make sure I didn't ruin it by being his smelly girlfriend at the first family event.

Where had Justin gone, anyway? When I'd stepped into the kitchen to get a glass of water, he'd been talking to one of his uncles, but now he was just...gone.

I'd find him later, but first things first.

"Excuse me, could you point me to the direction of the restroom?"

"Of course, dear. There's one up the stairs and to the right."

"Thanks."

I stepped back into the large, open hallway on the first floor. Unlike Justin's home, his mother's place was kind of enormous and overwhelming. I'd never been in any houses that were this big before. Never. Even though I knew this was the world I was joining soon, it was still kind of unnerving.

As soon as I stepped out of the living room and started walking up the stairs, I heard everyone begin speaking in hushed tones. I didn't know what they were saying, but somehow, I could tell they were talking about me, and it was embarrassing and annoying.

I knew that this was fake.

Like, I got that. I understood that this entire arrangement wasn't real, but it still *felt* real in some ways, and the family wasn't rejecting some fake version of myself I'd made up. They were rejecting me. It hurt so much more than it should.

With little effort, I found the bathroom. Of course, it was just as big as everything else in the house. I headed straight for the sink and washed my hands and splashed a little water on my face.

"Pull it together," I told myself. "You can do this."

When I stared in the mirror, I wasn't sure if I really could do this. It was a horribly scary thing, wasn't it? And he was...

Well, Justin was hot. Dangerous. Sexy. Powerful.

He was so many different things, and I wanted a part of all of it. I wanted to be with him and to get to know him, and even though he'd promised sex was off the table...

Well, I was hoping there would be an exception to that rule.

"You can do this," I told myself again, and I started rummaging around in the drawers and medicine cabinet, looking for any sort of body spray. I wasn't so gross that I was going to use someone else's stick-on deodorant, but maybe I could find some spritzer or something that would stop whatever odor surrounding me was so offensive.

I was on my hands and knees, looking under the bathroom sink when I heard footsteps outside of the door.

"She's something else, isn't she?"

Who else could they be talking about? It had to be me, right?

"I don't know what he sees in her."

"And, I mean, she's *human*."

There was that word again.

Yeah, they were definitely talking about me, only I didn't know why. I didn't know what I could have possibly done to Justin's family that was so damn offensive. So, I was a *human*. Did that really matter?

And more importantly, why?

Why did it matter to them?

Weren't we all humans, anyway?

Maybe I acted a little more down-to-Earth than they were, but I was kind of a poor kid who had grown up in a normal, run-of-the-mill area. I hadn't been born into wealth, hadn't been bred into it, and I was kind of trying to find my way through all of this.

I quietly closed the doors beneath the sink and stepped over to the bathroom door. The two people seemed to have stopped right outside of the bathroom.

"It's no secret that she's dating him for the cash."

"At least he hasn't done anything crazy," one of them said.

"Yeah, like propose."

Yikes.

Well, as far as I knew, the proposal was still happening as planned, so these family members were going to have to get over it and fast. I couldn't tell who it was outside of the door, but I knew that more than a few of the relatives weren't super thrilled with me.

"Like he'd propose to her, too. She's not even a shifter!"

Shifter?

"Shhh. You know we aren't supposed to talk about that stuff today."

"Why the hell not?"

"Because Justin brought Rebecca, and she doesn't know, and Ally brought Kyle, and he doesn't know."

"Well, maybe our relatives should stop worrying so much about trying to impress these people. I mean, if Rebecca knew Justin could shapeshift into a polar bear, do you really think she'd stay?"

17

Justin

"She's cute," Kyle said.

My cousin, Ally, had always been one of my favorites, and despite the fact that her boyfriend was a human, he seemed like a good match for her. The two of them hadn't seemed to stop smiling at each other since the Thanksgiving event had started. Now Kyle and I had somehow ended up alone together. Dinner was going to start soon, and both of our girlfriends were strangely absent.

"Thanks," I told Kyle, glancing around the room. Where had Rebecca run off to, anyway?

"You two seem pretty happy," Kyle continued. He was obviously feeling a little uncomfortable being around so many relatives at once.

"Us? Oh, yeah. We are," I fumbled a little. I still couldn't figure out where she'd gone. The last time I'd seen her, she'd been heading off to find a glass of water, but she'd never come back.

"How'd you meet?"

"Wow, this is just a lot of questions, Kyle," I looked at the human, who had the decency to blush.

"Sorry," he muttered, "I guess I talk a lot when I'm nervous."

"Why are you nervous? Haven't you and Ally been together for like, a year?"

"Well, yeah," he nodded, grinning. "In fact, I'm going to ask her to marry me."

"You are?" This was news to me.

"Yup. Turns out, I'm her mate."

"What?" I looked at Kyle, and my jaw hit the floor. He did *not* just use the "M" word. He was a fucking human!

Kyle seemed to realize that he'd done something wrong because he paled and shook his head.

"Nothing," he said. "I just care about her a lot."

"Kyle, why did you use that word?"

"Marriage?"

"No."

"Mate?"

"Yes."

"Um, because...well, because...because we are!"

Kyle frowned, placing his hands on his hips.

"We both know that the family will never approve, but they just have to. I love her!"

Ally appeared in the doorway to the sitting room where Kyle and I were talking. As if sensing her mate, apparently, was unhappy, she hurried to his side. She placed a hand on his shoulder and gently started murmuring to him.

"Are you okay?"

"I'm fine."

Ally looked up at me and her eyes narrowed. I'd seen that same look on her face before plenty of times when we were kids. Anytime she thought I might be cheating at chess or trying to steal money in Monopoly, she'd look at me with that same unhappy frown.

"What did you say to him?"

"Me? Nothing!"

"You obviously said something to upset Kyle."

"Why would you blame me? Ally, I'm your favorite cousin."

She stared at me for a moment, as though she wanted to argue with that, but then she just rolled her eyes as though the entire situation was ridiculous.

"Yeah, well, I suppose you are my favorite cousin, aren't you?"

"I suppose I am," I agreed.

"So," she looked from Kyle to me and back again. "What happened here, boys? I'm not a fool, you know."

"No one thinks you're a fool," Kyle said.

"So, what is it?"

"I don't think that Justin approves of the fact that I'm human."

"Why wouldn't he approve? He's dating a human, too."

"I don't think she knows," Kyle murmured, looking right at me. He was right.

Rebecca didn't know. There were so many things that she didn't know. She didn't know my life history or all of my favorite stories. We hadn't read my favorite books together and she hadn't seen my favorite films. Well, not all of them, anyway. We'd made a good chunk of progress through some of my early favorites, like *The Goonies* and *The Princess Bride*, which she somehow hadn't seen before.

There were still so many things she needed to know, though.

"Wait, you haven't told her?" Ally seemed shocked.

"I have to admit I'm pretty damn shocked you told Kyle," I snapped.

"Why wouldn't I tell Kyle?" Ally's face contorted into a mix of confusion and disappointment. "He's the guy I want to marry one day. He's my mate."

"Because our existence isn't something we're supposed to share openly."

"I'm not sharing it openly. I'm sharing it with the person I'm supposed to love forever," she said. Ally's eyes narrowed and she looked at me. "Do you really think you're going to be able to date this girl and not tell her? Like, long-term? How are you going to pull that off?"

"We're living together, and I've already pulled it off," I said smugly, crossing my arms over my chest.

She didn't know.

She wasn't going to know.

"Are you serious right now? You're living together?"

"Yes."

"I didn't know that. Does your mom know?"

My mom was the only one who did know anything about anything.

"Yeah," I nodded. "She knows."

Luckily, she knew, and she was happy for us. She had been instrumental in making sure this entire thing was going to go according to plan. Then again, it *had* been her idea.

"So, your mom knows you've got a girlfriend who lives with you, and your girlfriend is happy living with you, yet she doesn't actually know the first thing about you? Dude."

Ally shook her head and gestured for Kyle to follow her out of the room.

"It's not like that," I started to say, but Ally turned around and shook her finger at me: a gesture she hadn't used since we were kids.

"It's like that, Justin. It's like that. You had a choice. You could have told her who you were. Yeah, maybe she wouldn't have liked it, but that's not your decision to make. You can't control how people react to the truth. You can literally only control whether you're going to be honest or not."

"Easy for you," I said.

"Easy for me? No, Justin. Not easy for me. Being honest is never easy, but it's the right fucking thing to do."

I stared as Kyle and Ally left the room. Kyle looked back and gave me a look that said, "Sorry, bro." I deserved that. I deserved all of it.

Collapsing on a nearby couch, I dropped my head in my hands. So much for having the perfect first Thanksgiving. Not only had I pissed off Rebecca before we'd even arrived, but I'd then made it completely awkward between my favorite cousin and me.

Shit.

I wanted to yell at Ally for revealing herself as a shifter to Kyle, but I knew that she was right. I couldn't be mad at her. She had chosen to be honest with the person she loved, and it really was the right thing to do. If he was actually going to propose to her, then it was the perfect choice.

"Knock-knock," a soft, sweet voice said from the doorway. I looked up to see Rebecca standing there looking lovely as ever. For what seemed like the millionth time, my heart seemed to start racing.

"You don't have to say it," I pointed out. "You can just knock."

"I like saying it," she smiled.

"I was wondering where you'd run off to."

"Had to find the bathroom," she told me. Rebecca walked into the room and sat down beside me on the couch. She reached for my hand and squeezed it. I hadn't even told her I was feeling tense, but she could somehow just tell.

"It's almost time to eat," I told her.

"What do you think? Showtime before or after?"

"Let's do it before," I told her. "I have a feeling Kyle is going to pop the question after, and I don't know if my mother can handle two proposals that close together."

18

Rebecca

We walked into Rita's dining room, which was really more of a banquet hall. In the center of the room was a huge dining table. It spanned the entire length of the room and was nothing short of lovely. In fact, it was the most beautiful thing I thought I'd ever seen. The table was filled with all sorts of foods ranging from traditional turkey and stuffing to an assortment of fruit pies to vegetable side dishes and at least a dozen different kinds of bread.

"Wow," I murmured.

"We like to go all out," Justin said, as though that explained everything.

An hour ago, I would have thought he meant his family when he said "we." Now, I couldn't stop thinking about what the cousins had said while I was in the bathroom. Was Justin a shapeshifter? Were all of them shapeshifters? I'd done a quick Internet search before I'd come out of the bathroom to brush up on my mythology and folklore. Even though I'd heard of shifters, they'd kind of been...well, they'd been out of sight and out of mind.

They'd never been anything or anyone that I concerned myself with.

Now, though, I was wondering exactly how much I'd missed. If Justin was actually a shapeshifter, that would explain a lot of things, now wouldn't it? It would explain his weird clothing while running. I'd read that if a shifter wants to change into their animal form, they have to be naked first. Otherwise, they tear their clothes. So, maybe Justin's walks and runs into the forest weren't normal adventures. Maybe he was changing into his animal self.

And he didn't want me to know.

I was almost certain I'd somehow waltzed into a family of animal shifters. That would explain so many different things. People were still sniffing me, for example. They were trying to be discreet, I knew, but it wasn't working too well.

I wasn't used to people smelling me.

It kind of stood out.

Now, I wondered whether Justin was ever going to tell me. I felt like I shouldn't be able to get mad. After all, this was a paid arrangement. It wasn't like he loved me. It wasn't like I was his fated mate, which was another thing I'd read about before leaving my bathroom hideaway.

"Well, it looks great," I said, turning to him and smiling. Justin nodded and took my hand, and he led me farther into the room. We sat down side-by-side at one end of the table. We were close to the foot of the table, where Judy was sitting, along with Ally and Kyle, whom I'd met. Then there were a group of triplets who were probably eight or nine. There were a couple of family sets, a few solo cousins, a really funny girl named Jezzie who promised to tell me silly stories about Justin if I ever got her alone, and then Rita sat at the head of the table.

"Welcome everyone," Rita said. "And thank you so much for joining us. Before we begin, let's bless the food."

I bowed my head, glad that my own family was traditional enough that I knew how to behave in a setting like this. Rita spoke some words of gratitude over the food, and then everyone looked up again. Rita introduced a game where we'd go around the circle and each person would say something they were thankful for. She started on the opposite side of the table from where Justin and I were sitting.

The first few answers were slightly predictable.

"I'm thankful for my family."

"School's going well."

"I'm happy about my health."

Each answer was nice, but not terribly serious until it was Ally's turn. I knew even before she spoke what she was going to do, and judging by the sudden tension radiating from Justin, I'd say he knew, too.

"I'm thankful for Kyle," Ally said. Kyle opened his mouth, like he was going to take his turn, but something in her posture must have tipped him off, too. "And I'd like to tell everyone something very important."

Everyone fell silent as we looked at Ally and Kyle.

Ally pushed her chair out from the table and stood. She tugged Kyle to his feet, too.

"What are you doing?" Kyle whispered. It was kind of a stage-whisper, though. We could all hear.

"Something I should have done a long time ago," she said. Turning back to her family, she spoke again, "Kyle is the most incredible person I've ever met. He's kind. He's funny. He's generous. He always knows just how to make me laugh. He's always there for me when I'm having a hard time, and most importantly, he's wildly loving."

"Aw," Judy clutched her hands to her chest.

"That's gross," the triplets snickered until Judy shot them a nasty look. They quickly quieted.

Ally dropped to her knees beside Kyle, and she reached for his hand.

"Kyle, I love you. Will you marry me?"

He laughed and tugged her back up, pulling her into his arms.

"A bit unconventional, are we?"

"I mean, I did ask your dad for his blessing," she laughed.

"Seriously?"

"He said he'd only give it if I took him fishing."

"That's why you and my dad went fishing?"

"Yeah."

"Well, a girl that's going to fish with my dad is a girl worth keeping, I'd say," he laughed and kissed her brightly. I wasn't sure whether I was supposed to clap or stay quiet or stare or look away, so instead of doing anything else, I just looked at Justin.

He seemed frustrated. I knew why. This was supposed to be the moment when he proposed to me. I knew that was how he'd been planning on doing it, but I didn't really mind. We could let Ally and Justin have this perfect moment together. We could let them shine.

"I have something to say," Justin said.

Or, apparently, we could share the moment. That would work, too.

"Justin?" Aunt Judy seemed shocked that Justin would dare interrupt Ally and Kyle's moment. A few other people seemed shocked, too. Rita was the only one who appeared strangely calm. She was *eerily* calm. If I didn't know that she was in on this, it would make me uncomfortable.

As it was, I just smiled at Justin, pretending like everything was okay.

Inwardly, I was completely freaking out.

"I have to admit that my beautiful cousin's plan to propose was not something I was ready for, but at the risk of being seen as an ill-timed copy-cat, I'd like to follow suit."

There was a gasp as Justin pushed his chair back and dropped to the floor. He took my hand and smiled at me. His eyes twinkled, and I knew what he was thinking.

"Rebecca, we may have had a whirlwind romance, but every day when I wake up next to you, I can't help but feel like it's going to be the greatest day of my life. Will you make me the happiest man alive? Will you marry me?"

What else could I say but yes?

"Absolutely," I grinned, laughing. I reached for him, tugging him into my arms, and then I gave him the kiss of a lifetime. I could tell from the gasps and awes and sighs that it looked damn good. It felt good, too. Everything about the moment felt perfect.

There was just a tiny, itsy bitsy part of me that wished it wasn't all for show.

There was a part of me that wished it was real.

19

Justin

"You think they bought it?" Rebecca asked excitedly once we were in the car.

I pulled out of my mother's driveway and hopped back on the road, shaking my head.

"Yeah," I said. "Absolutely. We put on one hell of a show."

And I couldn't believe it.

We'd pulled it off without a hitch, and everyone had truly gone for it. After my aunts and uncles had freaked out a little bit, everyone hopped up to welcome both Rebecca and Kyle to the family. Luckily, Ally was a good sport about the whole thing, and I pulled her aside later to apologize. She hadn't cared. She'd just laughed.

"Great cousins think alike," she'd said, and that kind of stuck with me.

I really was lucky to have a family who cared so very much about me and who were so flexible when it came to on-the-spot marriage proposals.

When we got back to the house, I headed to take a shower and Rebecca started getting ready for bed. I was aching to go for a run, but I didn't. Even though I wanted to, I didn't want to tip her off to the fact that I was kind of a total freak.

Oh, I knew she'd be nice about it. Rebecca was definitely the type of girl who was *nice*, but I didn't really want to start off our

123

fake marriage with bad ideas or thoughts. It was strange, I supposed, how much I wanted her to like me. There was a part of me – probably the shifter part – that wanted her to like me for who I was and not for my money.

I stepped into the shower and let the water pour over me. I stood there, spacing off for what seemed like a solid eternity. What would it be like to invite Rebecca in to shower with me? Yeah, we'd said no sex, but that didn't mean we couldn't do other things... did it?

Oh, fuck.

I was losing my damn mind.

I couldn't tell her.

That much was for certain. My mother had been right. This was a secret that I had to keep to myself. Even though I didn't approve, it was different for Ally and Kyle. They really loved each other. They were fated mates and they both knew it. Their relationship was honest and open and pure on so many levels.

Rebecca and I...

Our relationship was made up.

Make believe.

A pretend fairy tale that my mother had dreamed up to save my public image.

Fucking hell.

I finally got out of the shower and grabbed a towel. I wrapped it around myself, brushed my teeth, and then headed into the bedroom. Rebecca was sitting in bed reading a book. She looked up when she saw me, and the faint scent of arousal flooded my nostrils.

Fuck.

She liked the abs.

I peered over at her as I started rummaging around the dresser. She kept her eyes firmly on her book, but she was biting her lip, as though she couldn't believe what she was seeing.

I couldn't resist the urge to have a little fun with her.

"I just forgot my clothes," I told her.

"Ah...yes."

"You don't mind, do you?" I turned toward her, so I was facing her head-on. Rebecca looked up and eyed my chest. If she bit her lip any harder, it was going to start to bleed. That was no worry. I'd go kiss it all better. It wouldn't be a problem at all.

"Um, no," she said.

"You don't mind if I get dressed right here?" I clarified. I'd be a gentleman. I'd give her the chance to say no if she didn't want to see.

"That's okay," she nodded, looking back toward her book. "It's your room, after all."

"Well, I figure that you'll be seeing me naked plenty of times over the next year, so we might as well start now."

"Makes sense."

She was shaking as the towel dropped to the floor, but I'd give her full credit. She didn't look. She stayed totally focused on the book in front of her. She was doing a damn good job of pretending that this wasn't affecting her in any way because oh, it was affecting her.

I took my time turning around, reaching for a pair of boxers and then slowly stepping into them. I fought the urge to turn around and see if she was watching my backside. I didn't really need to know, now did I?

No....I didn't need to know.

There would be plenty of time for fun and games in the future, and right now, I could rest assured that I'd at least gotten to have a little fun teasing my soon-to-be-bride.

I hung up my towel and then came to bed wearing only the boxers.

"No pajamas tonight?" Rebecca asked quietly.

"Not tonight."

"I see," she said quietly.

She closed her book and set it on her nightstand before flipping off her light. Then she stayed quiet for a few moments on her side of the bed. I listened as her breathing slowed and regulated as she started to calm down for the night, but I also knew that she wasn't asleep.

"Rebecca?"

She was quiet.

"Becca?"

Nothing.

"I know you're not asleep."

Silence.

"You snore a little."

"I do not!" Rebecca sat up abruptly and put her hands on her hips. She didn't know it, but as a shifter, I had excellent vision. I could tell exactly what she looked like in that tight little tank top. I could see the way her nipples were hard and poking at the fabric.

"I know," I said. "But it got your attention."

"You're insufferable."

"A little," I agreed, rolling over onto my side. I propped my head up with my hand and just *looked* at her. This was her. This was the woman I was actually going to marry. We still had to actually hold the ceremony and everything, but this was it.

It was really going to happen.

"What are you looking at?" Rebecca whispered.

"You."

"Why?"

"Because you're pretty," I said simply. I hadn't meant to say that. I was probably more surprised than she was that I'd actually gone so far as to say that, but I meant every word.

"You don't have to do that," Rebecca told me. "You don't have to pretend to like me."

"But I do like you."

"Don't make this harder than it has to be, Justin," she whispered. I was surprised when she settled back on the bed but faced me. Her position mirrored my own. She propped her head up.

"Why would this have to be hard? It's just an exchange, right? You're selling me your time."

"I think it will be hard, though."

"Why?"

"Because you're not what I expected," she admitted. "I thought you'd be this pompous, arrogant prick who was away all of the time. I didn't think you were going to be the kind of guy who wanted to watch *Buffy the Vampire Slayer* reruns with me."

"Hey, everyone who's anyone likes Buffy," I laughed.

"You know what I mean."

"I know what you mean," I agreed.

"It's just that...today was pretty intense."

"That's a nice way of putting it. I'd probably describe it more as chaos wrapped as a turkey dinner."

"It wasn't that bad. Your mom seemed really happy."

At least that much was true. My mom hadn't just been happy. She'd been ecstatic. She'd loved the way Rebecca and I had spent so much time together. She'd loved the way we were happy and laughing together.

"She really likes you. Not just as a fake mate, either."

"I'm glad. I like her, too."

I didn't want to think about my mom too much because of what her diagnosis meant. I knew that soon, I wouldn't be able to see her anymore at all. Soon I'd have to say goodbye for the very last time, and I didn't want to.

I didn't want to have to tell my mom goodbye. I didn't want to have to lay her to rest. Cancer was a horrible bitch, and I was tired of facing her. When my mom passed away, at least she'd do so surrounded by people that she loved. She'd have me, and now she'd have Rebecca. She'd also get to die having seen my wedding, no matter how fake that was.

"What's wrong?"

"I was just thinking about my mom."

"She's a good lady. A nice lady."

"I know."

"I'm sorry about her being sick," Rebecca whispered.

"I'm sorry, too. She didn't deserve this."

"It's not the first time, right? She fought it once. Maybe she can fight it again."

"I don't know."

"She's strong," Rebecca reminded me. "Really strong."

"She can definitely do anything she sets her mind to, but I don't know if she can do this," I admitted.

"Well, let's keep hoping, okay? Let's keep hoping."

Rebecca surprised me by reaching out and pressing her hands against my chest. The gesture was tender and sweet, and it wasn't something I thought she'd be doing. Not on a day like today. Not on a night like tonight.

"What are you doing?"

"I'm touching you."

"Why?"

"Because you're sad."

"You don't have to sleep with people just because they're sad."

She laughed.

Oh, that sound was something I could listen to a million times over and never grow tired of. Rebecca's laugh was the sweetest, loveliest sound in the whole world.

"I'm not going to sleep with you. I'm just touching you."

"Touching me because you want to sleep with me," I teased.

"No," she said, but she kept stroking my chest. She touched me softly, gingerly, like she wasn't quite sure how to do it and she didn't quite want to hurt me.

"You're not going to hurt me."

"Just making sure."

"Are you always this gentle?"

"In bed?"

"Yes."

"Sometimes," she admitted. "What about you?"

"I'm not usually very gentle in bed."

"Are you like, a dominating kind of guy?"

"Sometimes."

"I thought so. So, do you like to tie people up and spank them?"

"That depends."

"On what?"

"On whether they like to be tied up and spanked."

Her breath hitched. She liked the idea. Curious. I wouldn't have taken the sweet English graduate as the curious type. I certainly wouldn't have pegged her as the type of girl to ask such questions late at night in bed.

"What about me? Would you tie me up?"

"Are you propositioning me, Rebecca?"

Silence.

She wasn't sure.

She was scared, and she should be.

"It's time to say goodnight," I told her. I pressed a soft kiss to her forehead, and then I rolled over onto my side, facing away from her. Rebecca was quiet, but agitated, and she finally laid back down on her side, too.

I was quiet until I was sure she had fallen asleep, and then I peeked over to look at her. She was so perfect, so quiet, and so sweet. I hated that I'd turned her down, but I knew it wasn't right. Whether she wanted kinky sex or vanilla sex or something in-between, I'd give it to her if I thought we could both handle it, but I knew that neither one of us could.

We'd promised that this was going to be a marriage of convenience, but so far, the only thing we'd achieved was getting attached.

Awesome.

20

Rebecca

"You're going to be a beautiful bride."

"This is the prettiest dress I've ever seen."

"It was made for you."

"What do you think?"

I stared at myself in the mirror. I really couldn't believe this was it. I was at my final fitting for my wedding gown. It was really happening.

"I love it," I said. A smile spread across Rita's face, and I knew I'd said the right thing. Not that there was anything else I *could* say in that moment. She'd brought me for the final fitting despite the fact that she hadn't been feeling well lately.

The wedding was in just a few days, and I was constantly checking on Rita to make sure she was doing okay. She'd been a total godsend when it came to planning everything and getting it all put together. If it hadn't been for her, this wedding never would have been planned. Not even if we'd had a year to bring it all together.

Justin had been busy with work, so Rita and I had been spending most of our days together. My evenings were Justin's, but my days were filled with afternoons on the town, shopping, and for the last few days, reminiscing over old photo albums.

When we left the dress shop, I spotted a little cookie store on the corner. Rita started heading directly to the car, which was parked out front, but I grabbed her arm gently.

"Have you ever had a hot chocolate chip cookie topped with frosting?" I asked her, grinning.

Rita seemed surprised. I knew her answer was going to be *no* before she even said it.

"No, I don't think that I have," she admitted. "That shop has been there for a long time, but no, I don't think I've ever gone inside."

"Want to try it out?"

"You and me?"

"Yes! My treat," I said. I hooked my arm through hers and guided her away from the car and over to the little shop. "Variety is the spice of life, right? I love little shops like this."

"They're wonderful," she agreed. "What's your favorite treat to get?"

We stepped inside and were instantly greeted by two different team members. There was a huge menu over the bakery display, and I led Rita over to it.

"Shops like this usually have a special menu item they're known for," I told her. "Look, it's there."

Sure enough, there was a little bear-shaped cookie with frosting on it. The bear was covered with sprinkles, too. It looked like someone's childhood dream creation.

"Excuse me," I asked one of the staff members. "What's your favorite thing to eat here?"

Each of the team members offered their suggestions, and eventually Rita and I each decided on a little treat. I paid, and we carried our wrapped cookies to one of the little tables that was located just outside of the shop.

"Are you ready?" I asked her.

"To try my cookie?"

"Yep. We both need to bite in at the same time."

"Same time?"

"It'll taste better that way," I promised. I didn't know if that was true or not, but it sounded pretty good to me.

"Okay," she agreed.

We held our cookies up and I counted out loud for us.

"One...two...three!"

Together, we shoved our cookies into our mouths and yes, we sighed with contentment. The cookie I'd chosen was by far the best thing I'd ever eaten. It definitely outshone everything else I'd ever tried on my own. Rita started laughing as she quickly devoured her cookie, too. Apparently, we both had the same opinion: the cookies were winners. By the time we finished giggling and eating, Rita looked at me thoughtfully.

"I have to admit, you're not what I expected."

"What were you expecting?" I was honestly curious about that. When she'd dreamed up this idea, had she been expecting someone kind of stuffy? Someone mean? Maybe someone who didn't have any manners?

Rita considered me for a long moment. It kind of seemed like she was sizing me up and trying to decide whether I was worth an honest answer. Luckily, she seemed to decide that I was.

"I figured you'd be a spoiled rich brat," she shrugged. "Maybe someone who wanted a little extra to pad their trust fund."

My jaw dropped. I could practically feel it hitting the floor. A trust fund kid? A brat? What the hell was she talking about? My confusion must have shown because she quickly started talking again.

"Obviously that isn't true. I mean, it seems as though you're quite perfect for Justin."

"Perfect?"

"You know, if this wasn't a fake relationship from the get-go," she lowered her voice, "I'd say he's falling for you."

I swallowed hard and nodded, and then I looked away because there was no way I could keep staring at her without giving away the fact that I felt the same way. Only, I felt like I was the one falling. I hated that he still had secrets from me. Those stupid, early morning "jogs" he took hadn't stopped. I still wanted to know what he was up to.

Was he really a bear shifter?

I had to know.

Before I even thought about bringing up the idea of us maybe, actually like, dating for real, I should probably try to find out the truth about him.

"Rita," I said. "Can I ask you something?"

She tensed but nodded. So, she probably knew what was coming. Surely, she had to realize that I was going to ask at some point.

"Is Justin a shapeshifting polar bear?"

Rita looked like she was going to throw up, and then like she was going to scream, and then like she was going to lie. I was prepared for all of those reactions, but the one reaction I hadn't predicted was pure, unadulterated laughter.

Rita laughed and laughed until her sides were obviously hurting, and then she snorted.

"Are you okay? Do you need a drink?"

"I wondered how long it would take you to figure it out," she said. "You're smarter than I thought. Like I said."

"So, it's true?"

She looked at me, cocking her head.

"Why do you think this place is called Rawr County? It's not for the wild animal population."

"Could have fooled me," I muttered.

"He didn't tell you," Rita suddenly said. "Did he?"

"He did not tell me."

"So, what made you come to this conclusion?"

I laid out the evidence I had. Rita had talked about Justin being a tiny "cub." I also brought up the fact that her relatives had called me a human several times. I talked about the weird jogs, about the sniffing, about everything. By the time I finished, Rita was rolling her eyes.

"Sometimes I wonder how we, as a species, have managed to survive," she said slowly. "It seems we haven't been as discreet as we're supposed to be."

"Is there anything wrong with me knowing?" I asked carefully. "Do you think I should tell Justin I know?"

"I won't tell you what to do. Real or fake, it's your relationship. Justin has his own way of handling conflict in his life, and he's always been a very private person."

"It seems like part of that is because of the company," I pointed out.

"Part of it, yes. Justin has a big role to fill."

"From what he's said – again, bits and pieces here – it seems like he has some enemies, too."

That concerned me a little. I didn't like the idea that someone might be mean to Justin. It pained me a little, too, if I was being honest. Despite all of his flaws and the incredible secretiveness, he was a kind person at his core.

"There are people who would do anything to take the company," Rita told me. "And those are the people you and Justin both need to watch out for."

"No one in particular?" I asked, raising an eyebrow.

"There are a few companies who want to merge with us," Rita said. "Sometimes companies do dangerous things when they're desperate: things like photoshopping pictures to destroy someone's reputation," she sighed. "These are all things Justin should fill you in on, but since he hasn't, I guess I'm stuck doing it."

"Gee, sorry," I rolled my eyes.

"I didn't mean it like that. It's just that this feels like a conversation he should be having with you."

I couldn't exactly disagree. I liked Justin. A lot. I liked him so much more than I ever thought I would, but he really was a mystery to me in so many ways, and I didn't know if I was ever going to be able to figure him out.

I just didn't know.

21

Justin

"**D**id you see the pictures?" Phil burst into my office, once again obsessed with pictures of me and Rebecca. It was getting a little old. At first, I hadn't really cared about his weird obsession, but now it had been weeks. Even though the entire point of Rebecca and I going out was to get pictures and to validate our relationship in the public eye, it still felt weird and a little creepy that Phil was bringing them up to me.

"Yes, Phil. I saw the photos."

Rebecca and I had spent the night before at a cute little restaurant downtown. My mom had actually recommended it as a place she liked going with her girlfriends, so the two of us decided to check it out. When Rebecca went out by herself, she wasn't really noticed or followed. Maybe that was because she went out with my mother. When the two of us went out, though, there was always someone ready to snap a photo.

"Well, what do you think about them?"

"I think that if you spent half as much time working as you do worrying about gossip, we wouldn't have the supply chain shortages we've been having this month."

He frowned and nodded, but then finally left. As soon as my office was empty again, I pulled up one of the gossip websites to see exactly which pictures had been taken and shared. Hopefully,

I wasn't doing anything stupid like wiping sauce off of my face. Unfortunately, I'd had more than a few pictures like that before.

"What do we have here?" I muttered, looking through them. The series of pictures that had been posted featured me and Rebecca, of course, but the thing that surprised me the most was just how happy I looked. I seemed calmer than I ever had before. During the dinner, I'd felt wildly relaxed. That showed through in the pictures.

Well, it looked like it wouldn't be hard to get people to buy I was in love with her. If I didn't know better myself, I'd say that I definitely was in love with her. Of course, that was impossible. This was a business arrangement designed to protect my business.

Nothing more.

Nothing less.

The morning flew by, and I resisted the urge to text her. It was silly, but I felt like if I texted her, even just to say that I missed her, that it would make things harder for myself. I already felt like I was getting wildly attached to the human.

Did I really need to make things harder on myself?

Reluctantly, I closed the website with the pictures of us, and I turned back to work for the day. Luckily, it seemed like the media had chosen to focus on my budding relationship with Rebecca and had shied away from things like talking about whether or not I was an alcoholic.

That was the way I wanted it.

My morning was filled with meetings that could have been emails, but my father had always believed in seeing employees face-to-face, and I felt that he was right. It was a good idea to get to know people on a personal level because then they'd feel safe at their jobs. They'd also feel like they could trust me.

There was a knock at my door around noon.

"Come in," I glanced up, half-expecting to see Rebecca walking into the office, but it was my head of marketing, Heather.

"Lunch?" Heather asks, holding up a couple of carryout bags.

"Of course," I said, leaning back. I was surprised. Heather and I almost never had lunch. "What do I owe you?"

"Nothing," she said. "I used the company credit card."

"Funny."

"I did."

"That's what it's there for," I shrugged. I cleared off my desk and Heather pulled up a chair. The two of us started eating right away.

"Gosh, were you hungry?" Heather laughed, gesturing to my empty food dish. She leaned back, crossing one leg over the other.

"I guess I was," I admitted sheepishly. "I suppose it doesn't look well for the boss to forget to eat breakfast, now does it?"

"Not so much. Listen, I didn't come here to have lunch with you."

"You don't say?" I asked, feigning surprise. "Why, Heather, do you have a secret reason for your visit?"

"Slightly," she admitted. "It's about the Cougar account."

"What about it?" I asked, suddenly serious. It was one of our oldest accounts. Honey Bear Software supplied their company with all of its security software. Because their company dealt actively with monitoring and managing personal data, making sure they weren't hacked or didn't have any soft areas in their programming was essential.

"Their orders have slowed down a bit, for one," she said carefully.

"That's natural, though." I wasn't worried about that. There was always an ebb and flow to these things. Some months, they'd acquire tons of software. Other months, they'd get very little. With any sort of company, consistent ordering wasn't something that really happened. Needs changed monthly. Hell, sometimes they changed weekly.

"There's something else, though," she said. She placed a single piece of paper on the desk.

"Why do I have the feeling you warmed me up with good food in order to soften the blow or whatever is on this paper?"

Heather pressed her lips firmly together. "Cougar Data's new marketing plan includes information about a new product that sounds dangerously close to some of our top security software."

"That's not wholly unusual. We have plenty of competitors. Why does this one make you so uncomfortable?"

"Because I have it on good authority that the Cougar Data company is partly to blame for your problems with the media."

"Excuse me?" That *did* get my attention. "What are you talking about? What authority?"

"Let's just say I had a date last weekend that went really well," Heather said dryly.

"You slept with someone from Cougar Data?"

"I wouldn't say we did much sleeping."

"Heather..."

"Okay," she shrugged. "I was messing around on Team Shifter. You know it, right?"

"Yeah. It's an app that's supposed to help you find your fated mate," I sighed. "I try to stay away from apps like that." In my experience, they only ever led to heartbreak and anxiety.

"Well, I don't. I love shit like that." Heather and I had known each other a long time. I didn't particularly care if she swore. Not while we were on lunch, anyway. "My date let it slip that they work for Cougar Data, and they started talking. They drank too much – or maybe not enough, depending on how you want to look at it – and you know what they say about loose lips."

"Uh, no? What do they say?"

"Loose lips sink ships," Heather stared at me like I was an idiot, "or, in this case, deals with that company. You should think about cutting ties."

"What exactly did your date say, Heather?"

"They said that Cougar Data hates your guts and that they have a dedicated photo team who manipulates pictures and sells them to tabloids to make it look like it's you."

"How do you know that any of this is true?"

"Because my date is the one who changes the photos, and I got to see the entire setup."

Suddenly, I felt like I was going to be sick. I felt literally and completely ill. My stomach churned, twisting inside of me.

"So, what, they're just trying to destroy Honey Bear Software? That doesn't make sense."

"They want to branch into the security world, and if they discredit you enough, you'll be forced to sell to them for cheap."

"Shit."

"Shit," Heather nodded. "But, I mean, you have options. This thing with Rebecca couldn't have come at a better time."

My eyes narrowed. It almost sounded like she knew the truth about our setup, but she couldn't know. There was no chance in hell Heather could know that Rebecca and I were a scam. We were a total and complete scam designed to improve my self-image, but this kind of changed things, didn't it?

Suddenly, I felt like I was putting Rebecca in harm's way, and I had never meant to. Before this conversation with Heather, I'd known people didn't like me, but I hadn't realized that there was going to be a specific plan for bringing down my company, so to speak.

"Tell me something, Heather. You know a lot about my company."

"Gee, thanks. I've only been your marketing director for like five years."

"Is Rebecca in danger?"

"What do you mean?"

"This thing with Cougar Data...are they going to go after her?"

"I've worked for you for a long time," she agreed slowly, "and I've seen a lot of strange things, but I've never seen anything quite like this before."

"It's weird."

"It's weird for sure. Listen, Justin, I can't say whether she's in danger or not, but if Rebecca was *my* girl, I'd start taking precautions. Judging by what my date said, the people at their company aren't too pleased about your newly reformed status. It's harder for them to spin dirt on you now, and that interferes with their plans for a takeover."

"What are you saying?"

"I'm saying, you need to protect the woman you love. You can start by protecting your company."

22

Rebecca

"What movie should we watch tonight?" Justin asked, looking over at me. He was holding an old-school DVD case filled with his favorite flicks. We'd seen quite a few of them, but not all of them. He wasn't selfish, either. We'd also spent time watching *my* favorite movies. I'd introduced him to some not-so-well known movies like *The Babysitter's Club* and *My Date With the President's Daughter*. There were some amazing movies that were just so funny and wonderful that they made my heart happy.

"How about *Arctic Tale*?" I asked, looking over at him. What was he going to do? This was his chance! This was his shot. He could tell me right now.

"I don't think I have that one," he said, carefully looking back at his DVD collection.

"Hmm," I sighed.

"We could watch *Titanic*. That's romantic."

"What about *Scamper the Penguin*? It's about a brave little penguin."

Justin looked over at me, confused.

"What about *Alaska* or *Balto*?"

"I don't have those, sorry," he shrugged.

"Well, for dragon's sake, Justin, we could rent something digitally. We don't just have to rifle through your stupid DVDs every night."

Instantly, I knew I'd gone too far. His face fell, and he closed the DVD case.

"You're right," he said. "Sure. Let's rent something."

"Nah," I shook my head. "I'm just going to go to bed. Sorry. I kind of killed the mood."

I headed out of the room and upstairs to the bedroom. I plopped down on the bed and closed my eyes. Why had I gotten so upset over something so small? Oh yeah: because he still wouldn't tell me. He still didn't trust me.

My soon-to-be-husband could turn himself into a polar bear, yet he didn't seem to want to share that with me. I didn't understand why, and that lack of understanding really hurt. I wanted him to be able to share with me, to open up with me. I wanted him to be able to explore this part of his life with me, but that was never going to happen if he couldn't be honest with me.

I was almost certain that the type of relationship we were going to have was going to shift back from slightly sexy and flirty to complete business casual.

That would probably be best, though, right?

I was a literature nerd.

I wasn't some billionaire heiress who understood his world.

I certainly wasn't a shifter who could change her body shape at will to meet what he needed, and there was a part of me that hated that.

I really, truly hated it.

I rolled around in bed for a few minutes, but then I realized it just wasn't going to happen. None of it was. I couldn't sleep. I couldn't go to bed this mad. I needed to just tell him. I had to.

Justin was never going to feel comfortable enough with me to admit the truth, so I needed to just go find him and tell him that I knew. If he couldn't handle me knowing, then, well, maybe we shouldn't have been trying to do this fake wedding thing, after all. Maybe there was a reason fake weddings weren't a thing.

Maybe we were just fooling ourselves to think it could work.

I climbed out of bed and went back downstairs. I'd just tell him. I could do that, right? I'd just go up to him and be like, "Hey, sorry I was crappy. I know you're a bear and I feel like you don't trust me."

Even in my head, the fake conversation sounded wildly cringy.

It didn't even matter, though, because when I got downstairs to the first floor, he was nowhere to be found.

"What the fuck?"

I looked around, walking through the kitchen, the living room, and even the back patio, but he was gone.

Then I noticed a little pile of clothing by the back door, and I realized what had happened. I scurried to the edge of the patio just in time to see a flash of white fur darting into the trees.

"Not this time," I muttered, slipping on a pair of mud boots that were by the back door. "You aren't getting off that easy."

This was my chance.

I was going to get to see that he really was a polar bear. This was my chance to see that he really was all of those things I thought he was. Besides, I'd always loved animals.

As a kid, my favorite adventure books were always the ones where people were brave and curious. They were the stories where people weren't scared to do what was right or hard or tricky.

Real life was pretty different from the storybooks, though, and I just didn't know if I was strong enough or brave enough to actually do what I was supposed to do.

"Where do you think you're going?" I muttered to myself, stepping closer to the forest. I was slow at first, but then I realized that if I didn't hurry, I was going to get myself in trouble. He was already in his bear form, so if I wanted any hope of seeing it, I'd need to scurry along.

The sun was setting, but it wasn't completely dark out yet. Still, it was hard to see much of anything once I stepped under the cover of the woods. I walked quickly, trying my best not to trip or step on anything that could hurt me.

Still, I knew I wasn't being as quiet as I should have been. A million years ago, I'd been a Girl Scout, and one of the things we'd learned was that you can't go traipsing around in the woods and expect that you won't disrupt the animals.

You will.

It's basically impossible to avoid.

Still, I found myself slowing down, trying to focus on not making *too* much extra noise. I did want to actually catch this guy, after all.

And then what?

There was a quiet voice in my head that told me I wasn't going to be able to hold back once he knew that I knew. I was either going to get completely pissed and go crazy on him, or I was going to try to sleep with him. There really wasn't going to be an in-between, and I wanted it to be the latter.

Yeah, I wanted to kiss him. Straddle him. Tease him. Sleeping in the same damn bed with Justin had been like a slow burning torture. I had no idea how people managed to stay celibate for years because I certainly couldn't do it. I couldn't do any of that. The idea of not being able to touch him for the entire year seemed like an even more exquisite form of pain.

What the hell was I going to do?

I didn't really know where I was going in the forest. I had a general idea of where I'd come from, so I didn't think I was going to get lost, but I wasn't exactly being a tracker. I had no idea where polar bear shifters liked to hang out, so I just walked around aimlessly for a little while, kind of trusting the idea that perhaps I'd just stumble across him.

Who knew?

Maybe I'd get lucky.

Eventually, I came to a swimming hole that seemed nice. The sun was setting even more, and the moon was up now, but I walked to the water's edge and sat down. I kicked off my mud boots and dipped my toes in the water.

"I should probably go back soon," I muttered to myself. I was already out farther than I thought I'd go. I wasn't sure why I kind of thought I'd be able to easily locate Justin. He hadn't managed to make it to this point in his life without giving away his existence by accident.

Nope.

He'd gotten this far because he was very careful, very precise, and very cautious.

What made me think that I'd be lucky enough to see him?

As I sat there, kicking my feet in the water, I started to think about all of the decisions that had led me to this moment. There had been moments when I'd been sad and lonely and lost. There had been moments when I'd wondered how the hell I was going to be able to feed myself.

Then there was this.

There was this moment.

I had chosen to come and marry Justin because I didn't have anything else to do this year, but was that really the only reason?

Was it really all about the money?

When I met him, there had been this instant, lightning connection. I'd felt right away that he was incredible. He was unlike anyone I'd been with before, and he made me feel so young, and so new, and so alive.

Was I really going to throw away this entire adventure over the fact that he didn't want to share as much about his personal life as I thought he should?

Wasn't that a little bit selfish of me?

I was just about to get up when I spotted something down in the water coming up toward me.

Fast.

At first, I wasn't sure what it was: a white blob of some sort. Then, all at once, I realized that it was him. He was in the water.

I screeched and leapt back, splashing as I fell away from the swimming hole. He came up hard and fast and breathing heavily. He was absolutely mammoth as a polar bear. His body was so big that it seemed to stretch on forever. Justin-as-a-polar-bear went to the opposite side of the swimming hole, climbed out, and stared at me.

He didn't run away.

He didn't change back.

He just looked.

I couldn't pinpoint why, but I had the feeling that this was a test somehow. It felt like some strange sort of quiz where nobody wins. What did he want me to do? What did he want me to say?

"Hello," I said, waving.

The polar bear waved back.

There was no doubt in my mind that it was him. The polar bear looked confused, surprised, and honestly, a little bit sad. Was he worried? It hit me then, all at once, that maybe he hadn't told me because he was worried.

Did the sweet bear think I was going to judge him?

Was he afraid I was going to pick on him or run away?

"You could have just told me," I said.

The polar bear shrugged, as if to ask, "What?"

"You could have told me you were a bear."

He sat down but didn't change back.

"I read on the Internet that you can't talk when you're in your bear form, but since everyone around you is sworn to secrecy, apparently, I have no damn idea if that's true. Is it true?"

He blinked, but kept his mouth shut.

I slipped the mud boots back on and walked around the side of the swimming hole. In the summer, I bet this place was dope. It was probably wonderfully refreshing to dive down and just enjoy swimming in a place like this, but right now...

Well, right now I had the idea that things were about to change, and not for the better. When I reached Justin, he was going to have to make a choice. Would he change back and talk with me? Or would he run off into the woods and pretend this interaction had never happened?

Things really could go either way.

I approached him slowly, worried that if I moved too quickly, I might scare him off. That was the thing I wanted to do the least. I didn't want to freak him out or make him panic. If I could move slowly, simply, quietly, then maybe he'd be able to stay calm enough to change back and to talk with me.

I stood in front of the polar bear. He was standing, towering over me, but not attacking me.

"I hope you really are Justin," I said to the bear. "Because if you aren't, I must be the dumbest human alive."

The bear looked nervous but still didn't move. He also made no attempt to change back into his human form. Fine. If that's the way he wanted to play it, then I wanted to see what I was getting myself into.

"You know, you really should have advertised the bear stuff on your bridal ad," I told him, walking around him. "Some girls are into that."

The bear snorted.

Good.

He was relaxing.

"Personally, I've never slept with a bear, but I'm not opposed to the idea. It's pretty badass you can change back and forth."

I stopped in front of him and looked up. Those big, beautiful eyes looked down at me. Justin's eyes. It really was him. There was literally no denying it in any way, shape or form. It was him.

Somehow, it had always been him.

"Can I touch you?" I asked.

The bear nodded slightly, letting me know that it was okay. Whatever I wanted to do, it was okay.

I stepped closer, reaching for him. I wasn't sure where to touch, but he held his hand out, and I started there.

"My, what big paws you have," I chuckled to myself.

He didn't seem to think it was funny.

"I see that your bear side isn't a joker," I muttered. "We'll have to work on that."

I stroked the soft padding on the inside of his paw before touching his claws, which were slightly extended. They seemed sharp, so I was careful not to cut myself on them. Who knew what spilling blood out here would do? It would probably attract some other animals.

It would probably make something even more dangerous happen.

He moved my hand to his chest, letting me know that it was okay to touch him there. I pressed my hands against his fluffy chest and started rubbing him there. I'd never touched a bear before. I'd never even been this close to one. The closest I'd ever personally been to a bear was at the zoo, and this was very, very different from that.

"You're softer than I thought you'd be." To be honest, I wasn't really sure what I expected. His fur felt softer than a dog or cat's. It was more like I was playing with a stuffed animal, stroking an animal I was planning to snuggle and hug.

I looked up to see the bear watching me with those bright, wonderful eyes.

"You could have told me," I whispered again. "I wouldn't have freaked out."

And then he changed.

One moment he was a bear.

The next, he was Justin.

23

Justin

I believed her.

There wasn't a single reason I should have believed a word pouring out of Rebecca's mouth, but I did. There she was, sweaty and tired in the woods, wearing my stupid-ass mud boots, and she was pouring her royal heart out to me.

She'd come after me.

"Why did you come?" I whispered, reaching for her hands. I held them tightly and looked at her, searching her eyes for answers. I needed something. Anything. I just needed a clue.

I needed any reason to let her know that this thing between us was more than just a business arrangement. It was special to me. *She* was special to me.

Did she *want* to be my mate?

"Because I'm sorry."

"For the fight."

"It was a stupid fight."

"I thought it was weird you kept suggesting movies with polar bears in them," I muttered. "How long have you known?"

"Since Thanksgiving."

"What the fuck?"

She'd known that long? It was almost Christmas now. She'd known that long, and she hadn't told me. She hadn't pressured me. She'd just waited...patiently. For the last couple of months, Rebecca and I had been inseparable. That was important as part of our arrangement. We needed to appear like a real couple, didn't we?

Only, somewhere along the line, our hearts had gotten tangled up in each other, too.

Now there was more going on than I could really wrap my mind around. She had come to me, and she'd seen me under the water. She'd seen me as a bear, and she hadn't panicked. She hadn't run. She'd just accepted me.

"Sorry," she shrugged. "I thought you'd tell me, though."

"I was never planning to tell you."

"Why not?"

"Because it's my secret."

"Your family knows, though."

"That's different."

"Why?"

"Because they're my family, Rebecca."

"And I'm what? Some contract?"

"You started out that way," I admitted. "It was only ever supposed to be a contract between us."

"But you don't feel that way anymore?"

No.

No, I did not feel that way any longer.

Now I had more emotions than I knew what to do with, and that was quickly becoming a problem for me. I didn't want confusing emotions clogging up my brain or my heart. I wanted things that were easy and fast and true and real. I wanted simple. I didn't want complicated.

Only, ever since Rebecca had arrived, things *had* been complicated. They'd been more than complicated. They'd been unbelievable.

"You've read about shifters," I said.

"A little. I mean, I didn't know about the underwater thing."

"Underwater thing?"

"Yeah, with you hiding under there and breathing. How long were you down there, anyway?"

"Like, a minute," I admitted. "I heard you coming and hid the first place I saw."

"Brave of you."

"Apparently, it was also kind of stupid of me."

"You're not stupid."

"What else did you learn about shifters?"

"That you take mates," she said. "I assume that's what you want to do after our divorce?"

"What, take a mate?"

She nodded, but the scent of sadness wafted up to my nostrils. I sniffed the air. Sure enough, it was her. She was sad about this idea. She didn't like the idea of us splitting up or she didn't like the idea of me finding someone else. I wasn't sure which it was.

"When I met you, my bear seemed to think *you* were our mate," I told her.

"Why do you talk like that? Why do you talk about your bear like it's separate from you? Aren't you the same?"

"In some ways, yes. In other ways, no. It's like when I'm in my human form, my bear form is at the back of my mind, whispering to me. When I'm in my bear form, I still have all my memories. I'm still me, but everything seems a little more wild. It's easier to be kind of...feral. Untamed."

"So, when you saw me as a bear, what did you think?"

"That I wanted to marry you. For real."

"What?"

She looked up at me and her jaw dropped. I knew – *knew* – this was a terrible idea, but I didn't care. It really was what I wanted. It was what I needed, and it was most certainly what I thought was right.

"Over the past few weeks...months...I've just..."

"I know," she whispered. "I feel the same way."

"I've fallen for you."

"I've fallen for you, too."

"Really?"

"You couldn't tell?"

"No."

"Maybe you are a silly bear," she said, giggling.

"Come here."

I reached for her and tugged her close, planting a soft kiss on her lips. It was the first of many to come. I had a feeling that I was never, ever going to grow tired of loving this girl.

"Why didn't you tell me sooner?" Rebecca asked.

"It wasn't safe."

"I thought you didn't trust me."

"It wasn't about you. It was about protecting the company," I admitted. "That's what this entire thing has been about. My mom doesn't have much time left, but she wanted to know that the company was going to be okay. She wanted to know that when she passes, it'll be well taken care of."

"I get that," she said. "It still hurt, though."

"I'm sorry," I whispered.

I was, too. She was my mate. She was my true, forever mate. She was the person my bear wanted more than anyone else ever. She was the one. It was all her.

"I should have talked to you sooner," she said, looking up at me.

"I wasn't ready," I admitted. "I should have been, but I wasn't."

"It's okay," she told me. "Let's get back to the house."

"Let's get back to the house."

I took her hand and started to walk.

"Wait," she pulled her hand away. She was still standing still. "Doesn't it hurt your feet?" Rebecca pointed to my bare feet. Now that I was back in my human form, I was completely naked. I'd left my clothing at home, after all.

"No."

"It has to," she said, cocking her head to the side. I'd forgotten what it was like to be around humans who didn't really understand the shifter lifestyle.

"It doesn't," I laughed. "I promise."

"How could it not?"

"Maybe we have thicker skin," I shrugged. "I'm not sure."

"Look, I like you, a lot," she said seriously, "but your company is going to kill me if I send the CEO to work with fucked-up feet. You *can't* walk through the forest like this."

"What would you suggest?" I asked.

"You change back to a bear."

"And?"

"And...race me home."

She turned and started running. Before I could even ask if she was serious, she was darting through the forest and trying to get back to the house before me. I was so shocked that I didn't shift. I didn't move. I just stared at her.

What made the little human think she'd be able to beat me?

I was a *bear* shifter, after all. I wasn't about to be bested by a human. Not in a silly race like this. I shook my head, changed into my bear form, and started walking slowly. I should give her a head start, I thought. Wouldn't that be nice of me? She deserved it after the time she'd had dealing with me.

Then I realized that she had tricked me, somehow, and that she didn't deserve a head start at all! She was the one who wanted to race. That was all her!

I started running, feeling happy as I did. My bear felt happy. All of me felt happy. In every possible future scenario of my life, none of them had included something as simple as *playing* with my mate.

Maybe this was one of the reasons people liked the idea of finding their true mate so much. When you found someone that you could connect with forever, you found someone who made your heart sing. Finding someone truly wonderful, the way that Rebecca was wonderful, was kind of incredible.

And so, I ran.

I tore through the underbrush, scurrying through the forest. I ran as fast as I could until my throat hurt and my mouth was dry, and then I ran a little bit more. I kept going, unable to stop. I was unable to slow down, unable to do anything at all except just keep on running.

I heard her laughing up ahead, and I knew I was close. I had no idea how she'd managed to sprint so far ahead of me, especially with the setting sun, yet she had. I kept moving, making my way toward Rebecca...

I kept making my way toward my mate.

Damn, that felt so fucking good to finally and truly accept. It had taken me far too long to stop fighting myself, to stop fighting her. It had taken too much time and energy and pain. I should have just done things right the first time. I hadn't, and I had paid the price with all of that lost time.

"Come on, slowpoke," she laughed from up ahead, and I burst out of the woods to find Rebecca...

And she was naked.

24

Rebecca

I knew what I was doing, and I knew it was a bad idea.

Still, I couldn't talk myself out of it.

When I'd reached the edge of the forest first, I'd been both shocked and pleased, and I'd wanted to keep feeling that rush. I'd stripped down, stepping out of my clothing as quickly as I could. Hopefully, it wasn't anything too crazy for good ol' Justin. I was mature enough to know that neither one of us were virgins. This wasn't going to be our first time, but oh, hopefully it would be the best time.

Judging by the look on the polar bear's face when he emerged from the woods, I'd managed to catch his attention.

He stared at me, and I felt like I could practically read his thoughts. I couldn't, of course. I wasn't even sure if that was a thing that bear shifters could do, but he was staring at me like he wanted to devour me.

"I'm pretty fast," I told him. "I ran track in high school and in college."

That wasn't a lie. It had been a long time ago, and I hadn't run at all during my undergrad, but apparently, my muscles hadn't forgotten their old skill, nor their love of speed. Feeling the wind in my face had always made me happy. To me, the rush from running was second only to reading a wonderful book.

Justin just kept right on staring at me. He looked at me different in his bear form, I thought. He wasn't looking at me like he was sorry I'd bested him, though.

He was looking at me like he wanted to eat me up.

"It's not hard once you get the hang of it," I continued speaking. "I mean, I used to practice every day. I'd say the biggest factor in becoming a fast sprinter is actually following a healthy diet."

"Stop."

He'd changed back.

He was back in his human form and he was on the prowl. He was coming toward me the way he would march toward a predator he hated, only he didn't hate me. He wanted me. He was craving me.

If there was ever a doubt in my mind that Justin wanted me, it was gone now: vanished like my clothing.

Soon he was in front of me, and then he was grabbing me, tugging me into his arms. He pulled my naked body flush against his, but before I could really even begin to enjoy or analyze the sensation of that, he started kissing me.

Hard. Fast. Passionate. His kiss was everything I wanted it to be. Kissing him was like fire burning my body and then ice chasing the pain. I wanted all of him and more. I needed him.

We were outside in the backyard, and the moon was now high in the sky. I'd never really been one to get too wild with sex. Yeah, I'd teased him about spanking me, and I'd been open to stuff like that before, but outside?

Never outside.

Not that I'd ever really had the chance.

My previous partners had been strangely timid, not ready to explore this sort of thing at all. Justin had no qualms, though. He wasn't scared, reserved, or shy. He was the type of person who knew what he wanted, and he took that.

As he kissed me, his hands began to wander down my chest. He ran his fingers over my breasts so softly that it felt like butterflies rushing over me. I reached for him, too, tracing my hands down his abs and then lower. I grabbed his cock, wrapping my hand around him, and I started to stroke.

"What are you doing to me?" Justin's words were almost a whisper against my lips. Almost. It almost felt like a promise.

"Everything," I whispered. At least, that was what I hoped. "Everything."

"I like the sound of that."

"I like it, too."

"Tell me what you want, Rebecca."

"You," I said. "I want you."

He kissed me over and over as I continued to touch and rub him. His hand found its way between my legs, too, and I stepped apart so he could reach me a little more easily.

"Such a pretty human," he murmured. "So fucking pretty."

I didn't know why those words worked so well for me. Something about the way he spoke made me feel like my heart was soaring. My entire body felt like it was on fire as I grew closer and closer to orgasm.

I wasn't sure what I was supposed to say. Did shifters do anything weird or special during sex? Did they bite or growl or anything like that?

Only, it didn't seem to matter. Somehow, I had a feeling that all the shifter sex in the world didn't matter right now because Justin and I were locked together in this moment.

We hadn't planned on this. We'd expected to go ahead and have our fake wedding followed by our fake marriage and our fake one-year breakup, but that hadn't happened, had it? Instead, true love had taken over, locking us into this immortal embrace, and I didn't know how I was ever going to be able to live without him.

When I came, it was like an explosion. It was a good thing Justin lived next to a huge, empty forest because I was definitely loud. He didn't seem bothered, though. He didn't seem upset at all by the sounds. If anything, it seemed to turn him on even more. He growled, watching and holding me as I fell apart. Then my knees were weak. They felt like Jell-o, and he lowered me to the ground.

"Oh, sweet girl," he murmured.

"You ruined my legs," I chuckled, accusing him. He didn't seem upset, though. He didn't seem to care. Instead, he sat down on the grass and tugged me onto his lap.

"We can stop," he told me. "We don't have to do anything else right now."

"I want to."

"You need to be sure," he murmured. "Once we do this...Rebecca, I'm going to want you forever."

"That almost sounded like a real proposal."

"It was."

I stilled, looking at him. He was serious. He wasn't playing around, was he? After all of this time together, after all of the promises about how we'd secretly keep things businesslike and professional, he was actually admitting that he had feelings for me. Wasn't he?

"What are you saying?"

"I want you for real. My bear knew the moment I saw you that you were the one for me. It just took the rest of my brain a little while to catch up." The look in his eyes said that he'd been scared and nervous. He hadn't been ready. That was okay. I hadn't been ready, either, but I felt ready now.

"Are you sure about this?"

It felt big. Huge. This was so much more than the contract we'd signed at the start of all this. This felt intense. Powerful. Crazy.

And it felt *good*.

It felt so damn good.

"I'm sure."

Instead of saying anything else, I pushed him back into the grass and straddled him. I watched his face in the moonlight as I lowered myself onto him, and then I rode the polar bear in the moonlight. It was weird to feel so wild and happy in a moment like this. It was wonderful. It was wild. It was incredible.

And I felt like my heart was going to explode.

When Justin came, he reached up and grabbed my hair, tugging it. He murmured my name as he came, and then he grabbed me, tugging me into his arms.

"I love you, Rebecca."

"I love you, too."

25

Justin

Waking up the next morning with Rebecca felt like a dream. It felt like a beautiful, incredible dream that I never wanted to end. I didn't want to have to get up or go to work. I didn't want to leave. I just wanted to stay there with her: with my mate.

"Mmmm," she murmured, rolling over. She opened her eyes and smiled at me. "Time to start the day?"

"Regretfully, yes." I didn't want to go, though. I didn't want to leave. The only thing I was interested in was staying beautifully, wonderfully put. She was incredible, wasn't she? Lovely and sweet.

"What are you thinking about?"

"We should have done this a long time ago," I groaned.

"I know," she laughed, shaking her head. I loved the way her hair shook, her wavy locks bouncing as she moved her head. "It was practically torture trying to sleep next to you every night."

"Torture for you?" I laughed. "Try for me. My bear kept trying to claw his way out."

"I don't want to be alone today," she said, reaching for me. "Let me come with you to the office."

"The office?" I asked, raising an eyebrow. "You've never come to the office with me before." I should have taken her before, but things had been crazy getting ready for the Christmas season. I'd given her plenty of information about the company, and she understood what we did and how we ran. She'd even accompanied

163

me to a couple of professional outings. She hadn't seen the inner-workings of the office itself, though.

"There's a first time for everything, right?"

"There is," I agreed slowly. Now that I was thinking about it, I kind of liked the idea of her coming to work with me. Rebecca could be a lot of fun when the two of us were just hanging out. What might it be like to have her come to work with me?

"You know," she told me, "if I got a job nearby, we could have lunches together."

"A job?"

"Yeah," she nodded again. "I don't really want to just sit at the house all year, you know. It's not that I don't *love* hanging out with your mom and Hector all day." As if on cue, Hector meowed loudly. "But I'd like to do something more, too."

"You were looking for a job when you accepted my bridal offer, weren't you?"

"I was."

"What do you want to do?" I realized that even though I'd spent the last few months getting to know Rebecca and her personality, almost all of our conversations about the future revolved around me and my company.

"I wanted to work in high schools," she told me. "I wanted to teach English. It's kind of a bitch to try to find a teaching job, though."

"You'd be a great teacher."

"Thank you. I agree," she laughed. "But seriously, it's hard to find jobs like that."

"You know," I said thoughtfully. "Ally works at the high school by my office."

"There's a high school near your office?"

"There is," I nodded. "It's a few blocks away, but yes."

"And she works there?"

"Yeah. Do you want me to ask if she has any openings for English teachers?"

"Are you being serious right now?"

"I'm serious," I said slowly, not ready for Rebecca to launch herself at me. She did, though. She threw herself right at me, pushing me back onto the bed. She straddled me, laughing and kissing my neck and chest, and then she moved back to my lips. She ran her tongue over my lips and then she sat there, pressing her hands to my chest.

"Thank you."

"It's nothing," I said. "I haven't even talked to her yet."

"I just appreciate that you're willing to do this for me. Even the fact that you're thinking of me kind of blows my mind," she laughed.

"I get the feeling you're not used to dating people who are very friendly."

"My exes are all fine," she shrugged. "I don't really have any bad memories or anything, but no, nobody has ever really gone out of their way for me. I appreciate it. Thank you."

"It's nothing," I said again.

"It's not nothing."

She kissed me then, and I closed my eyes as I just allowed myself to be surrounded by her. Rebecca was...everything. She was like passion and chaos and wonder wrapped around me in one beautiful package. I couldn't believe that I was lucky enough to be kissed by her.

I couldn't believe I was lucky enough to be loved by her.

WALKING INTO THE OFFICE with Rebecca on my arm felt a little bit like bragging. She was so damn pretty, and the office was so damn boring without her. I hadn't even realized how much I'd been dreading going to these meetings until I got the chance to take her with me. Walking in with her made me feel like I was damn lucky to have ever met her.

"Good morning," I said to the receptionist as we walked in.

"Morning," she said, glancing up at Rebecca.

"Nice to see you," Rebecca said, smiling.

We walked through the lobby and to the elevators, where we headed up to the top floor.

"I've got a couple of meetings this morning," I explained.

"Are they in your office?"

"Nope. I'll be meeting a couple of people in the conference rooms."

"That's fine," she smiled. "I brought a book. I can read while you're gone."

"It's pretty nice taking you to work," I smiled. It was a strange sort of feeling. I'd never taken anyone to work before. As a kid, I'd always loved accompanying my father to work. It had always been our special time to bond and spend time together. Now, it was almost like I was doing the same thing with Rebecca.

Excitedly, I gave her a quick tour of the entire floor where I worked. I showed her the office, introduced her to a few of my team members, and even helped her get a cup of coffee from our little kitchen. There were fresh cookies in there and an assortment of fresh breakfast items. Rebecca grabbed a soft chocolate chip cookie to eat with her coffee and I grabbed a bagel. Then we headed to my office.

"Good morning," Phil said, meeting us at the door. His eyes opened a little when he saw me with Rebecca. "And who is this?"

"I feel like you know," I glared at Phil. I couldn't quite pinpoint why he was rubbing me the wrong way. He was grating on my nerves and I didn't have a very good reason for it. Phil wasn't the one who had created those fake pictures of me. He wasn't the one trying to steal my company.

Still, his obsession with Rebecca had pissed me off one too many times.

Ignoring my sour attitude, Rebecca offered Phil her hand. He grabbed it greedily, shaking it far too hard and fast. Her entire arm shook.

"I'm Rebecca," she said. "I'm Justin's fiancé."

"Phil Burton," he said.

"Nice to meet you."

"Believe me, the pleasure is all mine."

"All right," I said, looking at their hands. "That seems like enough."

"What? Oh," Phil seemed to realize they were still touching, and he dropped his hands.

"I'll see you in the meeting at 10," I said to Phil, and then I opened the door to my office. Rebecca and I stepped inside. I closed the door before Phil could say anything else, and we headed inside.

"He was..."

"Crazy?"

"I was going to say *enthused*. What's the story?"

"Phil is one of my assistants. He's actually great at what he does, but he's also a nosy guy. He loves looking at paparazzi pictures, too, so don't let him get too close to you. He might try to snap a few 'exclusive' photos to sell."

"You don't really think he'd do that, do you?" Rebecca gasped, drawing a hand to her lips.

"If he did, I'd have to fire him on the spot," I told her. "There's no chance I'd let that happen."

26

Rebecca

After a relaxing hour just hanging out in Justin's office, it was time for his first meeting. He had to go talk with his team members about a new marketing plan they were launching. Then he had to talk with his attorneys. Apparently, he was about to tell his lawyers that he was going to terminate all contracts with a company called Cougar Data. The organization, according to Justin, was responsible for taking pictures of him and editing them to make him look bad. They also crafted their own pictures and basically Photoshopped his head into the pictures.

While he was gone, I made myself comfortable in his office. I curled up in his desk chair and spun around so I could face the windows. From up here, I could see so many different things in Rawr County. This particular city was just lovely. I loved looking at all of the tall buildings. There were plenty of old things, too.

I managed to spot the high school he'd been talking about. Would I manage to get a job there? Would I be able to make a name for myself here? Now that I knew Justin and I were getting married, like for-realsies, it seemed like it was time for me to think about putting down roots.

I tugged out my phone and sent Earl and Gabe each a quick message. I wanted them to know that I was okay, that everything was going well, and that things between me and Justin had kind of gotten a little bit crazy.

Perhaps most of all, I wanted them to know that I was okay. They'd already left for their world adventures, but they still had phones. Regular text messaging didn't work in every country, but we had other messaging apps we could use. No, they weren't going to be able to make it to the wedding since they were now on the other side of the world, but they could still watch it live. I could have Rita hold a tablet or something and stream the ceremony. I'd figure something out.

I set the phone down in my lap and just kept staring out the window. It really felt like one big dream, didn't it? It really seemed like everything was just wonderful. Incredible.

Justin's mom had done so much of the wedding planning that I hadn't even needed to stress. I probably should have worried more about making sure that everything was perfect and personalized to me, but it was good enough. It was nice enough that I was happy with how everything looked. I was happy with what our big day was going to be like.

I heard Justin's office door open quietly, and I smiled. He'd come back early from his meetings. This was it! I spun around, eager to see how everything had gone, but I was shocked to see that it wasn't Justin in the office. It was a woman. From the look on her face, she hadn't been expecting to see me sitting in his chair. I realized that when I was turned around, she hadn't been able to see that I was sitting in the chair.

She'd thought that she was alone in his office.

Instantly, all of my senses were on high alert.

I stared at the woman, but didn't say anything right away. She was dressed to impress in a nice, tight dress-suit with heels. Her hair looked absolutely perfect. Like, it looked so much more perfect than my own hair would *ever* look. She had earrings that matched the gold necklace around her neck, and she was...flustered.

She looked flustered, like she was trying to figure out what to say next.

"Can I help you?" I finally asked.

"I'm looking for Justin," she told me. "We had an appointment."

I knew that was a lie. He'd shown me his schedule, and a meeting with a random woman wasn't on it. He had his appointment with Phil and the other marketing people at 10, but then his only other morning meeting was with the lawyers. Glancing at my watch, I realized he was probably just sitting down to talk with the attorneys.

So, who exactly was this woman?

She didn't know about his lawyer meeting, so she couldn't have been someone too wild, right?

"I'm so sorry," I told her politely. "He must have forgotten."

"No, I don't think that's it. You're his fiancé, aren't you?"

"The one and only," I said. I stood, smoothing my skirt. I didn't look as dressed up or as professional as this woman, but that was okay. I wasn't an employee here. "I'm so sorry, but I don't believe we've met." I held my hand out, but the woman just looked at it. Then she looked away.

"No, I don't believe we have," she said. "I'll see if I can find Justin," she said. Then she turned, and just as easily as she'd walked into the office, she left.

Weird.

WHEN JUSTIN RETURNED from his meetings, he brought lunch with him. I looked up from reading *The Vampire Lestat*, which was only the second vampire novel in the series I'd just started. Luckily, I had looked up local bookstores and found out that there were three within walking distance of Honey Bear

Software, so I had plenty of ways to buy the next books once I'd finished this one.

"What is it?" I asked, rubbing my hands together.

"Something special," he said. He pulled out two little boxes and glanced at them. Each of them was labeled. He handed one to me, and I read the label out loud.

"No shellfish?"

"Because of your allergy," he explained.

"Perfect. What's yours say?"

He rolled his eyes and held it up.

"No cherries," he said.

"Same reason?" I asked innocently.

"Maybe I just don't like cherries."

"It's nothing to be ashamed of," I pointed out. "Lots of people have allergies."

"My mother told you, didn't she?"

"Yes, she did," I nodded, and I opened the box. Instantly, my nose was filled with the scent of flavor. There were multiple flavors. There were so many flavors that my eyes started to water as I soaked it all in.

"Please tell me what this is," I said. "It smells insanely good."

"So, there's this little restaurant next door," he said. "They do these surprise boxes for lunch. If you have any dietary restrictions or preferences, you just let them know, and then they prepare you a box they think you'll totally love."

"Mine looks like chicken, noodles, and a bunch of vegetables," I said. "There's a bunch of sauce, too."

"No shellfish, though," he pointed out.

"No shellfish," I agreed. "Thank you for remembering."

"I wouldn't forget something like that," he admitted. "You're too important."

"I feel the same way about you," I murmured. I looked at him and smiled. He really looked at peace. It seemed like this was the first time I'd ever seen him truly and totally happy and calm, and it was kind of a wonderful feeling.

When I first responded to his ad, I had no idea what kind of adventure we'd end up going on together, but I was so damn glad it was with him. The idea of us falling in love was something that I hadn't really expected or counted on, and I still felt like I had so much to learn about Justin. Even though we'd been *living* together for a few months, it seemed like every new day was fresh. Every new day was complete.

"So, what did you get?"

He peeked into his box and smiled. Then he tilted it slightly over so I could see. Bright bits of green peeked out of the white cardboard.

"A salad," he said.

"Do polar bears often eat salad? I would have taken you more as a salmon filet kind of guy," I winked at him.

"No teasing," he told me.

"Why not? It's so fun."

"Not everybody likes to be teased," he whispered. "Besides, you might hurt my fragile bear feelings."

"No, I wouldn't want to do that," I reached for his hand, running my fingers over it. His skin was soft and smooth. "I would never want to make you sad."

"I'm glad to hear that. Now eat your food," he gestured toward the noodles.

"I'm not about to say no to that."

I reached for a fork and started digging in. I was thrilled to be eating something hot, tasty, and relatively healthy. One of the best things about being with Justin was that he loved trying new things. Nothing ever seemed to slow him down. He wasn't scared to try new foods or explore new recipes. He was always happy to eat, and thanks to his shifter-sized appetite, he could eat a lot.

That was fine by me.

There was a knock at the door, and before Justin could even say anything, it opened slowly. The woman from before peeked her head inside. She smiled brightly, which was very different from the way she'd acted earlier. I hadn't even had a chance to tell Justin that she'd stopped by. It was a little strange, the way that she'd just stepped into his office without even knocking. While she'd done that this time, I had a feeling it was because she knew I was here.

Earlier, she hadn't known, so why had she come in?

Maybe she really did think she had a meeting with Justin, but I wondered if the real reason she'd come into the room was because she wanted to be in his office alone.

I pushed the thought from my head because Justin lit up when he saw her. Obviously, this was someone he knew and trusted. I probably just had the wrong idea.

"Heather," he said. "What can I do for you?"

"Hey," she wiggled her manicured fingers in a friendly little wave. "I stopped by earlier. Weren't we going to talk about the Cougar Data client today?" She cocked her head, looking innocent.

"No, I don't think so," he said. I took a bite of my food as he considered this. "I just had a meeting with my attorneys, though. We're drawing up contract termination papers and will be pursuing a lawsuit against them for defamation."

Was it just me, or did Heather pale a little bit?

"You...what? Why did you do that without consulting me?"

Even Justin picked up on the slight edge of hostility in her tone.

"Because it's my company, Heather. Last time I checked, I didn't have to talk to my marketing director about any of this stuff. Weren't you the one who suggested terminating the contract, anyway?"

Heather didn't say anything right away. She sort-of sputtered for a moment, as though she was struggling to get the words out in the right order. What was going on with her?

"Oh, and speaking of you being the marketing director, you weren't actually at the marketing meeting this morning. Is everything okay?"

"Everything is fine," she said, gritting her teeth. "No problems at all." Changing the subject, she nodded her head toward our food. "Bon Appetit in a Box? I thought only people with food allergies ate there."

"Then it's perfect for us," I said. "Check it out. Justin told them no shellfish for me, and the entire meal is just chicken and pasta. It's amazing. Totally worth checking out."

"Nice," she nodded before turning back to Justin. "Anyway, Justin, if you don't actually need me, I'll be going. I just thought maybe you had questions about the situation with Cougar Data."

"Not at all," he said. "I'm not about to let them soil the name of my company, though, so if they're actually the ones who have been making these pictures, as your date said, then it's time for them to pay for it. If it wasn't them, then it's probably time we open up an investigation into who the real culprit is, don't you think?"

Heather pressed her lips together tightly. "Understood," she said. Then Heather walked to the door, opened it, and left. As soon as the door closed, he turned to me.

"That was weird."

"What was weird?"

"Heather was really anxious the entire time she was here," he said. "I scented her."

"You...scented her?"

"Yes. As a shifter, I can scent emotions. It's not just the emotions of my mate, either. I can tell if someone is experiencing any sort of strong emotion...anger...frustration...even jealousy."

"She did seem tense."

"There's something else, too," Justin said. "She didn't even introduce herself to you. That would have been the first thing I would have expected from her, but she didn't. She didn't seem surprised that you were here, either."

"I didn't tell you because we started eating, but she came by earlier. She walked right into your office. Not sure if that's normal or not. She didn't see me at first." The more I thought about that, the more uncomfortable it made me. It *so* wasn't okay that she had done that. Even if she did have a meeting with Justin, it would have been much more professional to knock before walking inside.

"She walked right in?"

"Yeah."

"She didn't knock?"

"Nope."

"Was she looking for something?" Justin asked.

"I have no idea," I admitted. "I thought it was pretty weird, though. She said she had a meeting with you that you'd forgotten about."

Justin sighed and started eating again. He shook his head.

"Heather is the one who warned me about our client trying to steal our company. My attorneys were just as surprised by the accusations today as I was when Heather brought them to me. Cougar Data has been a trustworthy client for years."

"So, why would you terminate your contract with them?"

"I didn't," he said.

"But you said..."

"I said what I said, but as you know, I'm quite good at lying." Justin winked at me, and I wondered why he'd been so insistent in talking about his meeting. He'd told me, and he'd mentioned it to a few other people. He'd been *very* clear about his intention to end his contract with Cougar Data.

"You *are* good at lying, are you?"

"I wanted everyone to believe it was happening in case word got back to whoever was behind this set-up. I'm a bit suspicious of Heather, but I don't know if she's the one leaking those forged pictures to the press or if she's actually dating someone who is. She made quite a plea for me to blame Cougar Data, but I'm not about to end such a long-lasting business relationship until I know for certain they're the ones responsible."

I was beginning to see why Justin was such a good businessman. He was a master manager. He had the ability to tell when someone was being deceitful or withholding information, and he did a great job analyzing when he thought someone was trying to trick him. It was a skill that was going to serve him well for a long time, I was sure. He also had the ability to lie, too, though. He didn't like to show all of his cards all at once and being sneaky enabled him to keep some things to himself.

"I had everyone believing that we were really in love even before we were, too," he pointed out.

"Why do you seem so proud of this? Most people wouldn't be bragging about their ability to lie, you know."

"I'm not most people."

"Why would you lie about that, though?" I asked, taking another bite of chicken. "The company thing, I mean. Why not just say nothing at all?"

"I have my suspicions about Heather," he said. "She was very quick to point the blame as to who was causing these problems for me."

"And you think, what, that she's behind it?"

"Maybe," he shrugged. "Her or Phil. They're both pretty damn obsessed with the paparazzi news about us. It makes me uncomfortable," he said.

"So if your meeting today wasn't ending the contract, what did you do?"

"Oh," he laughed. "I just increased the price of doing business. If I'm going to do company with a group of cats, I'm going to make them pay for it."

27

Justin

The day of our wedding arrived.

We'd chosen to get married on Christmas morning, which may or may not have been a good decision, but it just so happened to be one of my favorite days of the year, and besides, it fit in well with our original timeline.

Rebecca looked absolutely beautiful in her long, white gown. It was embroidered with navy blue flowers and she carried a bouquet of deep red roses. She wore her hair down, and when I saw her walking down the aisle toward me, I thought my heart was going to explode.

She was perfect.

Everything about the moment was perfect.

Her friends Earl and Gabe hadn't been planning to make the wedding. They'd recently relocated to another country and flights back to the United States weren't cheap. As a gift for Rebecca, however, I'd flown them in to accompany her down the aisle. With one of them carefully planted on either side of her, they guided her down the aisle and to me.

She was glowing.

I stood at the altar with Kyle as my best man. Ally stood as Rebecca's Maid of Honor. The three of us stood, along with our officiant, and watched her make her way down the aisle. I finally understood why all of those YouTube videos featuring crying grooms were so popular. I felt tears starting to well up. This was it. This was our moment. It had started out fake, but it had evolved into something very, very real. It was all real.

When Earl and Gabe reached me, they both leaned over and started whispering into my ears.

"Don't you dare hurt her," Gabe said.

"Not at all," Earl added. "If I hear you made her cry, then I'll fly out here again, and I'll make you cry."

"Gentlemen," I assured them, "I will not be making Rebecca cry. I adore her."

"Oh, good, because she's really happy!"

"And she likes you so much!"

They both hugged me, and Rebecca somehow got tangled in the middle, so our wedding started off with all four of us hugging at the altar. Finally, Rebecca managed to wiggle free, and her two friends went to sit down.

"Wow," I said, looking at her.

"Wow to you," she smiled, gesturing to me.

I suppose I cleaned up pretty nicely in my tuxedo. I wasn't a huge fan of dressing up, but for her, I'd do anything. Once Rebecca and I had decided to get married *for real*, she'd gotten a little more serious about the things she wanted.

I liked that, though. I liked that she got to plan part of the wedding, but that she didn't have to stress about all of the tiny details. I enjoyed hearing all of the things she especially liked. It was great to see how passionate she got when she was working on seating arrangements with my mom.

She was incredible.

"Shall we begin?"

We both looked to see our officiant standing there ready. We smiled, nodded, and the ceremony began. It was strange to experience my wedding day. When I'd thought about this day in the future, I had pictured it differently. For one thing, I thought both of my parents would be alive. I missed my dad. I also thought my old friend, Basil, would have stood for me as a groomsman. He wasn't even at the wedding. I'd also figured that I would marry a shifter, and Rebecca was absolutely, totally, completely, one hundred percent human.

She was wonderful and sweet, and she'd somehow managed to worm her way right into my heart.

After the ceremony was over, we headed to the reception hall. We kept things light and breezy with lots of different kinds of finger foods, cupcakes for our guests, and lots of dancing. Rebecca and I danced for hours, just enjoying one another's company.

Although I'd never really considered myself much of a wedding kind of guy, I couldn't help but enjoy myself because I was with her. Being with Rebecca was everything I wanted it to be. During one particularly slow song, I tugged her into my arms, holding her close.

"Having fun?"

"The most fun," she admitted.

"Is it everything you hoped for?"

"Absolutely it is. What about you? Is this the wedding of your dreams, or what?"

"It's pretty damn incredible. I never really considered myself to be the kind of guy who dreamed of my wedding day, but this is a pretty good time."

"I have to agree," she leaned up and kissed me. "Not too bad for fated mates, huh?"

"Not too bad," I agreed.

The song changed and I took her hand, leading her away from the dance floor. I was beyond parched and if I was thirsty, my sweet human bride probably was, too. We headed back to the head table and took our seats. Everyone else from the wedding party was absent. They'd all gone off dancing or were chatting with other guests, so it was just the two of us.

I reached for my glass of wine and Rebecca did the same. We'd chosen an assortment of red and white wines for each table at the reception. There was a bartender who was ready to mix anything else anyone needed, of course. Shifters liked to party hard, and after all, it was Christmastime. Even though we'd chosen to get married the weekend before the holiday, we were still in the heart of the Christmas season.

"These are cute," Rebecca said, gesturing to a couple of *his* and *hers* cakes that were sitting on tiny little plates in front of us. She looked around. "I didn't notice these over at the buffet. Did you?"

"Nope. They must have just brought them out. Shall we give it a go?"

Rebecca laughed and nodded.

"Wait a second," she reached under the table and grabbed her tiny white purse. She pulled out her phone and held it up. "Let's get a picture. These are cute."

She snapped a photo of the two little cakes. One said HIS and one said HERS. Setting down her phone, she grabbed a fork and handed me one.

"Okay, let's do this."

We each grabbed our forks and broke off a little bite of the cakes. Just as we were about to bring them to our lips, we heard a scream.

"DON'T EAT THE CAKES. DON'T EAT THE CAKES!"

Instantly, we dropped our forks and looked toward the source of the sound. The DJ cut the music and everyone at the reception turned to see a man coming in one of the side doors. He was hauling someone by her elbow, and they were both yelling.

"Phil?" I stood, shocked that he would interrupt our reception like this. "What are you doing? Is that...is that Heather?"

"There's poison," Phil said. "Don't eat those cakes, boss!"

Rebecca and I looked toward the cakes on the table in front of us.

"What do you mean, they're poisoned?"

"She found out about your allergies when she saw your lunch boxes," he said, hauling her close.

"Let me go!" Heather screamed, wiggling and fighting. I gestured for a couple of the bigger shifter guests to grab her and hold her in place. Even though Heather wasn't a shifter, she kind of seemed like she'd wiggle away like a snake if we weren't careful. Phil was obviously dedicated, but he also wasn't a huge guy.

I didn't want him to get hurt.

"What are you saying?" I asked.

"Holy dragons, Justin," Rebecca tugged at my sleeve. "Look."

She held up a forkful of my portion of "cake" to reveal the red interior. She sniffed it and nodded.

"Yeah, that's cherries."

"And yours probably has shellfish," I sighed.

How could I not have seen what Heather was up to?

"All right," I said to her. "What exactly is going on? Why would you try to poison us?"

"It's not that simple," she shook her head. "You don't know what's going on."

"I do," Phil said. "I know what's going on." He handed me his phone. It was open on a folder of images of me and Rebecca.

"Phil, I know you're obsessed with these pictures, but please, man, just let it go."

"I know you think I'm nuts," he said. "I'm just a fan, but please, scroll through. Look in the background of the pictures. Really look."

So, I started to scroll through. I scrolled through picture after picture and sure enough, in at least one shot in every series, Heather was in the background of the photos in some capacity.

"You've been following us?" I asked. "What the fuck?"

There was an audible gasp as I realized everyone was watching us and trying to see what was going to happen.

"Mom, can you please call the police?" I called out.

"Already on top of it," Aunt Judy said, holding up her phone.

"Heather, you're the one trying to destroy my reputation? You're the one who's behind all of the Photoshopped playboy pictures of me?" I didn't say it out loud, but it was kind of starting to look like she was the one who was behind me and Rebecca getting together, actually. If she hadn't been on such a horrible mission to try to screw up my reputation, then I never would have tried to find my one true mate.

"You never deserved your position," she snapped. She fought, trying to free her arms from two of my cousins who were holding her in place, but they weren't about to budge. They didn't even look bothered by her attempts to weasel away. They just looked bored.

"Are you serious right now?"

"Your father wanted ME to become the CEO after he died!"

"What the fuck?" Mom stood up, walking forward. She stared right at Heather's face, and then she slapped her. "You selfish little snit," she said. "What have you done?"

Now it was my turn to gasp. I'd never heard my mom using language like that. I hadn't even known that she could. And what the hell was a snit? I had no idea, but it sure sounded bad.

"Something you should have done a long time ago," Heather sniffed, looking away. "You always were bad for the company."

"Heather, you're the marketing director. You were never in line to be CEO," I said carefully. "Is that what you thought? Did you think that by discrediting me and ruining my image, I'd be forced to hand the company over to someone like you?"

"It should have been mine," she said again.

"She tried to get you to view Cougar Data as the ones causing the problem so it would draw any attention away from her," Phil added. "When you said you were ending your contracts immediately, she panicked. She knew that when the pictures continued, you'd realize it was an in-house problem."

"How do you know all of this?" Rebecca asked.

"I listen a lot, and Heather likes to talk. It's not really a secret around the office that she doesn't like Justin too much." Phil looked back to me and shrugged. "Sorry," he said sheepishly, "but it's the truth."

"It's fine," I said. I was just glad that Phil had rushed into the reception when he did. Without Phil's warning, it might have been too late. I was far too distracted by everything that was happening to sniff my food. If I had, I would have noticed the scent of cherries. I honestly felt like a fool. Thanks to the fact that I'd been distracted, I had almost lost myself a bride.

Rebecca seemed to be getting agitated with the entire situation, and I was getting tired of dealing with Heather. Needless to say, she was definitely fired. I looked at my cousins.

"Can you take her outside to wait for the cops?" I asked them.

They both nodded and a few other cousins joined them just to make sure Heather didn't try to make a run for it. They headed outside and I looked back to the table. I wanted to ask someone to take the poison allergen-laced cakes away, but I knew the police would need them.

"I guess the party's about over," I said to Rebecca.

"All thanks to Phil," she said, looking at my colleague. He was staring at Rebecca with happiness in his eyes. "Thanks for your sharp eye," she said. "I think I speak for everyone here when I say I'm very happy that Justin and I didn't die on our wedding day."

"I'm happy to be of help," Phil said.

"You know," Rebecca looked over at the DJ. "We have a few minutes before the cops arrive to take our statements. How about a quick dance, Phil?"

"Really?"

"Really."

I thought poor Phil was going to start crying tears of happiness as he and Rebecca went to the center of the dance floor and started to dance. I watched with the crowd as my beautiful wife showed everyone just what a big, wonderful heart she has, and of course, I took plenty of pictures for Phil.

28

Rebecca

By the time we got home after the reception, I was exhausted. Hector meowed loudly at us as we walked in the door.

"Apparently, somebody thinks we were out too late," I squatted down in my dress and started scratching behind his ears. Hector seemed a bit suspicious of all of the lace, but he soon calmed down and started purring loudly, letting me know that all was forgiven.

"I also think we were out too late," Justin laughed. He closed the door, locked it, and then offered me his hand. I accepted, and he pulled me to my feet and into his arms. "Welcome home, my beautiful bride."

"Why, thank you. Are you going to carry me to bed now?"

"Would you like to be carried, or would you like to walk?"

"I'd like to run," I laughed. I bopped him gently on the nose and whispered, "race you." Then I raised my skirts up as high as I could and started running up the stairs. Unfortunately for me, the dress slowed me down considerably and it didn't take much for Justin to grab me. Laughing, he hauled me over his shoulder and carried me the rest of the way to the bedroom. He dropped me gently on the bed and crawled up there next to me.

Then he reached for me, tugging me into his arms, and just kissed me.

"So, today was crazy," I admitted.

"More than you bargained for?"

"A little bit," I told him. "I mean, not that I ever planned to have a huge, beautiful wedding, you know? It's just that there was a lot of...extra...excitement that happened with that wedding."

"I'm sorry," he told me.

"It's not your fault."

"It is, a little bit. I should have known that Heather was bad news. I'd suspected she was up to *something*, but I didn't know what. I certainly didn't think she was the one behind the pictures or that she would ever try to hurt either one of us."

I shivered, trying not to think of what might have happened if either one of us had eaten those cakes. We both would have ended up in the hospital, at the very least, I was certain. It was scary knowing that there were regular, ordinary foods that could make us sick or that could kill us entirely.

It was like living knowing that there were hidden traps that could catch us at any time if we weren't careful.

"I should have smelled it," he muttered.

"Hey...I know your shifter senses are great," I chuckled, "but you can't be expected to deal with that kind of overstimulation and still know everything. Am I right in assuming that there were a *lot* of smells and scents at the wedding?"

"Yes," he agreed. "A lot."

"And if I was the shifter who couldn't quite smell everything I thought I should, would you be upset with me?"

"You know, I see where this is going, and I'm not sure that I like it."

I reached for his face and pressed a kiss to his forehead. I was so wildly comfortable and at ease around Justin that it wasn't even funny.

"I just think you need to remember to be kind to yourself," I told him. "You do so much for other people. Don't you deserve a little break sometimes, too?"

"Maybe," he said. "But right now, I think I have everything I need."

When he kissed me again, I closed my eyes, melting into him. Justin was everything I'd ever dreamed of, and to think that it all started from an ad.

Epilogue

Justin
Three months later

GROWING UP, I ALWAYS thought that funerals were supposed to be drizzly and dreary affairs. It always felt wrong to think that a funeral was the type of place the sun could shine. After all, if I felt nothing but sadness in my heart, it seemed wildly unfair that a day where I was broken hearted and devastated could act so normally.

Yet there we were.

My mother's funeral was held on a sunny afternoon in the middle of March. She'd survived long enough to spend three wonderful months seeing me married, which was kind of wonderful in and of itself. It was strange to think that if things had progressed normally, or at least according to plan, that Rebecca and I would only be about a fourth of the way through our one-year commitment to each other.

As it was, we were going to be committed for a lot longer than that.

She reached for me, squeezing my hand. We'd never told anyone about the arrangement. Nobody. I had a feeling that my cousin, Ally, suspected something was awry, but she'd been kind enough not to call me out. Now, as we stood watching my mother's casket being lowered into the ground, I realized that my mother had been right.

Maybe it had been her plan all along. Maybe she'd been trying to help me find my soul mate. Either way, she'd succeeded remarkably well because Rebecca was everything I'd ever wanted.

She was *everything* I'd ever needed.

"Thank you for being here," I murmured. I didn't need to say anything else, and maybe that was one of the nicest things about loving someone like Rebecca. She didn't need for me to say anything else. She didn't need the big words. She didn't need huge, grand gestures.

All she needed was for me to be okay with this.

With everything.

All she needed was to know I was safe.

When the funeral ended, we went back to my mother's house to eat and spend time together. It felt strange hosting the event at her house, but she'd specifically requested this. Both Rebecca and I had been honored to be able to help prepare my mother's house for this day, and instead of hiring caterers, we'd held a potluck in my mom's honor.

All of the family members, cousins, aunts, and uncles came to join together as we celebrated my mother's life and reminisced about how we missed her. At one point, I needed to take a break. I just couldn't bear to be in her house anymore. Rebecca seemed to sense this, and she nodded to me.

"It's okay," she said. "Take a break. I'll be right here when you get back."

"I don't know where I'd be without you," I told her.

She kissed me softly and then smiled, letting me know that it was okay to run off for a little while without her. I stepped out onto the back porch and then wandered a short distance into the woods. Within seconds, I was naked and in my bear form.

Then I was running.

I let out a long, fierce growl. It was more like a cry of pain than anything else because that was what I was feeling. Pain. Loneliness. Isolation. I was feeling like nothing was going to be okay again. Shifting was supposed to help, but it didn't. At least, not right away.

I started running, and that was when my mind started to clear.

I raced through the woods, running as fast as I could. As a polar bear, I loved the water, and I raced toward one of my favorite swimming holes. Nothing mattered in that moment. Nothing mattered at all except burying myself beneath the cool, icy liquid. It might be sunny and warm outside, but in March, the water was still going to be cold. As soon as I located a place to swim, I dove right in, letting myself sink down, down, down.

I let myself become wrapped up in my thoughts. I let myself become wrapped up in everything that was happening. The wildness. The chaos. The sadness.

The pain.

When I emerged from the water, I was only slightly surprised to see two golden eyes peering back at me. My friend, the lion, was sitting there looking at me. Luckily, it was a lion I recognized, so I didn't attack him on sight. Instead, I shifted back to my human form and glared at him.

"What do you want, Basil?"

The lion just stared at me. He was big and had an incredible mane. That was really the giveaway as to who he was. Everyone thought all lions looked the same, but if you were careful, you could see the subtle differences. Basil's mane was his own personal pride and joy. He spent more time staring at himself in the mirror than anyone else I'd ever met.

"I know it's you. Nobody else has a mane like that."

More staring.

I sighed. I was going to have to fight dirty if I wanted him to change back.

"Wait...is that a grey hair?" I pointed to his mane.

Instantly, he shifted into his human form and started reaching for his chin and head.

"What? Where? Really?" Basil stopped touching himself when he noticed me laughing, and then he glared. "You did that on purpose."

"Yeah. What do you want?"

"Can't a friend visit a friend?"

"Not like this."

"I wanted to see you."

"Cool. I don't want to see you."

"Why not?"

"Because it's a bad time."

"Because of your mom."

So, he knew.

Everyone knew.

Then again, my mother had been an incredible cornerstone of the community. She'd always been kind and helpful to the people around her, and she'd gone above and beyond with keeping people safe and helping them to lead happy lives.

I hoped I'd live up to that legacy. She and my dad had built Honey Bear Software together, and they'd done it on a platform of community involvement and caring.

Would Rebecca and I be able to live up to that legacy?

I sure as hell hoped so.

"Yeah, because of my mom," I finally said.

"Sorry, brother. I know the pain."

Basil's parents had both passed away, too. It was a few years ago, and it had hurt him very deeply. He'd thrown himself into work and partying, and that was around the time the two of us stopped spending as much time together. Like me, he had a reputation as being a bit of a playboy.

Unlike me, he didn't seem to mind.

"I'm sorry about your folks," I told him.

"Me too. It gets easier."

"Thanks."

"She was a good lady."

"Thanks."

"Heard you got married," he offered up.

Basil hadn't come to the wedding. I'd invited him, but he had been out of town on business, and with such short notice, anyway, it wasn't surprising. I hadn't felt snubbed or anything like that.

"I did," I said.

"Is she a shifter?"

"Nope."

"Really?" Basil looked at me. "You went for a human?"

"It's complicated, but she's the one."

"You just knew, huh?"

"I just knew."

"That's how my parents said it was for them," Basil told me. We rarely talked about his parents. I was surprised we were doing this now. Once upon a time, the two of us had been close friends, but we'd really grown apart. Now, I kind of missed that companionship.

"They told you that?"

"They said falling for your mate was like getting slapped in the face by a tidal wave...but in a good way."

I laughed.

"Funny comparison," I admitted. The two of us were sitting on opposite sides of the swimming hole with our feet kicking in the water. It reminded me of the good old days when we were kids and nothing else really mattered. Once upon a time, we'd been calm and relaxed and the world had seemed...

Well, it had seemed simple.

"I'm happy for you," Basil said.

"What about you? Anyone special in your life?"

"Not right now," he said, but I thought I detected a tone of wistfulness...or maybe it was hopefulness. Like me, Basil ran a large company, and he likely didn't have a lot of time to date. If he did find time, it was for single one-off events that he was forced to attend to keep up with his public image.

Basil and I talked for a few more minutes, and then we went our separate ways. I headed back to the house where Rebecca was entertaining our guests and keeping everything running smoothly for me. Damn, I was so lucky to have her. I didn't know what I'd do without her. Literally.

Life was hard enough on my own. Having someone by my side who would help me, cherish me, adore me, and just be happy with me was really and truly life-changing.

It was calming.

And it was nice to know that no matter what happened next, I'd always have her by my side.

I just hoped that Basil would find that same happiness.

THE END
The adventure continues with Basil's story in THE LION'S FAKE WIFE: SHIFTERS OF RAWR COUNTY #2.

The Lion's Fake Wife
Sophie Stern

ONE LION. ONE HUMAN. One important lie.

Melinda

I don't have much going for me until I see an ad in the local newspaper. Wanted: one bride. It seems like a total scam except for the fact that it'll get me out of Kansas. After dealing with *my* past, I'm more than happy to claim this Get Out of Kansas Free card. After spending a year in prison, staying married to a CEO for half of a year doesn't seem too bad, now does it? Yeah, some weird things seem to happen in Rawr County and the people there aren't exactly welcoming to outsiders, but it can't be all bad...can it?

Basil

I'll do whatever it takes to improve my image at the company. Apparently, my shareholders don't look too fondly on the fact that I've been something of a playboy in recent years. All that's about to change, though, because I'm getting married. The moment I see Melinda, I know that she's the one. My inner-lion knows, too. She's not just the woman I'm going to marry for the sake of improving my personal image. She's the one I'm going to marry because she's my fated mate.

Only, Melinda doesn't know I'm a shifter, and she's got a few secrets of her own. When an enemy from her past resurfaces in Rawr County, we're going to have some hard decisions to make. We're going to have to fight for what we believe in, and we're going to have to fight for her safety.

Luckily for Melinda, I love a good challenge.

For my Jack Cat

Author's note: this story takes place in Rawr County, Colorado. While this is sadly a fictional location, my love of the mountains is anything but fictional. I had the incredible chance to live in Colorado for a few years with my husband and we spent many hours driving through the mountains, listening to music, and just enjoying ourselves. It's my hope that this story will make you laugh, make you gasp, and hopefully, make you forget about life's troubles for a little while. Now, put on some music and turn the page so we can begin our adventure...

1

Basil

My front porch was angled perfectly so that every day when the sun set, I could sprawl across it and feel the setting sun on my face. It was a wonderful experience, really, and not just because the sun felt good on my face. The sun felt good on *all* of me. Everything from my mane to my paws felt warm and relaxed, and then when the last rays of sunshine finally disappeared, it was over.

Everything was gone.

Usually, after the sun set, I went inside of the house, closed the door, and went to bed. I never fell asleep right away. Instead, I'd lay there for hours just thinking about everything and nothing all at once. My sleep had never exactly been good, but lately, it had been downright horrible.

Tonight, though, I didn't move after the sun set. Instead, I stayed on the porch in my lion form. My mane was moving ever-so-slightly in the evening breeze, and the air was cooling already. Summer was going to be here before I knew it, and the weather would grow hot and sticky. I wouldn't be able to just hang out on the porch into all hours of the evening.

I might be a lion shifter, but I was also half-human, and that carried with it certain preferences.

I didn't *like* feeling too hot.

I didn't like flies swarming around my mane.

I didn't like a lot of things.

Then again, maybe that was one of my problems. Perhaps I needed to learn how to let things go and just *live* a little. My assistant would argue that I lived far too much. My reputation as a playboy was a bit out of control these days, but I never let that get to me. It wasn't really what I enjoyed. It never brought me peace the way just sitting on the porch watching the sunset did. This was where I really wanted to be.

I heard my phone ringing from inside the house. I'd have to get up sooner or later and go find out who was calling me, but it was a weekday evening, so I had a pretty good guess as to who it was, and I didn't really want to answer.

She was persistent, though.

The phone stopped ringing only to immediately start again, and I knew that if I didn't get up and answer the phone, she'd come over to the house. I didn't want that. I appreciated everything that my assistant did for me, but showing up at night?

I didn't need that.

Slowly and laboriously, I pulled myself up and walked across the porch. I might run a multi-million dollar company, but I lived outside of the city in a rustic farmhouse that cost almost as much as a penthouse apartment. The farmhouse was custom built just for me and to my very specific needs.

Mostly, I wanted luxury with privacy, too.

I wanted a place where I could relax, and where I could be myself.

I wanted a place where the world would just leave me alone.

Once I reached the door, I shifted into my human form, reached for the handle, and pushed it open. Instantly, I was reminded that living alone was terrible. My house smelled clean and sanitary, but it smelled like disinfectant, too. A farmhouse like this should smell like apple pie or blueberry tarts.

It shouldn't smell like someone was just scrubbing the floors.

I appreciated having my place be clean and tidy, and I appreciated my privacy, but every so often, I resented the fact that I lived alone. I knew it was for the best. I was a crabapple of a lion, after all, but it still bothered me from time to time.

Heading to the phone, which was still ringing, I lifted it and swiped to answer. I didn't bother looking at who it was because I already knew. Still, I answered professionally just in case I was wrong.

"This is Dixon."

"Basil," a frantic voice said. "Basil, have you seen the news?"

The news?

She *really* did sound panicky. I had no idea what could have happened to make my assistant sound so damn worried. Surely there wasn't some sort of national incident that would warrant a phone call this late in the day. No, whatever the problem was, it was much more localized, which meant it involved either me or my business.

"No, Sherry, I haven't. What about the news? What's wrong?"

Sherry was a kind woman, but she also tended to overreact to things that didn't require overreacting. She was in charge of keeping me in one piece, but sometimes she took that a bit far and I had to help her rein it all in. She was a bundle of stress wrapped up tight. Sometimes I wasn't sure how her wife handled all of Sherry's anxiety and worries. Still, despite all of her tension, Sherry was detail-oriented and driven.

She was a badass, and she was responsible for saving my company more times than I could possibly count.

So why call me tonight?

It *had* to be about the company.

"It's you, Basil. It's you."

Or about me, apparently.

"Hold on."

I walked over to my open laptop and pulled up the local news website. Sure enough, it was plastered with headlines about me partying and debasing myself in all of the very best ways. There were a couple of pictures of me drinking the weekend prior at a club. There wasn't anything factually untrue about me on the news site, but it certainly wasn't flattering.

It wasn't going to look good for the company.

At all.

"You're looking at the news?" Sherry spoke with slight hesitation in her voice.

"I'm looking at the news," I agreed.

"And you think it's bad, don't you?"

"It's pretty bad," I sighed.

We were supposed to announce the new launch of a product next week, but this was going to set us back significantly. If local shareholders and potential investors saw this, which they would, they were going to be pissed. The news painted me as irresponsible and unpredictable. Both of these things were true, but neither meant that I was bad at my job.

In fact, work was the one thing that I had always been consistent with. Working kept me grounded and it kept me focused. When I was talking about product development with my team, I shined. It was the one time when I felt like nothing else could bother me or touch me.

It wasn't until later, when I was home, when I was alone, that I let the world start to get to me.

A lion shifter who was sad didn't sound good for business, but I *was* good.

No, scratch that: I was great.

I excelled. When I was pitching products to my team or coming up with new ideas to help our company grow, I was incredible. It was like I finally came to life and all of the things that had bothered me before no longer mattered.

Now, though...

Well, this could change everything.

"What do you want to do?" Sherry asked. "I've already drafted a press release, but I need to get your okay on it before I submit it for release."

"What's it say?"

"The usual stuff: the pictures have been doctored, that it's not your usual behavior, and that over the weekend, you weren't even out at the club."

All lies.

The pictures weren't doctored, it's absolutely my normal behavior, and I was definitely at the club.

If Sherry submitted the press release she'd dreamed up, it wouldn't go over well. It wouldn't actually solve any problems. I could deny, deny, deny until I was blue in the face, but if people began to doubt me as a leader, then my company was going to collapse.

I couldn't have that.

I'd already lost more than anyone else should ever lose. Both of my parents were gone, and they were never coming back. I would have suspected that losing them as an adult would hurt less than losing them as a kid, but the pain was still harsh and raw. I tried not to think about them too much because it was always too painful when I did.

Still, we had to do something. There had to be some sort of damage control.

I sighed and ran my hand through my hair. What would my dad have done? What would Mom have done? They both always seemed to know exactly which choices were going to be best. Anytime I'd ever struggled, they had always been there for me. Now they weren't. Now I was alone, and I had to make a choice that could impact the future of my company.

Maybe Sherry's press release really was a good idea. At the very least, it would buy us some time for me to get my shit together. I knew that I needed to reform my image. I understood that. Nobody wanted to invest in someone who drank too much or who liked dancing a little too much. The world was still a place that equated partying with being unreliable, which meant my shareholders really would believe that I wasn't able to keep things together.

I took a deep breath, and I was just about to tell Sherry to just go for it anyway when I suddenly had an epiphany. Maybe there was another way. Oh, there was *definitely* another way.

"Wait on the press release," I told her.

"Sir?"

She was surprised. In the past, I would have told her to send it out. Damage control was super important and it was one of the biggest roles Sherry had. She wasn't just my personal assistant. She was also my PR professional. She was my guide. She was basically my manager.

But I had an idea. It was a crazy one, but maybe it would work. Maybe we needed a little bit of crazy and unexpected.

My friend Justin's company, Honey Bear Software, had made a miraculous comeback and swung back toward stability when he'd announced his marriage. It was only recently that Justin suddenly produced a wife. He had this whirlwind romance that spanned only a few months, from what I could tell.

Everyone loved it.

The romantics who invested in his company were thrilled, his mom got to attend his wedding before she passed away, and Justin got to marry the girl of his dreams.

Everyone won.

What if I did something like that?

Oh, I didn't have a girlfriend, a fiancé, or a wife, but I could. I'd learned over the years that there wasn't much money couldn't buy. When it came to happiness, there actually was a price tag attached, and if you had enough cash, you could acquire anything you needed in life. This situation was no exception.

"Don't release that, Sherry. We aren't going to say that the pictures are fake," I told her. There was a pause, and I could hear her gasp. She was surprised.

"Basil, you know I never tell you what to do..."

"Sherry, you *only* tell me what to do."

"Fair, but hear me out. If you tell everyone the pictures are real, they're going to think that the pictures are real."

"They are real."

"Yes, but we don't want people to think that they are," Sherry insisted.

"If we lie, people will know. They aren't fools."

"Basil, we need to negate the narrative that you're some sort of playboy."

"I think I have a solution."

A pause.

She was thinking about what I said. I could practically hear the wheels turning in her head. She had no idea what I was about to say because it was absolutely crazy, and I knew it. What was worse is that Sherry couldn't tell anyone because if word got out, it would ruin everything.

"You aren't going to tell everyone the pictures are fake," I repeated.

"Okay..."

"You're going to admit that the evening got out of hand, but that it was a rare occasion because I was celebrating."

"Celebrating, sir?" Sherry still didn't know what I was getting at, and I still wasn't sure if it was an idea I should even be sharing out loud, but I had to. This had to be the solution we needed.

"Yes. Announce that I was out celebrating my recent engagement."

"Basil?"

"Sherry?"

"You're engaged?"

"As far as the company needs to know, yes."

"But Basil, you aren't even dating anyone!"

"I know. Sharing that I was celebrating my engagement with a sort of bachelor party is going to sound a lot better than telling everyone I was out drinking because I was sad."

Silence.

Sherry didn't know what to say, and I felt a little bad because I knew I was putting her in an awkward position. She wanted to know what was going on. She wanted to be able to help. Sherry was nothing if not resourceful, and she was always helping. When Sherry encountered a problem, she tried to get it fixed as quickly as possible.

"So, what are you going to do when people want to know who you're marrying?"

"I'll host a party," I said quickly. "In two weeks. Everyone will be there, including my bride-to-be."

"Who?"

"I'll find someone, Sherry."

"So, let me get this straight," she said slowly. "You're not actually engaged."

"No."

"You're going to find a girl who says she'll pretend like she's going to marry you."

"Yes."

"And you're going to have a party and introduce her as the woman you're going to marry."

"Correct."

"So, what are you going to do in a few months when everyone wants to know when the wedding is? Stage a public break-up?"

"That's just the thing, Sherry. There won't be a breakup. I'm going to get married."

"You're going to get married?"

"Yes."

"Basil, do you hear yourself? You sound crazy."

"I'm not crazy, but I do need to get off the phone, Sherry. I've got a lot to do."

"What could you possibly have to do?" Sherry sounded totally exasperated.

"Why, haven't you heard? I've got to find myself a fake wife."

2

Melinda

I read through the ad five times before I decided that it probably wasn't a scam. If it was, it seemed like a really good one. The ad started out with a jaw-dropping headline: WANTED: ONE BRIDE.

The terms of the agreement were pretty clear-cut. A private businessman wanted to arrange for someone to marry him. The terms were that the marriage would span half a year, no sex was required, and there would be money involved.

More important than any of that: there would be privacy involved.

I could use a little bit of that.

As it was, I had no money, no job, and soon, I'd have no place to live. The little motel I'd been shacking up in was going to be kicking me out soon when they realized I no longer had any money to pay them with. I'd been in jail just long enough to not lose touch with reality, but also just long enough to lose any of my former friends.

Nobody wanted to associate with a villain, so my friends had left as soon as they possibly could.

I felt like that had been one of the hardest things about going to jail. It wasn't the fact that I'd been convicted of something I viewed as stupid and unimportant. It wasn't that I now had this tarnish on my perfect record. Nope. It was the fact that when I'd been imprisoned, all of my old friends had bailed.

Not a single person had come to visit me in jail.

Nobody had tried to come connect with me.

Nobody had cared.

For me, that had been the worst of it. When I'd finally gotten out, I suspected that the world would be different, but I couldn't have possibly anticipated just *how* different things would be. Life was just as busy and hectic, but it was also lonelier.

And trying to get a job with a fresh criminal record wasn't proving to be easy. Nobody wanted to hire someone with a record. It didn't matter what I'd done. It didn't matter whether it had been a rightful conviction or not. People saw the little box marked on a job application that said yes, I had a criminal record, and they ran the other way. I was tired, and I was hungry, and I was almost out of cash.

So, would I marry a guy for money?

Yeah, sure.

I didn't exactly have a boyfriend of my own right now. I wasn't out picking up anyone. I had nothing to offer another person at all, and from the sound of this advertisement, this guy was slightly desperate. Desperate sounded good to me. It meant he might stoop low enough to hire someone like me: someone who was running from her past and who didn't see much of a future.

What was the harm in trying to apply?

The ad said that I was supposed to send an email with my qualifications. There was a list of requirements for submission. I had to include a headshot, a full-body shot, a resume, a list of my skills, and a brief commentary on why I'd make a good wife.

Seriously?

What the hell did I know about being a good wife?

I'd never been married before. Worse than that: all of my previous relationships had been dysfunctional and unconventional.

I'd never had a relationship where we'd had any sort of healthy dynamic, so I didn't know what to put on this application.

What made a good wife?

Did this guy want me to say that I could bake a mean apple pie or that I could make spaghetti really well?

I had no idea, but I had to come up with something because I was running out of options.

Quickly.

I reached for the vodka next to me and took a sip. I shouldn't have been drinking. Drinking wasn't something that ever led to good or clear decisions, yet there I was, drinking anyway. Vodka was something I'd missed very much while I was in jail, and right now, it kind of took the edge off of everything.

There was a certain fear that wrapped around me these days. Even though I was living anonymously in this motel, even though I'd changed my hair, and even though I never went out during the daylight unless I really, really had to, I was still scared. There was still this fear that seemed to hover over me, never going very far. There was still this *what if* that haunted me.

What if he found me?

Every so often, the hair on the back of my neck would seem to stand upright. I'd get this fear that washed over me, making me feel like he was there, watching. He couldn't have been, right?

I knew it.

I knew that reasonably, he couldn't have been there.

But I knew that he might be.

The man responsible for sending me to jail wasn't the kind of person who would forget. I knew perfectly well he'd kept a close eye on me while I was in the system, and even now that I was free, I knew that my freedom came at a cost.

I had nothing to lose.

If I stayed here and he found me, I'd be screwed. If I stayed here, and he didn't find me, I'd spend every day worried and scared. I'd spend my days afraid.

Now I had a very unique chance to do something most women my age would never dream of doing. At least, not if they had anything going for them. I was about to respond to an ad for a bride and become what, some mail-order wife?

That sounded messed up, even to my screwed-up head.

But I was desperate.

I knew I was talented when it came to schmoozing. Once upon a time, I'd been a damn good waitress. I'd thought about dancing, and I knew I'd be good at that, too, but I was too worried. Too afraid. The types of people who worked at gentleman's clubs were the types of people who might know the man I was hiding from. It was too risky.

I wasn't about to take any risks.

Not anyone.

"Except for this one," I muttered.

The time for risky behavior had come and gone. I wasn't interested in doing anything that might end up with me hurt or killed, but this was different. This situation had *crazy* written all over it, but I had a good feeling about it. I had a feeling that no matter what happened now, I was going to find a way to fight my way to freedom.

This just might be my ticket out of here.

Eventually, my hunter was going to give up on me. He was going to realize that I wasn't the tasty, delicious prey he'd left behind last year. He was going to stop looking for me, and when that moment came, I would finally have my freedom.

Maybe I could wait things out pretending to be someone's wife. If nothing else, it meant I'd have free food and free shelter. Besides, it *had* to be better than the motel. I glanced over at my little bed and frowned. There weren't any bedbugs, but I wasn't convinced this place was roach-free. Anything could be hiding in the thin walls of this place. Anything.

Gross.

I opened up my email. I used my real email address with my real name attached. The person who was running this ad was obviously very private, but he or she – the advertisement hadn't exactly specified – was obviously going to run some sort of background check. They'd probably run a credit check, at the very least. That was fine. I could let this person know that I'd been to jail. I didn't have to let them know why I'd gone, did I?

I just didn't want anyone else to know.

Hopefully, this wouldn't come up at all. I didn't need anyone to know I was running from the past or that I'd kind of started to craft my own future. I wanted to break free from all of the things that bound me to the hunter. I wanted to have something different in my future: something that wasn't painful or terrible or broken. Was it so hard to hope that I'd be able to find a life where I could just relax?

From my first impression of the ad requesting a bride, the person I would be dealing with didn't want anyone to know about the situation. That made me wonder whether this was a really old dude who needed to impress some young people or whether it was a younger man who was trying to get ahead in the business world. Was it a trust fund baby? I had no idea, but the person probably had money. They *had* to have money.

After all, they were offering cash in exchange for being a wife.

That had to mean something.

It meant that whoever this person was, they liked discretion. They liked to fly under the radar. They weren't going to be broadcasting my past, so even if they found out the truth, they weren't going to let everyone know.

Right?

Right.

I paused for a moment, staring at the computer screen. What exactly was I supposed to say in this application? I felt like there would probably be a lot of replies to the advertisement. If my response wasn't interesting enough, then the email would just be deleted. End of story. End of adventure.

If I could find a way to make it stand out, though, then things could be a little bit different: a little bit better.

This person was going to receive tons of replies. They would get at least dozens – if not hundreds – of responses. I needed to figure out how I'd be able to make my application different. I needed to get visible. I needed to make this person *want* me.

"You can do this," I said out loud. It was a stupid thing to talk to myself, but I'd always done it. Sometimes, just hearing the words out loud helped. Sometimes, we all just needed for *someone* to believe in us.

Even if that someone was ourselves.

"Dear sir," I started.

Then I stopped.

What if it wasn't a "sir"?

"Dear sir or madam," I started again.

Once more, I stopped.

What if this person didn't like being called "sir" *or* "madam"?

Finally, I decided to go with the old standby of, "to whom it may concern."

Once more, that didn't sound very good. It sounded formal and stuffy, and not at all like myself. The truth was that if I was going to be fake-married to this person for a while, they were going to get to know me: the real me. As much as I wanted to act and pretend to be someone I wasn't, the reality was that I couldn't hide forever. Eventually, they'd realize I was something of a joker and that I was annoyingly sarcastic.

Was that going to be a dealbreaker?

It was probably best to let a little bit of my personality shine through now before things got too serious. If this person hired me and then found out I like to be silly, they might not like that. They might fire me and then I'd be shit-outta-luck once more.

No, it was best to be myself.

My mom had always told me to believe in myself. She'd always said that it was important to be who you were even if people weren't going to like it. That was something a lot of people said, but very few actually believed.

I'd learned that the hard way.

In this case, at least, I figured it would be okay to be myself for a little bit.

"Dear Captain," I finally wrote. There. That was polite, friendly, slightly formal, and gender-neutral. "I'm writing to you about the ad you've put out looking for a bride."

I paused, once more wondering what I should write next. If I'd known my writing skills were going to be so needed, I probably would have paid better attention in English class in high school.

"I happen to be single," I continued, pressing my lips together tightly. Writing this was going to be harder than I thought. "And I am interested in applying for the bridal position."

I remembered reading about business proposals long ago. When I was in high school and later college, my writing classes had frustrated me endlessly – I was more of an artist than a writer – but I remembered that you were supposed to list your qualifications. If you wanted to prove to someone that you were worth their time, you needed to be very specific.

So, what were my qualifications?

Good at blowjobs.

Couldn't exactly put that in an email when the ad clearly said, "no sex."

Good at biting.

Once again, I couldn't put that.

Good at surviving.

I sighed, wondering whether I was ever going to be able to finish this email. I'd had to learn how to survive over the last few years, and the experience had been traumatizing. Maybe traumatizing wasn't the right word. Maybe it had just been devastating.

Something within me had broken. Once upon a time, I'd felt that everything in the world was good and pure and hopeful. I'd been optimistic. Now...well, now it just seemed like no matter what I did, I was always running.

Hopefully, this person would choose me as their bride and then I'd at least get a slight reprieve from running. I'd get to hide away wherever it was that they lived, and I'd get to be someone else. For months, I'd get to be someone else, and I wouldn't have to worry about running or hiding or being hunted.

I wouldn't have to constantly look over my shoulder.

Would I?

Use that. Use that passion.

I heard my favorite art teacher's voice in my head as I thought about what I would write. Mrs. Banton had always been telling me to believe in myself, to use my passion, and to harness my creativity so I could unleash it on the world.

Maybe she was right.

Maybe I'd use that passion now.

I continued my letter, outlining my experience in customer service industries and talking about how I was good with people. I explained that I was a good liar. I didn't say it was because I'd gone to jail and now had to learn how to survive on my own without people knowing about my past.

I did, however, explain that I would be able to blend in with whatever the situation that I was facing was.

Before I could think too hard about it, before I could talk myself out of it, I pressed the send button.

Then I closed my computer, went to my little motel bed, and closed my eyes.

3

Basil

Number twenty-three was perfect.

Less than a day after advertising that I needed a bride, I'd already received fifty responses. Most of them were pretty basic, a few were over-the-top, and a couple of them seemed like applicants who wanted to make a quick buck. Number twenty-three, however, was absolutely perfect.

Her message had started off strong, catching my attention with a "Dear Captain."

Captain?

I'd never been called that before, but oh, I loved it. It was less formal than "sir" and more formal than "hey you." It was absolutely what I wanted, and it stuck out above all of the other responses.

"Look at this," I said to Sherry. It was early in the morning, and we were at the office before everyone else arrived. I'd asked her to come in early and go over the responses with me. She hadn't wanted to, but I'd convinced her that I needed her. Sherry was the best, and I'd definitely be giving her some sort of generous bonus for helping me out: probably a few extra vacation days, too, so she could spend that bonus money however she liked.

"What is it?"

"Number twenty-three."

I'd printed off all of the emails, resumes, and pictures that had been sent to me, and I'd organized each applicant into their own little pile of documents. I was going to take this very seriously. My plan had been to narrow the applicants to about ten and do background checks before further narrowing it down to three. Those three people, I would interview, and then I'd make my final decision.

Now, though, I didn't need to do all of that.

Now, the only thing I needed was her.

I pushed the pile for number twenty-three over to Sherry. There was a picture of her on top of the pile, and I stared at it as Sherry reached for the papers. The woman really was lovely. She really did seem like she was the total package.

"Melinda South," Sherry read the name. She looked up at me. "Too bad your name isn't Basil North. You'd be perfect."

"Please," I gestured to the email. "Read the whole thing."

"Melinda South," Sherry read my notes on the file out loud. "31. Single. Never been married. A good liar." Sherry looked up sharply. "What?"

"It's in her email."

She looked back down. This time, she didn't bother reading out loud. She scanned the email a couple of times and then looked at the attached photos.

"Well, she's beautiful."

"She is."

Melinda had bronze skin and long, dark hair. Even though pictures never did anyone justice, I could tell that her eyes were the kind that sparkled. She was passionate, I gathered. I wondered what kind of things she cared about. She seemed like she was bright and energetic, and that was what I needed.

Of course, being a good liar was a plus.

"Why did she say she can lie?"

"Because that's what I need," I pointed out.

"Clever."

"She seems very clever," I agreed. I didn't need a wife who could suck me off or make my cock hard, although if Melinda wanted to add sex into our little arrangement, I'd be more than happy to. No, what I needed was someone who could schmooze. I needed someone who could bat her eyes at me and make the whole world believe that she loved me.

Out of all of the applicants I'd heard from, nobody compared to her. She was the best, and she was the one I wanted. Suddenly, I didn't even care what it cost.

"We need to make this happen," I told Sherry.

"Well, what's your plan for screening?"

"Background checks, interviews..." My voice trailed off as I realized that I didn't care about either of those things. I just wanted her. Something deep inside of me felt drawn to this particular woman out of all of the applicants, and I knew that I needed to make this happen.

I needed to make *her* happen.

This could be it. This could be the solution to all of my issues. I was an incredible businessman and I was an incredible closer, but I needed something more. I needed someone who could make the world believe that I was the total package. Would having Melinda by my side be enough? Could she really be what I needed?

"Okay, would you like me to give her a call to set up an interview?" Sherry was all business, and I appreciated that, but suddenly I didn't feel like being very business-like.

Suddenly, I felt like being wild. My inner-lion seemed to be clawing at me, threatening to break out, and I didn't mind at all. For once, I didn't mind. All I wanted was to be with this woman. I knew we weren't going to sleep together. I understood that, and more importantly, I accepted it. What I wanted was the knowledge that we were going to be physically close.

I wanted to touch her, grab her. I wanted to pull her into my arms and make her promise to be mine, even if it was just for show, which it would be. Melinda was going to be performing a service for me – that is, if she'd have me.

"I'll call her myself," I told Sherry.

"Oh?"

"Yes," I nodded. "I think I'll call her myself."

"So, do you even actually need me for anything?" Sherry frowned at me.

"I'm sorry, do you have somewhere you need to be?" I asked her. The last time I'd checked, Sherry was my assistant, so what was with her acting like she couldn't stand being here? Maybe she had something going on in her personal life, but I knew for a fact that she didn't have anything on her agenda for the day.

She rolled her eyes and crossed her arms over her chest. Sherry wasn't about to let me get away with talking to her like that, which was one of the things I liked about her. She was no-nonsense. She was factual and she always got right to the point.

"Boss, you know how I feel about this."

"No, actually," I leaned back in my chair and propped my feet up on my desk. Then I just stared at her. "How do I feel?"

"It's a dangerous game you're playing," she lowered her voice. For the first time, she looked worried. A pang of guilt shot through me. Perhaps she was right. Maybe she was right, and I was wrong, and this wasn't what I really needed to be doing.

"It's for the company," I said, and that was true. At least, I thought that it was true. What my company needed was for the owner to be stable and put-together. My company needed someone who could make things look like they were going well even when they weren't.

My company needed me to get my shit together, and this was how I was going to do it.

"Just be careful. I'll start with the party-planning today," Sherry told me. Then she turned and left.

Ah, yes.

The party.

My engagement party was in less than two weeks now, and I still didn't officially have a bride.

Yet.

I had a feeling that was all going to change.

I picked up the phone and dialed Melinda's number. Her file had been absolutely flawless, and I wondered if there was a catch. Nobody could be *that* perfect, that wonderful, or that absolutely kind without there being some sort of dark side to it all.

She answered on the first ring.

"Hello?"

Breathless. She sounded breathless. Had she been jogging?

My dick stirred.

Had she been masturbating?

What did sweet Melinda like to touch herself to? Was she the kind of girl who rubbed her body and played with her nipples when she got excited? Or did she start by dipping her hands between her legs and touching herself there?

"Hello?"

I realized that I still hadn't spoken. I'd gotten completely caught up in my fantasies and I hadn't actually told her who I was or what I wanted. I needed to talk fast before she hung up the damn phone and thought I was trying to spam her.

"I'm calling for Melinda," I quickly said.

Silence.

Her breath hitched, and even through the phone, I could tell that she suddenly felt anxious.

Why?

Who did she think was calling her?

"May I ask who's calling?"

A whisper.

She was scared, I realized. How strange. I knew a lot of women my age didn't exactly like talking on the phone, but getting anxious over someone calling and asking if it was you seemed a bit strange. It wasn't my place to judge, though. Besides, I had my own problems.

"My name is Mr. Dixon," I said, choosing not to use my first name just yet. There were plenty of Dixons in the world, but not too many Basils. If she felt like looking me up online, she'd have easy access to who I was, and I wanted to talk to her for a moment first.

"Mr. Dixon? What do you need with Melinda?"

"I'm calling about the ad you responded to," I told her, ignoring the fact that she was pretending not to be herself. Nobody used landlines anymore. It wasn't like she could pretend she had answered someone else's phone. That was a bit ridiculous, even for a situation like this.

There was a slight hitch in her breath as I said the words. Yeah. This was definitely Melinda, and she definitely knew what I was talking about.

"The ad?"

"The bridal ad."

"Oh. That one."

"Do you respond to a lot of ads?" I asked playfully.

"No," she said, and something about the wistful way the word floated from her end of the call to mine let me know that she was telling the truth. Whoever this girl was, whatever she was interested in, and whatever her dreams were...this wasn't the type of thing she usually did. Right away, I knew this wasn't the type of girl who took chances, but that was okay.

She didn't have to take all of the chances in the world.

I just needed her to take a chance on me.

"Well, I'd like to talk more about the ad you responded to yesterday."

"Okay," she whispered.

"All of that bravado I read in the email," I murmured. "It's gone?"

"What? No!"

"Sounds like it's gone," I pointed out. "Maybe I called the wrong number. If I recall, the girl who responded to my ad sounded like a badass. You sound like a scared puppy."

I was being a dick, and I was pushing her, but I had to. If this was going to happen, if she was going to be my "one," even for a fake relationship, then she had to be able to take the heat.

I lived a life that was under scrutiny. My company was big, and people turned to me when they were trying to figure out what to do next. I needed someone by my side who could handle that sort of scrutiny...that sort of watchfulness.

Was Melinda my girl?

Or was I going to have to go with one of the other applicants?

"A puppy?" There was a hint of laughter in her voice before she burst out into a huge giggle fit. "Are you fucking kidding me?"

I waited, not saying anything. I wanted to know what she was going to do. This was the kind of woman who didn't back down, wasn't it? That was what I was hoping for. I needed someone who could be strong and bold. Ideally, I needed someone who could be a bitch if the moment called for it.

"I'm no puppy, sweetheart," Melinda said. "More like a wolf. I'm loyal as hell, but if you fuck with me, I do bite."

"Good thing for us," I said slowly. "I bite also."

"I doubt it. You're the one who sounds scared. Have you never talked to girls before?"

"I've talked to plenty of girls."

"Then why do you have to resort to hiring someone from an ad?"

Unlike before, the teasing tone was no longer present in her voice. She wasn't laughing, but she wasn't accusing me, either. She was just...curious.

I could answer that.

"I have a job where I'm in the public eye," I explained.

"Ah."

"And I need to present myself as-"

"Stable."

"Yes."

"And dependable, probably."

"Exactly."

"And you think getting married is going to help with that."

"I'm hoping that it will, yes," I agreed.

"And you think I could be the girl for you."

"I'm hoping so."

I knew so.

I knew it.

She was *everything*. She was sassy and flirty and funny, and perhaps most of all, she'd already made me laugh. She'd already gotten me curious, and that was no easy feat. Most of the time, when I talked to a woman, I just felt bored.

I felt *tired*.

With Melinda, I didn't feel that way.

Instead, I felt wild.

Happy.

Inquisitive.

"So, what do I need to do?" Melinda said, bringing the conversation back to the point. She was good at that, I realized. She was good at redirecting the flow of conversation. That was an important skill. Not everyone could do that, and it would serve her well if she ended up coming to...

What?

Work for me?

Date me?

I still didn't really know how to label this relationship we were about to begin. I needed to figure out what to call it so that I could better handle things mentally. Sometimes planning helped.

Okay, planning *always* helped.

"I need someone who can be by my side," I explained. "At social events in particular."

"Well, as I said in my application, I'm pretty flexible. I'm good on my feet."

"A good liar?"

"A good liar," she agreed easily. She didn't seem embarrassed or bothered by this self-assessment. That in itself seemed strange to me, but also kind of wonderful. Not too many people could give themselves that sort of label with confidence.

"That's good," I murmured. "I need my shareholders to actually believe we're in love."

"Have you seen my pictures? That won't be hard."

So she was confident, too. I liked it. A lot of women struggled with self-image. Hell, a lot of men did, too. When you threw shifters like me into the bunch, the world was a huge, wallowing pit of self-doubt. Melinda didn't seem like she doubted herself, though, and I rather liked that.

I appreciated the fact that she seemed comfortable with who she was.

"I have seen the pictures," I said slowly.

"They don't do me justice," she offered.

"Are you trying to convince me that you're gorgeous?"

I was already sold.

"I'm just warning you. I can be intimidating, but I'll try to tone it down."

"I think I can handle it."

Were we flirting? Really? I was excited about this possibility. I'd hoped that I would be able to find someone who could meet my needs, but now it seemed like I had found someone who was also going to be interesting.

Yeah, I had a feeling that this thing was going to work.

"I'm sure you can."

We chatted for a few more minutes. I asked Melinda to tell me a little more about herself. There was no hesitation at all. She simply launched into telling me about her likes and dislikes. She was a huge chocolate lover, and she was slightly obsessed with vampires. She liked animals and when she was a kid, she had a pet cat.

That was a good sign, considering I was a lion shifter. I wasn't about to tell her that. I wouldn't. One day, I'd have to. I understood that perfectly well, but that reveal would have to wait for another day. Right now, I just needed to know that she could do the things I needed her to do.

It sounded like she could.

"Are you comfortable in crowds?"

"As comfortable as anyone."

"Can you think on your feet?"

"Absolutely."

"Are you okay with public displays of affection?"

A pause.

That was the first time she hesitated.

"I thought the ad said there would be no sex."

So, she was worried I was going to try to pull one over on her. Did sweet Melinda think I was going to hire her and then change the rules of the game?

I wasn't.

"I'm not expecting sex," I told her.

"But it might happen."

"That's not what I'm asking about," I clarified. "I'm asking if you're okay with me holding your hand or kissing you in public."

"Because you're a public figure."

"I run a huge company," I reminded her gently. "I'm in the public eye."

"I'm not big on public events," she said slowly. "Will I have to have my picture taken?"

"Yes."

A hesitation.

Did she not like the way she looked, after all? Was she just camera-shy? Why would this present any sort of issue?

"Is that a problem?" I asked. Unfortunately, public events were part of the deal. If that wasn't something that Melinda could do, then we weren't going to work. I felt my chest swell with disappointment. I was already attracted to her, and we hadn't even met. "It'll only be local events," I added, in case that mattered. "Nothing regional." My company matters were big news locally, but it was rare to have any sort of national coverage on anything that I did. There might be a magazine or two covering the wedding, but that would be in the future. As of right now, as long as Melinda could handle being featured on local blogs, we'd be okay.

"No, it's no trouble," she said quickly. "I'm a bit nervous about being in the spotlight," she said. "If I can blend in as much as possible, that would be great. Local stuff is okay. It's so...local."

"I can try to help you blend in," I said, "but even if you don't, I have a feeling that people are going to love you."

4

Melinda

He wanted me.

I couldn't quite believe that the rich guy I'd applied to work for had called me back *personally*, and when he offered me the position without even meeting me in real life, I was baffled.

I knew it was a bad idea.

It had to have been a bad idea.

Unfortunately for me, I was out of options. It didn't really matter if Basil was a murderer or if he was a freak. It didn't matter because I had no more money and no more options. It was this or nothing. It was this or death.

He asked if I needed time to get my affairs in order. That was how he phrased it. He wanted to know if I needed to sort out my *affairs*.

No.

No, I didn't.

I didn't have any affairs or anything personal holding me down. I had nothing. I literally could fit all of my things into a bag. That was it.

"I'll send a car to get you tomorrow, then," he told me. He said he'd have a car come pick me up and bring me to the airport. Then I'd fly to his city, which was in the heart of Rawr County, Colorado. I'd never been there before, but I liked the name. It sounded like the kind of place where anything could happen, and right now, I could use something good in my life.

I warned Basil that I didn't have much in the way of clothing, but he didn't seem worried about that. The fact that I wasn't going to bring a lot of personal possessions with me felt like a big deal, but he was surprisingly calm about my comment.

"I'll take you shopping," he said. I thought I could hear a hint of amusement in his voice. "It'll be fun."

"You like shopping?"

"I like a lot of things."

"Like shopping?"

He laughed. The way he laughed made me feel comfortable and at ease. I wasn't sure why. There was something so relaxed about his laugh. It was so different from people I'd known in the past. Then again, my last boyfriend had turned out to be a hardened criminal, so there was that.

No, Mr. Dixon didn't seem like a criminal. He didn't seem mean or terrible or rough around the edges. He seemed like he had the entire world at his fingertips, and he seemed comfortable with that.

While we were on the phone, I looked him up online. It seemed like everything checked out. As long as the person on the phone was, in fact, Mr. Dixon, and not an impersonator of some kind, I felt like I was going to be just fine. I wasn't going to get killed or be murdered. I really was, in fact, going to be a bride.

From my quick searching, I could see that he ran a company. It was a big one, and even though I'd never heard of it before this phone call, it seemed like he was quite a serious businessman. From my quick searching, I could see that Big Cat Technology was the kind of company that had made a name for itself by being on the cutting edge of just about everything. They were located close to another software company, Honey Bear Software, but didn't seem to be direct competitors.

The company's logo was cute: a giant cat who appeared to be napping on a rock with the name of the company scrawled beside it. The website design was great, and the best part was that there were pictures of everyone: including Mr. Dixon.

Oh, and he wasn't ugly.

At all.

I could see from my searching why he wanted to take a wife, too. He really did have a reputation as something of a playboy. It was the kind of reputation that could damage a business, I knew, so I understood, logically, why he wanted to change a little bit.

Once people had an idea of who you were and what you stood for, it didn't really matter what you did. They'd label you, and they'd decide what kind of person you were, and then you were done. Nothing else mattered.

People didn't care if rumors were true or not. They just cared about spreading them.

"Tell me what else you like," I murmured, closing my Internet browser. I didn't really want to look up anything else at the moment. I'd have plenty of time later today to find out everything there was to know about this guy, but right now, I just wanted to savor his voice.

He had a really, really nice voice. There was something sort of calming about it. He had the kind of voice you could trust. It was the type of voice that made you want to pour your heart out to him.

"I know you like chocolate," Basil told me, "but I'm more of a meat-and-potatoes kind of guy myself."

"What kind of meat?"

"Any kind."

"What kind of potatoes?"

"Mashed. Fried. Tots. French. I don't care. They're all heaven."

I laughed. Oh, I was already into this guy. I knew that there could be no feelings between us. This was a business arrangement after all. I wasn't sure if we were going to get legally married or just fake a wedding, but I no longer cared. The ad hadn't said his name or that he was young or that he was fun. He was around my age – early 30s – and I liked the fact that he seemed to know what he wanted.

He was comfortable with himself.

"You know, when I asked you what you liked, I thought you were going to say something dirty," I admitted. Maybe it had been far too long since I'd slept with someone. It had been. The last guy had been Shane, and that had been...

Well, it had been a long time ago.

Now, talking to Basil, I was starting to realize just how long a year can really be. I'd only been locked up for a year. One year in prison. One year where I wasn't allowed to do *anything*. One year.

One entire year and now I was starting to get wound up just by talking to some guy on the phone. Last year, I wouldn't have batted an eye at dirty talk over the phone. Now my panties were already soaked, and we hadn't even gotten started. Damn.

Something really *was* wrong with me.

"Is that so?" Basil's voice sounded breathy. Was he getting turned on by this? It kind of sounded like he was getting turned on by this.

I was.

We weren't even doing anything – just talking – and already, I was starting to get excited by this guy who liked mashed potatoes.

I wondered what else he liked. What was this guy like in bed? Was he rough and tumble? Was he shy?

No, he wasn't shy. Something told me that Mr. Basil Dixon wasn't the kind of guy who held back in the bedroom. He was the kind of guy who got all wound up and then went all out. He was the kind of guy who gave pleasure just as much as he received it. I already knew it. I could tell.

"Maybe," I said, trying to sound casual. Shit. How was I supposed to sound casual? I really couldn't remember how to. My flirting game was *off*. It had died. It was executed when I'd gone away and Shane had gone free. It had been buried, unable to be revived until this moment.

Now, it was like my whole body felt like it was on fire.

I wasn't a virgin, but I very well felt like one on the phone with this man. Basil Dixon. He was going to drive me crazy if I wasn't careful.

"Well, I'm not sure if I'm supposed to be talking dirty to someone I'm going to pretend to marry," he informed me, but I had a feeling that he was smiling. I could detect just a hint of laughter in his tone. I tried not to sigh with need and desire.

"Pretend to marry?" I asked, suddenly realizing this was my chance to ask my big question. All thoughts of sex seemed to leave my mind as I realized what he'd said. "So, are we going to get legally married?"

"Yes, we'll get legally married," his tone changed. Suddenly, he was all business again. The moment had gone, and I regretted that I was the one bringing up the change. I knew there would be other moments in the future when we could flirt and tease each other, but right now, I had bigger fish to fry than getting off over the phone.

Why did this man want to get married so badly?

And why would the marriage be legal?

"Why?"

"Excuse me?"

"Why not just lie?" I asked. Why did he want to actually get married on paper? Surely, there was a reason.

"I need people to believe we're married," he said. "And some of the people in my life...well, they'll check. This isn't something I can just casually lie about."

"I understand," I nodded, even though he couldn't see me. "They'll check the marriage records to see if you filed the right paperwork."

"It's unfortunate, but I have to be thorough. You aren't already married, are you?"

Basil made it sound like he was joking, but I was relieved that I didn't have to say yes. If there was one thing I didn't want to have to lie to Basil about, it was my marital status. I may have been stupid in the past, but luckily, I'd never done anything quite that permanent.

"No, I'm not married."

I'd never been happier to say those words.

5

Basil

Her plane was going to land in twenty minutes, and I was being a complete fool about it. I was nervous as hell, anxiously walking back and forth in front of the gate. I couldn't stop staring at *everything*. It was like I'd never been in an airport before. Hell, it was like I'd never been out of the house before.

"Calm down," Sherry was by my side. Her hair was pulled back in a neat, utilitarian bun. Her makeup was simple, and her lips were pressed tightly together. She was carrying a damn clipboard. Who the hell needed a clipboard at the airport?

Sherry definitely didn't need one, and yet there she was holding one. She had everything she needed to start planning my future right there on that board. She knew exactly what Melinda's schedule was going to be for the next week and half leading up to the party. She knew what Melinda would eat, what she would wear, and what she would do. Sherry had a plan, and that plan had been carefully detailed in excruciating detail.

Since Sherry and I had decided to find me a bride, it had only taken a couple of days to actually locate one, and we'd done a damn good job. The woman we'd chosen was better than anyone I could have possibly imagined. I still couldn't quite believe it was all coming together like this.

Melinda was perfect.

She was everything.

And I still didn't know if we were going to be able to pull this off or not.

What if she arrived and decided I wasn't worth it? What if she looked at me and decided I was so much lamer than she'd anticipated? I couldn't exactly go back to the drawing board on this one. Sherry had already released the press release explaining why I'd been partying, and she'd made it clear that there would be a large engagement party with an open bar – that bit had been her idea – and that invitations would be sent out shortly.

"I'm calm," I said to Sherry.

"You aren't."

"I'm calm," I repeated. I hoped that if I said the words enough times, I'd start to believe them. If I said the words enough, I'd start to think that they were true.

"You're shaking."

"I'm sorry, is your job to insult me or to make sure I attend meetings on time?"

"My job is to keep you alive," Sherry said simply, turning back to the gate. She glanced at her watch and then back up at the space where any moment now, a plane would land, and my future wife would emerge. We were at a small, local airport where the plane would stop out on the runway, everyone would debark, and then they'd walk across the far-too-hot pavement outside to the cool airport interior.

As soon as she stepped through the doors, I'd be on her. I couldn't wait. I'd dressed to impress, and Sherry and I had even picked up flowers on the way over. I hoped that Melinda liked flowers. I hadn't known what her favorite kind was, so I'd spent over half an hour at the florist's shop just smelling each and every flower until I finally decided on sweet peas.

"I haven't seen you like this," Sherry said, staring at me. She shook her head, as though she was slightly grossed out by how ridiculous I was being.

"You've seen me like everything."

"Not like this," she murmured. "Usually, you're just sort of sad."

"I feel like you aren't taking me very seriously," I pointed out.

Sherry looked over at me. "It's good to see you happy," she said, and then she turned back to her notes. She wrote something down, shuffled a couple of papers, and generally appeared to be busy. I looked back toward the gate. A plane had landed.

Her plane.

It was her.

In a few moments, she was going to be here. I'd be meeting with the woman I'd been wild about since I'd first seen her picture.

"You have to calm down, though," Sherry glanced over once more. "She's going to think you're bonkers, Basil."

"Call me Mr. Dixon," I suggested, but not in a mean way. "She'll like it."

"I'm not doing that," Sherry looked away once more. I was slightly rankled that she wasn't going to do something to make me look cooler or more exciting to my date, but I'd have to accept it. I didn't have a lot of choices, now did I?

I couldn't explain why I suddenly had the urge to try to impress Melinda. By all accounts, she was just a woman. She was just a *human* woman. She was someone who was going to have to do a lot, and who was going to have to put up with a lot because my life was a bit wild and unpredictable.

Still, I couldn't wait.

I closed my eyes, took a deep breath, and then she was there.

"She's there," Sherry said, nodding her head toward Melinda. I didn't need Sherry to point her out. I could feel her before I even saw her. She had her dark hair pulled up into two space buns. Her makeup was soft and subtle. Outfit? Jeans and a tight tank top. I loved it.

Her entire aesthetic was incredible.

She spotted me right away and waved nervously as she walked over. As she neared, I could scent her excitement to be here. I tried to resist sniffing the air. Desperate though I was to get a better whiff of the way my newfound wife smelled, I wasn't ready to tell her I was a shifter.

To be honest, I might never tell her.

Yes, people knew there were shifters in the world.

Yes, humans sometimes worked side-by-side with shifters.

Yes, there were even humans and shifters who had long-term relationships and who got married. My friend Justin was the perfect example of that. He'd chosen to marry a woman who was human. Even though the two of us were no longer very close, we'd been friends for years, and I sometimes found myself wondering if I'd ever find the happiness that he'd found.

This thing with Melinda was going to be a short-term solution to my business troubles, but it wasn't really something that was going to last for an eternity.

Was that what I wanted?

An eternity?

Sometimes, I thought that I did. My mom and dad had been so happy to have found each other. They'd been gone for years now, but I'd never forget the way they looked at each other and just always felt so at peace. No matter what they were going through, they always knew that they had each other. They'd always counted on each other, depended on each other.

Would I have that with someone?

Maybe.

Maybe far off in the very distant future.

For now, though, I just looked at the woman in front of me and wondered how the hell we were going to pull this thing off. The no-sex rule had been a stupid idea. That was my very first thought. It had been a stupid idea and I was a stupid person for suggesting it.

In fact, I was a damn idiot.

"Hello," she said, offering a little wave as she neared Sherry and me. Melinda looked from me to Sherry. She must have decided that Sherry was the person in charge – thanks, clipboard – because she focused her attention on her. "My name is Melinda. I'm supposed to be meeting Basil Dixon here."

"He's here," Sherry jerked her head toward me. Melinda looked over at me.

"You seem taller than I expected," she offered casually. Then she held out her hand.

"Oh, I'm afraid not, darling," I told her. "There are always people watching, and I can't have anyone thinking I just flew you in on a whim."

"What?"

Before she could argue and before she could tell me that it was a bad idea, I grabbed Melinda and tugged her into my arms. Yanking her close, I pulled her tightly against my chest, and I just held her.

It was the hug of all hugs. It was the best, most comfortable embrace I'd ever experienced, and I didn't want it to end.

Instantly, my inner-lion started fighting, clawing to escape. I was going to need to go run later. I was going to need to go swim or hunt or climb to get her out of my system, wasn't I? Right now, Melinda's scent wrapped around me like a warm hug. It was the most incredible thing I'd ever experienced.

I wanted more.

I already knew that spending a few months with this woman wasn't going to be enough. I already knew that being around her was going to drive me absolutely crazy if I wasn't careful.

Stay professional.

"Oh, you smell nice," she murmured, snuggling a little closer to me.

All thoughts of being professional faded away.

"Thank you," I whispered. "I showered."

For some reason, Melinda thought that was super funny, and she pulled back, shook her head, and looked up at me.

"You're goofy, Basil."

"And you're beautiful."

"And we're late," Sherry stepped forward. "Hello. I'm Sherry," she held out one carefully-manicured hand.

"Melinda," my bride said, accepting Sherry's hand. She shook it firmly. Good. She was confident, and she wasn't scared. I didn't think she was going to be, but seeing her personality shining in real life made me feel like this was the right decision.

"Pleasure," Sherry said. "Now, if you don't mind, we've got a tight schedule today. It's time for us to go. Do you have any checked bags?"

"Just this," Melinda held up a sad-looking backpack. It had definitely seen better days, and those days were probably at least twenty years ago.

Sherry wrinkled her nose at the monstrosity. The backpack was grey with black patches sewn over it. It looked dirty, and it smelled a little strange, and I wondered exactly what Melinda had been able to pack into the little bag.

"What is that?" Sherry asked, unable to resist.

"It's not much," Melinda shrugged. "It's got everything I need, though."

"Well, we'll be taking you shopping," Sherry explained. "We can buy you a new backpack."

"You really don't have to do that," Melinda insisted. "Really. I understand the terms of this...arrangement...and I don't need you to spend anything else on me."

"We aren't talking about that here," I said quickly, looking around. I doubted anyone at the airport was going to pay us any mind, but I'd learned long ago that looks could be deceiving. I didn't want to give anyone the wrong impression about what was happening here. Nobody could know about the arrangement we had.

Nobody.

If anyone so much as *thought* that Melinda and I were anything less than totally in love, I was going to have trouble on my hands. There would probably be a couple of naysayers at the beginning, but I was certain that my engagement party coming up would be just the thing to stop the gossip and rumors at the source.

"Of course," Melinda said quickly. "Let's go."

Together, the three of us left the small, local airport, and headed for the parking lot.

"I've never flown into an airport this small before," Melinda said as we made our way toward Sherry's car. Usually, I drove or hired a driver, but today Sherry wanted to listen to her music and test out her new car, and I didn't care.

"Oh, it's so beautiful out," Melinda murmured.

"You came from Kansas, right?" Sherry asked as we walked across the parking lot.

"Yeah," she nodded. "We don't have this there," she gestured to the mountains off in the distance. "We don't have *anything* like this."

"I'm a mountain person myself, too," I admitted. "I've lived around them my entire life."

"I moved a lot as a kid," Melinda admitted. "My dad was a military guy, so we were all across the country. We spent three years in Colorado and they were incredible."

"You'll probably find that not much has changed," Sherry offered. "At least, not as far as the views go."

"In the last fifteen years?" Melinda laughed. "I really thought I'd be surprised if anything was still the same at all, but damn..." She sighed, stopping in the middle of the parking lot. "Those mountains. You're right. They haven't changed a bit."

I glanced over at her. She really was something, wasn't she? Melinda had an expression of total awe on her face. It was like she couldn't quite believe what she was seeing.

"All right, out of the middle of the parking lot," Sherry grabbed her arm and gently tugged, pulling Melinda out of the way as a car drove slowly by.

"Sorry. I just got distracted."

"It's fine," I said.

We kept walking. We were almost at the car. When we arrived, Sherry tried to put Melinda's bag in the back, but Melinda wanted to hold it.

"Suit yourself," Sherry shrugged.

Melinda and I sat in the backseat while Sherry started the car up. Melinda looked over at me nervously as the car started to move.

"So," she said slowly. "Do you do this often?"

"What? Hire a bride?"

Melinda looked sharply toward Sherry, as if to ask whether this was a secret from her or not, but I shook my head.

"Sherry knows everything about my life."

"And he does mean everything," Sherry glanced in the rearview mirror. "Seriously, man, you need to learn some discretion. There are some things your assistant really doesn't need to know."

"Pshh," I waved my hand. "You love it."

"I know," Sherry laughed. "Listen," she said to Melinda. "You don't need to worry about Basil. He acts like a bear, but he's got the heart of a lion."

I glared at Sherry. What the hell was she doing? She knew I wasn't going to tell Melinda I was a shifter. Not unless and until I absolutely had to.

Although we were going to get married, the less I shared about my personal life, the better. There were some things that even my would-be wife didn't need to know about me, and that was one of them.

"Heart of a lion, huh?" Melinda looked over at me. Her eyes sparkled. "Does that mean you're very brave?"

"I certainly try," I said. My mouth suddenly felt dry. She was still looking at me, and she wasn't staring at me like she didn't know me. She wasn't watching me the way she might watch someone she'd only just met. She was looking at me like I was handsome, like I was sexy. She was staring at me like she wanted to absolutely devour me, and I didn't know what to do about that.

"So, no other brides? I'm not next in a series of failed marriages?"

"No," I told her. "You're the first."

"I'm honored."

"What about you?"

"Me? I've never taken a fake bride."

"Have you been married before?"

"Hey," Sherry called out from up front. "Don't you think you should have asked these questions before you flew her out?"

"I mean, maybe," I shrugged. "But it didn't come up in conversation."

"It's okay," Melinda said. "I'm not offended. I've never been married." She paused for a second, like there was something else she wanted to say, but maybe I was just reading into the situation because she quickly changed the subject. "Anyway, good to be here."

"It's good to have you," I said. "And I appreciate that you're here."

It was a relief to know that I was going to be able to reclaim my life and to reclaim my company. So far, it seemed like the announcement of my engagement had been taken with a grain of salt. Some local gossip sites had reported that my bride and I would *definitely* be breaking up long before the wedding, while others were speculating on when and where the wedding would be held, as well as what the ceremony would be like.

"Of course," Melinda said.

"We're heading to the lawyer's office first," Sherry offered. "We should be there in about five minutes."

"The lawyer?"

"We need to sign our contract," I explained. "It outlines the terms of our agreement, how much and how often you'll be paid, and what will be expected of you."

"Interesting." Melinda didn't seem nervous about going to an attorney's office, but the idea made her tense slightly. If I hadn't been watching her body when Sherry mentioned the word *lawyer*, I would have completely missed the way the muscles in her neck tightened just the slightest bit.

Interesting, indeed. Why didn't Melinda like lawyers?

"Why don't you like lawyers?" I asked, deciding that being blunt was the way to go.

"What? I don't have a problem with lawyers."

"I think you do."

"I don't."

Sherry gave me a look that told me to drop it, but I couldn't. Suddenly, I was like a cat with a mouse or a dog with a bone. I wanted to know everything there was to know about this woman, and it all started with this.

"Was a lawyer mean to you?"

"They just...it's just that most lawyers I've known were liars, okay?" She looked up at me, and I didn't say what I was thinking.

So, it wasn't lawyers that she disliked.

It was liars.

And unfortunately for Melinda, I was the biggest liar I knew.

6

Melinda

THE LAWYER'S OFFICE was cold and sterile. The three of us walked right in the front doors, past the receptionist, and into a small conference room. The air felt like it had been turned down ten degrees before we arrived, and I shivered.

"Would you like my jacket?" Basil leaned over and offered me his coat. I shook my head, not trusting myself to speak. If Basil actually did give me his coat, and if I wore it, then I was going to melt right out of my damn clothes.

I had known that he was rich, and I had known that he was confident, but I hadn't known that he was funny. The realization that he was slightly cocky and totally goofy caught me off-guard, but I kind of liked it.

Okay, I really liked it.

I'd dated plenty of people in my life, but none of them ever seemed as carefree or as happy and silly as Basil did. For someone who felt pressured into fake-marrying someone, the realization that he was actually pretty funny was kind of surprising to me.

I'd just thought that this was the type of person who might be stuffy, uptight, or arrogant, and to be fair, it was possible that he was any or all of those things. Right now, though, he was sweet, and he was thoughtful, and I couldn't wear his coat.

If I did, I'd never want to take it off.

I'd want to throw myself at him, wrapping my arms around him. I'd want to kiss him until I went crazy. I'd want to get on my knees for him.

"No thanks," I said. It was hard to force the words out.

"You're sure?"

"I'm fine."

"Suit yourself," he shrugged.

"He should be here any moment," Sherry tapped her fingernails on the conference-room table. "He knows we're here."

We hadn't checked in at the front desk, but Basil had waved at the receptionist when we'd walked in. Apparently, he was used to hanging out here. Apparently, it was the kind of place he came often.

My own personal experiences with lawyers had been volatile. In my experience, lawyers made a lot of big promises they weren't always able to keep. Then again, when I'd gone to prison, my attorney had shrugged it off and bid me farewell. She hadn't exactly seemed to mind that I was being locked up.

I knew that this was different. I understood, logically, that the person we were going to meet with wasn't the same lawyer who hadn't saved me from being sent away, but I was still nervous. There was still a sense of anxiety washing over me as we waited. With each second that passed, I felt myself growing more and more tense.

Finally, there was a gentle knock at the door to the conference room, and then the receptionist appeared. She smiled brightly. She might not be the attorney, but she seemed kind and friendly. Instantly, I felt the tension wash away. If she worked for this lawyer guy, then he couldn't be so bad, right?

After all, she seemed pretty cool. A cool girl like her wouldn't work for a jackass. At least, that was what I was going to tell myself.

"Can I get y'all anything while you wait for the big guy?"

"We're fine, Athena," Sherry smiled. "But thanks."

"You sure? I can grab some coffee." Athena wiggled her eyebrows mischievously. "I could order us some pizza."

Pizza sounded delicious. My stomach rumbled as it relished the memory of eating hot pizza. Once upon a time, that had been me. These days, I lived off of stale crackers and cheap microwavable ramen noodles. Yeah, I wasn't going to turn down pizza if Athena actually ordered anyone.

Basil shot me a strange look. No way had he heard my stomach rumble, and I hadn't said anything out loud, so why was he staring at me? I blushed, looking away. I hope he didn't think I looked hungry. I didn't want him to know that I was secretly completely poor, completely broke, and completely out of options.

That's why I'd chosen to give him my future.

I didn't have any other prospects and he was going to help me reclaim my life. Shane had taken a lot of things from me, but that was my life before. The person I was now wasn't going to put up with a guy crushing her under his foot. New me was strong and brave.

Still, new me wasn't going to turn down pizza.

"Stop giving away all of my money," a booming voice said. I heard loud footsteps in the hall. Athena chuckled and walked away, leaving the door open. Apparently, pizza wasn't going to happen because the attorney had decided to show up. Time seemed to pause and stretch. I held my breath, wondering what kind of person was going to walk through those doors.

Then he appeared.

The man who walked in was big. He was taller than I had expected someone like him to be. He was dressed sharply in a dark suit, and his eyes roamed from person to person until they landed on me. Then they narrowed as he honed in on me. He seemed fascinated with me for some reason that I didn't understand.

I wasn't anyone special.

I was just me.

"You," he said.

"Me."

"You must be Melinda," he held out a hand, and I scurried to my feet to shake it. I needed to make a good impression if I wanted all of this to go well.

"That's me."

"And you're sure that my dear friend Basil hasn't forced you to come here," he said, narrowing his eyes at Basil.

Oh, now wasn't that interesting?

It seemed that despite charging Basil whatever exorbitant amount of money he was charging to create this contract, he wasn't supportive of the idea. That was a little bit strange. For some reason, I had expected that Basil was the kind of person who just did what he pleased.

Apparently, that wasn't quite accurate.

"No," I shook my head. "I'm not being forced or coerced in any way. I'm here on my own."

I wasn't sure if I'd say it was of my own free will. I hadn't exactly felt like I had a lot of choices when I'd responded to the ad, but at the same time, it had been a ticket out of my life. It had been an escape.

Basil was giving me a chance to get back on my feet. I could save all of the money I earned from working for him, and when this was all over, I could go do something else. I could find some freedom.

Who knew?

Maybe I'd rent a little house out in the woods or get an apartment in a huge, random city where nobody knew me, nobody could find me, and nobody would ever bother me.

I could do all of those things, and it was all thanks to Basil.

"Are you sure?"

"I'm sure. I want to be here," I said. I glanced over at Basil, and he smiled at me. He seemed so genuine. I just really couldn't believe it.

Usually, when I was around men, I felt like they were wolves in sheep's clothing. The men I'd known in the past had always tried to trick me, and sometimes, that had worked. I'd certainly fallen hard and fast for Shane, and that had ended with me in jail and scared for my life.

Now I was worried. I was constantly afraid that he was going to find me and finish the job. I was always scared he was going to somehow chase me down and kill me, but I had one thing going for me.

This.

Now I had the chance to hide in a new place: a place where he wouldn't be looking for me. Basil had flown me out in a private plane, which meant there wasn't going to be some airline company passenger list with my name on it.

Was there another way Shane would be able to find me?

I didn't think so.

I *hoped* he couldn't.

No longer did I have a bank account. No longer did I have a cell phone plan through a company. My phone was prepaid and it wasn't linked to my personal name. I didn't have utilities or rent payments, and even when I'd stayed at the motel, I'd paid a little extra to keep my name off of the books.

If Shane found me, it was going to be utter and total bad luck. It certainly wouldn't be because of poor planning on my part. I'd thought of everything because I'd had to. I'd been scared for so very, very long.

With Basil, I didn't have that fear. I couldn't explain why I felt comfortable around him. Maybe it was that thing that Sherry had said. She'd told me that Basil had the heart of a lion. That sounded pretty nice to me.

It made me think that he was the kind of guy who was courageous.

Apparently, the lawyer was satisfied with my answer because he sat down and gestured for the rest of us to do the same. He placed a stack of papers in the center of the table and looked from me to Basil and back again. He basically ignored Sherry.

"You're sure about this?"

"I'm sure, Cosmo," Basil nodded. "It's what I want."

"It's a bad idea."

"Aren't you supposed to advise me of my options – not pass judgment?"

"We've been friends long enough for me to judge you," Cosmo said.

"Let's just get this over with," Sherry interrupted. "We've got other meetings today, Cos."

Cosmo sighed. Interesting name, wasn't it? Cosmo. I wondered if it was a family name or if his parents were just kind of quirky and cool.

"Nothing you have to do today is as important as this," Cosmo told her. "And we're going to take our time to make sure everything is signed correctly, and that the paperwork is appropriate for everyone." He turned to me. "You have the right to hire your own attorney, if you would like to. I understand that Basil wants this entire thing kept hush-hush for obvious reasons, but if you'd like someone who can represent you, I'd be happy to pull in one of my colleagues. They're all very trustworthy, which means they won't tell anyone, and they can act as an advocate for you."

"I..."

I didn't have any money. I didn't think I needed my own lawyer, but I also didn't have any money. Basil seemed to sense my hesitation, because he placed a hand on mine.

"I will pay any fees related to our legal expenses," he lowered his voice. "Would you like to talk with another lawyer today? We're going to go over everything in detail right now, and if something sounds bad or wrong to you, we can talk it out and modify the contract as needed. That said, I'm completely fine and not offended if you want someone else."

Really?

That was it?

He was going to pay, and he wasn't offended?

How the hell had I never met a guy like this before? I didn't even know people like Basil existed! If my panties hadn't been soaked before, they sure as hell were now. Apparently, nice guys did it for me.

"I think I'm fine," I said. "Thank you, though. I appreciate that." I did. I appreciated it so much. I didn't think Basil would ever be able to understand exactly what his words meant to me. Knowing that I could ask for assistance and be granted that meant everything.

Basil looked at me for a moment. He was trying to figure me out, I realized. He was trying to see if I was actually fine and if I was actually okay because if I wasn't, he was going to insist that I use another attorney. I could already tell.

He wanted me to be okay.

"If you're sure," he finally murmured.

"I'm sure."

Something about the way Basil talked to me just calmed me. He really knew exactly how to help me relax. He knew exactly what to say to help me calm down, breathe again, and feel like I was totally at ease.

"Okay," Cosmo nodded from across the table. "Then let's begin. First things first," he handed us each a pen. "Make sure your names are signed correctly on these and then initial beside them."

I took the first piece of paper from Cosmo, and I wondered – not for the first time - what I was getting myself into.

I started signing as we went through the contract. I was a little surprised with just how thorough this entire thing was. It outlined *everything*: how many events I had to go to, how I needed to act while we were out in public, and what our backstory was. The contract stated exactly how much I'd be paid per *week*, as well as the additional allowance Basil was going to give me for things like clothes and special events.

As long as I was part of this fake-relationship with him, he was going to take care of me.

That was calming to me.

"If you'll give me your bank account information, we can make sure you receive your funds each week," Cosmo tapped one line on the contract. We were on page 34 at that point, and I was starting to feel a little worn out, but I wasn't so tired that I felt like I needed to give out my bank account information.

The problem was that I no longer had a bank account. Once upon a time, I'd had one. Shane had drained it, though. He'd made sure that I wasn't able to escape from him. After I got out of jail, I didn't open another one. I was afraid he was going to find it and use that to find me.

Even banks weren't totally secure, and Shane had fake ID cards with my name and picture.

He could hire someone – or use one of his friends – to walk into a bank and pull up my information. Considering the type of people he liked to hire, it wasn't going to be very difficult for him.

No, it would be better not to have an account now. I couldn't risk it.

What if I made a bunch of money and he somehow figured out what bank I was using?

What if he stole from me?

"Would it be possible for me to be paid in cash?" I asked, blinking.

The room seemed to fall completely silent. Everyone stared at me for a minute.

Shit.

It was like I'd asked something a lot crazier than being paid in cash. Basil was looking at me like I'd asked if he ate babies. Why was this such a big deal?

Out of everything we were doing and all of the papers we were signing, the thing that tripped people up was me wanting physical money?

"Cash?" Sherry asked.

"Uh, yeah," I nodded. "Just for now," I lied. "Until I can get a bank account set up in Rawr County."

I wasn't going to set up an account in Rawr County, but they didn't need to know that. For now, I could just hide my money in my room. I'd keep things off the books as much as possible, if only for my own sanity.

"That's fine," Basil said, but I could still tell that he thought it was weird. They all thought I was weird.

Well, whatever.

I was doing my best. I wanted to save up some money, and even though I wouldn't be able to earn interest on cash sitting in my bedroom, I was going to actually be able to walk away from the entire situation with cash in my pocket.

Right?

Right.

7

Basil

"May I speak with you privately?"

Cosmo looked up at me after he handed both Melinda and I copies of the contract we'd signed. For privacy reasons, I didn't particularly want a lot of copies of this agreement floating around, but I also wasn't going to tell her she couldn't re-read what she'd signed.

I wasn't a monster.

If she wanted to negotiate the terms of our arrangement, I was fine with that. The only thing she'd actually tried to negotiate so far, though, was that she didn't want to be paid by direct deposit. She wanted cash each week, and even though I thought it was kind of strange, I was fine with that.

Was it really any of my business if she didn't trust banks?

I'd known plenty of people like that. My grandfather was one of the biggest anti-bank people I'd ever met. As a kid, I'd always been fascinated by how he'd carefully tucked his cash into his safe each week. He'd shown me how to count it, and he'd let me know how he arranged everything, and then he'd put it away. No, he hadn't earned interest on it, but it had always been there when he needed it.

I put Sherry in charge of making sure that Melinda got an envelope of money each week, and that was that. I wasn't going to bring it up again, nor was I going to try to convince her that

255

receiving cash was outdated and strange. Now, as Cosmo looked at me, I noticed the concern in his eyes. He wanted to talk to me privately.

"Privately?" What could this be about? We'd literally just finished signing the contracts. Why would he need to talk to me alone?

"Yes," he nodded curtly, but didn't offer any other information that might clue me in on what he wanted. Luckily, nobody seemed to think it was strange that my attorney wanted to talk to me without anyone else around. Sherry read the situation and quickly took control. She reached for her belongings and started walking toward the door.

"I'll take Melinda to the car," Sherry said, gesturing for my future wife to follow her. Melinda nodded and gathered up her own things.

"Thanks for everything," Melinda said kindly to Cosmo, who smiled brightly at her. It was hard to believe just how incredible Melinda was in real life. For someone being thrust into such a chaotic situation, she seemed wildly calm, collected, and in control of herself. She wasn't panicking in any way. Instead, she was just accepting these moments one at a time.

"It was my pleasure," he said. "Hope to see you again soon."

Melinda cocked her head, looking up at the dragon shifter. "Will you be at the engagement party?"

"Oh, I wouldn't miss it for the world," Cosmo told her seriously, but I didn't miss the way his eyes twinkled when he spoke.

Once Sherry and Melinda were gone and the door to the conference room was closed, Cosmo turned and growled at me, baring his teeth. It was quite the demeanor shift from less than ten seconds ago, when he'd been all good manners and polite behavior.

"What the fuck is that?" I asked, gesturing at his contorted face. "You're growling?"

"What the fuck is this? Who the fuck are you?" Cosmo snapped back.

"That doesn't make any sense," I stared at him. I didn't know what Cosmo was trying to say or what his point was, but his scent had changed. No longer was he calm and relaxed. Now he was angry. No, not just angry: pissed.

At me?

Why?

"Who do you think you are that you can just find yourself a fake wife, asshole?"

It was the first time he'd expressed any sort of discomfort with the entire marriage situation, and I thought that this was probably the first time I'd ever seen Cosmo truly irritated. Even though the two of us had known each other for many years, we'd never really argued. There'd never been a reason to.

Cosmo was a dragon shifter who had come to Rawr County after leaving Dragon Isle. He'd wanted a new place to live, and he'd told me that he preferred the mountains to the ocean, so it worked well for him. He'd made himself at home in the county and now he spent his days practicing law and his nights...well, I wasn't really sure what he did with his nights.

"What are you talking about? You really have an issue with this?" What could he possibly have to complain about? I wasn't tricking Melinda into this little arrangement. I wasn't forcing her to marry me. She had a choice, and she was choosing this lifestyle.

Besides, I was paying her. She'd be handsomely compensated. She'd agreed to it. Everyone thought it was fair.

Except, apparently, for Cosmo.

"I do," he nodded again.

"Then why did you just spend the last two hours helping Melinda and I with our contract?"

"Because I want to protect her from you," he said.

Now *that* surprised me.

"Aren't you supposed to be my attorney?"

"I am your attorney," he said. "And I'd say that you both got a good deal out of this contract, but you need to promise me something, Basil. You have to."

A promise?

Dragons didn't often ask people to promise them things. Maybe it was because other types of shifters were known for being sneaky and wild, especially cat-shifters like myself. Cosmo wasn't a cat, though. He was a proud, beautiful dragon who was loyal to the people he cared about, and for some reason, he'd chosen to care about Melinda.

A slight tingling of jealousy rose from within me.

Did *he* want Melinda for himself?

He couldn't have her.

She was mine.

I knew that the idea of claiming a woman as my own was archaic, but my inner-shifter didn't know that. I wanted her with a deep-rooted need I couldn't explain. Words would never be able to truly express how desperately I wanted or needed her. There was just *something* that made me crave her.

"A promise," he repeated. Cosmo nodded, as though he'd convinced himself this was the best plan of action for moving forward.

"What sort of promise?"

"You can't hurt her, Basil."

I stared at him, blinking.

He didn't blink as he stared back at me.

"Are you serious?"

"I'm more serious than I've ever been. You can't hurt her."

"This isn't some sort of rom-com, Cos. I'm not going to hurt her, but you also aren't going to pretend to be her big brother who watches out for her." He didn't even know her. Cosmo knew *nothing* about Melinda. Nothing. He had no claim to her. She wasn't his to protect. She was mine.

"I'm serious. She's running from something."

"What?"

What was he talking about? Melinda wasn't running from anything. She was just between jobs, which meant it was a good time for her to try a project like this. She didn't have a career right now. She didn't have a house or a lease. She was totally free and flexible, and she'd been trying to decide what she was going to do next with her life. This was it. This was what she'd chosen.

In Rawr County, she'd get to explore with me. We could go hiking, eat at restaurants, and see shows. We could try all sorts of things together that could help her decide what exactly she wanted as she moved forward.

At no point had she mentioned she was running from something or that she was scared of something from her past.

So what was Cosmo talking about?

"You really don't know?"

"Know what?"

I was starting to grow frustrated. I wished Cosmo would just tell me what it was that he was thinking. Stupid dragons. They always thought they knew everything.

"Know what she's upset about."

"Cosmo, I need to get going. Tell me or don't, but if you want to tell me, then just spit it out." I'd run out of patience, even for my attorney.

"What did Melinda say when you told her you were bringing her to an attorney's office?"

She'd been a bit surprised, and she'd tensed. She hadn't been scared, but she'd been slightly uncomfortable with the idea.

"She wasn't very happy."

"Because she's talked with attorneys before."

"Lots of people talk to attorneys," I pointed out the obvious.

"The type of people who get uncomfortable around attorneys are the kind of people who have experienced the legal system before. She might not have been married before, but she's dealt with a lawyer. Maybe she planned to get married and visited an attorney for a prenup. Maybe she dealt with a criminal attorney. I don't know, but she's been around lawyers before," Cosmo insisted. He said this like it was this great reveal.

Who cared?

Who cared if she'd talked to attorneys before?

"Maybe she bought a house," I shrugged. "Maybe she had to meet with a real estate attorney."

"That's not it." Cosmo looked worried, but I couldn't tell why.

"Are you afraid she's lying to me?"

"I'm afraid there's more to Melinda than being a gorgeous woman who can't get a job," he clarified.

I frowned at Cosmo now. For a dragon, he was really annoying. It was a good thing I was paying him to help me out because if I wasn't, I'd be tempted to end our friendship over this annoying interaction.

"I don't appreciate you not trusting her."

In this situation, I was the liar. Not her. Me. I was the one making things up to please my shareholders. Melinda was just the woman who was going to help me out. She was going to protect me, and she was going to keep me safe, and I was going to do the same thing for her. Only, I was going to protect her physically and she was going to protect me socially.

Having her by my side meant I wasn't going to have to deal with people speculating about my personal life any longer. People would know that I was married to someone beautiful and wonderful, and I wouldn't have to worry about dating or finding someone or accidentally finding the *wrong* person.

"It's not that I don't trust her, but I've had clients like her before. She kept her eyes on the doors, Basil. The whole time she was here, she was staring at them."

"Lots of people like to know where doors are."

"She kept glancing at the exits," he said again. What was this? Broken record day?

"You're repeating yourself."

"She sat with her back clearly to a wall: not the windows, and not the doors."

"Cosmo, I'm leaving," I said, pushing past him. "All of these concerns are fantastic, but they really don't have anything to do with me. I don't think she's hiding anything, but even if she is, it has nothing to do with you, either."

I paused in the doorway and looked back to see him watching me. Fear, concern, and sadness were present on Cosmo's face. Silly dragon. He really wasn't good at hiding his feelings, was he? Normally, I'd say that he was. His ability to hide his emotions was part of what made him such an incredible attorney, but now...

Well, now he just seemed kind of down.

Maybe I was being too hard on him. I knew that Cosmo was just looking out for me. He didn't want Melinda to get hurt, and he didn't want me to get hurt, either. Probably, I should have been more patient with him. He was just trying to be a good friend.

"Just be careful," he said again. "I think she's been hurt before, Basil. I don't want to see it happen again."

I nodded, suddenly appreciating the fact that my friend really was so tender-hearted. He was truly kind, wasn't he?

"Thanks, Cos."

"Stay safe, brother."

8

Melinda

The rest of the day flew by. After we signed the contract – which took an eternity – Sherry dropped Basil off at work, and she took me shopping. She made sure I had new *everything*: socks, shoes, underwear, jeans, dresses, and hair supplies. I couldn't remember the last time I'd gone on a shopping spree.

Had I ever done this?

I couldn't remember.

As a kid, we'd never been able to afford the huge back-to-school shopping extravaganzas many of my friends got to have. I'd usually go to the thrift shop with my mom where I'd choose a couple of severely discounted items that were still in one piece, but that was it.

I wasn't the type of person who just went crazy and bought new things.

Sherry seemed to sense my discomfort because she kept reassuring me that everything was fine. Three or four different times, she commented that Basil was practically made of money and that I didn't need to feel nervous or anxious.

"I'm not nervous," I lied.

"You seem nervous," she shrugged.

Did I? I'd tried really hard to stay calm and put-together this entire time. I didn't think I was doing anything that would give her the impression I was nervous or anxious. If anything, I felt like I seemed far too calm about this entire ordeal.

There I was: marrying a stranger.

That was messed up no matter how you looked at it.

"He's a good person," Sherry said, holding up a shirt to me. She nodded after a second, letting me silently know that I'd be wearing it at some point in the future.

"Basil? You've known him a long time, huh?"

"Feels like forever," she shrugged.

"And you and he..."

"What?"

I felt a little rude asking, but nosiness quickly won over nervousness. "Did you and he ever date?" I raised an eyebrow as I asked the question, hoping it would seem innocuous and not jealous. I wasn't jealous. Every single person in the world had a past of some sort. Even me.

To my surprise, Sherry just laughed and shook her head.

"He's not my type, sweetheart."

"What? Tall, dark, and handsome isn't your type? Rich guys with hearts of gold aren't your type?" I bristled, finding myself personally offended that she said he wasn't her type.

Why did it even matter?

It wasn't like Sherry was the one marrying him, and for that matter, it wasn't like Basil and I were actually in love. Sherry seemed to find this very funny, though, and she laughed and shook her head.

"Melinda, you've got me all wrong," she laughed, and she held up her phone. Her lock screen was of a beautiful woman with long dark hair and a big bright smile. "This is my wife," she said.

"Your...wife?"

"Yes."

"So..."

"Yes."

"So when you said Basil wasn't your type, it wasn't that you think he's ugly."

"It's that he's a man," she told me gently. "And that's not the type of person who captures my heart."

"Looks like your heart isn't up for grabs, anyway," I gestured to the picture.

"Not anymore," Sherry smiled, and she shoved the phone back in her pocket.

Somehow, the two of us managed to get past the awkwardness of the situation I'd just created, and we finished buying more clothes than one woman could possibly ever wear. After that, we had a different, more exciting stop. Sherry took me to the world's cutest bookstore. It had a giant bear out front that had been carved out of the trunk of a tree, and the sign with the name of the bookstore was also carved out of wood.

BIG BEAR BOOKS was a cute, locally-owned bookshop that looked wildly adorable. Everything about the exterior screamed "cute," and I knew right away that despite my inner-whining about having to go shopping for clothes, I was going to have a damn good time buying books.

"You have no idea how dangerous this is," I said as we walked into the bookstore. By the time we walked out, we'd collected four bags of books between the two of us. I made Sherry pick out a few things for herself, and she'd easily complied.

"Buying books? Dangerous? Maybe. Only because you're going to run out of space for them. Don't worry. Basil has a lot of bookshelves at his place. At least, he did the last time I was there."

"You haven't been over in a while?"

"Not really," she shrugged. "Then again, we mostly meet at the office."

I wondered, just for the slightest fraction of a moment, if Basil liked to bring a lot of women to his home. He didn't seem shy. Was he the kind of person who dated a lot? Sherry seemed to sense my curiosity because she just shrugged.

"Basil's dating past is complicated, but I'm sure he'll fill you in."

"I could probably just Google it," I pointed out. I didn't really want to have an intense heart-to-heart about our pasts. If we did, there was a chance that I'd end up telling him about Shane or about my fears. There was a chance he'd end up just finding out about my past because I'd accidentally reveal too much information.

Something I'd learned in prison was that you really couldn't trust people as much as you wanted to. Even people you viewed as super trustworthy and committed could let you down, and that was okay. It was just the way that life was.

I needed to protect myself, though.

One of the ways I'd do that was by carefully selecting the conversations I chose to be a part of. A talk about the who's-who of our collective dating pasts? That didn't sound like something *anyone* needed.

"You could look it up online," she agreed, "but if you do that, you'll never really know what's real and what's not. It's best to just talk with him."

"I'm not going to be his *real* wife," I reminded Sherry. Maybe I didn't need to know everything about his past. "I probably don't need to ask."

"You do because people will bring things up to try to trick you or scare you," she informed me. "Look, Melinda, Basil is kind of a big deal around here. He can be reclusive, sure. A lot of guys around here can. He's in the public eye a lot, though, which means you need to be ready for anything. If someone name-drops an ex, you need to be aware of that."

"I understand," I told her as we reached the vehicle and dumped our books in the backseat. I climbed up front to sit beside Sherry. She was right, I knew. I didn't like to admit it, but she was right. People were going to scrutinize this relationship from every angle, and while Basil was something of a local celebrity, he really was just that: a local icon.

I wasn't worried about people taking pictures of us while we were out and about because my name was going to change. People wouldn't be able to look me up online and find pictures of me if they searched for my current name. To be honest, the name "Melinda" was simple and common enough that it wasn't going to raise any eyebrows.

It wasn't like a bank account. It wasn't like something tangible that someone who had my name could use to track me.

I had asked Basil that when he tell people my name, he use my middle name instead of my last name. He'd been fine with that, so he'd introduce me as Melinda Lee. Nobody needed to know my real name, and I didn't think I'd have a problem with it being published.

Besides, Shane was a whole state away. Unless he felt like randomly wandering to Rawr County, Colorado, he wasn't going to find me.

I was going to be fine.

"You okay over there?" Sherry asked.

"Oh, yeah, sorry. I guess I spaced out for a minute."

"That's perfectly fine," she said. "Everyone needs time to themselves sometimes. Care like sharing any of your thoughts?"

"Not really," I shrugged. "It's just a lot to take in."

"What? The money?"

"That, and the lifestyle."

"Basil lives a busy life," Sherry agreed, nodding. "There will be days when he's gone far past dinner. You could get a job if you want something to do, you know."

A job?

That was an interesting idea. I still wasn't sure how I'd get a job with the legal record that I had. Somehow, Basil had managed to miss my past when he'd looked me up. Well, either that or he hadn't actually run a background check. I was afraid to ask.

"I could?" If nobody was going to run a background check, maybe it would work. Maybe I actually would get something around Rawr County. A job could keep me busy and entertained, and it would give me a good chance to meet people around town.

"Yes, I made sure that was included in the contract," Sherry told me. She had? How cool of her. Sherry really wasn't half bad.

"Oh, hey, thanks," I told her. I meant it, too. It was something really thoughtful that she didn't have to do, yet she had. She'd gone out of her way to make sure I was comfortable and that I was taken care of, and it meant a lot to me.

Sherry smiled. "Us girls have to stick together," she told me.

"I appreciate that."

"You could do volunteer work, too," she pointed out.

"I guess I haven't really thought about that," I admitted sheepishly. Volunteer work was something I'd always thought about, but never really gotten around to.

"There's an animal shelter close to his house," Sherry said. "There are a couple of nursing homes, too."

"Wow, so there are a lot of choices."

"My wife and I like volunteering at the shelter," Sherry told me. "We're both slightly obsessed with animals, so it's fun for us. It lets us spend time together while also doing something to help others."

"That's a good way to live your life," I pointed out. "How long have you been married?"

"Sometimes it feels like forever," Sherry laughed. "Sometimes it feels like no time has passed at all."

"That's not a real answer," I pointed out.

"It's not, and that's what I want you to practice doing."

"What?"

"When you start meeting people in the next few weeks, they will straight-out ask you questions you don't want to answer. You don't have to. Remember that, okay? Remember it for me."

"Okay."

"If someone asks you something about you or Basil or anything regarding your life together...you can blow them off. You can change the subject. You can be vague. You have the control, okay?"

I liked Sherry so much, and I liked what she was saying.

Control?

That wasn't something I'd felt like I'd had in a very long time. Now, the idea of being fully in control of myself and my choices sounded pretty good to me.

"Thank you," I said. "That's a good reminder." It was.

"Anytime," she said. Sherry turned and we started driving down a road that seemed to lead away from the big buildings of the city.

"Where are we going?"

"Don't stress," she murmured. "We're just going to Basil's house."

I wasn't stressed, but my heart had started racing a little. Something about her gentle tone of voice made me feel a little more calm, though, and I felt myself relaxing.

"Basil lives outside of the city?"

"Yes."

"But he works in the city?"

"Yeah."

Sherry's hands gripped the steering wheel, and I got the distinct impression that she didn't really want to talk about why Basil lived so far away from work, but I found myself curious and unable to resist asking more about it.

"Why?"

"You know, you'd make a good cat."

"Because I'm curious?"

"Because you don't know when to quit," Sherry glanced over at me. "If you're going to make this thing work, you need to learn when to let things go."

"That's not my style," I said. Obviously, considering where I was coming from. After spending a year in literal prison, I felt like I had a pretty good read on people, and I had a pretty good understanding of when someone was going to hurt me. I could tell if someone was harmless. I could tell if they were going to cause me problems or not.

Sherry wasn't going to hurt me. I could tell that she was fiercely loyal to Basil, but she was also kind. Because she was a woman married to a woman, she was probably used to people judging her, which meant she was discreet when she needed to be. Sherry, too, had a good read on people.

So what did she think of me?

I wasn't sure if I wanted to know or not.

"I'm not telling you to change your style," Sherry said. She turned down a dirt road. "You do need to make sure you're reading people correctly, though."

"He seems like a good man," I pointed out.

"He's a good man."

"So, why would a rich, good, handsome man live in the middle of nowhere?"

Sherry laughed and made one more turn, bringing us in front of a huge, rustic-looking farmhouse with the biggest wraparound porch I'd ever seen in my life.

"I don't know, hon. Your guess is as good as mine."

But she was lying, and I didn't know why.

SHERRY HELPED ME UNLOAD everything we'd purchased. Together, we carried all of the bags and put them into the house, but before long, she had to get home for supper. She promised to invite me over sometime, but she wasn't sure when just yet. After I thanked her profusely for her help, Sherry took off and I was alone.

It was a little bit weird to be in Basil's house on my own. Even though I knew I was allowed to be there, and even though I knew I'd be living there for a good long time, it felt like being in a stranger's home.

Probably because he is a stranger.

With Sherry gone, I slowly walked around Basil's house and explored. Taking my time, I wandered around the house. It was big and carefully decorated, but I hardly noticed the paintings or the carpets or the furniture. I was too distracted wondering what Basil was doing.

Even though I had his number saved in my phone, I didn't call or text Basil. I didn't know where he was or what he was doing.

Was he the kind of guy who liked to go out for drinks after work?

Did he like to hang out with people from the office and socialize?

Did he stay late pouring over numbers?

Or was Basil the kind of person who hit the gym?

I'd noticed the way his hard, lean body filled out his clothes in all the best ways, and even though I'd tried my best to avoid staring at him, it had been difficult. That entire "act-like-you-like-each-other" thing wasn't going to be a problem, like, at all.

He was handsome as hell, and I had a feeling that Basil could have had his pick of ladies to marry. He didn't have to go online to find someone. Anyone would have been lucky to get to be with a guy like him.

Anyone.

I stared at my phone. There was zero chance I wanted this guy to think I was going to be needy. I knew I shouldn't text him or call him.

Besides, I was fine on my own.

Fine.

Except for the fact that this entire place was totally isolated, of course.

Except for the fact that we were miles outside of town.

What if something happened to me?

There would be no way to call for help. I wasn't even sure if my cell phone actually *got* service here. Unfortunately for me, I didn't really have any friends I could call to test it out.

Whatever.

I tried to focus on familiarizing myself with the house. It was a pretty straight-forward layout with a living room, kitchen, and bathroom on the first floor. There was a cute little office, too, and a door that opened to a basement.

I stayed away from there.

I'd seen far too many scary movies to be interested in going wandering down into some dude's basement.

No thanks.

The second floor had a couple of different bedrooms. There wasn't anything scary like a sex dungeon or a murder room, which was a relief. I was pretty sure Basil wasn't going to murder me, but I still wanted to be extra safe.

For a moment, I thought about hauling all of my things up and tossing them into one of the rooms, but I didn't know how the house worked or what Basil was thinking.

Was I supposed to sleep in his room?

Would I stay in a guest room?

I just didn't know.

After a little while, I got bored and made myself a turkey sandwich with lettuce and cheese. Basil had a nice kitchen that was fully stocked with all of the groceries a girl could possibly want. He had a great wine collection, too. None of the wine bottles were opened, but I found an open bottle of whiskey and took a couple of shots to help myself calm down.

Where was he?

It was after seven, which meant he was probably leaving the office. Right? Maybe he'd already left. I had no understanding of times. Once again, I thought about texting, but I didn't want to seem needy, so I decided to walk around outside and explore a little more.

I stepped out onto the porch and closed the door behind me. It was so beautiful out here in the country. I could see why Basil liked it. I had a wonderful view of the mountains, and there was a nice, wooded area nearby, too. Straight ahead, there was a huge tree with a little treehouse in it. There was a barn, too.

I decided to start exploring by checking out the treehouse. I couldn't imagine that Basil liked to go play out in there, but you never knew for sure, did you?

Trotting over to it, I looked around his property as I did. I'd never been much of a country girl. I'd always considered the country to be a place where bugs roamed free, and horses ran wild. That had never been something that interested me. Not even a little.

So, for me to walk around on Basil's land like I owned the place, I must have really wanted to know what I was up against.

At least, that was what I told myself.

When I met people – and I would have to meet a lot of people, I knew – I'd have to talk with them. I'd have to share my thoughts.

I'd have to let them know that I knew the ins and outs of Basil's property.

If I didn't know, then it would stand out. People might question whether I was really the woman he loved.

"Get it together," I said to myself.

There was nothing to be afraid of. There was nothing to feel scared about. This was it. This was my moment to prove to myself that I wasn't going to be scared off by something tiny. I wasn't going to be scared away because I couldn't handle walking around in nature by myself.

I approached the treehouse. There was a long rope ladder hanging down, but if I reached up, I could touch the end of the platform where the house stood. I wondered if it would be easier to climb up the ladder or to simply grab the platform and tug myself up.

I figured that first, I'd tried to pull myself up top. In the past, there was no way I would have been able to do that, but a year in jail had left me bored. I hadn't just sat around.

I'd put my time to good use.

One of my cellmates had shown me her daily routine, and I'd quickly adopted it as my own. Every day, the two of us would do push-ups, sit-ups, jumping jacks, and a bunch of other random exercises we managed to modify enough to do in a cell.

When I got out, I'd continued doing those exercises in my motel room, and now they were finally paying off. Reaching up, I grabbed the edge of the platform and jumped up, giving myself a natural boost so I could swing one leg over. As soon as my leg hooked, I pulled the rest of my body up and onto the platform.

Then I was there.

Carefully, I stood up and looked at the outside of the little treehouse. Why the heck was this thing here? It didn't really fit with the aesthetic, but it was kind of wonderful, too. It was old and rustic-looking, and it seemed like it had been built by hand.

How interesting.

I reached for the tiny door with its little doorknob. Then I turned it and pushed the door open. A billow of dust poofed up, shocking me. I coughed, sputtering and sneezing, and then I realized that I wasn't alone.

There was a kid in there, and she looked up at me and screamed.

9

Basil

I couldn't stop thinking about her.

I hated the way she had looked at me like she needed me, like she wanted me, and I hated the way that I wanted her back.

This was supposed to be a normal, run-of-the-mill arrangement. It was supposed to be ordinary. This entire thing we were doing, this game we were playing...it was supposed to be something that didn't involve our feelings.

Only, my feelings were involved.

I'd been caught, ensnared in her delicious trap as soon as our eyes had locked. I knew that I was a goner. The entire time we'd been signing the papers, I'd been fighting not to touch her, not to comfort her. I found myself wishing that this was a real arrangement and not something for money.

Why the hell was I so drawn to Melinda?

She was *human*.

She was human, and she didn't know I was a lion, and she could never know.

That wasn't part of the deal.

This was a simple thing between us. We were going to pretend to be in love for a few months, get married, make some public appearances, and then in a year or so, we'd quietly separate. Couples did it all of the time. Lots of people had quiet divorces that nobody paid attention to. That could be us. We could be those people.

Only right now...

Now, the idea of leaving her made my heart hurt.

Fuck.

Closing my eyes, I slouched down in my office chair. I knew that it was a bad idea to have bad posture, but right now, I didn't care. The only thing I cared about was figuring out how I was going to handle this arrangement. The engagement had been announced, the bride had been found, and the groom...the groom was falling in love.

Big time.

My phone rang. I picked it up, and this time, I *did* look at it before I swiped to answer. If it was anyone but Sherry, I would have ignored the call, but it was her. She was probably calling to let me know she was leaving the house. She'd promised to take Melinda on an incredible afternoon of shopping. I'd get the credit card bill to prove it.

"Your bride-to-be is safely in her cage," she told me cheerfully.

"Her cage?"

"Yeah, isn't that what guys always want? A woman tucked neatly away at home who will cook and clean?"

"Is that what you want from your wife?"

Sherry laughed. I could picture her shaking her head. Her wife Wendy was a sweetheart, but I knew they both liked the give and take of being a dual-working couple. Sherry worked for me and liked keeping me organized and busy. She liked the hustle and bustle that went with running a company. Her wife, on the other hand, was a soft-spoken teacher who worked with little kids and taught them to read.

They were very different, but they worked.

"That's not what I want from my wife. The idea of locking a woman up at home horrifies me."

"Then don't call my house a cage," I told her. "It's actually a pretty nice house."

"I'm not arguing about that," she said. "It's definitely nice."

There was a pause, and I knew it was my chance to get real. This was my opportunity to ask what I really wanted to know. It was the question that had been bugging me.

"How was she?"

I hoped my voice didn't give away the fact that I was desperately curious about her. More than that: I was needy. I wanted to know exactly how she was doing...exactly *what* she was doing. I hadn't been able to stop thinking about her and it was driving me absolutely mad.

"What?"

"How was she? Was she...did she seem happy?"

"Woah, boss," Sherry laughed again. "Did you catch feelings already?"

"No."

"Sounds like you did."

"I'm just making sure that my guest is having a nice time," I said.

"I'm sure she's fine," Sherry was calm. "I showed her around the house. Wasn't sure what the bedroom situation was, though, so I didn't help her get settled in one of the guest rooms. I figured you two could work that out later."

"Smart."

"Yeah, well, I'm almost home. See you tomorrow," Sherry said. She ended the call before I could say anything else, but I didn't mind. Sherry was always busy, just like me, and that worked well for the most part. Sherry wasn't offended if I cut a conversation short or if I had something I needed to do.

I set my phone down on my desk and walked to the window.

It had been quite a week, hadn't it? I'd gotten in trouble, I'd hatched a plan, and I'd executed that plan. Oh, the engagement party wasn't until next weekend. We still had plenty to do when it came to planning. My phone had already been going nuts with old friends and colleagues wanting to know if they were invited and why I hadn't said anything sooner, but none of it bothered me.

I didn't care about any sort of mess that was happening because I had found her.

I had found someone who made me feel...

Wild.

Untamed.

And most of all, curious.

I knew that Cosmo was right about Melinda. There was something she hadn't told me, something she hadn't confided in me yet. I didn't care. I could wait.

Melinda and I really were strangers. There was no reason she needed to tell me her entire life story just yet. I could wait for her just as I knew she'd wait for me.

By the time I was ready to leave work, it was after six and I knew that I needed to get home. I stopped by a little restaurant and grabbed some takeout before hopping back in the car and driving to my house.

I was forever happy I'd chosen to settle just out of town. My friend Justin had done the same thing. He'd opted for a rustic, comfortable home. His was more of a mansion than mine, but it still felt cozy all the same.

Turning off the main road, I drove for a couple of minutes before I noticed the fact that there were wildflowers lining the sides of the road. Now that I had a fake fiancé, maybe I should start thinking about ways to make her feel better or happier.

What if I picked her flowers?

On a whim, I stopped the car and hopped out, grabbing a handful of the blue and yellow flowers that grew wild and free. I was just about to get back in the car when I heard a scream.

It was her.

Instantly, I knew.

It was Melinda.

I didn't even think. I just shifted, changing into my lion form. My mane probably looked terrible and messy, but I didn't have time to care. Instead, I started running toward my home. It took me less than a minute in my animal form, and then I was there.

I was in the yard, and I was looking up at the treehouse where my neighbor, Sora, liked to play. Melinda was standing on the little porch of the treehouse, and she was staring inside of the tiny house.

Sora's family and I had spent a lot of time last summer building that thing. Her parents lived nearby and didn't have a solid tree like I did, so last year, we'd all gotten together and built the treehouse in my yard.

It was a fun project that had taken my mind off of things like work and business. Sometimes, it was nice to just relax at the end of a long day. Sora still came over frequently and hung out in the treehouse. Her parents didn't mind. Sometimes they'd come too and read a book while she drew or worked on decorating the inside. Every so often, my cousins came, as well.

Now, Melinda was standing up there, and she was staring inside of the treehouse.

I knew Sora was up there. I could smell her. If I wasn't wrong, I'd heard her scream, too. I'd heard both of them.

Sora was a shapeshifter, like I was, but she couldn't shift yet. Most shifters weren't able to actually change until after puberty, but Melinda wouldn't know that.

Why had she screamed?

Had Sora surprised her?

From the looks of things, the two of them were fine now. Apparently, I'd overreacted by running up in my lion form. I needed to get back to the car before they noticed me, I realized, and I needed to get inside of the house.

Before I could back away, though, and before I could try to sneak off, Melinda glanced over her shoulder.

And she spotted me.

"Shit!"

Her voice was loud, and it carried.

"What is it?" I heard Sora asking gently.

"Don't move," Melinda whispered, blocking the entrance to the treehouse with her body. She was trying to protect Sora from me. "I don't know how this is possible, but there's a line. It's a big one. Don't move. Don't make a sound."

"A lion?" Sora tried to push Melinda out of the way, but Melinda wasn't going to budge.

"Shhh."

"If it's a lion, then we don't need to be scared."

"Sora, hush," Melinda urged the little girl.

I watched for a moment, looking up at Melinda. She was so damn brave. I could scent her fear. I knew she was scared. I didn't want her to be scared of me. Not now and not ever. I appreciated the fact that she was protecting my neighbor, though.

She was looking after a kid she didn't even know.

She was going all out with making sure that Sora stayed safe and cared for.

"If it's a lion, you don't need to be afraid," Sora said again. "It's probably just-"

But I wasn't ready.

I didn't want her to know it was me.

I didn't want Melinda to know that I wasn't a man the way she was used to.

I was different.

Being a lion through-and-through meant that I had different needs. I *needed* to shift. That was non-negotiable. I needed space to run around. I needed peace. I needed silence.

And I needed to know that I was totally ready before I told her what I could do.

Being a shifter was a huge responsibility. It meant I was stronger, faster, and more agile than most humans. Cat-shifters in particular, like me, were able to do things like scent other people really well. We could climb, and we could hide, and damn, could we hunt.

But our identities weren't things we usually revealed.

Not right away.

And never like this.

So even though I hated myself for doing it, I opened my mouth and growled. I let out a damn loud growl before Sora could finish her sentence. In no world did I want Melinda finding out like this that I was a shifter, but I didn't know how to stop Sora from telling her.

After all, I couldn't speak as a lion.

So, I growled.

I let out the biggest, most feral roar I could. It was so loud that the trees practically shook, and it was so loud that it scared Melinda.

The scent of fear that wafted from her was unbearable to me. It was terrible. Melinda started to cry, and she shoved Sora back into the treehouse and slammed the door shut. She was sobbing loudly, obviously scared out of her damn mind, and that was when I realized what I'd done.

I hadn't just silenced Sora.

I hadn't just tried to keep my secret.

I'd made Melinda think that she was about to die.

I'd made her think that this was the end.

And now, now I didn't know what to do. I couldn't shift and climb up there. I had no damn clothes with me, and with the treehouse door closed, I didn't want Melinda to think that I was the lion climbing up.

What if she kicked me or tried to hurt me?

What if she panicked even more?

So even though I regretted the decision more than I'd ever regretted anything before, I turned away from the treehouse, and I ran back to my car. I collected my clothing, I pulled it back on, and then I drove the rest of the way to the house. As soon as I parked and climbed out of the car, I started walking directly toward the treehouse.

It was time to talk to Melinda.

We had a lot to discuss.

10

Melinda

"There's a lion," I whispered, wishing that I wasn't crying. Why did I have to cry?

It seemed like such a silly thing to cry over, but I was scared. I was afraid. I didn't want to be trapped in this treehouse with some kid I didn't even know. I didn't want to die here today.

Not when I was so close to my freedom.

Maybe that was the thing that hurt the most. I'd only just gotten out of jail. I'd only just realized that there was something I could do. For me, choosing to get married to this stranger and come live in this place had been an escape.

It had been everything.

And now it was all going to end.

"Don't look," I told the little girl with me. "Maybe he'll go away."

"But he's not a scary lion," she said. Her name was Sora. She'd told me. After I'd scared the ever-living crap out of her and after she'd scared me right back, we'd had a moment where we'd exchanged names. I'd told her that I was going to marry Basil, and she found that surprising and funny at the same time.

Then the lion had appeared.

To be fair, it was the most incredible lion I'd ever seen. It wasn't like the type of lion you'd see walking into, say, the zoo. It didn't look sad. It didn't look bored.

It was majestic.

"It's a wild lion," I told her quietly. I fought the temptation to look out of the window of the treehouse. If I dared to peek, I'd realize just how screwed we really were.

Was there *any* chance at all that this lion would go away?

I tried to remember my scout training. When I was a kid, I'd been in so many different clubs and activities designed to teach me about the great outdoors that it made my head spin, but now I couldn't seem to remember a single thing that I'd learned.

Had any of them ever mentioned wild lions?

I knew that I was coming to Colorado from Kansas, so that probably made a difference. There were cougars from time to time, but were there ever straight-up lions? I didn't think so. I hadn't realized that Colorado had lions in the wild, and I hadn't thought one might wander to Basil's home.

"It's not dangerous," Sora said again. She was staring at me curiously, as though I was missing something very important.

"Sora, you can't go out there," I said.

"Why not?"

"Because it might eat you."

She started laughing and shook her head.

"He doesn't eat humans. Are you joking right now?" Sora cocked her head, staring at me. What did this kid know that I didn't know?

"Do you know this lion?"

"Of course, I know the lion," she put her hands on her hips.

"How? Does he come 'round here a lot?"

Her eyes narrowed, and I realized, all of a sudden, that whatever information I was missing was very important.

"I thought you were going to marry Basil."

"I am."

"Then how could you not know?"

"Not know what?" I was starting to get frustrated and a little irritated. What did Basil have to do with the lion?

And then it hit me.

All at once, it came rushing over me, and I collapsed on the treehouse floor and stared up at Sora. She was right: how could I not know? It was so obvious, and it was staring me right in the face.

It was him.

He was the lion.

That was why its mane looked so good.

That was why he'd growled right before she told me who he was.

That was why...

"Why didn't he tell me?" I whispered, looking up at her. She was a kid, for dragon's sake. She was just a kid, and she didn't need to be involved in matters like this, but she was.

"Have you not met a shifter before or something?" Sora stared at me like I was an idiot.

"I haven't."

"Why not?" Sora put her hands on her hips and stared at me just a little bit harder. She tapped her foot on the treehouse planks. She resembled an irritated schoolteacher who was tired of her students.

Why not?

Why hadn't I met a shifter?

I didn't know. I didn't have an answer. I'd been running around with Shane, and then I'd gone to jail. Everyone's blood was tested when they went into prison. If you were a shifter, you had to go somewhere else. You couldn't be with the general population. Everyone knew that. Nobody wanted someone to change into an animal and attack a guard randomly.

We all knew that shifters existed. Everyone knew. Shifters kept to themselves, though, and they stayed out of sight.

"I don't know," I finally whispered.

"Anyone up there?"

It was him. Basil was here. He was outside of the treehouse, and he was calling to us.

No, he was calling to me.

Sora looked over at me. I was still sitting on the floor, so I scrambled to get to my feet.

"Are you going to tell him you know?"

"No."

"That's funny," she laughed. "You can tease him."

She pulled open the door and stepped out onto the platform.

"Hello, Mr. Dixon."

"Hello, Miss Watson," Basil called out with a smile.

I stepped out onto the platform and looked down at him. I gave him a little wave. He looked slightly disheveled, but if I hadn't been paying close attention, I might not have noticed that. His suit was just slightly wrinkled and, if I wasn't mistaken, it had torn a little bit.

Had he rushed to get out of his clothes before shifting?

Or had he rushed to get back into his clothes after I'd started sobbing like a madwoman?

"Darling," I said, looking at him. I realized he had a bouquet of wildflowers in his hand, and he held them up.

"Gift for you," he murmured.

"Pretty," Sora clapped. "Hey, Basil, you won't believe what just happened!" The little girl's eyes twinkled mischievously, and she looked over at me and wiggled her eyebrows.

"What happened?" Basil wanted to know.

"We saw a lion, and he made Melinda cry."

11

Basil

I felt like a perfect ass.

I'd gone and scared her, hadn't I?

I didn't mean to. I didn't mean to freak her out and make her cry, but now, as I stared up at Melinda with her tear-stained face and her racing heart, I wished I could take it all back.

I should have told her.

"I've got to go," Sora said, climbing down the ladder. "My mom will wonder why I'm not back. She'll complain. Then she'll call you."

"Can't have that, can we?" I winked at the neighbor kid and waved as she ran off into the woods. She lived next door, and there was a small path that led from my yard to hers. Even though it looked like she was running off into the wilderness of the woods, she would have no more than a five-minute walk back to her home.

"Thanks for the flowers," Melinda said. She sat on the platform in front of the treehouse and let her legs dangle down. I took a few steps over to her, and then a couple more.

She was wearing shorts, so I could see the soft skin of her thighs as she swung her legs back and forth. Oh, she was gorgeous. Suddenly, I didn't feel quite as bad. My remorse was quickly replaced with a different feeling: one I was more comfortable with.

Arousal.

I wanted her.

Did she want me the same way I wanted her?

"You're welcome. I picked them myself."

"I can tell," she said, but there was no judgment in her voice. She wasn't displeased that I'd grabbed them myself by the side of the road. She didn't mind.

I wondered if anyone had gotten her flowers like this before. Had anyone gone and purchased her flowers? Or had Melinda dated people who didn't really think of her?

I hated the idea that her previous partners had been selfish. It bothered me more than words could ever express. She was beautiful, and she was sweet, and she deserved to have every happiness.

"Do you like them?" I took a step forward, and then another. Melinda didn't move. She just watched me as I slinked toward her, never letting my eyes stray from her. Not even for a moment.

"I like them."

"What else do you like?" I asked, finally reaching her. She opened her legs slightly. I wasn't even sure if she realized she was doing it, and I took the moment to step between them. Melinda looked down at me.

"I like a lot of things."

"Tell me some of them."

"I like pizza."

"Don't we all?"

"I like movies."

"I like them, too."

"I like snuggling up with a good book."

"A wonderful choice," I agreed.

"And I like being licked right...here," she said, tapping the inside of her thigh.

"Right here?" I asked, tapping a slightly different spot.

"Nope. Right here," she touched the original spot once more.

"Oh, right here?"

"That's it," she smiled brightly. "But, I do think I said I like being licked there. Not tapped." Melinda raised an eyebrow, watching me.

"It sounds like you're teasing me," I murmured.

"A little."

"Or maybe you're taunting me."

She shrugged.

"I just want to see if you're scared."

"Melinda, I'm getting ready to marry you. I'm not going to waste a single chance to touch you. I'm not scared," I said.

I leaned forward and swiped my tongue across her leg. Instantly, her leg was covered with goosebumps, and she quivered ever-so-slightly.

"Is this the right spot?" I murmured, pressing my lips to that particular patch of thigh.

"You got it," she whispered.

"What about this spot? Do you like to be licked here?" I kissed a different spot on her opposite thigh, and she nodded.

"I like that, too."

"Does that mean I get to taste you here?"

"Please," she whispered.

"Such good manners. How can I resist that?"

"Hopefully, you can't."

I moved my mouth, sliding my tongue up and down each of her legs. Kissing, licking, teasing: I loved every second of it.

"Basil..."

"Shh," I reached up, pressing my finger to her lips, silencing her. "Just enjoy this."

I was surprised when she laughed and sucked my finger between her lips, tugging it effortlessly into her mouth. I was so caught off guard that I took a step back, stumbled, and fell right on my ass.

Melinda thought it was hilarious. She started laughing lightly at first, but soon her laughter turned into a bellow.

"Hey," I protested, hopping back to my feet, but it was too late. The moment was over, and she was climbing down from the treehouse.

"Thought a cat would have faster reflexes than that," she said, crossing her arms over her chest.

"A cat?"

Oh.

So, she knew.

Well, crap.

I looked at her for a moment, trying to gauge the situation. Was she mad? Was she panicked? Did she think it was completely weird?

"Aren't you going to say anything?" Melinda asked, looking at me. "And when was I going to find out about the surprise?"

"The surprise?"

"That my husband is actually a secret shapeshifter."

"Oh, that surprise."

"That surprise," she agreed.

"I wasn't going to tell you, actually," I offered. At least, I could be honest about that. I wasn't really sure whether it was the right thing to do. I didn't exactly want to burden her with the information, of course, but I also wasn't really ready to share that part of me.

Shapeshifting was personal, of course, but it was also an integral part of who I was.

When I shifted, it was like coming home. It was the one time when all of the sadness and pain from my past seemed to morph into nothing but faded memories. It was the one time I could feel at peace.

So, no, I didn't often talk about the fact that I was a shifter. I rarely – if ever – told women I was dating that I was a shifter.

It wasn't that I was ashamed of what I was. I wasn't.

Most humans weren't ready to know, though.

"You weren't going to tell me?"

"No."

"But we're getting married."

"I realize that."

"You don't think I should have that information before signing my life over to you?"

"Technically, you're not signing your life over to me. Just your time."

"I understand," she said carefully. Melinda looked like she wanted to say more, but she wasn't going to, and I appreciated that.

What I appreciated most of all was the fact that she didn't yell.

She didn't panic or freak out.

She just waited carefully, looking at me, and then she spoke again.

"You could have told me."

"I know."

"Your neighbor knew."

"I realize that."

"Why did you tell her?"

"She's a shifter, too. Well, she can't change yet, but she'll be able to in a few years."

"Is she a lion, like you?"

"Bear. Her entire family can shift."

"Kind of incredible," Melinda nodded, looking back toward the treehouse. "So it's like a little cubby for bears."

"Something like that."

"Interesting. Well, I'm starving. Do I smell food?" Melinda jerked her head toward the car. The sudden conversation shift was slightly jarring, my stomach rumbled in response to her question. I, too, was completely starving. I'd been nervous and excited all day, which meant I'd completely forgotten to eat: an oversight that would quickly be remedied.

"There's no way you could smell our food."

"Perhaps not," she laughed. "But I like the flowers, and I have a feeling that any guy who is going to go to the trouble to get me flowers is also the kind of guy who is going to bring me dinner. What do you say? Let's eat."

She marched toward the car, opened the door, grabbed the food, and headed into the house. I stood there, staring at her, wondering what the hell I'd gotten myself into.

Melinda was cool, and I felt cool because I got to be around her.

I couldn't wait to see what she'd do next.

12

Melinda

After a huge dinner, a long bath, and an oversized glass of wine, I was ready for bed. Basil and I talked a lot during dinner, after which I was wildly exhausted. Shifters. Who knew?

Not me.

I knew they existed, sure, but that was about it. I hadn't exactly planned on hanging out with one or dating one. I definitely hadn't expected to end up married to one.

By the time bedtime rolled around, I'd figured one thing out for certain: it was kind of cool. Basil explained that he had a couple of special things he could do: he had overdeveloped senses, for one. He had incredible strength, for another.

The idea of being married to a lion probably should have scared or worried me, but it didn't. When I thought of Basil being able to completely change into an animal, it didn't make me worry the way I worried when I thought about Shane coming to find me.

He's never going to find you.

Actually, finding out that Basil was a shifter made me feel better, if that was possible. Even if Shane managed to find me – which he definitely wasn't going to be able to do – Basil could protect me. He could keep me safe.

I felt a little bad for viewing our relationship in those terms. Not only was I accepting money for fake-dating this dude and then legally marrying him, but now I was relieved that he could protect me from the demons of my past?

Messed up.

The entire situation was messed up. There were a lot of things I hadn't considered before I'd come to Rawr County, and shifters were one of them. Oh, I'd known that shifters existed, but getting to be up close to one, and getting to *talk* to one, well...that was a different story.

At bedtime, I padded down the hall to Basil's room. I was wearing my slippers, pajamas, and my hair was pulled back in a low, loose ponytail. I knocked before walking into his room. He was sitting in bed reading and looked up when I walked in.

For just a moment, I paused to look at him. This was my life now. This was what I was getting myself into. I was getting myself into a situation where I was going to get to walk up to this guy every night and hug him. I'd get to kiss him. I'd get to spend all of my time with him because we'd agreed to do it.

We'd agreed.

"Hey future wife," he smiled.

My stomach flip-flopped. I liked Basil. A lot. I liked him more than was appropriate, and I already knew that when this thing between us was over...well, it was going to hurt.

Like, a lot.

He wasn't going to stay with me after the terms of our contract had been fulfilled. I understood that. The two of us were never going to have sex. We were never going to passionately make out on his couch because we just couldn't hold back. We weren't going to do any of that because...

Well, because this thing between us was impossible.

And it wasn't what he needed.

Or wanted.

"Hello, future husband," I responded, trying not to let my emotions get the best of me. I'd been with him less than a day, and already I had emotional whiplash from the extreme feelings I'd been experiencing all day.

He patted the bed beside him, and I walked a little deeper into the room, still feeling a little unsure of myself.

"Are you sure you don't want me to have my own room?" I offered lightly. We'd dumped all of the shopping bags in one of the guest rooms and I'd wasted no time making the little space my own. The clothing had filled the closet and two separate dressers. My makeup had filled the little vanity.

"I think you should sleep in here," he told me again.

He had everything planned. I could keep all of my belongings in the guest room. That was where they'd stay for the most part. They'd be carefully tucked away and out of sight, but they'd also give me my own special space where I could keep things separate from him.

I knew that in the next few days, weeks, and months, our lives would begin to blur closer together. We'd become more and more of a couple, which meant I'd probably struggle more and more to keep my identity separate from him.

The real question was how I'd manage to do that.

Would I be able to keep my world my own?

Would I find myself melting into Basil?

Would I become the type of person who wasn't scared of anything?

Would Shane find me?

Even though I now knew that Basil was a lion shifter, and even though I now knew that he was the type of person who could literally tear someone apart, I wasn't scared of him.

Instead, I found myself relieved. I was wildly relieved and wildly happy to find someone who could protect me if Shane ever came for me.

I just hoped that the situation never came to that.

13

Basil

Perhaps sleeping in the same bed as my would-be wife was a terrible idea, but I didn't really care. The only thing I cared about was her.

I liked her.

A lot.

My inner-lion liked her, too.

While Melinda fell asleep almost as soon as her head hit the pillow, I was awake for a long time. The entire situation was crazy, but it was turning out to be just fine. Melinda was exactly the type of person I always thought I'd end up with if anyone was crazy enough to marry a lion like me.

She was funny and sweet, kind and gentle. I liked the way she asked questions about what it felt like to be a lion. She didn't seem angry or upset that I was a shifter. She wasn't disappointed in any way. She was just...herself. She was curious.

The next morning, the two of us got up early and went on a walk around my property. I showed her the little touches I'd added to the treehouse and talked about my plans for the future. Mostly, I thought it could use more books.

Melinda agreed.

Breakfast consisted of bacon, eggs, and two cups of iced black coffee. Once we were satisfied, showered, and dressed, it was time for me to leave for work. Melinda loitered as I got ready, never leaving the room. She fiddled, messing with her shirt and her hair and her new books.

"What is it?" I finally asked.

What was bothering the sweet human?

"It's just that you're going to be gone all day," she finally said. "I'll miss you."

Me?

She was going to miss me?

"Really?"

"Really."

"Why?"

"Because being with you makes me feel safe," she said.

"I hope it makes you feel more than safe," I told Melinda. "I hope you feel safe, and I hope you feel adored, and I hope you feel happy."

"That wasn't in the contract," she whispered.

"Happiness?"

"Yeah."

"Want me to call Cosmo? I can tell him to add it in."

"I don't know if he's going to like having to make changes to it," she said slowly.

Crossing the room, I made my way toward her. I reached for her cheek, but I didn't kiss her. Instead, I just looked at her for a long minute that seemed to stretch out into an eternity.

"Melinda."

"Basil."

"Spend the day with me," I blurted out. Once the words had left my mouth, I wondered why I hadn't thought of it before. Of course, she should spend the day with me. The two of us had a lot to talk about. We still needed to get to know each other. We still needed to start learning about the other person's little quirks.

What better way than spending the day together?

"Don't you have to work?" Melinda looked confused, as though she'd misunderstood my previous comments about going to the office.

"Yes, but it's a big building. A curious girl like you could do a little exploring."

Right away, I knew I'd said the correct thing. The grin that spread across her face was contagious, and that was how I found myself standing in my office with Melinda dressed in her new business-casual attire that Sherry had purchased.

I made a mental note to give Sherry a raise. She really did deserve it.

"It's time for my meeting," I finally told Melinda regretfully. I didn't want her to leave, but she understood that I had meetings she couldn't attend. I wasn't abandoning her, though. I arranged for two different employees to take her on tours. It would be her first time being out of the house as "my fiancé," but it would also give my team a chance to start to get to know her.

If they felt the way about Melinda that I did, then I was going to be a happy person.

Lunch rolled around, and the two of us sat in my office eating sandwiches that Sherry had ordered for us. Most of the time, I just ate quick meals in my office between meetings, but every so often I'd wander into town to eat at a restaurant or diner. Today, being alone in the office felt good.

Melinda licked her lips as she started to eat her sandwich. My eyes were drawn to her, and I had to force myself to be normal. I'd promised her no sex, hadn't I? I could respect that.

Only, in retrospect, it really had been a stupid thing to put in the contract.

"What did you think about everything?" I asked. "Did you like the office?" It was important to me that she approve of my building and my company. I'd never craved anyone's approval before, but I wanted her to think it was interesting, at the very least.

Big Cat Tech was a company that did a lot of good in Rawr County. Yes, we produced a variety of different software products and offered technical services, but we also donated an incredible amount of our profits to local animal shelters and charities. Despite the fact that my company did well now, I'd tried to never take anything for granted. That was where donating came back in.

"It's nice," Melinda nodded. "Big, too. I almost got lost a couple of times," she laughed. Then, she paused and cocked her head. "Is everyone here a shifter?"

I stared at her over the top of my turkey-and-cheese French roll. "What?"

"Shifters. Is your entire office full of them?"

I took a bite and chewed slowly. Okay, so maybe I should have had a better talk with Melinda about shifters before we'd come out today. It wasn't that there weren't other shifters here, but rather, that there *were*.

And the shifters here didn't like to be bothered.

They liked to be left alone.

They liked to be left to do their own thing and in their own time.

"There are a few," I told her.

"I thought so."

"Getting curious again, are you?"

"A bit," she nodded. She started picking at her sandwich. "You know, I had never met a shifter before you."

"I hope I haven't disappointed you."

"You haven't. Not at all."

"I'd hate to disappoint you," I murmured, and it was true. I didn't want to let her down or have her feel like this thing between us wasn't going to work.

"You've never let me down," she whispered, and when she looked up at me again, heat had filled her eyes. She wasn't worried about me. She wasn't scared of me. She was *excited* with me.

"Well, don't worry," I chuckled. "There's plenty of time for that."

My sandwich was forgotten. Now, all of a sudden, the only thing I could think about was her. The only thing I could think about was touching her and teasing her and playing with her. Oh, I wanted to run my hands through her hair and tug her close. I wanted to kiss her like there was no tomorrow.

I wanted to make her feel the way she made me feel.

Standing, I walked around the desk to her. I sat on the edge and looked down at her. Melinda looked up.

"What's going on?"

"You know, I've been thinking."

I had been thinking.

A lot.

Ever since she'd arrived, I hadn't done much *besides* think. It was crazy to me how the idea of going out and forging a future with someone like Melinda had never crossed my mind before. After my parents had passed away, I'd sort of lost myself a little bit. I'd poured myself into work and distractions, but I'd never just put myself out there. I'd never done the work to find someone who could bring joy to my life, or who I could bring joy to.

"About what?"

"We're going to be married, right?"

"That's the general idea," she chuckled nervously.

"And when we get married, we're going to be seen together a lot. Hell, throughout the entire engagement, we'll be seen together a lot."

"What's your point, Basil?"

"I'm getting there."

I swallowed hard and just *looked* at her. Soft skin, big eyes, and pouty lips: Melinda made my cock stir without even trying.

"I think we should kiss," I finally said. "I think we should kiss each other."

14

Melinda

I stared at him.

He wanted to kiss me.

Right here, right now: Basil Dixon wanted to tug me into his arms and kiss him, and I wanted exactly that from him. The idea of getting to just cut loose and let myself go...it seemed perfect to me. For so long, I'd had to be strong. I'd had to stay firmly in control of myself so I didn't get hurt.

Now, it seemed like I was being offered a chance to just *feel*.

I wanted it.

I wanted to take that chance.

"Say that again," I whispered.

I could hear the husky arousal that filled my voice, but I didn't care. I wasn't ashamed of how he made me feel. He made me feel like I was wet and needy and turned on. He made me feel like a damn cat in heat.

I wanted to stand up and start rubbing myself against him, purring with desire and need. I wanted all of that and more. I wanted *him*.

Needed him.

"You want me to kiss you?"

"I think we should," he nodded.

Then I was on my feet. Basil stayed where he was: casually perched on the edge of his desk. I took a step forward and pressed my hands against his chest. I moved tentatively at first, but then, as I moved my hands up and down, my confidence began to grow.

I tried not to think about the hard body beneath the carefully-fitted shirt. He was definitely the kind of guy who had his clothes tailored, and I could see why. He might have the heart of a lion, but he had the body of a damn god, which meant everything beneath him was hard as rock.

Everything, I thought, glancing down between his legs.

Yeah, he was hard thinking about this. He was turned on thinking about sharing a kiss with me, and the truth was that it turned me on, too.

"You know," I murmured, running my hands up to his neck. I cupped his throat, stroking my thumbs over his soft skin. Time seemed to stand still as I stood gently touched him, gazing into his eyes. "This sounds like a line. Saying you think we should kiss. It's a line."

"Oh, it's a line," he agreed.

"Are you sure it's a good idea?"

"It's necessary," he told me. "What if we go to the engagement party, and we have to kiss in front of all of those people?"

"Oh, I understand," I nodded. "You think we should practice ahead of time, you know, to um, perfect everything."

"Exactly," he nodded.

"It still sounds like a line."

"I've already admitted that it is."

His eyes seemed to sparkle as he looked up at me, and my hands were still on his neck. I moved them up slowly, resting them gently on his cheeks, and then I nodded.

"I like this idea," I murmured, and then I brought my lips down to his.

Basil Dixon could fucking kiss.

I'd had plenty of experience kissing plenty of different people, but this was different. This was more intense than anything else I'd ever experienced. The way his tongue gently probed, his lips moving over mine, was incredible. It was like every move had been carefully rehearsed, carefully practiced.

Even though I knew it hadn't been.

"Basil," I whispered.

"Shhh."

He stood, getting to his feet, and my hands fell to my sides, but Basil wasn't slowing down. It was his turn to reach for me, sliding his hands into my hair, tugging me close to him.

He was grinding against me, deepening the kiss. It was easy to feel exactly how this moment was affecting him, and oh, it was affecting him. Everything about this was making him *feel* things, and I loved it.

Or maybe I just loved him.

"Basil," I said his name again. It was a request. It was a promise. It was a million things wrapped into one, but most of all, it was me begging him not to stop.

I didn't want this moment to end.

He lowered one of his hands to mine, grabbing it while he kissed me. It felt strange to be holding hands with the lion while I kissed him, but it mostly felt intimate.

I knew that no matter what happened after this moment, there was no going back. Basil might be pretending that we needed kissing practice, but I knew in that moment that my heart was going to be his.

No matter what happened next...

I was going to be his.

I groaned against his mouth, and suddenly, his hands weren't locked on my hands anymore. Suddenly, they were on my ass, pulling me closer to him.

I could feel everything.

I could feel his cock pressing against his pants. It was dying to get out and oh, I was suddenly dying to free it. Basil and I had been taunting and teasing each other this entire time. We'd wanted so much from each other, and we'd just denied ourselves.

Wasn't it time that we stopped?

Wasn't it time that we stopped resisting this thing between us?

"Basil," I whispered.

"Melinda."

"I want you."

He pulled back and looked at me, and then he cupped my cheek.

"What do you want?"

"You."

"You have me, little human."

"That's not what I mean."

I licked my lips. I felt like he was going to make me say it. He was going to make me be blunt and bold, and I didn't really want to be, but I could. I could do it for him if it meant getting what I wanted, and what I wanted was his cock inside of me.

"Then what you do mean?" Basil asked innocently. He placed his hands on my waist and gently brought them up to my breasts. I closed my eyes as he started massaging my chest, taking his time in the most deliciously dangerous way.

"I mean..."

What *did* I mean?

Suddenly, I couldn't remember what I meant. It was hard to focus when he was touching me like this. It was really, really hard to focus. I knew that I wanted to ask him to...

What?

What did I want?

"Tell me," he whispered, leaning down. He moved forward and nipped at my ear. I squeaked in surprise, but it didn't hurt.

"I want you to fuck me," I finally said. The words came out all in a rush, and I was embarrassed that I'd asked it, but I got the distinct impression that my embarrassment just turned Basil on even more. Maybe he was one of those guys who liked to make women beg for what they wanted. Maybe he liked the power and control that came from making someone beg for your cock.

"Is that what you want, princess?"

"Yes."

"I thought we had an agreement," he murmured.

"I don't...we don't need to...fuck the agreement, Basil, and then fuck me!"

I didn't need to tell him again. I didn't need to *beg* him again. Almost instantly – and I had no idea how he did it – Basil removed all of our clothing. We were completely, totally naked in his office, and he was kissing me.

All of me.

He moved his mouth swiftly from my neck to my breasts, and then he lifted me up, carried me to his desk, and sat me down right on top of it.

"Basil..."

I wanted to ask what he was doing, but I didn't care anymore.

I wanted to ask if this was a good idea, but it didn't matter.

We were too far gone to stop. We both wanted this. Needed it. We craved each other.

There was something electric about this relationship, and I knew that neither one of us was going to stop until it was over.

We needed this moment.

"Please," I whispered, and he chuckled as he got to his knees in front of me.

"Such a pretty pussy," he murmured.

Oh...well, oh damn. Did I like that kind of talk? Apparently, I did, because I was so wet that I worried I'd leave a mark on his desk.

"Basil..."

"Has anyone ever told you that, Melinda? That you have a pretty pussy?" He slid a finger through my lips, feeling just how wet I was. I was already close to coming, and I had a feeling he was going to start teasing me until I came for him.

"No," I whispered. Nobody had ever told me that before, but I kind of liked it.

Okay, I really liked it.

"You do," he told me. "It's the prettiest thing I've ever seen, and I'm going to kiss you there now," he told me. "You're going to be a good girl, Melinda, and you're going to come for me."

It wasn't a request.

And then he started licking me.

I threw my head back and closed my eyes. Basil wasn't holding back at all, was he? He was acting like this was the best damn dessert he'd ever eaten in his life, and if I didn't already feel like a damn goddess, that moment would have done it for me.

When I came, Basil reached up and covered my mouth with his hand, making sure that I didn't alert the *entire* office as to what we were doing, but I had a feeling that with shifters and their weird noses, everyone already knew.

"Basil, that was..."

Fire.

Lightning.

Magic.

It was everything I'd ever wanted, and everything I'd never had. It was perfection, and I'd barely had a chance to recover before he was back on his feet, and his cock was nudging at my entrance, begging to be let in. Oh, I was going to let him in. I was going to let him do whatever he wanted.

"Please," I whispered. "Give me your cock, Basil. I need it."

I needed it more than I'd ever needed anything in my damn life.

Fortunately for me, he didn't hold back. He thrust his hips forward, sheathing his cock to the hilt, and then he made love to me right there on the desk. He was wild and passionate and wonderful, and when he came, it was the sexiest thing I'd ever seen in my life.

He whispered my name.

It was more than just a word.

It was a promise.

And I knew that when it came to me and Basil, everything had changed.

There was no going back now.

15

Basil

T he engagement party was held at a local hotel known for its
beautiful fountains. There were three fountains outside of the
hotel and each one boasted a different theme. One had mermaids.
One had bears. The final one, of course, had a huge, majestic lion.

I'd been responsible for commissioning that one.

"Wow," Melinda whispered as we walked past the gorgeous
fountain and into the hotel lobby. She looked in awe of everything
that was all around us. It truly was a beautiful place to have our
party.

"Wow indeed," I murmured, but I was looking at her: not the
fountains. She'd chosen to wear a low-cut yellow dress that showed
off all of her beautiful curves. It fell just to the tops of her knees. She
was so damn perfect, and the last few days had been a whirlwind
of happiness and excitement as we'd spent our days texting and our
nights making love. If I wasn't careful, I knew I was going to start
feeling like the entire thing was real.

It wasn't real, but oh, when I looked at Melinda, I really, really
wanted it to be.

Why had I asked her to be my fake wife, again?

Why hadn't I just asked her to be my real wife?

Melinda noticed me admiring her right away. A sly grin spread
over her face. Oh, she wasn't going to let me get away with oogling
her in public. Not my Melinda.

"Why Basil," she chuckled, pressing a hand to her chest. "Am I right in assuming that you like the way I look?"

"I like the way you look," I agreed.

"You're going to make me blush."

"Good," I reached for her and pulled her into my arms. People were watching, but that wasn't why I was holding her. It was just a good excuse. I heard the snap of a camera, and I knew that people were eating up what we were selling, but at this point, I already wasn't sure what I was going to do when it was all over.

Melinda, however, didn't lean into me. Instead, she pulled away. Her eyes widened, and she looked toward the source of the sound.

"What's that?"

"It's just a camera," I murmured. "Probably for the engagement spread."

"Engagement spread? For the local newspaper, right?"

"This one is going to be national," I explained. "There's going to be a piece on us in *Intrigue* magazine."

"Really?"

I scented the air just then, smelling something strange coming from Melinda. I had expected her to be excited about the magazine article, which was why I hadn't mentioned it, but she wasn't excited about it at all, was she?

She was...nervous.

"Really. Is that a problem?"

"No," she said quickly, but I had the distinct impression that it *was* a problem. I thought about Cosmo's words when we were filling out the forms for our contract. He'd been certain that she was hiding something, and now I wondered if he was right.

Was there a reason Melinda didn't want our names or pictures in the magazine?

"We don't have to publish your last name," I told her. "If that's what you're worried about."

"I'm not worried," she laughed, brushing it aside, but there were some things Melinda hadn't told me yet. I wasn't so naïve that I didn't realize she was hiding a couple of big items from me.

For one, I still didn't really know why she wanted her money in cash. I'd only paid her twice so far, but each time, it had been with an envelope full of cash. Melinda said she'd get a bank account soon, but she hadn't.

That felt strange to me.

She paid for everything in cash, and she never showed her ID card unless she absolutely had to.

There had been nothing strange in her background check, I knew. She hadn't been convicted of a crime or a DUI or even drug possession.

So, what was it that had her so rattled?

Before I could press the issue, a familiar face appeared.

"Hey, there you two are," Sherry said, grabbing us. "Let's get a couple of photos by the fountains before we head into the party. It's in full swing." Sherry shook her head. "Being late to your own party, Basil? I feel like that wasn't necessary."

"It's not a big deal," I insisted.

"It's not," Melinda agreed quickly. A little too quickly. She was taking my side, which was fine, but she was also still nervous and tense.

What had happened?

What bothered her about pictures?

"Whatever," Sherry motioned for the photographer to come over, and together, the two of them posed us in front of the fountains for the next fifteen minutes. After that, though, I couldn't take the scent of Melinda's agitation anymore, and I insisted that we were ready to go into the party.

The photographer and Sherry walked ahead of us as we made our way into the hotel and through the lobby. Melinda was tense and didn't look at me. She walked straight ahead with her shoulders back and her head high, but I needed answers.

And she was going to give them to me.

I reached for Melinda's arm and tugged her aside, pulling her into a little alcove just off the hotel lobby.

"What's going on?" Melinda asked, surprised.

"I could ask you the same question," I told her.

"What?"

"What's wrong?"

"Nothing's wrong, Basil," but she wasn't meeting my eyes.

I reached for her chin and tilted it up, forcing her to look at me.

"Try again, love."

"Nothing's wrong."

I narrowed my eyes. I wasn't mad, but I was irritated that she still didn't trust me. I was disappointed that I hadn't been able to earn her trust just yet, but I knew it hadn't been much time. She'd been with me for less than two weeks, and that wasn't a lot of time in the grand scheme of things.

"One more try," I murmured. I lowered my lips to her ear and whispered, "or I'm afraid to be forced to paddle that soft bottom of yours before the party, darling, and I don't think you want a sore ass while we're dancing."

She gasped.

"You wouldn't."

"I would," I laughed darkly. I reached for her hand and tugged, placing it on my cock, which was rock hard at the very *thought* of getting to pull this beautiful woman over my knees.

"Basil..."

"What do you think, little human?" I murmured, growling into her ear. I nipped at her earlobe with my teeth, tugging just enough to feel a shudder shoot through her body.

This was turning her on just as much as it was turning me on, which was good. It had been the goal. It was what I was going for.

I wanted Melinda to want me: to crave me. Probably, it wasn't fair. This had been an arrangement, after all. It had been something where our feelings weren't supposed to be involved, but that was the problem with situations like this.

Feelings always got involved.

Humans and shifters: we were all complicated. We weren't simple beings with straightforward emotions or feelings. Sometimes even when we thought something should be simple or easy, it wasn't. It became hard.

Right now, this was hard.

I could see Melinda wrestling with whether or not she was going to tell me. I could see the fire in her eyes as she thought about having my hand come down across that sweet ass of hers.

"One more chance," I whispered, but she didn't say anything. She froze, not speaking, and I laughed.

"All right, darling," I said. "You lose."

I took her hand and led her down the hallway. To people walking by, it probably looked like we were going to the party, but we had a little detour to make. There was a small "family bathroom" in this hallway, which was basically a room with a toilet. Because it was a nice hotel, however, there was a small, separate room with the sink, as well as a sitting area. We went into the family bathroom, and I closed the door behind us, locking it.

Melinda looked around the room.

"On the bench," I pointed to the little sitting area. Across from the sink was a small, velvet bench.

"What?"

"Hands and knees," I told her. "On the bench. Oh, wait," I reached for the bench and tugged it out, pulling it so that it was crossways in the room. Melinda climbed onto the bench, and I positioned her on her hands and knees so that she was facing the sink and mirror.

"Basil," she whispered. "I can't tell you."

"I understand that," I told her honestly. "I also understand that you had a chance to be honest, and you chose not to be."

"But..."

"No buts," I told her. "We're going to be married, and this might not be a real relationship, but we're going to trust each other."

"I can't trust anyone with this."

"You can trust me," I murmured. "Now look at yourself in the mirror."

She looked up, watching herself. I reached the hem of her dress and pulled it up so that it hung around her waist.

"So pretty," I ran my hands up the backs of her thighs and to the edge of her lace panties. They were yellow, like the dress, and I loved being able to see her in them.

"I'm glad you like it," she said.

"Keep your eyes on yourself," I told her. "Melinda, have you ever been spanked before?"

"Yes."

"Tell me."

"I've been spanked, and I've spanked people," she bit her lip. She wasn't embarrassed by this idea. She smelled excited, aroused. She *liked* the idea of someone spanking her. A lot of people did.

"Did your boyfriend use his hand when he spanked you? Or did he use an implement?" I always liked to use my hand. I liked feeling someone's skin beneath my palm, but I was experienced enough to know that not everyone felt the same way as me.

"It was my girlfriend," she whispered. "She used a flogger. Sometimes her hand."

"Which did you prefer?"

"Hand," she said quickly. No hesitation.

"Why?"

"It's more intimate," Melinda admitted.

I felt the same way. I wasn't into hardcore BDSM by any means, but I liked spanking. I liked tying people up. Occasionally, I liked to be tied up.

The thing about a spanking, though, was that it didn't have to be a punishment. Even now, I wasn't really going to hurt Melinda. We were playing a game, her and I, and it could stop at any moment. If I suspected, even at all, that this wasn't going to absolutely delight and excite her, then I wouldn't do it. I would back down.

If I suspected that sweet, wonderful was going to feel scared or hurt or fearful of what we were going to do, then I would stop.

She didn't seem fearful, though.

She was excited about this.

"I'm going to spank you," I told her. "Tell me why."

"You want me to know I can be honest with you."

"Why else?"

"You want me thinking of you," she said breathlessly. Our eyes locked in the mirror, and I could see how damn aroused she was. I hadn't even really touched her yet, and already, she was excited.

"I want you thinking of me," I agreed.

And then I reached for the soft lace of her panties, and I tugged them down, pulling them so they pooled at her knees, and then I touched her skin.

Oh, she was so fucking soft.

So perfect.

So completely wonderful.

How the fuck was I going to let her go when this was all over?

I wanted to mark her. Claim her. I wanted to make her promise that she'd be mine for real. I wanted to make her promise that when this was all over, it wouldn't be. I wanted forever.

The thought scared me, but tonight wasn't about being scared. It was about us. It was about celebrating our "love," however make-believe that might be.

I brought my hand onto her bottom, and she flinched just a little. I smacked her again, admiring the way her bottom gently bounced with each swat. Over and over, I smacked her, until Melinda finally started groaning and wiggling.

She wasn't crying.

I stopped when I realized she was pressing up, back against my hand. She *wanted* this, I realized. She *really* liked this.

"Melinda, darling, I think you're having fun."

"They call it a *funishment* for a reason," she whispered.

"Tell me what you're thinking."

"I'm really glad we broke the *no sex* rule in our contract."

I stilled.

Had she really just said that?

"What?"

"I'm just saying," she looked over her shoulder. "You and I could have a lot of fun, Basil. A lot of fun."

She was right. We could. The two of us could have more fun than a pretend couple was possibly supposed to have. We'd already had quite a bit of excitement in my office, and I was delighted to find that she wanted more. I wanted more, too. Melinda was the type of woman I didn't think I'd ever grow tired of.

I wanted her more than words could possibly express. She was incredible, and I found myself thinking about her constantly when we were apart. It reminded me of a high school relationship: passionate, wild, and crazy.

"If I slide my hand between your legs, Melinda, what am I going to find?"

"My tight, wet pussy," she whispered. "Basil, I'm so wet right now."

"Can I touch you?"

The words caught in my throat. It was hard to get them out for her, but somehow, I managed to do it.

I wanted to touch her.

I wanted to make her fall apart.

Oh, her bottom would be a little tender at the party, and of course, she'd think of me that way, but maybe I'd give her something else to remember me by.

"Please," she whispered. "Please make me come."

How could I refuse such a request?

Slipping my fingers between her legs, I started to stroke Melinda as she watched herself in the mirror.

"Such a good girl," I murmured. "Such a pretty girl."

She groaned, pushing back against my hand once more, and this time, I slipped a finger inside of her. I quickly followed it with a second, filling her, and started to move my fingers in and out of her body.

"Basil..."

"I can't wait until it's my cock inside of you," I found myself saying. That was what I wanted: what I craved. I wanted to fuck her again so badly, but I wasn't going to do it here in the hotel bathroom. I'd wait until later when we were alone, so I could spread her out and devour her like a damn feast.

"Oh, I want you to be," she admitted.

"Not here," I told her. "Soon," I growled. "I need you, Melinda. I need to feel my cock slide inside of you and I need to feel that pussy gripping it. Is that what you want?"

"Oh, yes."

She closed her eyes, and she was so close to the edge of orgasm that I couldn't even demand she keep them open. I just wanted her to feel good. I wanted her to feel great.

I wanted Melinda to fall apart right now, just for me, and I wanted this to be the best orgasm she'd ever had in her entire life.

"Come for me, pretty girl," I said. "Little human, come for me. Show me what a good girl you can be."

And she came.

It was like watching a falling star on the Fourth of July. It was like watching the world explode. She started to cry out, but I covered her mouth with my hand until I'd wrung the last remaining quivers from her body. Then I pulled my hands away, helped her back into her panties, and tugged her up to her feet.

"Wow," she whispered.

I nodded, unable to speak, and I pulled her close. Planting a kiss on her lips, I placed my hands on her lower back and pulled her closer. I was still harder than ever, which was something I'd have to deal with, but what I wanted more than anything else was her.

Mine.

My inner-lion seemed to agree with her. I wasn't sure if I believed in the idea of fated mates the way some people did, but I knew that there was something wonderful about Melinda.

Something incredible.

And I knew that I never wanted to let her go.

"You still didn't tell me your secret," I reminded her.

"Your spanking didn't scare me that much," she teased.

"I'll try to be scarier in the future."

"No, don't," she looked up at me, cupping her hand on my cheek. "You're perfect, Basil. Perfect."

"What?"

"You're perfect the way you are," she said. "Don't try to be anything other than what you are. Any girl would be lucky to have you."

"You have me."

"Then I must be the luckiest damn girl in the world."

Before I could say anything else, before I could try to remind her that this situation was all a big, fat, fake set-up, there was a knock at the door.

"Let me in! Please! Let me in! I'm about to explode!"

Melinda and I exchanged looks and she started laughing.

"Just a second," she called out.

It was time for us to go.

16

Melinda

The party was beautiful.

He'd really gone all out with all of the careful planning, I realized. The more I got to know Basil, the more I realized how thoughtful he was. He was trying to save his ass and seem more responsible, sure, but there was more to it than that.

He wanted me to have a good time.

We'd been socializing and chatting with people for the better part of an hour when Sherry sidled up to me with a beautiful woman who towered over me. She was so tall that I had to really tilt my head up to see her.

"Hello," I said, holding a hand out. "I don't think we've met. I'm Melinda."

"And I'm charmed," the woman said. "I don't shake, though, dear. I hug!" She reached for me and pulled me into a warm embrace that was probably the softest, sweetest hug I'd ever gotten in my life.

Sherry didn't seem to mind at all. She just smiled and shook her head, as though this kind of behavior was something she was totally used to.

"Melinda, this is my wife, Wendy," Sherry told me.

"Nice to meet you, Wendy," I laughed as I pulled away.

"I've heard so much about you," Wendy gushed.

She had?

What had she heard?

It probably wasn't surprising that Sherry had talked about me to her wife, but the idea that anyone would find *me* interesting was still weird to me. I wasn't anyone special. I was just me. I was normal and I was ordinary, and despite having a very weird relationship with the one and only Basil Dixon, I wasn't exactly someone to write home about.

"You have?"

"I have!" Wendy clapped her hands.

"What have you been telling Wendy about me?" I turned to Sherry.

"Only the good bits. Don't worry."

"The very good bits," Wendy agreed. "I heard you've really made Basil happy."

"I hope so," I smiled, ready to play the part. "He's an incredible man. I'm really lucky to be marrying him."

Wendy and Sherry exchanged *looks*, and I realized that Sherry hadn't kept the secret as close to her heart as she'd said she was going to.

"Does she know?" I asked Sherry.

"She knows."

"I won't tell anyone," Wendy insisted. "Promise."

"There's nothing to tell," I said with a smile.

Especially since now, I really was starting to have feelings for him. I really was starting to fall for the lion man. I knew that it was wrong, that I shouldn't have developed an attachment to him, but I did.

I liked the way we hung out together and watched movies in bed. I loved the way he kissed every inch of my body before completely devouring me. I even loved the way that tonight, he'd dragged me into the bathroom and spanked me.

I liked all of this.

"Of course," Wendy nodded.

There was a soft vibrating sound and Sherry reached into her pantsuit pocket and pulled out her phone. Staring at it for just a second, she looked up.

"Excuse me," she said. "I need to take this."

She stepped away, and Wendy and I stood there for a moment. I wasn't really sure what I was supposed to do. Basil was off socializing and now that Sherry was gone, I wasn't sure whether I was supposed to start making the rounds and meeting people at the party or if it would be okay for me to just spend time with Wendy.

To be honest, Wendy made me feel wildly at ease. She seemed nice and friendly, and I could use that. Even though I'd eventually have to start learning the ins and outs of the people Basil worked with and spent time with, at the moment, I just wanted a few minutes to relax with someone who was friendly and non-threatening.

"I could go for a drink," I offered, and Wendy agreed, nodding. "Me too. I'm parched."

"Parched?"

She fanned herself and smiled. "Doesn't it feel a little hot to you in here?"

It didn't, but I laughed and nodded, anyway. The two of us made our way over to a bar that had been set up against one wall, and we each ordered drinks: vodka Redbull for me, red wine for her.

Together, we stood at the bar with our drinks for a moment and just stared out at the crowd. I could see Basil laughing and chatting with a couple far off in the distance. He always seemed so comfortable and at ease. No matter what he was doing, he never seemed to struggle.

I was a little jealous, if I was being honest.

Wendy watched him, too. I wondered if she was like me. Was she the type of person who had a hard time meeting new friends? Or was she like Basil and Sherry: social and comfortable in new situations?

"Have you met a lot of people?" Wendy asked, sipping her wine.

"A lot," I agreed, nodding. "I'm going to have a hell of a time remembering names."

"You probably should have asked everyone to wear nametags," she teased.

"Probably."

It wasn't a really bad idea. That would have made it easier for me to keep everyone straight. For now, though, I was content to hide out at the bar with my new friend who had an easy name. I wasn't sure how much Sherry had told Wendy about my personal situation or my relationship with Basil, but Wendy didn't seem particularly interested in quizzing me, which was nice.

As we watched the party from our little lookout, I spotted the photographer, who was still circling around the room. A few other people with cameras had joined him, and I watched them warily, not wanting to let them get out of my sight.

No matter how safe I felt with Basil, I was still worried that somehow, Shane was going to find me. Taking the marriage contract hadn't seemed so bad when I thought that I was going to mostly be dealing with local pictures, but the idea of nation-wide photos that *anyone* could see kind of freaked me out.

What if Shane was still watching for me?

I had almost been certain that he'd known which motel I was staying at back home. I had constantly been afraid that he was going to figure out where I was and come get me.

What if he realized where I was hiding?

The thought sickened me. Our relationship had ended poorly, but there was more to it than that. He'd framed me. He'd let me take the fall for his crimes. A year in jail for weed possession didn't seem so bad to come people, but he'd literally done it so that I couldn't go cry to the cops and tell them the truth about him.

Shane Winchester was a fucking creep.

We'd been dating for a couple of months when I discovered that not only was he a creep, but that he was embezzling from the company he worked for and had no plans to quit. The very worst part of it all was that the company he worked for was a charity organization that was supposed to help kids with cancer.

There he was, though, funneling those funds from the accounts he worked with right into his own.

Who the hell *did* that?

When I'd approached him and tried to talk with him about it, he'd brushed me off. He'd made it sound like I was totally wrong and totally crazy, and then he'd planted weed in my car and in my purse, so when I was searched going into my office the next day, I'd been arrested.

It had been easy-peasy for him to ditch me, but the worst part was during my arrest. The worst part was that when he was actually pretending to be upset and shocked and sad, I could see the look on his face.

I could tell that he was thrilled.

He'd written to me in jail, especially during the last few months. He'd sent people to talk to me, too, making it clear that I wasn't going to ever be able to talk about what he did.

Never.

Now, being around Basil, I was finally starting to feel like I was going to get a fresh start. When I was with him, I got to talk about books and movies and food. Our relationship was so ridiculously *normal* that I sometimes forgot that it was supposed to be fake.

This entire marriage was supposed to be a second chance to have a new life, but that wasn't going to happen, was it?

Nope.

"Normal" didn't happen for girls like me.

So, as I watched the photographer stopping different people and taking an assortment of shots, I wondered how long my relationship with Basil was really going to last. How long would it be before someone found out who I really was?

How long would it take for the entire contract to fall apart?

"You don't like photographers, huh?" Wendy asked, noticing my nervousness.

"Not really."

"Me neither," she admitted.

"Why not?"

Wendy was tall, lean, and beautiful. She had the kind of body most women would kill to have, but she just shrugged.

"It's not easy being a gentle giant," she joked lightly, but I could tell there was some pain there. She added, "nobody really thinks there's anything wrong with making fun of tall girls."

Cringe.

She was right, and I could see on her face just how much that bothered her.

"I understand," I nodded. "Want to get out of here?"

"Oh, yeah," she agreed. "Let's go."

We started to walk toward the doors that led to the hall. Basil was busy talking with a couple of business associates. I noticed that he didn't seem to have any relatives at the party, which I'd have to ask him about. It mostly seemed like the party was filled with colleagues and acquaintances. He was definitely a popular guy who knew a ton of people.

It was easy to see how Basil had been so successful with his company. Despite the fact that he himself tended to shy away from serious relationships – friendships or otherwise – he was actually pretty social. When he was working the room, he did an incredible job moving from person to person. He somehow made the flow of moving throughout the room feel natural, so nobody felt like they'd been shorted.

Wendy and I had just reached the doors when she placed her hand on my arm.

"Wait," Wendy paused. She was watching a couple who were canoodling in the corner. The woman was short and curvy with bright, frizzy hair. She reminded me of Miss Frizzle from *The Magic School Bus*. The man had her hands pinned over her head, but they weren't kissing. They were just sort of eye-fucking each other.

"Do you know them?"

"I know him," she laughed. "I'll be damned. Hey Lincoln!" Wendy yelled loudly. The man abruptly dropped the woman's hands and looked over at Wendy. A huge grin spread over his face, and he waved at her. His date waved, too, and then they turned back to each other.

"Who was that?" I asked as we left the room, heading into the hallway.

"An old friend."

"Boyfriend?"

"Something like that."

We headed outside of the hotel, where Wendy lit up a cigarette. She offered me one, but I shook my head.

"I'm good with my drink," I held it up.

Wendy just shrugged and started talking.

"So that," she told me, "was Lincoln. He runs a service for people who need a date."

"A service?"

"Yeah. He's not a prostitute. Not really. Well, maybe. Depends on your definition."

"Basically, he sells you an evening, not sex?"

"Yes! Exactly!"

"And you've been out with him before?"

"Not personally, but one of my friends needed a date to my wedding. She didn't want to come alone, so she hired him. It was great because she didn't have to worry about people asking her when she was going to start dating someone or when she was going to settle down."

"He was just there for her?"

"Yeah," Wendy nodded. "Exactly. Kind of like how you're being there for Basil."

"Ah," I nodded, and I leaned against the side of the building. "Exactly like that."

"You like him, don't you?"

"Of course," I nodded. "I'm marrying him, aren't I?"

I didn't know who was listening. I didn't know who was around that might overhear our conversation, so I wasn't about to admit that any of this had been a setup, but it didn't matter. Wendy seemed to know what I was talking about.

She seemed to realize that I hadn't been able to stop thinking about him.

It was the spanking that had done me in, really. Who the hell spanked their bride-to-be right before their engagement party? Like, *was* that something people thought was okay? It wasn't something I thought was okay.

There I was, though: thinking about it.

The orgasm that he'd followed up the light spanking with had been over-the-top and wonderful, and even now, just thinking about it, I wanted more.

I'd meant it when I said I wanted his cock.

"No," Wendy looked at me. "You *really* like him."

"Yeah," I whispered. "I really do."

I sighed because it was a stupid problem to have. What kind of person started to fall for their fake husband? Like seriously, who *did* that?

Only, it was me.

I did that.

I fell for my fake husband.

I was the kind of person who totally, completely, absolutely started to fall for the guy I was fake marrying, because why not?

Maybe I was just a glutton for punishment or maybe I just liked pain. I didn't know. What I did know was that no matter what happened next, somebody was going to get hurt.

Maybe Shane would find me and hurt me.

Maybe Basil would end our marriage before I was ready, and I'd get emotionally hurt.

Or maybe Basil would start to fall for me, too, and we'd both get hurt.

No matter what, someone was going to be injured. Agreeing to this relationship had been a terrible decision, I thought, but I wasn't about to back out of it. I wanted him. I wanted as much of him as he was willing to offer.

I wanted to be his.

"What are you going to do?" Wendy asked me gently. "Are you going to tell him?"

"No."

"Maybe you should," she offered.

"We literally had one rule: don't fall in love."

Not really. Our one rule had been *no sex*, but we'd almost broken that like an hour ago when he'd locked us in the bathroom and tugged my dress up. I wasn't about to tell Wendy, though. I knew she was Sherry's wife, but I didn't want to overshare with someone I'd just met.

"Sometimes rules are made to be broken," she told me.

"Not this rule."

"You never know. When I met Sherry, she didn't want something serious, either."

"Really? But Sherry seems so..."

"No-nonsense?"

"Yeah."

"She is. She's also really headstrong, determined, and organized. She's totally business-oriented and professional, and then she met me. I'm a teacher and an artist and to me, a healthy diet consists of bagels and coffee and pastries. We're total opposites in every way, but..."

"But you work together?"

"Yeah. We just *work* together."

Was that how Basil and I were?

Was that how we were going to be?

Were we going to be able to make something between us just *work*?

I didn't know, but suddenly, I kind of wanted to find out.

I knew that before I did, though, I was going to need to tell him everything.

I was going to need to tell him the truth.

17

Basil

I was talking with Justin and his wife Rebecca, who both seemed surprised that I was getting married. Justin was slightly suspicious of the entire situation. I knew perfectly well why he was suspicious – he'd just gotten married, after all, and maybe he thought he'd planted the idea in my head.

His own romance had been as much of a whirlwind as mine. Maybe he had a secret he hadn't shared with me.

Had his own marriage been a sham?

Maybe it had started out that way, but I knew without a doubt that his relationship now was wildly incredible and special. I could tell just by looking at them that it was something for the ages. Rebecca lightly held onto Justin's hands. Their fingers were intertwined, and she kept looking up at him and smiling, like she couldn't believe how lucky she was to be married to someone like him.

It really was kind of magical.

"The food is great," Justin said.

"Absolutely delicious," Rebecca agreed. "Thanks for choosing things that are so allergy-friendly," she added, lowering her voice. Both she and her husband had food allergies. I'd tried to make sure there were plenty of things they could both eat at the event.

"I try to be accommodating," I smiled, glad they appreciated the gesture. I didn't have the same problems they did, and I didn't have to live my life quite as carefully as they did, but it didn't take a lot of time or planning to think about other people.

I liked to think that was one of the things that made me a good leader, but I wasn't sure if it did or not.

"Excuse me," Sherry approached, placing her hand on my arm. I looked at it before glancing back up. Sherry wasn't exactly a touchy sort of person. She wasn't the kind of person who would just randomly touch me without a good cause, and I didn't understand why she was touching me now.

Not unless it was something important.

Not unless it was urgent.

Or bad news.

"Hey Sherry!" Justin gave her a wave. Justin and I didn't often do business together, but he knew Sherry and Wendy.

"Justin," Sherry nodded. She looked at Rebecca and her look softened. "Rebecca." Then she turned back to me. "I'm so sorry, Mr. Dixon, but I'm afraid I need to pull you away from your guests for just a moment."

Mr. Dixon?

Oh, shit.

Something really was wrong.

"Will you please excuse me?" I turned back to Justin and Rebecca, who seemed to understand. Justin placed his hand on Rebecca's lower back and steered her away from us, while Sherry grabbed my forearm and started tugging me out of the room.

"We can't talk in here," she said. "Too many ears."

Too many shifters was what she meant. Shifters were wonderful and wild and obviously, we both *were* shapeshifters, but we all had different kinds of enhanced senses.

One thing many shifters could do?

Hear.

Shifters could hear incredibly well.

Whatever the problem was that had risen during the party, Sherry wanted to talk to me *away* from prying ears. She wanted to talk to me in a place where nobody could hear, and I was instantly nervous. Looking around, I tried to spot Melinda, but Sherry knew what I was doing.

"She's with Wendy. They went out for a smoke."

"Melinda doesn't smoke," I pointed out.

"Doesn't matter. The two of them are gossiping: probably about us. We have a few minutes. Come."

She led me from the party and out into the main hotel hallway. Then she guided me down to what appeared to be an unguarded coat room. The clerk's table, which usually had an attendant, was empty. Sherry pushed past it and into the coat area, dragging me with her. She closed the door to the coat room, essentially locking us together in the silence.

"What is it?"

What could be so important that we had to talk now?

And in a room filled with coats?

"I need to tell you something."

"Yes, I got that part," I said drily.

"Listen, I just got a call from Fletcher."

"Fletcher?"

"Yeah," she nodded.

"Why would Fletcher be calling you today?" I stared at Sherry, trying to figure out what she was getting to. Fletcher was one of our security professionals, and for him to call during a party that he was supposed to be at, there must have been a problem.

What could it possibly be?

A million thoughts raced through my head. Was someone trying to hack me? Had someone managed to get past our security? Had they accessed private employee files?

Nothing could have prepared me for what she had to say, though.

"It's about Melinda."

Instantly, my heart fell.

Not Melinda.

Not my bride.

I didn't want to think that there was something wrong or that she'd lied to me. Even though I knew perfectly well that there was something she was hiding from me – after all, I'd spanked her for it right before the party – I hated the idea that she was somehow up to something malicious.

Was *she* trying to hack the company?

Stay calm.

My inner-lion seemed to roar, and it took everything in my power not to shift and run away. I wanted to. There were so many times in my life when running away had solved my problems. Running away meant I could hide. It meant I could stay tucked away from everyone and everything until I was ready to be open and honest and *share*.

It meant I could protect myself.

Sherry's eyes flashed a different color. She was a pigeon-shifter, which wasn't as common as one might think. She was good at blending in, though. Nobody saw a pigeon and thought, "Oh, I'm going to stop and stare at you." Instead, people walked right by pigeons, and that was one of the reasons Sherry was such a great assistant.

She saw things other people didn't see.

She noticed things other people didn't.

And now she was about to tell me something that I really, really didn't want to hear.

Oh, I didn't want to hear this.

"Just tell me," I finally said.

"I'm so sorry to tell you tonight," Sherry whispered. She looked nervous, and that was strange because Sherry never, ever looked nervous. Instead, she was the type of assistant who *always* looked wildly put-together and wildly brave. She was always on top of things. She was a great planner, and she always did a wonderful job making sure that I stayed on top of everything I was supposed to be doing.

"Spit it out."

"Fletcher made a mistake on the background check," she said.

"What do you mean?"

"The background check came back totally flawless," Sherry pointed out.

"I'm aware."

"That's because he accidentally only ran a credit check instead of a full criminal background check."

"What are you talking about?" I didn't understand how that was even possible. It seemed like a huge oversight, actually, and it seemed like something I wasn't going to be very happy about moving forward.

The entire point of having Fletcher run a background check was to make sure that there was nothing other people could use against me or my bride. If she had a criminal history, then I needed to know. I wasn't the type of person who held judgment or who was ashamed of someone who made mistakes, but I needed to know.

I was in a precarious position with my shareholders. The whole reason I'd hired Melinda – and I had *hired* her – was to make sure that things between us went smoothly. I wanted to know if there was anything shady in her past so that I could get ahead of the press.

Marrying someone was only going to work to improve my reputation if the person I married actually had a good reputation.

So, what had we missed?

"I'm really sorry."

I was starting to get irritated. Sherry didn't want to tell me because she knew how I felt about Melinda. She *knew* that I liked this girl. She *knew* that I cared for her.

"What did she do?"

"A year in jail," Sherry whispered, and my heart fell.

18

Melinda

The party flew by with dancing, speeches, toasts, and celebrating. It was so much fun, and I had a wonderful time, but something was wrong. When I came back inside with Wendy, both Sherry and Basil were slightly cold to me. I wasn't sure at first if it was a mistake, or if I'd done something wrong. Basil pasted a smile on his face, but as soon as we were alone in the car and driving home, I finally got the courage to ask him about it.

"Basil?"

"What?"

His hands were gripping the steering wheel so hard that it looked painful.

"Is something wrong?"

"What makes you think that?"

His words came out tight. Tense. Gone was the carefree man from earlier in the day. Gone was the man who had locked me in a bathroom with himself and made me come apart. Gone was the man who had nipped at my ear, nibbled at my skin, and made me feel like I could freaking fly.

That dude was long gone: dead and buried.

Basil, or whatever version of Basil I was left with, was as cold as ice. Right away, I knew that I'd gotten my hopes up prematurely. The last week and a half with Basil had been incredible. It had been damn near perfect. We'd kissed, we'd slept together, and we'd

337

talked. Oh, we'd talked *so* much. I should have known it was too good to be true, though, because this version of Basil was one I didn't recognize.

Was this angry man the real Basil?

Or was he just upset about something?

I hated how my voice quivered a little as I spoke. I sounded weak. I sounded scared.

"It's just that you don't seem as friendly as you did before," I whispered.

"Back when my fingers were in your pussy?"

It was my turn to flinch.

"You don't have to be crass."

"Oh, now it's crass?" Basil shook his head. "Earlier, you seemed to like it just fine."

"Please stop," I whispered. Suddenly, I was embarrassed about what we'd done. I was embarrassed that I'd let him touch me. I didn't orgasm easily with most people, but with him, it was like he knew what I wanted before I did. Basil touched me, and I seemed to come alive so easily.

It was like my body was getting turned on just for him.

It was like I'd put on a show just for him.

And now...

Now things were different.

Basil didn't say anything else until we pulled up to the house. It was dark outside. The exterior light had flickered out the night before and needed to be replaced, which meant that outside of the car, everything was pitch black. A small light shone from the front porch, but that was it.

There weren't even stars outside.

"Were you ever going to tell me?" Basil asked tensely.

"Tell you what?"

Surely, he couldn't have found out about Shane. I hadn't said anything. I hadn't had any contact with him. I'd also been careful not to do anything that might cause Shane to want to track me.

Before I'd come to stay with Basil, I'd even ditched my phone "just in case." Instead, I'd picked up a prepaid one with a new number that only Basil had.

So, what was he talking about?

He sighed loudly, and I knew asking what he meant had been the wrong decision. Whatever he had on me, he was irritated about it, and I understood why.

Basil was the kind of man who liked honesty. He was the kind of person who liked when other people told him the truth. He had to demand honesty from the people around him, after all. That was part of how he'd managed to grow such an incredible business.

"About jail," he said, turning to me.

"Jail?" My mouth suddenly felt dry. So, he'd found out. How hadn't he known before? When he'd hired me, I'd assumed that my records hadn't appeared on my background check just yet. After all, I'd only just gotten out of prison. Apparently, I'd been wrong. I thought I'd have a bit of time before things showed up in my history.

Maybe he'd gotten swept up in meeting me and hadn't bothered to do a proper check.

I didn't know.

"Jail."

"Basil, I can explain."

"Yeah," he snapped. "You explain, Melinda. You explain how you didn't tell me you were in jail for a fucking year. You explain that to me. And for drugs? What the hell? What kind of drugs were you doing? Were you dealing?"

Shame washed over me. I felt my face grow hot with embarrassment as he stared at me there in the car. Gone were feelings of excitement or happiness about this arrangement.

Suddenly, I realized I had bigger problems than Shane finding me.

I had lost the man I'd fallen for.

Oh, I knew this was pretend. Logically, I knew. Only, I didn't really. My head knew, but not my heart. The only thing my heart knew was that this guy was sweet, sexy, and completely hot for me. The only thing my heart knew was that my body ached with need every time Basil was near.

"No," I whispered finally. "I wasn't dealing."

"Then what the fuck happened? And why didn't you tell me?"

I took a deep breath. I couldn't talk about this. Not now. Suddenly, I felt like my entire body was on fire. I felt like I was burning up alive, and I felt like I was going to burst into tears.

Never let them see you cry.

My cellmates in prison had taught me a lot of things. They'd taught me how to be strong and how to defend myself, and they'd taught me that you can't let people see you cry.

"First of all," I finally said. "Prison and jail are two different places."

"That's not what this is about."

"Well, then, since you seem to know so much, why don't you tell me what the hell you're talking about?"

"I want to know what you did."

"Why? So you can judge me?"

"Because I just told the entire fucking county that we're getting married, Melinda. This shit is bound to come out. You should have told me so I could have-"

"What? So you could have left me? So, you could have found someone else?"

"Yes," he said coldly. "That's exactly why. It's too late now. Breaking up with you would make me look even more unstable than I did before I told everyone we were getting married."

And there it was.

There was a reason I hadn't wanted to tell him.

I wanted to trick myself into believing that Basil and I were going to be something special. I wanted to trick myself into thinking that the two of us really had something going.

When he'd touched me in the hotel, it had been like my entire body had sprung to life just for him. I'd felt like a wildflower.

Now I felt like a fucking pebble under his shoe.

I slid out of the car quietly, closing the door behind me. Then I walked up to the house. I hated the darkness. I hated the way it wrapped around me like a cloak, locking me in. I hated the way the darkness seemed to wrap over me, sucking me in.

I'd always been scared of the dark.

Always.

It was always bad things that happened in the dark.

Now, as I slowly made my way up to the front porch, I was well aware of the fact that Basil wasn't following me. I didn't even care. He could go fuck himself for all I cared.

I just wanted to be alone.

I wanted to get inside and just be by myself and figure out what I was going to do.

So I climbed the porch steps up to the wraparound deck, and I made my way to the door. Fumbling with the keys Basil had made just for me, I let myself into the house and closed the door behind me. From what I could tell, he was still in the car.

What was he going to do?

I didn't think Basil was going to do anything crazy. He wasn't going to hit me or throw things at me. He wasn't going to hurt me more than he already had, but he might go out. He might go get drunk somewhere. He might go to a strip club or find some different girl to be with tonight.

I understood, and this had never been a real relationship, so it wasn't like I could even really get mad.

But I was.

I was mad, and I was sad, and I was hurt.

Most of all, I felt broken.

I kicked off my shoes, leaving them in the middle of the floor, and I walked upstairs to the guest room where my clothes were. I understood how this worked. I knew the drill. The two of us would not be sharing a bed any longer. There would be no playing footsie under the bed. There would be no touching. There wouldn't be any teasing or taunting or licking.

I'd ruined everything.

Well, one of us had.

I didn't want to think that it was me, but there was a definitive possibility that it had been me.

Maybe I should have told him.

Once I was in the guest room, I closed the door behind me. I plopped down on the bed, allowing myself to finally relax, and then I burst out crying.

Never let them see you cry.

He wasn't here to see me cry, so it didn't matter. I hadn't cried in a very long time. I couldn't remember the last time I'd cried. It had been before I'd gotten out of prison. It had been before I'd ever even been taken away. It had been a very, very long time ago.

And now...

I was crushed.

19

Basil

I'd been a prick.

I'd been a total fucking prick, and I didn't know what to do.

I'd seen the way her body tensed when I asked her about jail.

No, not jail.

Prison.

She'd been sent to prison, and I didn't know why. I wanted to know why. She didn't seem like the kind of person to sell drugs. Then again, I wasn't sure what a drug dealer was supposed to look like. Maybe I'd misjudged her. Or maybe I'd judged her when I shouldn't have.

Maybe she'd been in a bind and a friend had offered her a chance to sell weed in order to make ends meet. Maybe she hadn't even been dealing. Maybe it had been a friend's drugs. Or maybe...

Well, I didn't know, and I didn't have the full report on what she'd been convicted of. All I knew was that it was a drug-related offense and that she'd done a year in prison.

A year.

I thought of sweet Melinda and the way she snuggled up against me at night. I thought of the way her toes pressed against mine and the way she draped her arm over me when she slept.

She was so sweet and so perfect, and she was everything I wanted in a woman.

I'd blown it, though.

343

Well, one of us had.

I wasn't sure whether it was me or her that had screwed things up the most. She should have been honest with me, I thought. That much was for certain. You couldn't expect a marriage – even a fake marriage – to work if you couldn't tell the person the truth about who you were and what you wanted from life.

Right?

You just couldn't.

That wasn't the way these things worked.

So, why hadn't she told me?

Because she knew you'd react like this, asshole.

I pulled out my phone. I knew it was late, but I needed to talk to someone before I went crazy. I wasn't about to call my therapist or my lawyer. I wasn't going to let Cosmo in on this one. He'd told me that she was hiding something, and he was right. If I knew Cosmo well enough, and I thought that I did, he'd probably hidden some sort of clause in the contract regarding situations like this.

No, I didn't need a lawyer.

I needed a fucking friend.

Sherry was going to be at home with Wendy. The two of them were early-birds. They were probably already asleep.

So, I called the next best person.

I called Justin.

He answered on the first ring.

"I thought I might be hearing from you."

"How could you possibly have thought that? We never talk."

"Call it instinct," he said.

"I need to meet with you."

"When?"

"Now."

"Where?"

"The place I saw you after your mom's funeral," I told him.

"I'll be there."

Justin ended the call without any sort of hesitation or pause, and I knew he was probably already on his way. Justin was nothing if not reliable, and I appreciated the fact that I could count on him now.

I slid out of the car and stripped out of my clothes. Setting them on the front seat, I set my keys on top and closed the door. Nobody was going to come out and steal my car. Not tonight. Besides, I needed to do this. I needed to get away.

I shifted quickly and quietly. My body morphed all on its own. One moment, I was a man. The next, I was a lion with a long, luxurious mane. I was proud of my mane. It was my best feature, I thought, and it was something that made me wildly happy.

My paws hit the ground before I even realized what was happening, and then I was moving.

Running.

I tore across the grass and into the woods, moving swiftly through the trees. I passed the opening to Sora's house and then I kept running, moving into another wooded area and heading toward the mountains.

There was a reason I liked living out here in the isolation, and this was it. I loved the fact that I could just run and be myself in the woods. No matter what I was dealing with, I could shift into my lion form and just move.

Sometimes, a man needed that.

Melinda had been so wonderful, but she'd lied to me. When I'd tugged her into the bathroom and spanked her, it had mostly been playful. She'd been right when she'd called it a "funishment." It hadn't been designed to scare her or hurt her. Not really.

It had just been something special for us to share.

It had been an excuse to touch her.

The reality was that even though I knew she was hiding something, I thought it was something silly or dumb, the way I'd hidden being a shifter from her. I hadn't thought it was something big. Not like this.

I kept running until I reached the swimming hole where I was going to meet Justin, and then I stopped. I sat down beside the water, and I just stared at my reflection. I wanted to know who I was and what I was supposed to do. This was a place I came often to just sit and reflect on my life.

It was a place that brought me peace.

And then I heard the polar bear.

I didn't look up as he approached and sat on the opposite side of the watering hole. He shifted back into his human form and splashed his feet in the water.

"You look sad, lion," he said.

That was when I looked up.

Justin didn't look sad. Not at all. Justin had recently lost his mother, but he'd dealt with it really well. He'd dealt with it far better than I'd dealt with the loss of my own parents. Probably, it was because he had Rebecca in his life. She'd been wonderful to him. She'd been everything he'd needed and more.

That was what I'd wanted with Melinda.

I'd wanted that peace.

I'd wanted that hope.

I'd wanted to know that above all else, we were going to mean something to each other.

Apparently, that had been too much to ask.

Feeling sorry for myself, I changed back into my human form. My fur-covered body was quickly replaced with sweaty skin and nudity. Luckily, Justin didn't care. We didn't have that type of friendship.

The two of us had known each other for years. We went way back. Long ago, we'd been buddies, but we'd grown apart over the years. Mostly, that was my fault. After my folks died, I lost interest in a lot of things. I lost interest in people. I lost interest in being a better person.

I even lost interest in trying to figure out what I wanted to do with my life.

In many ways, Melinda wasn't just here to help me save my company. She was here to help me save myself. Once upon a time, I'd thought that my life wasn't worth saving, but she'd shown me something else, something new.

She'd shown me that together, we really could make this thing work.

And then Sherry had dropped the news that she'd lied.

"What happened?"

I looked up at Justin. I'd known the polar bear shifter forever. We'd grown apart, as friends sometimes do, but somehow, we always found our way back to each other. I knew that I could trust Justin with anything I needed to say, and this...

Well, this was hard to say.

"It's Melinda."

"Is she okay?" Justin asked, cocking his head. I didn't scent anger or frustration or concern. Not for Melinda. He knew perfectly well that she was fine, but he was giving me a chance to explain what worried me.

How could I put this into words?

"She's fine."

"But there's a problem."

"Yes."

"Did you have a fight?"

"A bit," I nodded. A fight. Somehow, it sounded so small and silly compared to what I was feeling. I felt like my entire world was exploding, but yes, we'd had a fight.

"What happened?"

"She lied to me."

"I'm guessing it was about something big."

"Very big."

"But you found out."

"Yes."

"And you confronted her."

"Oh yeah," I nodded.

"How'd she take that?"

I appreciated that Justin didn't ask me what the lie had been about. He didn't push me to tell him what she'd done. That was important to me. I liked Melinda a lot. There was a part of me that thought I might even love her.

I wasn't ready to share the personal details of what had happened between us, though. There was a part of me that still felt obligated to protect her and keep her safe, even if that was from someone thinking poorly of her. Even though I was mad, I didn't want anyone to think badly of her.

Not now.

Not ever.

"She didn't like it."

"How can I help?"

"You've been married a long time," I pointed out.

He laughed and shook his head. "I've been married a few months, my friend, but sure. Long time," he laughed again.

"Well, what do you think? What do you do when you and your mate have a fight?"

"So, she's your mate, is she?"

Shit.

I hadn't meant to say that out loud.

I hadn't meant to admit that.

"I didn't say that."

"You did, actually, but it's okay. I feel like I'm missing something about your relationship with Melinda," Justin said slowly. "A few months ago, I met you here on the day of my mother's funeral. The two of us talked, and I got the distinct impression that you were not otherwise engaged or involved with someone."

"Make your point."

"Just seems like this relationship happened fast," he shrugged.

"It did."

"Is it fair to assume that you may have chosen to engage in a stable relationship for...business purposes?"

Fuck.

Sometimes I hated how observant Justin really was. I hated the idea that he *knew*. He knew. Well, he couldn't *know*, but he definitely had an idea that something was wrong.

And I wanted to tell him the truth.

"I can't confirm or deny this," I said simply.

"So, yes."

"Yeah," I sighed and pushed myself off the edge of the little swimming pool. I landed in the water and let myself float down, down, down. I didn't love swimming nearly as much as some of the other shifters. Polar bears in particular *loved* swimming, but not me.

For me...

Well, I loved to run. I liked to feel the wind in my face and the gentle way my mane flew behind me. That was what *I* liked.

But I could suddenly see the appeal of sinking under the water and just letting go of everything else. I kept my eyes closed tight – I wasn't one of those people who opened my eyes under water – and

I just let everything melt away. A moment later, I swam back up, bursting out of the water, and I looked over at Justin, who was still sitting there.

"Feel better?"

"No."

"That's fine. Look, marriage is tough," he shrugged.

"Quality advice."

"You don't have to like it," he said. "But it's true."

"It just seems a bit simplistic."

"It's easy and hard at the same time," Justin explained.

"It seems like you and Rebecca are very happy together."

"We are," Justin agreed. "That doesn't mean our relationship has been easy, though."

"You two fight?"

"Everyone fights, Basil. All people in all relationships sometimes fight. It's our nature."

"I just...I've screwed this up, Justin. I know I've screwed it up, but she lied to me. She tricked me."

He looked at me carefully, and then he nodded.

"I can tell that you feel betrayed."

Betrayed was a hard word to accept, but yes. That was how I felt. I felt betrayed. I felt like she'd told me one thing when something entirely different had been true.

That wasn't quite it, though, was it?

"I do."

"Let me ask you something," Justin said, "and don't get offended."

"Okay."

"Did she lie to you on purpose? Or are you upset about something she just hadn't told you yet?"

I paused. It was the latter. She hadn't actually come right out and said *I don't have a criminal history*, but I felt like that was something I should have known.

Maybe that was how she felt about me being a shifter.

"It was a lie by omission," I finally said.

"Do you think she was ever going to tell you?"

"I don't know."

"Okay, let me ask you something else," he said. "Realize that I don't know what the situation is, okay? So, you can always go tell me to pound sand. That's fine. I won't be upset. That said, maybe she has a reason for not telling you."

"What kind of reason?"

He shrugged. "You haven't known each other very long. I'm guessing that you're rushing into things – either that, or this entire situation is a sham-turned-true-love, but we won't go there – and that there's a lot you don't know about each other. Maybe she's scared. She could be worried about her safety or your safety. She could be afraid of something from her past. Hell, maybe she's just scared you'll be sad if she's honest, which it sounds like you are."

"I hate you," I told my friend.

He laughed and shook his head.

"Well, I *love* you."

"Thanks for meeting me. You make a lot of sense, and I'm going to think about everything you said."

He nodded, kicking his feet in the water. It splashed a little.

"Love is hard, Basil. It's not always worth it, but for the right girl? It's definitely worth it for the right girl."

Was she the right girl?

I thought that she was.

She definitely was.

Melinda was *everything* to me. She was kind and she was sweet. She was everything I'd ever hoped for in a wife, but she'd deceived me.

Only, maybe she hadn't. Maybe she'd been waiting for the right moment to be honest, and I hadn't given her enough time or chances to share with me.

Maybe I hadn't been patient enough.

"Thanks, friend," I finally said, and I stood and stretched.

"Time to go?" Justin smiled.

"Time to go," I agreed. "Give Rebecca my love."

"Not a chance in hell," he chuckled, "but I'll tell her you said hi."

Before I could say anything else, he shifted and took off running. He was in his bear form, so he'd probably be home in just a few moments. A quick shift later, and I myself looked like less of a man and more of a cat.

It was time to go home.

I needed to talk to Melinda. He had been right. He'd been right about everything. Justin didn't need to know the details of our situation to realize that this thing between me and Melinda really was special and that our relationship was something I wasn't going to let go of. Not easily.

Not ever.

So, I ran. Racing home, I didn't stop to enjoy the feeling of the air on my face. I just ran, racing. I jumped over trees and branches and scurried around as quickly as I could until I finally reached my house. Changing back into my male form, I grabbed a couple of wildflowers that were growing by the driveway, and I marched up to the house.

I needed to see her, and I needed to apologize. I'd overreacted, and I'd made a mistake. I was ready to tell her that I was sorry, though. I was ready to let her know that I understood she probably had reasons for keeping this secret.

But when I pushed open the door to the house, I realized that I was too late.

The house was empty.

She was gone.

20

Melinda

The tiny motel I checked myself into was the kind of place you should never go. Not alone. It was dingy and run-down, and the door to my room had only a tiny sliding lock that needed to be screwed back in. They took cash, though, and they didn't ask many questions.

Leaving Basil felt wrong and hurtful and scary, but I knew when he didn't come into the house that the relationship between us was over.

I wasn't going to be his fake wife.

I wasn't going to be his fake girlfriend or his fake fiancé or his fake mate.

I would be nothing to him because I had hidden something big from him and he'd learned about it before I ever had a chance to tell him.

I should have just been honest, I knew, but I couldn't. I couldn't tell him because I was scared. Besides, what was Basil going to do about Shane?

Nothing.

At least when I was with Basil, I'd known that Shane couldn't come find me. He couldn't hurt me. I knew that he wanted to hurt me. He'd made it very, very clear during my time in prison that he would come for me as soon as I got out.

I just couldn't give him the chance to do that.

354

Well, now I was in Rawr County, Colorado. He couldn't find me here. Yeah, Shane might see the pictures, but if the wedding was off, they'd probably never even run, so I was okay. I'd be safe. Protected. I could lie low for a week or two, and then I could move on to the next place.

Where would that be?

I didn't know.

I had enough money from Basil to last me at least two or three months if I was careful. Yeah, it was safe to say that the guy overpaid. Still, I wasn't going to complain. I'd take a couple of days to cry and feel sorry for myself. I'd nurse my wounds and then I'd figure out what I would do next.

I could do this.

I could survive.

I had to.

A WHOLE WEEK WENT BY.

I had no idea if Basil had tried to call me because I turned my phone off. I wasn't about to allow myself to be tempted into answering. Not for him. If I heard his voice, I'd want to be with him. I'd beg him to forgive me and I'd ask him to give me another chance. That was seriously bordering on a "real" relationship, and that was something that the two of us didn't have.

It had been fake.

Pretend.

And I'd broken the contract.

We were allowed to fight. I knew that we were allowed to fight. We were allowed to screw up and make mistakes and have a hard time with each other, but I'd left him.

Maybe it had been the wrong choice.

I'd only planned to stay at the Hungry Bear Inn for a couple of days, but it had been seven, and I didn't have any idea where I was supposed to go. The owner seemed to take pity on me, and was okay with me just coming down and paying daily for my room. I didn't ask them to send housekeeping in or anything, and she knocked a couple of dollars off of my daily bill, which I appreciated.

Now I was just sitting.

The Wi-Fi service was spotty at the motel, which was a nice way of saying it was non-existent. If I was going to ever get out of Rawr County, I probably needed to visit a library to use the Wi-Fi and start doing research on other cities.

Surely, there were small towns where I could hide. I hated the idea that I was going to be running and hiding for the rest of my life.

What were my other options, though?

I could go back to Kansas and hope Shane left me alone. Who knew? Maybe he'd died. Maybe he'd gotten locked up himself.

I could hire an attorney and ask how I could report what had happened. Maybe the right lawyer could help me figure out how to explain that I'd been framed and punished for something I hadn't done.

What if I was able to somehow report Shane for embezzlement? What if I could prove it? What if I could get *him* locked up so that he didn't hurt me or scare me ever again?

Only, I didn't know how, and I didn't have the money for that, and besides...

Maybe I was overreacting.

Finally, I managed to pry myself out of bed. I showered, cleaned up the room a little bit, and ate a granola bar. After I ran a brush through my hair, washed my face, and brushed my teeth, I headed out to my car.

I had the distinct feeling that someone was watching me, which was stupid. Nobody here knew me. I parked my car behind the motel, so Basil would never see it. Not that he ever drove to this part of town. He probably didn't even know it existed.

Still, I couldn't help glancing around as I made my way to the car and got in.

"Calm down," I told myself. "Settle down. You're being a panicking Patricia."

The library was only a couple of blocks away. Honestly, I could have walked, but I took the car. I headed inside, found an empty corner, got connected to Wi-Fi, and started researching. It looked like Rawr County actually consisted of a lot of little towns. Most of them were probably full of shifters, like this one, but there was one particular town called Bitesville. I couldn't tell if it was a meme or not, but I had the sudden feeling that it might be filled with vampires, and that wasn't something I had any interest in at all.

One of the little cities, Bear Town, seemed like it could be a good choice. They had a lot of restaurants, several cheap motels, and a couple of little rental apartments that offered month-to-month leases. That was me. That was what I needed.

Bear Town it was.

Satisfied with my choice, I hopped back in the car and headed back to the little motel room I'd been staying at. As soon as I walked in the room and locked the door, I started packing. It took almost no time at all. That was because I'd left almost everything Basil had purchased for me at his place.

I hadn't brought the dresses or the shoes or the hats. Yes, he'd made sure that I had hats. I wasn't interested in bringing those with me.

I did, however, take the bras and panties, along with the swimsuits. He wasn't going to need those things, and he wasn't going to give them to anyone else, so I didn't feel bad. Those were items that weren't exactly reusable.

Once I was packed, I sat down on the bed and closed my eyes.

Maybe I should have turned the phone on. Maybe I needed to know. Before I actually left town, maybe I should find out whether or not he'd tried to reach out. I sort of expected that he'd thought it was a good thing that I'd left him, but what if he didn't feel that way at all?

What if he hoped I'd come back?

I took a deep breath and turned my phone on. Then I waited. It took a couple of moments for my phone to fully power on, load up my emails, and receive all of the texts that had come through during the past week.

As it was, there were a lot of texts.

As in, dozens of them.

There were messages from Basil and texts from Sherry, and there was even a message from Wendy asking if the two of us could get together soon because she'd had a good time. I scoured the texts, wondering what the narrative was now that I was gone. I didn't get the impression that Basil had actually told Sherry I'd left him.

After all, she hadn't asked me why I'd broken the contract or anything like that. She'd just asked if I wanted to meet up and get lunch or if I needed anything. Judging by how vague her texts were, I was guessing that Basil had told her I was busy or that I'd gotten some sort of hobby.

And there were the texts from him.

Basil was sad.

My heart clenched a little as I looked through message after message from him.

I miss you.

I'm sorry.

I completely screwed up.

I read message after message where he wanted to know if I was okay. Not a single message was mean or cruel. He just wanted to make sure that I was fine.

And then there was a text from Cosmo, Basil's attorney. The message was short, simple, and to the point, and it made me realize that Basil was looking out for me even as I'd been nursing my wounds.

It's Cosmo. Basil filled me in on the status of what's happening; however, he'd like to continue paying you. Please call me at your earliest convenience to set up a time for me to give you your latest payment.

What the hell?

He still wanted to pay me?

But I hadn't fulfilled the contract. The wedding wasn't planned. The dress wasn't purchased. I hadn't set up florists or caterers or chosen a bridal party. I hadn't done anything, and we hadn't set a date. I hadn't made any appearances or anything, either.

How was the lion supposed to have a wife if I was hiding away?

And that was when I realized that I didn't want to keep hiding away. I wanted to tell him the truth. I wanted to tell him everything.

He would understand.

He would understand, and he would forgive me.

That was the kind of man Basil was. He wasn't the kind of guy who was going to run away scared like I had. He was going to fight for me, and that was the kind of guy I wanted. I wanted someone who was going to fight for me, who was going to love me.

I wanted someone who was going to be there for me no matter what happened.

I wanted him.

I pressed his name and the phone started ringing. Standing up, I spun around in a circle, wildly excited that I was going to go for it. I was going to give this another chance, and I had a good feeling that everything between us really was going to be okay.

Only, when I spun around, I realized that I wasn't alone.

I realized that I hadn't checked the bathroom when I'd gotten back to the motel.

And I realized that Shane had, in fact, found me.

"After all of this time," he smiled maliciously.

I dropped the phone.

21

Basil

———◆◇◆———

IT WAS A HELLISH WEEK, but she called. I was in the middle of a meeting with a couple of investors when I felt my phone vibrate. I wasn't expecting a call, and most people knew not to bother me during a meeting, but something told me to peer at my phone, and I was so glad that I did.

I stared at my phone for half a second until my brain registered what was happening, and then I answered right there in front of everyone.

"Melinda," I said right away. "I'm so sorry."

I was.

I had been wrong.

I'd hurt her, and I'd scared her, and I'd done so many things that were hurtful to her. I'd chased her away with a lack of understanding. I could have asked her about what happened in such a better, gentler way, yet I hadn't.

Now I was paying the price because I'd had to spend a week without the woman who made me crazy. I'd had to spend an entire week without the woman who made my heart soar.

But she'd called.

Only, Melinda didn't say anything. Instead of her beautiful voice, I heard a man.

"After all of this time," he said, and then I heard a crashing sound.

Had she just dropped the phone?

I wanted to call out for her, but I didn't. Instead, I waited for a moment to see if she was going to say something else. Was she in trouble? Had she been captured? What the hell was going on?

The entire room I was standing in fell silent. Everyone knew that there was a problem.

"What are you doing here?" Melinda's voice came out loud and clear. She wasn't talking to me. She was talking to whoever was with her.

"Not even a *long time, no see*?"

"No."

"Why, Melinda, I'm hurt."

"You aren't hurt at all. Not compared to what you put me through, Shane."

Shane?

Who the hell was Shane?

I muted my phone and put it on speaker. This Shane guy wouldn't be able to hear me, but everyone would be able to hear what happened.

"My fiancé is in trouble," I told the room. "Listen for any clues as to where she might be. We need to go help her." I looked at Sherry. "Get Fletcher on this. Have him try to track her phone."

"On it," she said.

"And find out who Shane is."

"Done."

We listened as a group. The fact that the people in my meeting were professional investors didn't matter. I didn't care. There were plenty of ways to make money, but there was only one way to find a woman to fall madly in love with.

I'd found her, and I'd almost lost her for good. I wasn't going to waste this chance. I was going to find her.

I'd spent the last week scouring Rawr County for any signs of Melinda, but I'd had to do it discreetly because I didn't want anyone to know she was missing. I wasn't embarrassed about having a fight with the woman I loved, but I didn't want to spread gossip or start rumors unnecessarily.

"You should fuck off. That's what you should do. How did you even know I was at the Hungry Bear Inn?"

She'd dropped the name.

We all heard it at the same time, and I started walking out of the room with the rest of my group following me. I was still muted so that whoever was with her wouldn't realize she was on the phone with someone who could help. My hope was that she'd dropped the phone and kicked it under the bed or out of the way so that nobody realized she had someone.

She had someone who loved her, who cared about her.

Sweet Melinda had someone who cared, and she had someone who was going to come fight for her no matter what that took.

"Get the cops," I said out loud. Instantly, Sherry and three other people pulled their phones out, but I didn't stay to hear what they had to say. I was too busy running down the hall to the elevator. I'd shift soon, but not before I started recording the call, and not before I got out of the building.

I couldn't exactly push elevator buttons with my paws.

Sherry raced to catch up with me, and the two of us rode down in the elevator. Everyone else scattered. Some people hurried to the stairs to go that way. I shoved the buttons, slamming the doors shut, and the elevator started to move.

"Who's the guy?"

"No clue."

"You've been separated, haven't you?"

"Yep."

"You could've told me."

"Just did."

She sighed, and I knew what she was sad about. I hadn't let Sherry in, but I hadn't wanted to talk about it. Still, my obvious moping at work probably made the situation pretty apparent. That, coupled with the fact that *nobody* had talked to Melinda, made keeping this relationship hiccup impossible to hide.

I didn't care about any of that, though. I just cared about her. I cared about Melinda. I cared about making sure that the woman I loved was safe, no matter what.

When we reached the first floor, I'd heard enough of the conversation to know what was going on.

"I'm going over," I told Sherry.

"I'll fly."

"Don't," I shook my head. "Take my phone with you. Make sure it doesn't disconnect. It's recording, and we might need this."

I knew from what I'd heard so far that it might be the only shot she had at getting any sort of justice. From how the conversation was going, it was pretty apparent that this person, Shane, was her ex-boyfriend.

It was also apparent that he was the reason she hadn't told me about her prison time.

Apparently, she'd been framed, and I had no problem at all believing it. I only wished I'd done so earlier when I'd had the chance. I hated that I hadn't trusted her, that I hadn't let her in. I hated the fact that I'd forced her to hide who she was.

She was incredible, and no matter what happened next, I was going to make sure that Melinda knew how much she was loved.

I had to save her first, though.

Before Sherry could argue, I shifted, tearing my designer suit and completely destroying the shoes. I didn't give a shit. The only thing that mattered was Melinda.

The only thing that mattered was my mate.

Hang on, baby. I'm coming.

22

Melinda

It took Shane less than a minute to have me bound and perched on the bed like some sort of exotic bird he didn't really like all that much. I was embarrassed that he'd found me so easily. Apparently, despite my "separation" from Basil, he hadn't told anyone we'd split, which meant the magazine had still run the article with the pictures and my name.

And it had, in fact, been a national thing.

I felt stupid for getting myself into this situation. When I'd first met Basil, he'd assured me that any pictures or photos we took would be for local websites, magazines, and newspapers. I'd believed him. I'd accepted that as truth. Even when I'd gotten nervous about the idea of my picture being in something more national, I'd accepted my fate. I hadn't fought it the way I should have.

And oh, I should have.

Shane *had* seen it, and he'd come to Rawr County. Shane hadn't been able to find me at first, but luckily, there were only a couple of motels in town, and he'd happened to find himself staying at the exact same one as me. It was cheap and easy, and apparently, it had allowed him to blend in.

Nobody really noticed the kind of people who frequented motels. This type of facility hosted the kind of people who were trying to hide, which meant you didn't pay much attention to the other guests. Everyone just wanted to keep to themselves. The less attention you drew to yourself, the better. The less you interacted with other people, the better.

I'd made the mistake of thinking that this meant I was safe.

Unfortunately for me, getting caught by Shane had happened not because I'd done anything to make myself stand out to the other guests, but simply because I'd gone to fill the ice bucket one afternoon while he was standing outside smoking.

I hadn't even noticed him.

But oh, he'd noticed me.

Now I was trapped in my hotel room. I didn't know if the phone was connected to Basil. I'd dropped it, kicking it under the bed so that Shane wouldn't realize I'd tried to call someone. At the very least, I hoped Basil would have a missed call from me and try to track it somehow.

If he could do that, if he could track me, then everything would be okay.

Right?

He loved me. He'd made it clear in his texts and messages that he loved me. He cared about me very deeply, and he wasn't going to let anything bad happen to me. I just had to keep hoping. I couldn't afford to lose hope.

"Why are you even here?" I asked Shane again. He still hadn't told me. Now that I was bound and non-threatening, though, it was starting to become clear.

"Because you're one last loose end," he said.

"What are you talking about?"

Loose end?

How the hell was I a loose end?

I'd never told anyone what he'd done. I didn't care. I didn't care about justice or having Shane sent away. I just wanted to move on.

My time with Shane had been a nightmare I wanted to forget. Nobody wanted to live trapped in the past, including me. I wanted to forget I'd ever known Shane, and I wanted to spend the rest of my life doing things that brought me happiness, peace, and joy.

Remembering Shane?

That didn't bring me joy.

"How am I a loose end?" I asked when he didn't say anything. For a long moment that seemed to stretch on forever, Shane just stared at me. He was looking at me like I was either really stupid or really naïve: possibly both.

"You threatened me before you went to prison," he said.

"I didn't threaten you. I just asked if you'd actually been embezzling. It's illegal, and it's also kind of a shitty thing to do."

"It might be illegal," he sneered, "but that doesn't make it shitty."

"It does."

"You're shitty," he muttered.

"Nice comeback, asshole," I rolled my eyes.

Fuck.

What the hell had I seen in this guy?

Oh yeah. He had a big dick...even if he didn't know how to use it. I didn't care. Basil's was bigger, and he *did* know how to use it. I'd *never* come with Shane the way I'd come with Basil. Hell, with Shane, I'd never come at all. Sex had been mediocre at best, and cringe-worthy at worst.

I hated myself for having ever dated him at all.

"Excuse me?" Shane was in front of me almost immediately. His hand wrapped around my throat as he forced me to look up at him. There was nothing good about this guy. There was no love in his eyes: no happiness. There was nothing there that would ever reveal the two of us had ever had *anything* in common. "Mind your manners, slut," he hissed.

I closed my eyes.

So, this was it.

I had a feeling that Shane was going to kill me. As he said, he had loose ends to deal with. Loose ends, and I was one of them. I was one of the reasons he couldn't move on with his life of crime, or whatever the hell it was that he was doing.

"Try again," he snapped.

"No."

"What?"

"No," I whispered.

Shane's hand constricted more tightly around my throat.

No.

I wasn't going to beg.

I wasn't going to be polite.

I wasn't going to be kind or nice or *good* to the dude who had sent me to prison and who was now going to end my life. I wasn't going to do any of that stuff.

I simply wouldn't do it.

"You and I could have been so fucking good," he whispered. I kept my eyes shut, but I could feel him watching me. "You had to go fuck it all up."

"We were never good, and you were a thief who didn't care that you sent me away."

"I should have let them kill you in prison."

He'd tried. Oh, I was certain that he'd tried. I'd had a couple of close calls when it came to my time in prison. There were at least two different occasions I could think of where someone had randomly tried to fight me. Luckily, my cellmates had prepared me for just about anything, and I'd been okay. I'd made friends on the inside, and I'd learned to keep my head down.

"Why did you just kill me in the first place?"

"If I had, we wouldn't be having this little talk, now would we?"

"I don't understand."

"I needed the cops to stay off my back," he told me. I opened my eyes. "If I'd killed you, then it would have been obvious. They always look at the boyfriend first, don't they?"

I knew he was right. Plenty of people were convicted for killing their spouse or partner because it was always really obvious when it happened. If Shane had killed me when I'd discovered his secrets, then the cops would have arrested him and he'd be the one in jail. Instead, he'd sat, biding his time, and he'd waited for me to be released.

Well, I'd been released, and apparently, it was time.

Now, my hourglass had run out of sand. It was over. Basil hadn't made it to me in time, and Shane was going to kill me. I saw the knife in his hand. It glistened in the dim motel room lighting, and I knew that this was it.

It was time.

I hadn't apologized. Maybe that was my biggest regret. I hadn't told Basil that I loved him for real or that I was sorry. I hadn't told him that he'd hurt me, but that I should have been a bigger person. I shouldn't have run away.

It was all too late now.

I stared at Shane, unwilling to close my eyes again. If he was going to kill me in the middle of a seedy motel room, then that was it. There was nothing else I could do.

I'd gotten good at fighting, but Shane was much, much bigger than me. He'd overtaken me easily, tied me up, and plopped me on the bed. It hadn't even been a fair fight. Not at all.

"Any last words?" Shane asked.

"Fuck you," I whispered.

And then the glass shattered.

At first, I didn't realize what was happening. A huge mass of fur shot through the motel room window, shattering the glass. I threw my body back on the bed and rolled off, trying to avoid getting hit by all of the pieces of glass.

There was a roar, and then Shane was screaming, and I realized all of a sudden what had happened.

He'd come.

He'd come to save me.

It was Basil.

Somehow, I managed to get myself up and to my feet. Basil, in his lion form, had Shane pinned to the ground with a paw on his throat. He hadn't killed him or even cut him, but he was pinning him down and not moving at all.

Shane looked like he was scared out of his mind, and that was when I realized that Shane didn't know Rawr County was a collection of shifter towns: each filled with different kinds of beings. There were lions here and bears. There were tigers and pigeons and swans. There were even a couple of snakes, if I wasn't mistaken.

Yeah, this wasn't the place you wanted to cause a ruckus.

A moment later, I heard sirens followed by the pounding of feet. The door to the motel room burst open and a second later, there were police officers and shifters filling the room. So many people came in that I found myself pushed against the back wall: carefully tucked out of the way.

Shane was arrested. He was hauled out of the room in cuffs. By the time he got to the police car, he was crying and begging and saying that it had all been a mistake, but Sherry appeared and came over to me. She held up Basil's phone.

Basil was still sitting on the floor in his lion form, not moving.

"Basil got everything," Sherry said. "Shane's confession and everything...it's all recorded. We clearly have him attacking you, and, if I'm not mistaken, it sounds like he's confessing to a few other things, as well."

"Having me imprisoned," I murmured.

"Yes, that," Sherry nodded.

"I'll take that," Cosmo appeared and took the phone from Sherry. He looked from me to Basil and back again. There were still officers in the room, but somehow, Cosmo convinced everyone to leave so that I was alone with Basil. A moment later, it was just the two of us.

And then he was a man again.

He stood there in the center of the room, and tears streamed down his face.

"I thought I was going to lose you," he said.

I stared at him, not believing what was happening.

"I thought you were going to lose me, too," I finally said, and something about the way I blurted that out made him laugh. He shook his head and reached for me, tugging me into his arms.

"I'm so sorry, Melinda."

"I'm sorry, too."

"I shouldn't have leapt to conclusions."

"I should have been honest."

"I should have been patient."

"Well, I probably should have sucked your dick more."

He laughed and kissed me. It was like no time at all had passed. It was like we'd been together the entire time and everything was going to be okay.

"I can't resist offers like that, baby."

"I know," I hugged him again, just glad to be with him. I was so damn glad that this was all going to be over.

I'd been scared for so long that I hadn't really remembered what it felt like to be safe...to *not* be chased. If Sherry was right, and if there really was enough evidence to convict Shane for assault and possibly embezzlement, then maybe I was going to be okay after all. Maybe I was finally going to get to live my life.

When I looked up at Basil, his eyes flashed with heat and excitement and satisfaction. The two of us had had to fight for each other, but it had been worth it. We were still going to have to fight. This wasn't over, and it wasn't going to be easy or simple or pretty, but we were going to make it work.

"I'm getting the vibe you didn't tell people I disappeared," I whispered.

"I didn't."

"Does that mean you still want to fake marry me?" I whispered.

"Princess, I want to for-real marry you," he told me. "That is, if you'll have me."

Basil looked at me like he couldn't wait to find out what my answer was, but there was only one thing I could possibly say.

"Of course," I whispered. "For now and for always."

Epilogue

Basil
Three months later

THE TWO OF US SAT ON my front porch, watching the sunset. I was in my lion form, the way I almost always was on these evening hangouts. I was in my lion form and she was...

Well, she was perfect.

I still didn't quite understand how I'd managed to get so lucky with Melinda. How the hell had a lion like me managed to find a beautiful woman who would steal my heart? How had that happened?

Seriously, how?

It wasn't very long ago that I'd been floating through life, just existing, and now it was like my entire world was exploding in the very best way. Each night with Melinda was like the 4th of July. Watching the sunset with her was like watching fireworks, only better.

It was better because I didn't have to wait to do this. It wasn't some once-a-year sort of event.

It was always.

It was every day.

It was with her.

I looked over at Melinda. She was sitting beside me with one hand on my mane and the other in her lap. She smiled at me when she caught me staring.

"I love you, lion," she whispered, and I knew that it was true.

This thing between us had started as a sort of farce designed to save my company's image, but it had morphed into something incredible: something true. It had morphed into something that was going to change *everything*, and I couldn't wait to find out exactly where our love was going to lead us next.

THE END

The adventure continues in THE TIGER'S FAKE DATE: SHIFTERS OF RAWR COUNTY #3.

The Tiger's Fake Date

Sophie Stern

One date. One wedding. One enormous lie.

Ivy

If Susan wasn't so uptight, none of this would be a problem. It wouldn't. Not really. As it is, she's the biggest Bridezilla I've ever seen, which is why I'm stuck interviewing actors to play my boyfriend at her upcoming nuptials. The guy I choose is tall, hot as hell, and...nerdy. Like, ultra-nerdy. He plays video games and reads comics, and he's seen more anime than me, which is no easy task. Lincoln has a secret, though. It's something beyond the normal nerdiness. It's something that he doesn't want anyone to know about. I want to know about it, though. What is this guy hiding? And why do I have a feeling that it'll change everything?

Lincoln

When I started running my fake date service, I didn't expect to meet someone like Ivy. I didn't expect to want more than just a single date. I couldn't have possibly planned any of this. That's exactly what's happening, though. Just one date, and my inner-tiger lets me know that yeah, she's our mate. Unfortunately for me, she doesn't know I'm a tiger shifter, and she doesn't know I think she's my one true love. Is Ivy strong enough to handle the truth?

Am I?

The Tiger's Fake Date is book three in the SHIFTERS OF RAWR COUNTY series; however, it can be enjoyed as a standalone story. It features a snarky human heroine and a tiger who doesn't believe he's good enough for love. Expect spicy scenes and a happily-ever-after.

1

Ivy

Staring at my older sister, who was busy trying on wedding dresses, was basically the worst experience of my life. It wasn't so much that the weird peppermint smell at the bridal shop was overpowering or the fact that everyone who worked here wore these frowny expressions that made me wonder if they'd been left at the altar themselves, but the fact that Susan was the worst bride in the history of brides. She'd gone full-on bitch that morning, and I was still wondering if there was some chance I'd figure out a way to skip the wedding and still be able to stay a valued member of the family.

I was leaning towards "no," though.

"What do you think of this one?" A brown-eyed bridal attendant, who had the cutest freckles sprinkled on her nose, looked up at my sister. Susan was standing on this giant pedestal thing the brides were supposed to stand on. She was surrounded by mirrors. The woman helping her, Isabella, couldn't have been older than 25. Out of all of the attendants, Isabella was the only one that wasn't looking dour.

"What do I think?" Susan said. She pressed her lips together and I knew that whatever came next was going to be irritating as hell. "I think that I look like I gained twenty pounds since I walked into the shop." She gestured to her tummy. In Isabella's defense, my sister had recently gained weight. She looked good at any weight, so I didn't understand what the big deal was, yet Susan was desperate to hide her weight gain from anyone who looked at her.

Isabella's face fell. Okay, so maybe that was the reason the other bridal attendants all looked so pissy. If I had to deal with crabby brides all day, I might be fussy, too.

"That's not necessary, Susan," I said. "She's trying to get a feel for the style you want."

"Well, whatever style I want, it's not this."

"Good," I nodded. "Now we can go from there."

My sister's eyes narrowed. Awesome. Now she was going to come after me. She really made defending other people quite difficult, didn't she? Susan was definitely going to ask me whether or not I'd found a date for the wedding. She'd reiterate the fact that it was *vital* that I bring someone special with me.

"Oh, little sister," she started. Her voice had turned sickly sweet the way it always did. Of course, that was exactly where this conversation was going to go. "Tell me about your date for the wedding. I don't think I've met him yet."

"What makes you think it's a boy?" I asked, crossing my arms over my chest. Oh, she was driving me crazy.

"Girls, don't do this." That was Tameka, Susan's maid of honor. Tameka was Susan's best friend since forever, and luckily, she was able to keep Susan calm most of the time. It wasn't *too* terribly often that I had to deal with my sister's wrath personally. It was still more than I would have liked, but Tameka did a good job making sure that everything was okay. "Let's just stay focused on finding a dress."

"Great idea," Isabella said. She stepped forward. "If it's okay with you, let's get you out of this dress. We can find something in a different style that may highlight some of your other features, okay?"

"What is that supposed to mean?" Susan glared.

"It means she's going to find you a dress that shows off your tits instead of your stomach," I snapped. Tameka and Isabella visibly cringed. I just rolled my eyes, walked over to a chair, and dropped down into it. This was a nightmare that I couldn't escape, wasn't it? I wasn't even the one getting married, yet already I hated weddings.

Isabella stood there for a second, confused as to what to do. Luckily, another bridal associate came up and knew what to do. As the two of them distracted my sister, coaxing her, talking to her, I stared out of the window.

I had no idea what the hell I was supposed to do next.

THERE WAS A COFFEE shop just three doors down from the bridal store. My sister had dragged us all the way to Howlton in Rawr County, which was nearly an hour away from Wishton, where I lived. I'd made the mistake of saying that I'd just ride with her and Tameka. For some reason – and I couldn't *possibly* think of one – I'd accepted that offer. It had been a terrible decision.

Despite the fact that my sister refused to let us listen to music and instead insisted on talking the *entire* drive, I'd tried to keep up a good attitude. Now, though, I had a few minutes while she finished up at the bridal shop. Tameka was with her still, but I'd slipped out to grab a coffee for the drive back. I needed a little bit of a pick-me-up before we hopped back on the road.

I needed this.

Stopping in front of the little café, I looked up at the name. This coffee shop didn't even have a proper name, I realized. Usually, coffee shops had these sweet, catchy names that made you want to stop in. This one, however, just said COFFEE in big, bold letters. The shop itself was only one in a row of shops in the same building. This part of Howlton was really small and quaint. It definitely gave me retro-town vibes. I kept looking around waiting for a video game quest to start. It was *that* kind of place.

There were two large glass windows on either side of a glass door that had a little bell tied to it. Grabbing the door, I pulled it toward me as I walked inside. The bells announced my arrival.

Was it my imagination, or did every single person turn and look at me when I walked in? One person even looked like they were *sniffing*. What the hell? I sighed. Had I gotten sweaty when I was helping my sister? Had I? Like, I hadn't meant to, but sometimes you couldn't control whether you were sweaty or not.

I tried to ignore all of the people looking at me as I approached the counter to order a drink. Why was the counter so far at the back of the coffee place? Also, why was it just called COFFEE? Why didn't it have a real name?

When I got to the counter, a pink-haired woman with a nose ring greeted me. Like Isabella, her nose was dotted with freckles and her smile was bright.

"How can I help you today?"

I didn't have a lot of time before my sister inevitably showed up or started calling me, so I wouldn't order anything crazy or hard to make. Frappes were off the menu for me today.

"Hey, could I just get a..." I scanned the menu quickly. It was a little chilly outside, so maybe something hot would be a good idea. "Could I get a regular hot mocha, please?"

"Sure thing, love," the woman said. She told me the total and I handed her my card while I kept looking at the menu. They had so many different things and most of the drinks seemed to be animal-themed. While I had ordered a plain mocha, they also had tiger cappuccinos, lion's heart lattes, and even white fang mochas, which appeared to be white chocolate mochas with a fancier name.

After I finished paying, I moved to the pickup area and looked around while I waited for my drink. The shop, despite its simple name, was a cute little place. The counter was at the back of the coffee shop and there were ten tables scattered throughout the space. Along one side of the coffee shop, there were floor-to-ceiling bookshelves and they were all filled with paperbacks. I found myself drawn to that part of the space, so I walked over.

How had this tiny, small, middle-of-nowhere café managed to accumulate such a collection of books?

"They're all used," a friendly voice said from beside me. I glanced over to see a guy sitting close to the wall of books. He was sitting alone at a tiny round table that only had one chair. I noticed that the table beside him had three chairs. Had he ditched one? If I wanted to appear unfriendly and cold, that would be my first move, too, but this guy didn't seem either of those things.

"Used?"

"Yeah," he nodded. "It's a bring-a-book-leave-a-book kind of deal."

"Interesting," I looked up at the shelves. All of these books had been brought here by patrons? That was crazy to me. "Have you ever taken a book?"

"Everyone at COFFEE has taken a book."

"Is that really the name of this place?" I asked.

"Yeah, and every letter has a meaning."

"Really?"

"Yeah, it's something like Can't Outlast Fiery Fairies Eating Eggs or something like that."

"What does that even mean?"

"It means that if you don't drink enough caffeine, you're going to be weak."

"Weak?"

"Yeah," he nodded. He set down the book he was reading. "If you're going to go off fighting fairies, you need coffee."

I couldn't tell if he was joking. Was this a man who believed in fairies? Was this someone who was playing with me? Or was "fairies" a code word for something else? When he said "fairies," did he actually mean something like, personal life challenges? Was that what was happening?

"I suppose that's fair advice," I said. "I'm Ivy, by the way."

SHIFTERS OF RAWR COUNTY: BOOKS 1-3   383

"Lincoln," he smiled. He was handsome, wasn't he? He was also the only one in this place who hadn't stared me down when I'd walked in. In fact, for some reason, Lincoln had been so very still while reading his book that I hadn't even really noticed him. It was like he'd become one with the wall of books.

"Do you come here a lot?" I asked.

"Is that a line?" Lincoln's eyes twinkled. Fuck. If I wasn't careful, I was going to get distracted. That was one of my biggest problems, according to Susan: I was easily distracted. I was easily caught up in the random aspects of life that were intriguing to me.

"What? No. I don't want to date you."

Shit, that came out wrong. I *so* didn't mean to say that out loud. Besides, I would definitely date this guy. He was *exactly* the kind of guy I would date. In fact, I'd date the hell out of him. Just from looking at him, it was fair to say there wasn't a single thing I didn't like about him. There wasn't a single thing that turned me off about him.

The fact that he was hanging out at a local coffee shop *reading* was even better.

"That's not what I meant," I quickly backtracked. "I just mean-"

"Mocha!" The barista was staring at me, holding out my drink. Apparently, she'd been trying to get my attention for a few moments. Yikes. I turned and hurried over, mumbling an embarrassed apology that earned me a frown, and then I went back to Mr. Book.

"Mocha, huh? Good choice, even if you don't want to date me."

"I like mochas."

"I'm more of an iced coffee sort of person myself," he smiled, gesturing toward his empty glass.

"Guess it was good," I said.

"I've been here for a little while," the guy smiled. He leaned back in his seat and crossed his arms over his chest. I tried not to stare at his muscles. His shirt was probably once a normal-fitting shirt, but this dude definitely worked out. The shirt was stretching over his muscles, like it practically was straining to break free from his body. "You aren't from around here, are you?"

"I'm from Wishton," I admitted. It was a bigger city and it was in a different county. "To be honest, I don't come to Rawr County very often."

"No? Why's that? Don't like all of the scenery?"

He was joking because Rawr County was like half open fields and half cities with a dash of little ranching towns mixed in. There were forests and hills and wilderness, and because we were in Colorado, there were also mountains. It was kind of an incredible county, actually.

"I just live a bit far," I admitted.

"But today you decided to venture out and have yourself a bit of fun. Is that it?"

"Something like that," I agreed. I wasn't really ready to tell this stranger that my sister was a crazy bitch or that I'd gotten roped into this journey. This guy just wanted to enjoy his coffee. He didn't need to hear anything else crazy.

"Well, what do you think so far?"

"It's a nice town."

"Lots of shops," he told me. He seemed fully invested in our conversation now, which both delighted and terrified me. I was suddenly worried about seeming boring or uninteresting: two things that rarely bothered me otherwise.

"Yeah, I was just over at the bridal shop," I blurted out. His eyes instantly darted to my hands. Nope. It wasn't me. "I'm not engaged," I told him quickly. Was it my imagination or did he seem a little relieved about that?

"What were you doing at a bridal shop? Just window shopping?" Lincoln winked at me. Oh, shit. I was in so much trouble. I was barely five minutes into the conversation and I was already smitten. I bet that wink got this dude whatever he wanted.

If he winked at me again, I would *definitely* give him whatever he wanted.

"Something like that," I told him. My phone vibrated in my pocket. That would be Susan. She was probably done and ready to get going. Either that or she was on the warpath and Tameka was messaging me to come find them. "What about you?" I ignored the vibrations. "Are you a big shopper?"

"I'm honestly more of a reader," he laughed. "But I spend a lot of time here, so I'm familiar with the shops. You should check out the boutique off 3rd Street if you haven't already."

"Is it a wedding shop?" I asked.

"The best one in town," he agreed. "It's not on many websites, so it's kind of this undiscovered little treasure."

That *was* helpful.

"Thank you," I told him. "I appreciate that."

"Cool," he smiled. "Glad to be of service."

Just then, I glanced up to see my sister peering into the front window of the coffee shop. She had her nose pressed against the glass and her hands were on either side of her eyes so she could get a better view into the space.

"Friend of yours?" Lincoln asked, arching an eyebrow.

"Something like that," I sighed. "I have to go. Thanks, though." For everything. Damn, this guy was cute. I wished I could stay and hang out more. I wanted to ask for his number or invite him on a proper coffee date. That was definitely the kind of thing *I* wanted to do.

But it just wasn't meant to be.

"Anytime," Lincoln grinned.

I nodded awkwardly, holding my coffee so tightly I was certain the lid would pop off if I wasn't careful. Then I headed for the door and pushed it open.

"Finally!" Susan threw up her hands in irritation. "What were you doing?" She eyed my mocha and glared. "A coffee shop? Really?"

"Actually, I was asking for information about other bridal shops," I lied smoothly. "Someone recommended a boutique off 3rd Street."

Tameka looked surprised.

"Someone suggested that place?"

"Have you heard of it?" I asked her. "I didn't get the name, just that it's a good place to find a dress."

"It's worth checking out," Tameka said. "I stopped there once before with friends. Susan originally turned down the idea of going there. Said she wanted to go to this shop in particular," Tameka pointed to the shop we'd spent the morning at.

"I did," Susan agreed. "But only because the prices were supposed to be good. This other place is probably more expensive."

"If you wanted cheap, you should have been more flexible," Tameka told her firmly. It wasn't the first time she'd had to remind my sister that money was what bought you your dreams. If you wanted to be cheap, that was okay, but you had to accept that you couldn't get everything you wanted.

"Oh, whatever," Susan glared. She turned back to me. "Fine. We'll check out the place you suggested. If it sucks, though..."

"Then we'll keep trying," I said, trying to keep my voice cheery. "We have plenty of time, right?"

"The wedding is in three months," Susan reminded me for the millionth time. "It's not exactly a long way away."

And whose fault was that, exactly?

I didn't say that. I didn't say anything. I just closed my mouth and nodded.

"You're totally right. Let's get going."

It was going to be a damn long day.

2

Lincoln
Two Months Later

"WHAT AM I LOOKING AT?" I asked Athena. She'd handed me some small, weird-looking ball. It was green, but it also looked kind of like it was covered in sprinkles. "And is this edible?"

"It's edible," she told me. She grinned. "I made it myself."

"You made an edible ball yourself?"

"It's for the office party this weekend," she rolled her eyes.

"Office party?"

"Don't tell me you forgot," she laughed. "You planned it."

"I haven't forgotten. I just haven't thought of it as a party," I admitted. As one of the attorneys at Dragon's Law, I was definitely both expected to be at the party *and* required to be there. Cosmo was a pretty decent boss, for the most part, but he also had high expectations for his team. Lawyers who didn't show up to client appreciation parties were frowned on.

"Really? How do you think of it, then?"

"An obligation," I admitted. I wasn't proud of that. I probably should have been more excited about the weekend event, but it was always kind of a struggle to get through these things. The main idea of the party was to show our clients how much we appreciated them. In my opinion, it was a huge schmoozefest where we spent the money our clients had given us to show them we appreciated them. I'd once suggested to Cosmo that we simply charge less. That hadn't been a fun talk.

"It won't be that bad," Athena said. "Come on. It won't be that bad. I'll be there."

"I'm sure you will," I laughed. "As if Cosmo would let you miss this thing." Anyone with two eyes could see that he was smitten with the receptionist. She was kind, funny, and silly in all of the best ways, and it was easy to see what the dragon-shifter attorney saw in her.

Athena, however, was clueless.

"What's that mean?"

"I think you know what it means."

"It sounds like you think he'll notice if I'm not there," she pointed out.

"That's exactly what I'm saying."

"I just don't think that's true, Lincoln." Athena frowned and leaned back in her chair. She spun around slowly in a circle, taking her time. Then she looked back at me. "We both know he won't miss me."

"Don't be silly," I laughed. "He's crazy about you."

"You're wrong," she said. She shrugged, though. The phone rang and she took a deep breath before she reached for it. "Take more of the balls with you," she gestured toward the plate on her desk. Then she smiled as she answered the call. "Dragon Law, how may I assist you?"

I grabbed two more of her candied balls and popped them in my mouth as I walked down the hall to my office. Pushing the door open, I stepped inside to the familiar scent of vanilla. I was kind of an incense slut so I burned it almost constantly when I was at work. As long as the door was closed, Cosmo didn't bitch at me, and most of my clients were into scents as much as I was and they appreciated it.

I couldn't really pinpoint exactly when my sensitivities to smells had started, but as a tiger shifter, it was often overwhelming for me to scent all of the different people who happened to live and be in Rawr County. Sometimes there were so many different smells that I felt like I was going crazy.

While all shifters could smell things, not everyone's scenting ability was as strong as mine.

For me, it was a little bit overwhelming.

A little bit stressful.

A little bit agitating.

So every day when I got to work, I lit incense. When I was off work and headed to my part-time job, the job I did just for fun, I would be overwhelmed with all of the different scents and sounds and sights. Working at weddings tended to do that. Here, though, this was my safe place. This was a place where I could just *be*, and so I did whatever it took to make sure that I was as comfortable as possible when I was meeting with clients and working to help them.

Sitting down, I opened my laptop and checked my schedule for the day. I had a couple of meetings, but they were all very straightforward appointments. Two of my clients needed wills drawn up. One of them wanted to talk about options for legally dealing with a neighbor. There was one person who had questions about setting up a power of attorney. I could deal with all of that.

Easy peasy.

Then tonight, that was where the fun started. I had a meeting with a potential client. Cosmo may or may not have been aware of the fact that I moonlighted as a boyfriend for hire. A lot of people didn't like dealing with familial pressure to have a boyfriend, so they'd hire me to help them out.

And I did.

I helped them.

I'd done everything from attending a college graduation as someone's fiancé (we staged a breakup at the after party), going to weddings as a date (the brides never had a clue), and even attending a grandmother's birthday party (she immediately knew the date wasn't real, but kept it together for her grandkid).

Tonight's client was a woman who needed a date to her older sister's wedding. The wedding itself was a month away, but if we were going to pull this off, we'd probably need to make a few family appearances together. I sent off a text to the woman I was meeting confirming the details of our first appointment, and then I settled into my chair, reached for a bottle of water I kept on my desk, and got ready to start the day.

LION'S STEAKHOUSE WAS one of the best places in Rawr County to get a decent meal. Despite its name, it was an affordable restaurant where you didn't have to spend *all* of your money just to be able to enjoy something decent and tasty. In fact, most of the time I left spending less than I would have spent to cook all of the same food myself at home.

While I generally met with clients at a coffee shop for the first time, this was going to be a longer commitment than just a single date. I wanted to get to know my client in a slightly formal environment so I could really get a feeling for how she acted in public.

I was choosy about my clients. The rent-a-boyfriend thing was something I charged for, but I did it for fun. It wasn't my main source of income, so I could afford to be as picky as I wanted to be. As an attorney, it was important to me that I chose clients who lived out of town, who could be discreet, and who wouldn't cause a huge fuss.

This was a business transaction.

Nothing more.

Nothing less.

I wasn't a sex worker. I was a freelance friend. In fact, that was what my business card said: Mr. Lincoln: Freelance Friend.

It was stupid.

I never gave out my real name.

Ever.

Clients called me Lincoln, but they all thought it was my last name. They could call me whatever first name they wanted to. Most of the time, by the point someone got to me, they'd already made up a fake date or fake relationship in their head. They'd already told their family that I was called Mark or Phillip or Sam. I just went with it. My job wasn't to make this the most perfect, romantic experience in the world.

My job was to make sure that no matter what happened, the people around us really felt that the person and I were dating. I wanted them to have a good experience, after all. The goal was for them to basically trick their loved ones, which felt a little bad, but which also saddened me.

Why couldn't people just be free to be who they were?

My parents had never pressured me one way or another. Both my mom and dad lived close to me in Rawr County. I met up with them about once a week for lunch or dinner and the three of us would hang out and have a good time. They never asked me when I was getting married. They never asked whether I'd found someone to date. They just asked how I was. They wanted to know about me – not who they imagined I *should* be.

I appreciated that.

Now, as I waited outside of the steakhouse for my date, I wondered whether this was going to be a positive meeting or a negative one. I only took word-of-mouth referrals. If someone had my contact information, it was because they'd been given the information from a former client or someone I trusted.

That was it.

My phone vibrated. I glanced down to see a text from one of my old buddies. Basil was sending a message to me, Justin, and our mutual friend, Fletcher.

"Dinner on Saturday? 7 @ The Polar Bear's Banquet Hall?"

I stared at the message. Justin replied right away that he'd be there. Fletcher did, too. Seriously, were these guys all just staring at their phones waiting for an invitation to go have fun?

"Be there." I texted back my reply. I hadn't seen any of the guys in some time. It might be fun to get together and catch up. Then again, if Basil was inviting us out, it could mean trouble. I had no idea what the invitation was for. The Polar Bear's Banquet Hall was, as its name implied, a formal banquet hall. There were parties there almost every weekend, though, so I was pretty certain it was going to be some sort of theme party.

Sure enough, a second later, Basil texted again.

"Cool! It's a costume party. Dress up like an animal – CAN'T be one that you are!!!!"

I stared.

Okay, so tiger stripes were out. I'd probably end up going as a polar bear like Justin was or a lion like Basil was. It would be fun to mess with my friends a little bit. They were easily teased, so it wouldn't be a big deal. We'd all just have a good laugh about it.

My phone buzzed again.

"I'm here! Are you inside?"

It was her. The woman I was meeting hadn't given me a first name at all. I'd asked her what I could call her, and she said to call her Miss X. I said that there was no way I was doing that. This wasn't a spy movie. Besides, I'd told her my real name.

Sort-of.

Okay, I hadn't told her my real name.

Still, I'd have to know who she was eventually.

"I'm by the front doors," I told her. I was sitting on a little bench outside of the restaurant. It was a cool night, so I was wearing a jacket. I glanced around the parking lot. A few older people were heading toward the restaurant. That was fine. I was in my early 30s. There was nothing wrong with me taking an older woman to a wedding as her fake date. It would definitely give her family members something to talk about.

None of the women walking past me even noticed me, though. A group of three women headed inside, followed by another woman who was on her own. There was a couple next.

Shit.

Should I have made reservations?

Suddenly, the entire place seemed to be swelling with popularity. Usually, I was right on top of making reservations and ensuring that we were able to do anything and everything we needed to, but I'd been distracted lately.

I'd *let* myself become distracted.

"Hello."

She was there.

She'd sneaked up next to me and I hadn't even noticed. What the hell was wrong with me? Turning, my jaw dropped.

"Ivy?"

"Lincoln?" Ivy cocked her head. She was obviously surprised. "Are you..." She started laughing. "You're *the* Lincoln. I should have guessed. I didn't. Obviously. I would have said something if I'd figured. It's just that when I met you, it was like your first name was Lincoln and then now, booking this whole thing, I thought that your *last* name was Lincoln, so I didn't really get that you were the same person."

"I'm the same person," I smiled.

"Shall we go inside?"

"Let's do it."

I opened the door and allowed her to walk first, but my inner-tiger was growling at me that this was a bad idea. It was a bad idea to agree to fake-date a woman I was actually attracted to. It was going to get me in trouble, but I ignored my tiger. I ignored him. That fucker could suck it up.

She was too perfect to turn down.

3

Ivy

The restaurant he'd chosen was really nice. It was fancier than most of the places I was used to eating. Actually, this seemed like the kind of place my sister would choose to eat. She was always trying to go to the most expensive places for food. I didn't really understand why.

Was she trying to prove something?

Was she trying to make it clear that she had high expectations when it came to her relationships?

I had no clue, and to be honest, I didn't really *want* to have a clue. The only thing I *wanted* was to survive the next month of meetings. The wedding itself was going to suck – no way around that. Still, having someone on my side, on my team, was going to make a big difference.

At least, that was the idea.

Once we were seated, I looked over at Lincoln. Fuck, this guy was hot. He was so far out of my league that it was crazy, and that bothered me only because it meant my sister was going to comment on that. I could already picture her asking Lincoln why he would choose to be with someone who was a little curvier, a little plumper. She wouldn't say it like that, though. She wouldn't be so bold.

She'd be passive aggressive instead.

"Oh, you like her? Well, I guess you don't only have to date pretty girls..."

"You're dating someone like my sister? I know she has a nice personality, but there's more to finding someone than that..."

My weight didn't bother me. It bothered Susan, though, and it *definitely* bothered our mother. As a pair, Mom and Susan were both obsessed with looks, which was one of the reasons I was glad it was a short engagement. If there had been more time before the wedding, the two of them definitely would have tried to put me on a diet, and then it would have been this huge, all-out brawl.

As it was, they hadn't brought up my weight very much, which was quite a relief.

"You look deep in thought," Lincoln said.

"I was thinking about what my mom is going to say when she sees you."

He raised an eyebrow. "Because I'm Black?"

"Because you're hot," I corrected him. "My future brother-in-law is from Japan. My mom doesn't care if my sister and I date people who don't look like us. She cares if we date people who are hotter than us."

"Meaning?"

"Meaning you're super hot," I repeated. "In case you didn't know that."

He laughed. He threw his head back as he did. It was a funny gesture. He looked happy. Content. Relaxed. That was the thing that was so strange about Lincoln – he was hot, but he didn't seem tense.

"Thank you. I feel the same way about you," he said. He seemed a little surprised that he said that. "I'm sorry," he said quickly. "I shouldn't have said that."

"Why not?"

"Because we aren't dating for real," he said. "So I'm not supposed to be saying things like that to you."

"Ah," I nodded. I understood. It was business. Everything between us was business. This entire experience was simply because I was paying him.

Nothing more.

Nothing less.

Besides, if this was his full-time job, then he probably had multiple people he was "dating" right now. There were probably a lot of people he saw himself with. Lots. Maybe he even slept with all of them. Was he going to want to sleep with me?

I looked up at Lincoln sharply. To avoid saying anything stupid or weird, I grabbed the menu in front of me a little too quickly and held it up in front of my face.

"What's good here?" I asked quickly, desperate to change the subject. Oh, I *so* couldn't be falling for this dude. I couldn't do it. I wasn't supposed to do it.

"Everything's good," he practically purred the words. Why was he like that? Why was he doing this to me?

"Like the burgers?"

"There are burgers, salads, steak, and even some seafood. Hey, Ivy, are you okay? We can skip eating if you're not feeling it and just get a couple of drinks. No hard feelings if you don't think we'll be a good match."

No hard feelings?

Maybe not on his part. On my part, there would *definitely* be hard feelings. Definitely.

I liked this guy. I'd liked him when I saw him the first time and I liked him now. I liked the way he looked and the way he spoke. I liked the way he winked when he talked sometimes, like he was sharing a secret or a special story.

I liked so many things.

There was *zero chance* I was going to let this go.

Zero.

"No, I eat food."

"Excuse me?"

"I...food...I eat it," I tried to speak. Why couldn't I speak? "I would like to eat food...with you..." I finally managed to string together a coherent sentence.

Lincoln just laughed and nodded.

"Sure," he said. "Sure."

———— ⟨∾⟩ ————

ONCE WE'D ORDERED AND our appetizer arrived, it was time to start working out the details. Lincoln had already shared his rates with me. Basically, he offered a couple of "packages." You could rent him for one night for a set number of hours, you could rent him for multiple dates, or you could rent him "as needed" and basically keep him on retainer. That sounded far too expensive for me, so I pulled out my calendar and calculated how many dates I'd need to have with him.

"Four dates," I said.

"Four?"

"My sister's bridal shower. I know that usually, guys don't go to those things, but Susan wants everyone to bring their dates. I'm pretty sure she thinks she'll get better presents if it's a couples thing. Then there's the bachelorette party. I need you to make an appearance that night, but of course, you don't have to stay for the whole thing. Then there's the rehearsal dinner and the wedding itself, plus the reception."

"What about the day after?"

"The day after?"

"Some couples like to have a get-together the morning after the wedding so they can open all of their gifts."

"Okay, five dates," I said.

Lincoln wrote down a number and passed it to me on a napkin. I looked up at him, shocked.

"Seriously?"

"I know it's high," he said. "This is actually less than I normally charge, but a lot of work goes into being a date for someone. I have to make sure I know a lot about you – enough to make our relationship convincing. Then there's the actual event. If I have to buy a gift, that makes the cost go up. Also, sometimes I need to buy new clothes for a celebration. That plays a role, too."

"Oh, it's not that," I said. "Actually, I was thinking that your prices seem low."

"Low?"

"Yeah, if I'd known this was all it took to get a date, I would have done this years ago." I'd spent far too many holidays on my own when I could have brought a date and not been pestered by family members. I really was dumb, wasn't I?

"You're the first client I've heard say that," he admitted.

"Well, you come highly recommended."

"By whom?"

"My friend Kapono," I told him. Instantly, Lincoln's eyes lit up.

"You know Kapono?"

"Yeah, we go way back," I told him. "The two of us have been friends for about a million years. He never told me that he hired you, though."

"Yeah, for a wedding about a year ago. I want to say it was his cousin getting married."

"I'm surprised he didn't hire a woman to be his date," I said. "Some people still aren't very open-minded when it comes to dating a guy, you know."

"I'm well aware."

"How'd his family take it?" I asked.

"They were cordial," Lincoln said. "It was a straightforward experience."

"Did he earn a goodnight kiss?"

Lincoln laughed. "As a general rule, I don't kiss my clients. If something happens where I need to in order to save face, then I'll make it happen."

"But it's not something you generally do?"

"Correct," he agreed.

I wasn't sure if it was okay that I felt a little sad about that. It wasn't that I had been hoping Lincoln would kiss me on one of our dates...well, no, that was exactly it. I was hoping he'd kiss me on one of our dates.

The waiter walked by our table and paused, glancing at the untouched pile of onion rings, chili-cheese fries, and buffalo wings in front of us.

"Is everything okay?"

"It's perfect," I smiled, looking over at him. "We just got to talking and didn't have a chance to try anything yet." I reached for an onion ring and took a bite. Then I nodded. "Absolutely perfect," I said. "Thank you so much."

The waiter laughed and nodded before moving to check on another table. When I turned back to Lincoln, he was looking at me curiously.

"What?" I asked him.

"That was very polite of you."

"Um, thanks?"

"That was like, really polite," he told me.

"Okay?"

"Most people aren't very polite to servers."

"Well, I'm a bartender," I told him. "Kind of comes with the territory."

"You are?"

"Yep. Do you need to write that down?" I winked.

"Probably," he agreed. "Tonight is just about us getting to know each other to see if we'll be a good fit and if we'd like to go through with everything."

"How am I doing so far?" I asked him.

"I'd say pretty good."

I laughed.

Yeah, okay. I'd agree with that. Even though this wasn't a "real" date, it was something I was really enjoying. Talking to Lincoln was easy. Hanging out with him was simple. It felt less like being on a date and more like talking to an old friend. It was like the two of us went way back, like there was this friendly, comfortable air between us.

I liked it, and I liked him, and I knew that I needed to be careful.

Lincoln didn't kiss his dates. He didn't fall for them.

I'd do well to remember that.

4

Lincoln

When Saturday night rolled around, I found myself pulling into the banquet hall parking lot dressed an awful lot like a cheetah. In the end, I hadn't gone for anything too crazy like dressing like a friend's shifter counterpart. I also hadn't spent a lot of time or money on my costume. I'd gotten a cheetah-print onesie, painted my face, and driven over with a pocket full of cash.

I wasn't planning on leaving sober.

Parking my car, I made sure to lock it. If I did end up drinking too much, I'd take a rideshare to a local hotel. I didn't live in Wishville, where the event was taking place. I'd originally planned to get a ride *to* the event. Someone had set up a party bus thing, but I hadn't booked my ride early enough and there had been something of a scheduling nightmare with the party planning. Driving myself to Wishville had been my second option, but it worked. Now I was switching back and forth between not drinking at all and leaving early or getting completely sloshed and just passing out in my car.

I really didn't want to be there.

The parking lot was basically full when I arrived. I had no idea what this party was celebrating, but it looked like it was going to be a banger. Heading up to the front door, I pulled it open and stepped inside. I looked around to see animal upon animal upon animal. I was a little surprised that nobody had actually shifted and just come to the party in their animal form. Not that it would have been allowed, according to my friend's policy, but it would have been funny to see all the same.

A lion and a tiger and a bear hanging out among people *dressed* like lions and tigers and bears? We were all idiots for not making *that* happen.

Now, as I walked around looking at all of the different animals, I couldn't help but wonder if coming out tonight was a mistake. It had been a long day. It had been a long week, actually. Hell, if I was being honest, it had been a long year. Despite the fact that the entrance to the building was pretty interesting, I managed to find the actual room where the party was happening. Looking around, I tried to stay focused. I tried to stay in the moment.

That was harder than it sounded.

The next day was Sunday, and I was going to be meeting up with Ivy and taking her to Susan's bridal shower. According to Ivy, the entire wedding had been rushed. Most of the time, I would have assumed that the bride was pregnant and wanted to rush into getting married, but Ivy didn't seem to think that was the case. From what she'd described to me, her sister had been offered a chance to hold the wedding at a desirable location, so she'd jumped at the chance. When you had a very specific idea of where you wanted your wedding to be held, you had to be flexible with dates.

Apparently, you had to be just a few months flexible.

Sheesh.

And now, even though I was supposed to be focusing on hanging out with the guys, I was busy staring into space and thinking about Ivy.

Awesome.

There was something really cool about her. She was the type of girl I could crawl into bed with and just make wild, passionate love to, yeah, but then the two of us could hang out playing video games and reading comics. Ivy was chill. Laid back. She didn't seem like she let things get her down the way most people would.

"Hey," a friendly hand clapped on my shoulder. I turned to see Justin standing there. His makeup was on point and his costume made him look less like a bear shifter and more like a tiger. He grinned and held his drink up. Okay, so Justin was having some fun tonight.

"Hey Justin, what's up? Nice costume." Why hadn't I dressed like a tiger? Really, I was just kicking myself for not being brave enough to seriously show up as my shifter self. That would have been so much cooler than this dumb outfit.

"Thanks," he shrugged. "My wife thought it was cute."

"Your wife?"

"Oh yeah, got married a little while ago. She's running around here somewhere," he gestured vaguely. "She's dressed like a tiger, too. Matching. Had to do it. What about you?"

What about me?

Well, I was a miserable attorney who moonlighted as a wedding date so I could avoid real relationships and getting my heart broken.

That wasn't what he was asking, though.

"Not married."

"No? Not yet?"

"Nope." I definitely should have made Ivy come to this with me. It would be nice to have someone on my team who understood what I was going through and what it was like to be me. Then again, I was *her* fake date. Not the other way around.

"Well, don't worry about it."

"I'm not worried."

"I'm sure you'll find someone when you least expect it."

I cringed. That was one of my least favorite pieces of dating advice. I'd heard a *lot* of advice, but stuff like that never failed to piss me off. It wasn't Justin's fault. He'd probably heard that same advice parroted over and over, but...

"Justin, I'm not looking for someone."

The bear shifter shrugged like it didn't better. He sipped his drink. "Well, if you ever change your mind..." Justin's voice trailed off.

"I won't."

"Well, if you do..."

"I won't."

It was a lie. I would change my mind. Everyone did. That happened all the time. To everyone. Justin cocked his head, looking at me, and then he grinned like he'd just realized something silly, something he should have known already.

"Sorry, I didn't know you were seeing someone already."

"I'm not."

Ivy and I weren't together. Absolutely not. She was my client: nothing more. Not that I didn't *want* more. Not that I wouldn't have accepted more.

If Ivy walked up to me right then and asked me out, I'd instantly say yes. In fact, the day I'd met her at the coffee shop, I almost had. Something had held me back, though...something I couldn't quite put my finger on. I just hadn't felt like I was ready, maybe. Either that or I just didn't know whether it was a good idea. She had a lot on her plate with her family being crazy, and me?

Well, I was just some nerd who definitely didn't deserve her.

"Sure," Justin laughed. "Anyway, I notice that your hands are empty. Let's get you a drink, shall we?"

"Of course." I wasn't going to say no to a drink. Not after that conversation. It was starting to look more and more like I'd actually be Ubering to a hotel instead of driving home. That was fine.

As the two of us made our way through the crowd, we passed lions and tigers and a couple of rabbits. There was even someone dressed up like a sexy cat. It was kind of crazy. "What's this event for, anyway?" I asked him.

"Hmm?"

"What's the event for?"

"Oh, the wolf pack is having a thing," he said.

"The wolf pack?"

"Yeah, the Lone Ridge Pack. You've heard of them, right?"

I hadn't. I knew there were wolves in Rawr County, but I didn't realize there was a whole wolf pack. Tiger shifters didn't really run around in packs. We sort of just spent time with our own families. Wolves were different, though. There was this entire hierarchy that went with being a wolf.

"No, I don't know much about them," I admitted.

"Well, most of the people here tonight are wolves. Basil's friends with a few of them. They invited him and he wanted to make sure he wasn't the only non-wolf here, I guess." Justin rolled his eyes like it was the dumbest thing he'd ever heard.

"So, what are they celebrating?"

"The Alpha is going to retire soon," Justin filled me in. We reached the bar. He looked over at me and smiled. "And he's got to choose a new one. This is just one of many celebrations the pack is holding to finalize the transition of power."

"Interesting," I murmured, looking around. The room was packed. It was body-to-body with people dancing, laughing, talking, and drinking. The music was loud and the costumes were wonderful. I noticed that there were a few people sitting on a stage at one end of the banquet hall. That must have been the current Alpha and his family. The people on the stage were watching everything that was happening in the room. Their eyes never left the group. They just looked from person to person to person.

"They're watching everyone," Justin rolled his eyes. He seemed kind of unbothered by this. Personally, I found it to be a little bit creepy.

"Why?"

"It's their party. Wolves don't like strangers. Somebody invited a ton of non-wolves to the event and they don't know who it was."

"Someone besides Basil?"

"Yeah," Justin nodded. "Maybe it was Basil. I mean, he invited you and me. There are like two dozen non-wolves, though. I don't think Basil would have gone that far. I talked to Daphne before the party really got going. Apparently, the Alpha is super pissed."

"Sounds a little scary." Wolves often were. "Who's Daphne?"

"Uh, her," Justin scoured the room for a second before pointing to a woman wearing a tight black dress with a kitty-cat mask. She looked less like a shifter and more like someone who had dressed up for Halloween. "She wants to be Alpha."

"Think it's going to happen for her?"

"No clue," he shrugged. "But I wish her well."

HOURS INTO THE PARTY, I was drunk, Basil was drunk, Fletcher was drunk, and Justin was drunk. So was Mrs. Basil and Mrs. Justin. Fletcher didn't have a wife, but if he did, she'd definitely be drunk, too. There was just something relaxing about letting loose and letting my worries fade away behind the polar bear shots we were doing.

Our little group had settled at a table in one of the corners where we were munching on popcorn and cookies. In addition to polar bear shots, we were drinking purple cocktails. I had no idea what was in them. All I knew was that they were the best drinks I'd ever had in my life. I'd definitely have to order these again in the future.

"Think they've chosen a new Alpha?" I asked, looking toward the stage. The Alpha and his family had never moved. The entire night, they'd just stayed where they were while everyone else partied. It was really weird. They'd never made any sort of motion to move from the stage. As far as I knew, they hadn't even eaten anything. There was plenty of food, too. In addition to the usual party fare of sandwiches and crackers, there were burgers and hot wings and even trays of French fries. It was a bit much, but I wasn't going to complain.

"It's not that simple," Basil explained.

"It's a process," Fletcher agreed. "And it's something that takes a long time. The Alpha has to lead the pack and take care of everyone. It's a huge responsibility."

"You know a lot about the pack," I pointed out. As far as I could tell, Fletcher wasn't a wolf shifter. I couldn't tell what he was, though, and it was pretty rude to ask. I could ask Basil or Justin on the sly later. Maybe he was a wolf and I just wasn't paying careful enough attention. I didn't think so, though.

"I've spent a lot of time with them," he admitted, but then he left it at that. Whatever. I wouldn't pry. If he didn't want to share his deep, dark secrets over drinks, then who was I to judge?

"Let's talk about you," Justin's wife smiled at me. Rebecca was really nice. There wasn't really another way to describe her. She was just...nice. Friendly, smiley, and outgoing. I could see why Justin liked her. "Justin says you have a girlfriend. Is she your mate?"

Wow.

Okay, so I really hadn't seen the conversation getting *that* serious *that* fast. A lot of people believed in mates. A lot of people didn't. The idea was that once a shifter found the person they were supposed to be with, they were basically unhappy until they were together. It was obsessive and it was fast, but it was also this beautiful thing. Unfortunately for me, I didn't think I had a mate out there. If I did, I'd want it to be someone like Ivy, but that was just a dream, and I was far too buzzed to be able to have a conversation like this with a stranger.

"Seriously, dude?" I glared at Justin, who was chuckling.

"Sorry," he held up his hands. "She's human. She only recently learned about the mates thing. She's smitten by the entire experience."

"It's very romantic," she said, nodding dreamily.

Rolling my eyes, I managed to get to my feet. "Something like that," I said. Romantic my ass. "I'm going to take off." Everything was spinning, just a little bit. I'd stood up too quickly. Still, I'd been drinking water and snacking between alcoholic beverages. I'd sober up soon and then I could figure out what I was going to do.

"No, don't go," Rebecca and Justin said at the same time.

Justin batted his eyes playfully at me. "We were just getting started. We don't have to talk about mates anymore," he promised. Something told me that Rebecca wouldn't be able to keep that promise, though.

"It's late. I've got a thing tomorrow. Work thing."

"A work thing?" Rebecca asked. "Aren't you a lawyer?"

"He moonlights as a wedding date," Basil informed her. Holding up his glass to me, he winked. "Go get 'em, tiger."

"Yeah," I nodded. I gave everyone a wave and turned to leave. I took one last glance at the Alpha family sitting up on the stage. They all stared at me as I slinked through the crowd and toward the door. Awesome. What a bunch of weirdos. I wished them all the best, but I also wished they wouldn't stare at people. Maybe wolves were better at dealing with that sort of thing, but as a tiger shifter, I kind of just wanted to be able to peacefully leave a party without being leered at.

Then again, it did sort of sound like we weren't actually supposed to be invited. If there were a lot of non-wolves at the party and they hadn't planned for that, I could see why they'd be suspicious. As a tiger shifter, I could generally scent what type of shifter other people happened to be. Wolves were probably the same way. Aside from just differing scents, shifters had some other things that made us different. Some of us were tall and lanky and slinked around because we were cats. Others were clumsy because they were bear shifters. Then there were the bird shifters who were...well, they were really in a category all their own.

Once I made it outside of the party, I leaned against the building and closed my eyes. What was I supposed to do now? I'd gotten drunk, but I was thinking about Ivy. I was wishing that she was here with me. Damn, she was fun.

"Long night?"

I turned to see the woman Justin had pointed out earlier. It was the kitty-cat wolf who wanted to be Alpha. I could see it. Even in the moonlight, she looked fierce. Maybe it was *especially* in the moonlight, she looked fierce. Daphne seemed determined. Strong. Yeah, she'd probably make a good Alpha. It didn't look like she was scared of very much.

"Daphne, right?"

"The one and only," she nodded. She, too, was leaning against the building. She wasn't smoking. I wasn't sure what she was doing outside. Maybe she was hiding from the party, from the chaos. Someone vying for the position of Alpha wasn't going to be leaving the party while it was still going. She wasn't going to be sneaking away like I was.

"What are you doing out here? Aren't you supposed to be like, competing for Alpha?" I asked her, cocking my head. Shoving my hands into my pockets, I closed my eyes for just a moment. I needed to get out of here. I wanted to call Ivy. What was she doing tonight? Was she sleeping? Was she thinking of me? Waiting until tomorrow to see her was going to kill me. Opening my eyes again, I saw Daphne staring at me.

"You aren't a wolf," she eyed me suspiciously. "What makes you think I'm competing for Alpha? That's wolf business."

"I have nosy friends," I explained, hoping that would satisfy her. It wasn't a lie by any means. Justin and Basil were both fantastic, but they were nosy bastards. Most shifters were. Shifters were like little retired ladies who always knew what was going on with every house on the street. They watched people carefully. They knew what everyone was up to.

"I guess that makes sense," Daphne sighed. "I have some of those, too. You're here with Fletcher, right?" Her eye twitched just a little when she said that. Weird. Did she like Fletcher? Did she hate him? She definitely had some sort of strong feelings about him if her eye was going to get all twitchy.

"The one and only." While I wasn't Fletcher's +1 by any means, the two of us were amicable. Not like Fletcher and Daphne, I was guessing. The nosy part of me reared up, wanting to ask more. Was he her mate? Was that the situation? He wasn't a wolf, though. Was he? I didn't think so.

"He's a good guy," she said. "He doesn't think he is, but he's a good person." Her voice went quiet and she looked like she was lost in thought.

"Are you two..."

"No," she shook her head. "No." She spoke firmly, as though this was something she could never allow to happen. Why the hell not?

"Can I ask you something?"

"What?"

"Why are you out here instead of at the party? You aren't on a smoke break," I pointed out.

"I could be on a smoke break."

"You aren't. You've got no cigarettes, no lighter, and no bag to hide them in. You aren't smoking." I wasn't sure why I was being so intense as I argued about her lack of a smoking habit.

"Does it matter?"

"I'm just curious."

"It's just a lot, you know?" Daphne lifted one leg, pressing her foot back against the brick wall of the Polar Bear Banquet Hall building. "All of it. It's a lot."

"Trying to be the Alpha?"

"Yeah," she nodded. "More than that, though, trying to just stay on top of everything."

I knew what she meant. Fuck. I hated that I knew what she meant. This was our very first conversation, and yet I knew exactly what she was talking about. Trying to manage work with taking care of a house and managing a social life and then somehow finding time to date...it was all a lot to deal with.

"You ever just want to run away?" I asked her. I shouldn't have. It was a personal question, and I was drunk. It was inappropriate. It was something I shouldn't have been verbalizing. To my surprise, though, Daphne didn't tell me to fuck off. Instead, she nodded.

"Yeah," she said. "Sometimes I want to run away."

We stood there in silence for a few minutes, just letting the cool night air wash over us. I didn't know what I was going to do about Ivy. I hated that I liked her so much. She was getting under my skin in a way that was going to drive me insane if I wasn't careful. Yeah, I needed to be careful.

The doors to the banquet hall burst open and a man with long, shaggy hair came hurrying out. He looked from me to Daphne and back again. Whoever he was, he looked very sober and very flustered. I wished I still had a drink in my hand. I'd offer it to him.

"Daphne, you're needed inside," he said, completely ignoring me. "Right away," he added, as though his urgency hadn't been noted. This was a dude who was used to people giving him attention.

"Is that so?"

He nodded curtly.

She sighed and pushed herself off of the wall behind her. Nodding to me in a silent farewell, she headed back into the lively party. The man looked at me and frowned, obviously warning me to stay away from her. That wasn't a problem. I didn't have eyes for Daphne. I only had eyes for Ivy, and that was proving to be a problem for me.

"She's just a client," I muttered to myself.

Nothing more.

I stayed there, leaning against that wall. Finally, I pushed away and trudged through the lonely parking lot to my car. There were still plenty of vehicles here and with only a few stray streetlights for illumination, it was a little bit spooky. I didn't care about that. If someone tried to mug me in the parking lot, I'd just change into my tiger form and bite them.

When I reached my car, I closed my eyes for a moment. I wasn't going to drive. I was still way too drunk for that. It was chilly, though, and I was exhausted. I didn't want to loiter outside of the party until I sobered up. Climbing into the passenger seat, I shut the door and leaned the chair back for a moment.

What was I doing?

Like really, what was this thing I was doing?

Fake dating?

It was weird, and it was kind of stupid, and it was something that a grown adult shouldn't have been participating in. I should have been *real* dating. I should have been looking for a mate. Most people my age had a mate, didn't they? Yeah, they did.

I should, too.

Maybe my friends were right.

Shit.

I hated it when they were right.

I wanted to fall asleep in my car, but it was a bad idea. Besides, I wasn't a teenager. I wasn't in college. Passing out in my car was something that was going to leave me sore and crabby tomorrow, and I needed to be in good condition.

It wasn't my best judgment, but when I pulled out my phone, I didn't call an Uber. Instead, I texted Ivy. My fingers flew over the screen as I typed a heartfelt message – one I was certain would be wonderful for her to hear.

"Thinking of you."

Send.

What the hell was wrong with me? I leaned my head back against the seat and stared at the ceiling of my car. My head was spinning. I was exhausted. Coming to this party had been a bad idea. Seeing my friends with their own mates had stirred jealousy inside of me that I didn't even know existed.

Did I want a mate?

Was that what I'd been missing?

I needed to stop thinking about it so much. What I needed was to get out of here. I could unwind and read a couple of comics or slay some dragons in one of my favorite video games. There were plenty of things I could do that didn't involve daydreaming about Ivy, and yet there I was. I was drunk, dressed up like a cheetah, and texting a girl I had a crush on.

Pathetic.

A moment later, my phone beeped. It vibrated, too. It had to be her. What was she doing up at this hour? I looked at my phone, surprised to find that it was, in fact, Ivy. She didn't waste time asking me why I was messaging her, instead she wanted to know something else...

"What are you thinking about me?"

Oh shit.

Yeah, this conversation could get really dangerous, really fast. I had to be careful. I had to watch myself because if I didn't...

"Wondering what you're wearing."

Fuck!

No!

I sent it before I could stop myself. It was exactly what I'd been thinking, but that didn't make it appropriate. It didn't mean I should have just been telling her what I was actually thinking or wondering.

Crap.

I was in the middle of typing an apology when she responded to me.

"Nothing at all, Lincoln."

Then she sent a picture.

5

Ivy

It was Susan's fault.

If she hadn't been so overbearing about her stupid wedding flowers and her dumb wedding cake, then I wouldn't have gotten drunk as a way to deal with her. As it was, I *did* get drunk, and I *did* hang out alone at my house, and I *did* respond to Lincoln's text right away.

It was a bad idea.

Still, the truth was that I liked him. I was attracted to him. He was hot. Cute. Funny.

And we were supposed to be getting to know each other, right? Right.

The two of us were supposed to be getting to know each other well enough that people would believe we were dating. That was the *goal*. What better way to get to know each other than by sexting? You could learn a lot about people from the way they typed...

From the things they found sexy.

I sent a picture of my arms wrapped around my breasts. It was a good angle: a shot I'd perfected. I looked sexy, but not *too* slutty, in my opinion. That might not have been true. Okay, yeah, it was a pretty slutty picture. I just didn't care. Maybe it was the drinks or maybe it was just thinking about him, but I liked the idea of Lincoln thinking about me.

I didn't know where he was or what he was doing, but I *loved* knowing that he was out there wondering about me on a Saturday night. We were supposed to see each other the next day, of course, but that was hours away.

Right now, we had a chance to do something else.

Something fun.

Something much more rewarding than working the crowd at a wedding event I didn't even care about.

I *knew* that he didn't sleep with the people he took on as clients. I understood that. I respected it. I just didn't care.

Judging by the fact that he was messaging me, I didn't think he cared, either.

Now, as I stared at my phone, totally drunk off my ass, I wondered whether this was the right choice. I didn't have time to wonder for very long because a moment later, my phone rang. I stared at it in my hand.

A call.

He was *calling* me?

What the hell?

Why?

"Duh, because you're naked," I muttered, and I swiped to answer. "Hello?"

"Ivy. It's me. It's Lincoln."

I giggled. "I know who it is, Lincoln. What's...what's up?" I leaned back on my bed, resting my head on my pillow.

"I was just thinking about you."

Good.

I'd been thinking about him, too, and in so many ways that I shouldn't have - in the shower, in bed at night. Lincoln was going to be a very real problem for me, I knew. He was handsome as hell, kind, and funny. Those were all weaknesses I had, especially the "funny" thing. I liked it when I dated someone who could make me laugh. I liked it when I dated someone who made me smile.

Life was too short to be miserable, right? That was what my dad used to say. My mom was the epitome of miserable, but maybe that's why the two of them got divorced when I was a kid.

"I was thinking about you, too," I told Lincoln.

Thinking.

Hoping.

Daydreaming.

"What were you thinking about me?" Lincoln's voice was a low purr. A rumble. He sounded the way I imagined a lion or tiger would sound if they were sprawled out in a beautiful field just relaxing in the sunshine. Everything about his voice screamed "relaxation." Everything about his voice screamed that he was as drunk as I was.

"Probably things I shouldn't," I whispered.

"Were you wondering if I'm good at football?" Lincoln teased. "I'm not. I try my best, but it's not my thing."

"I wasn't wondering that."

"What were you wondering?"

"If you're good at other things," I whispered.

Dirty things.

Naughty things.

Deliciously wonderful things.

"Baking? Because I can bake, Ivy. I'm so fucking good at baking. You know what? I'll prove it. I'll bake you a cake."

"I won't say no to cake, but that wasn't what I was thinking, either."

"What were you thinking?"

"I was wondering if you liked the picture." I bit my lip nervously. I hadn't felt like this about a guy in ages. My entire body felt like it was burning up with excitement and nervousness. What was he going to say?

"It was perfect. Like you."

I paused. Had I heard him correctly? Had Lincoln really just said that to me?

"You think I'm perfect?"

"Perfectly gorgeous," he told me. "Definitely out of my league."

"I don't think that's true at all," I laughed. There was no way in hell I was out of *his* league. Seriously? He couldn't be serious.

Lincoln had his shit together. That was the thing that really impressed me about him. He knew who he was and what he wanted. He had this whole dating business down like it was no big deal at all. He had everything set up just the way he wanted.

And me?

I was a bartender who still didn't have a proper boyfriend. I worked nights and weekends and holidays – mostly because I volunteered so I could avoid being around my family. I didn't have the kind of stability or calmness that Lincoln seemed to exude.

Damn.

That guy was something else, wasn't he?

And I found myself wishing – not for the first time – that this business arrangement included more than just talking and showing off for family members. I wanted more. I wanted kissing and touching and teasing. I wanted taunting.

I wanted Lincoln to look at me and just *know* that I was a bad girl for him. I could be naughty for him.

"Either way," he continued, "the picture was fantastic. Thank you."

"You're welcome."

"I'd love to see more."

He would?

Really?

"Really?"

"I wouldn't want to just look at your breasts, though," he growled. "I'd want to touch them, too."

His words sent a fresh wave of heat throughout my body. He wanted to touch me. And do what? What would come next? I'd never considered myself to be the best at dirty talk, but damn if I wasn't going to learn fast. I was *super* into this. Oh yeah. I needed this.

"How would you touch me, Lincoln?" I asked him carefully.

Was he into massaging?

Licking?

Biting?

One of my friends dated a guy who liked flicking her nipples. Was Lincoln that kind of guy? Was that what he wanted to do? Or was it something else?

"Oh, I think I'd start slowly," he said.

"How slowly?"

"Slow enough to make you moan," he told me.

"I don't think you'd have to go slow to make me moan." If anything, going slowly was going to destroy me. I was already turned on. I was already more excited than I'd been in my entire life. I couldn't even think clearly anymore.

Not that I'd been thinking clearly before the call.

"No? You don't think so?"

"I don't think so."

"Do you think you'd groan for me if I flicked my tongue across your pretty nipples, Ivy?"

Holy.

Dragons.

Yeah, I did! I definitely thought that. Groaning, purring, meowing: I'd do it all. I'd make a million damn animal noises if Lincoln swiped his tongue across me.

"I think that might work," I said slowly, trying to sound as sexy as possible. My body was already aching with need. I was horny. I was more turned on than I'd ever been. For some reason, Lincoln just made me feel like my body was on fire and the only thing that could make me feel better was his penis.

"I'd love to taste you," he murmured. I heard a sound in the background of the call. Sirens? Did I hear sirens?

"Lincoln...where are you?"

"In my car." He sounded casual, like this wasn't a big deal. Was he driving?

"What are you doing in your car?"

"I was at a party. I sat here to call a ride home. I'm not driving," he told me, just in case I was worried. I was worried. I worried too much about him.

"I'm drunk, too," I admitted. "I can't come get you." I wanted to, though. I wanted to go pick him up and bring him home. Nothing would be hotter than bringing him into my apartment and pushing him back on the bed. Then I could climb all over him and kiss him and touch him and play with him.

"I'll be okay."

That might be true.

He might be okay to sleep things off in the car.

It was late, though, and I was making dumb choices tonight, so I threw out a random offer that was definitely a bad idea.

"What if you come over here?"

"What?"

"What if you come over here instead of going home?"

It was a terrible idea. A bad idea. The two of us were supposed to be working together on pretending to date – not dating for real. I wanted him, though. I wanted to touch him and drop to my knees in front of him. I wanted to kiss him and touch him. I was craving him.

I *needed* this guy.

"Come over?"

"I'm alone," I offered, as though that wasn't obvious.

"Text me your address," he said.

Then the call ended.

Oh shit. This was happening.

6

Lincoln

The car dropped me off in front of a row of buildings in downtown Wishville. Luckily, it was only about fifteen minutes from where the party had been held. I wondered why I hadn't realized she lived in Wishville. I was over in Howlton, which was still part of Rawr County, but it was on the opposite end. I found myself glad, now, that I'd texted her. I didn't have to sober up enough to drive the hour home. I didn't have to sleep in my car or Uber to some random hotel where I could pass out alone.

As the driver headed off into the darkness of the night, I stood where I was and stared up at the building in front of me.

Was I really doing this?

In front of me was a little bookstore. To the left was a restaurant and to the right, another restaurant. Above the shops were loft apartments. That was where Ivy lived. I stared at the texts she'd sent me. I was still buzzed as hell, but I had her address and directions to find the staircase. To the right of the little bookstore, squished between the edge of the shop and the restaurant, was a door that led to a staircase. I walked over to the door and pressed the buzzer. She answered right away.

"Hello?"

It was Ivy.

"It's me."

I hoped that didn't sound too lame.

Or creepy.

I didn't want to be creepy.

Not for Ivy.

"Come up," she said. "It's open."

I heard the lock click. I pulled open the door and I stepped into the narrow entry. There was nothing in front of me except for a narrow set of stairs leading up. This was the kind of place people went to get murdered. The scent of cigarette butts overwhelmed me. I knew I needed to get my anxiousness about scents under control, but it was harder to do than people realized.

At the top of the stairs was a small hallway. There were four doors: two on each side. Ivy's was the first door on the right. Her door had a little plant just outside of it that was nestled safely in a small red pot. I looked a little more closely. Jiji painted on the front. Jiji was the cat from *Kiki's Delivery Service:* a cute black cat who had a big attitude. Very nice. I wondered if Ivy painted that herself. I'd ask her.

For now, I just focused on getting inside. I knocked on the door. She opened it right away, grabbed my onesie, and pulled me inside. She was kissing me before the door even closed.

Drunk, sloppy kisses were my specialty, and I kissed her back. She hadn't even greeted me. She'd just kissed me, and I was all about that. Kissing was something I could handle. It was something I was good at. It wasn't like all of these other problems I had to deal with in the world. It wasn't hard.

Not with her.

My hands were in her hair as I pulled her closer, tighter. Ivy's scent wrapped around me. It didn't bother me. I didn't feel overwhelmed by her smell the way I sometimes felt overwhelmed with scents at work or in meetings. Nope. It was perfect. She was perfect. Everything about this moment made me feel like I was floating.

Finally, she pulled back long enough to tell me to close the door.

"Don't want to give the neighbors a free show," she chuckled.

I could do that. I could close the door. I shut it tightly, locking it, and then I turned back around and just about lost my balance from the hotness in front of me. She was standing there with her arms at her sides. She was only wearing a tiny pair of black panties.

"You don't have a shirt on," I pointed out the obvious.

"I don't have a shirt on," she agreed.

"You look gorgeous."

"I was promised that you wanted to touch me," she reminded me carefully.

Yeah. Yeah, I did want to touch her. I wanted to touch every part of her.

"Of course, I want that."

"Do you want a tour of my apartment first?"

"No. I don't care where you live."

"You might care," she cocked her head to the side. "I have cats, you know."

"Good. I like cats." I was a tiger shifter. I was damn good with cats. There was nothing about cats that I didn't like. I probably would have kept several hundred of them for myself if it wasn't for work.

As it was, I was far too busy to take care of cats. Instead, I chose to play with my clients' cats when I had the chance. Sometimes I volunteered at a local animal shelter, too. Just for fun.

"And I have cookies," she said. "Are you hungry?"

"Hungry for you," I growled, and I stepped forward and kissed her again.

Ivy practically melted against me. She purred as her hands wrapped around my neck. She kissed me eagerly, passionately. Her breasts rubbed against the soft fabric of my onesie. The sensation was driving me crazy.

I wanted her more than I'd ever wanted anything at all. I was still buzzed, so all of my emotions and feelings seemed to be even higher and crazier than they usually were. Everything that was happening made me feel alive. Crazy. Happy.

Ivy reached for the zipper on my onesie and tugged, pulling it. "Why are you so dressed up?"

I realized I hadn't actually explained everything that was going on.

"I went to a party."

"A dress-up party?"

"Something like that."

"Was everyone else dressed up, too?"

"Yeah," I nodded. "It was required." I didn't tell her we were all shifters dressed like other animals. It was a stupid sort of requirement, especially from a wolf pack, but it was also kind of fun and silly. It wasn't something I was normally up for, but I'd gone for my friends, and it had ended with me in Ivy's apartment, so I couldn't complain too much.

"And the drinking?"

"Open bar," I admitted.

"Sounds like a good night." Ivy looked up at me and licked her lips. "I'm glad you're here."

"I'm glad, too."

I was. I hadn't expected to end up here, at Ivy's place, but I was really, really happy that I was. She reached for my shoulders and pushed the onesie down off of them. It slid down my arms, down my body, and pooled around my ankles.

She looked down and raised an eyebrow before looking up with a smirk.

"No underwear?"

"No underwear."

"Did your dick bounce around while you were dancing?"

"A little," I admitted. It was a hazard I hadn't thought of, but nobody had complained. Ivy certainly wasn't complaining now as she reached out and wrapped her hand around my cock. She kissed me as she started to stroke, rubbing me faster.

"You feel so damn good, Lincoln," she groaned against my mouth.

Oh, I wanted this.

Wanted her.

Needed her.

My inner-tiger firmly agreed with me. While I went on plenty of dates – most of them fake – I didn't often get the feeling that the shifter half of myself was interested in the women I was sleeping with. As a tiger shifter, I was fully tiger and fully man. It was strange to try to explain to each other. It wasn't like I was half-man, half-tiger. Instead, I had a man form I could take. I also had a tiger form I could take. I could switch easily between both of my forms. It wasn't hard or painful.

I didn't always tell humans what I was, though.

Someone like Ivy was special.

Wonderful.

Oh, and exciting. She turned me on *so much*.

And then she got to her knees in front of me and I thought I was going to die from pleasure.

"Lincoln, you look good," she murmured.

"It's dark," I reminded her. "You can't see."

The lights to the apartment were off. There was only the soft glow of moonlight streaming into the room from one of the open windows. I could see her perfectly because I was a shifter. My eyesight was incredible even in the dark.

Her, though, she couldn't see me as well as I could see her.

"I can see you in the moonlight," she said. "And I like what I see."

Then she took my length in her mouth, sucking and licking me. I grabbed her hair, holding on as she played with my cock. Ivy was *super* into this. I couldn't take my eyes off of her. The scent of her arousal flooded my nostrils, and I knew in that moment that I wanted to keep her.

I didn't want this to just be one night.

I didn't want this to just be one fake relationship.

I wanted her for real.

And I had no idea how to tell her.

7

Ivy

He gently pushed me away and pulled me to my feet. Kissing me, he tugged me closer. Lincoln was hot as hell. I still couldn't really believe that I'd sent him that picture or that he was in my home. He was here with me, and I was...

Drunk.

I was so fucking drunk, but I didn't care. I was still able to make decisions. I still knew that this was what I wanted. More than anything else, this was what I wanted.

I wanted him.

I wanted to shove him down on the couch, straddle him, and ride his cock until we both came. I wanted him to play with my breasts as they bounced in his face. I wanted him to cling to my hips, thrusting up into me like it was the best damn ride of his life.

I wanted all of that and more.

I *needed* all of this and more.

"I want you," I whispered.

"I want you, too."

I looked up at him and our eyes locked. Then, almost like there was some sort of special effect happening, his eyes seemed to change color.

What.

The.

Fuck?

Lincoln seemed to realize that something had happened because he took a step back.

"What is it?"

His voice was no longer sultry or sweet. Instead, he sounded pained and a little bit scared. Nervous.

Was Lincoln nervous?

I didn't really like the idea of him being nervous around me. In fact, I really did pride myself on him being calm and comfortable around me. I did my best to make sure that I was a calm presence around other people. I hated the idea that he might not feel free to be himself in this moment.

"Your eyes," I whispered. I shook my head and closed my own eyes. Fuck, this sounded stupid, didn't it? "I think they changed color. Like, it looked like they turned orange for a second."

"Oh," Lincoln closed his eyes and then opened them again. They had returned to their normal brown color. "It's probably just the contacts."

"Contacts?"

"Yeah," he nodded. "When I dress up in costume, I love to wear contacts that change the color of my eyes. I think it makes them look better. Don't you?"

"Uh, they're nice," I nodded. I could see what he was talking about. The orange really did look cool. "I think your normal eyes are pretty nice, though."

Better than nice.

They were incredible.

I knew that I needed to stop crushing on this guy. From the moment I'd met Lincoln, I'd felt drawn to him. There was just something about him that was wildly attractive and wonderful. I felt safe with him, I'd come to realize. I felt safe and at ease.

So many times, when I was with a guy – or even a girl – I felt awkward and a little bit shy. It was like I never really felt free to be myself. With Lincoln, though, I didn't feel that way.

With Lincoln, nothing else mattered except that the two of us were together.

I stepped forward once more and reached up to him. Cupping his face, I kissed him over and over. Slowly, he started moving me toward the bedroom. I knew that we were both ready to take things to the next level.

This *so* wasn't like me.

Maybe it was the alcohol talking.

Maybe it was the fact that I hadn't dated anyone in a while.

Maybe it was just because my sister had stressed me out and pissed me off *again*, so I couldn't really deal with reality.

But I was happy with where I was: in his arms.

"We don't have to do anything you aren't ready for," he murmured against my lips.

He was giving me an out, I realized. That was sweet. I liked knowing that he was the kind of guy who wasn't going to freak if I told him I didn't feel ready, if I told him that this wasn't going to work for me.

"I'm ready," I told him.

We reached the bedroom, and I turned the knob to open the door. I'd closed it earlier when I'd heard him arrive. There was a loud meow and then two of my cats came running by. They hissed as they ran past both me and Lincoln. I looked up to see him staring at the direction the cats had run.

"They're nice cats," I said.

"They seem nice," he nodded. "They didn't even bite me, and I could tell that they really, really wanted to."

"That's not fair," I protested, laughing. It was fair. They were both big ol' meanies but I was convinced they secretly had hearts of gold.

"Come here," he took my hand and led me into my room. He backed up into the center of my room as he kept kissing me. The lights were still off, but in this room, there was no moonlight. It was almost completely pitch black. That, coupled with the fact Lincoln walked backward into the room, was the reason he didn't see my third cat, Mr. Fuzzypants, sitting on the bed.

So, when Lincoln sat down on the bed, inadvertently squishing Mr. Fuzzypants' tail, my cat let out a huge cry and swiped at Lincoln's back before leaping off the bed and speeding out of the room.

"Shit!" Lincoln cried out. He jumped to his feet, and I darted to the doorway to turn on the light. I looked at Lincoln to see him reaching for his back. "Sorry, kitty!" Lincoln called out. He looked at me. "Is your cat okay?"

"I...I...Lincoln, I'm so sorry," I said.

Suddenly, my buzz was almost completely gone. I didn't feel excited or horny anymore, I just felt embarrassed. I'd tried to be spontaneous and invite my crush to the house, but instead of getting to have hot, steamy sex, I'd inadvertently allowed him to be injured by my cat.

"It's okay," he said. "Is the cat okay?"

"That was Mr. Fuzzypants," I whispered. I was mortified. How had I let this happen? Oh, I was the worst at sex. How the hell had I let the events of tonight transpire?

I'd tried sexting, which I'd been proud of.

I'd sent a nude. Again, I'd been proud of that.

Then, I'd tried to have random sex with a guy I knew and...

My cat had basically picked a fight with him.

If there was ever a situation where I wished the ground would open up and swallow me whole, this was it. This was the moment I'd been waiting for. This was my chance.

"Mr. Fuzzypants, huh?" Lincoln asked. "Why don't you go check on him?"

"I think you might be bleeding," I pointed out to Lincoln.

"I'm totally fine," he said. "Go check on the cat. Is your bathroom through there?" He gestured to the bathroom door.

"Yeah."

"I'll get cleaned up. Just make your kitty is okay, all right?"

"Done."

8

Lincoln

As soon as she was gone, I darted to the bathroom. I couldn't heal my body instantly, but shifters generally healed much more quickly than humans did. Sure enough, the scratches on my back, which had bled slightly, seemed to be closing up very quickly. In a moment, they wouldn't even be visible. The casual observer would simply assume that I'd overreacted to the situation, which I probably had.

And he was named Mr. Fuzzypants. Really? For such a sweet name and such an obviously well-loved cat, he sure had sharp claws.

I felt super terrible for scaring the cat: possibly hurting him, too. I trusted that he was probably okay. I had to believe that he was okay. I'd grown up with cats – and I was a shifter myself – so I knew that cats were pretty wild and tough creatures, especially if you let them have their own space.

A moment later, Ivy knocked on the bathroom door.

"Are you okay?"

"I'm okay."

"Can I...can I see?"

"Yeah."

I opened the door and turned around so she could see my back. I heard her step forward and then felt her fingers tracing the place where Mr. Fuzzypants had scratched me just moments before.

"Oh," she said. "It doesn't even look like he got you. I was certain that he scratched your back. I thought it was going to be like, flayed."

"Nah," I shook my head and shrugged, as though it was no big deal at all. "I'm totally fine."

Totally fine except for the fact that I was *crazy* about her.

What the hell was wrong with me?

"I guess the mood is kind of ruined," Ivy sounded disappointed. I turned around to face her. While it was true that my buzz was wearing off, and I was sure that hers was, too, I wasn't ready to call it a night. Not just yet.

"Let's go to bed," I murmured. I reached for her hand and walked to the bed with her. Together, the two of us climbed under her covers and faced each other. It was kind of a strange feeling. It was almost like we were having a sleepover together, which was pretty funny to me. I hadn't had a sleepover since I was a kid. I wasn't going to complain about having one now, though. Not when it came to Ivy.

"What are you thinking?" Ivy whispered the words. She reached out beneath the blanket and felt around until she gripped my hand. Then she held it.

"I'm thinking that tonight was really different than I thought it would be."

"Thought you'd be hooking up with someone else?"

"I didn't think I'd be hooking up with anyone at all," I said honestly. Much less someone as pretty and sweet as Ivy. "I'm sorry Mr. Fuzzypants threw a little bit of a wrench in our plans," I murmured. I'd be lying if I said I wasn't nervous about the cat attacking me during sex. If we tried again, we'd have to lock the cats out of the room. I was under the impression that Ivy didn't often have guys over to the house, so her cats were probably very protective of her.

"I'm glad you came over."

"Me too."

"Listen, about tomorrow..."

"I'm sure everything will be okay," I murmured. "We've talked about everything that will happen." The bridal shower was something that Ivy wasn't looking forward to, which I could understand. I hadn't met her sister yet, but she sounded like a total bitch. The bridal shower was on Sunday evening, which was strange for many reasons. Most people planned this kind of event on a Saturday afternoon. Not Susan, apparently.

"Are you still okay going to lunch with me tomorrow?" The plan was that I'd go with her to lunch. We'd meet up with her mother and Susan and the four of us would have some time to get to know each other before the bridal shower. We'd worked the cost of the additional date into my fee, but to be honest, I didn't really care about the money. Even though I told Ivy I'd bill her when this was all over instead of in advance, the way I usually billed my clients, I wasn't planning on actually charging her.

That was bad.

I wasn't supposed to *not* charge people.

I liked her a lot; I was starting to realize. I liked her more than I was supposed to. The issue was that every time Ivy did *anything*, I seemed to find her sweet and funny instead of normal and ordinary. Anytime she said something silly, I'd get all goofy and excited like a little puppy.

"Absolutely. Lunch sounds great."

"I'm nervous," she admitted. Her words hung in the air for a moment. I scented her anxiety, her nervousness. Poor Ivy. I knew this was all a lot to bear.

"About Susan?"

"A little," she whispered.

"About your mom?"

"Yeah."

"Don't worry," I pressed a kiss to her forehead. "I'm very good with moms."

"Do you ever go on dates with women who are older than you?"

"Older than me?"

"Like moms or grandmas."

"Sometimes," I admitted. "Although, to be fair, someone could be a mom in their 20s or a grandmother in their 30s. A grandmother isn't always *very* old."

"Oh, I know," she nodded. "I know."

"And *I* know that you're very, very pretty," I whispered, brushing back a stray strand of hair.

Stop it, Lincoln. Don't get involved.

Oh, I wanted to get involved. I wanted so much when it came to Ivy that it wasn't even funny.

"That's very kind."

"Very few people have called me kind," I told her.

I usually heard things like "shark" or "prick."

Not kind.

"I think you're a nice person," she whispered.

"I'm not as nice as you think, princess."

"No?"

"No."

"So, you're kind of a bad-boy, huh?"

"A little." I liked the idea of that. Bad boy. It had a cool ring to it.

"Does that mean you're going to touch me more tonight?" Ivy whispered. "I think a bad boy would touch me more."

"Are you sure you don't want me to be a gentleman? I could go to sleep. We both could. Nothing has to happen."

"That seems very polite," she said. She reached between us, grabbing my cock. She started stroking it. Almost instantly, I was hard for her. Shit. How did she keep doing this to me? Ivy seemed to have the magic touch when it came to my penis, and try as I might, I couldn't really resist her.

And I was trying.

Oh, I was trying.

"That's not a polite way to touch someone," I pointed out, closing my eyes. I reached for her, too, and started stroking between her legs. She shifted, adjusting her position on the bed so I could reach her more easily.

"I don't want polite, Lincoln. I want bad."

"I think that if you want to be a bad girl, you should come for me," I told her. Leaning forward, I pushed back some of her hair and started nipping at her ear. Oh, she was hot as fuck, wasn't she?

Ivy was turned on as hell. Her breathing was heavy, and her body was tense and tight. She wasn't going to be long. If she didn't stop rubbing me the way she was, I wouldn't be long, either.

"Ivy..."

"I like this," she admitted. "I've been thinking about you when I touch myself, Lincoln. Did you know that?"

I could honestly say I did not know that.

I was happy that I did, though.

"Come for me, pretty girl," I growled at her. I wanted her. Needed her. Needed to feel her come against my hand.

"Make me," she laughed.

So, I kissed her.

Claiming her mouth, I kept touching her as she touched me. Rubbing her faster, I felt the exact moment she started to lose control. Then it came.

The orgasm hit her at the same time mine hit me, and together, we came right there under the blankets like a couple of damn teenagers.

It was the strangest and most wonderful thing that had ever happened to be on a fake date. Waves of pleasure washed over me as I wondered what I'd ever done to deserve a moment like this, what I'd ever done to deserve a moment with someone like her.

She was perfect and I...

Well, I was just the lucky bastard who got to hang out with her.

9

Ivy

My mother had a reputation for being a little bit...overbearing. In some ways, she was as bad as Susan was. In some ways, she was worse. Both Mom and Susan were the type of people who would stab you in the back if it meant getting ahead, regardless of how little that "ahead" really meant.

"You look great," Lincoln told me as we headed into the restaurant. His hand was on the small of my back.

"Not as good as you," I told him honestly. He was wearing a black button-down with jeans and converse. It was a combination I didn't really expect to see, but it looked good. He looked good. Shit. He looked *too* good.

After our not-sex, we'd passed out. In the morning, I'd driven him back to his car so he could get all of his stuff. Apparently, he'd packed an overnight bag in case he ended up staying in town instead of driving back last night. He'd driven back to my loft once more so he could shower and dress.

We'd spent a *lot* of time making out, but no sex.

I wanted sex.

Really, I wanted it. Like, in a bad way.

It was a little ridiculous just how horny being with Lincoln the night before had made me. Like seriously, what was my deal? Even though he had totally, completely satisfied me, I wanted to feel more of him. I wanted his cock. I wanted him to come in me.

There were a lot of things that I wanted.

Right now, though, what I wanted was to make it through lunch before I had to deal with my family again at the bridal shower. It was Susan's idea to bring me and Mom to lunch. Susan said that the three of us didn't spend enough time together, which was a lie. To be honest, sometimes it felt like all we *did* was spend time together.

"Why, thank you," he winked at me. "Seriously, though, that dress." Lincoln let out a long, low whistle. "You're killing it."

"Really?"

"Really."

I was nervous.

I was always nervous around my mother and Susan. I'd managed to finally come to terms with the fact that neither of them was ever going to like me very much. For most of my adult life, both my mother and my sister had managed to find things that were "wrong" with me.

They'd hurt me.

They'd spit out mean, cruel words that felt like they were tearing up my insides.

They'd done so much and still...

Well, still I couldn't stop myself from wanting them to accept me.

I'd spent way too much time choosing the perfect dress for lunch. This one was blue with white flowers sprinkled along it. The dress fell just to my knees and swayed a little bit as I walked. I planned on wearing it to the bridal shower later that day, too, but I'd probably change my mind on that one. Susan would inevitably say something shitty and then I'd let it get to me until I doubted myself enough that I changed my clothing.

That was how things always went with Susan.

"Are they already here?" Lincoln asked when we stepped into the little restaurant lobby. He glanced over at me.

"Yeah," I nodded. "I just texted them. They're in the back."

The two of us headed to the hostess stand. I let her know that we were meeting some friends and then the two of us headed back to find Susan and Mom.

Most of the little sports bar and grill was empty. It was lunchtime, so that was a little surprising, but I didn't mind the lack of fellow patrons. It would probably fill up soon, but even if it didn't, sometimes having a nice, quieter space to meet up could be nice.

I spotted Susan at the back of the restaurant tucked into a little booth, but it wasn't my mother beside her.

It was Tameka.

Both of them looked up, surprised.

"Lincoln?" Tameka asked.

"Ivy?" Susan glared at me. "What the hell is going on?"

"Tammy?" Lincoln grinned. Tameka slipped out of the booth and threw her arms around Lincoln. "It's been a hot second, hasn't it?"

I had no idea what was going on, but apparently, neither did Susan. The two of us were totally in the dark. I had no idea how Tameka and Lincoln knew each other.

"What are you doing here?" Tameka asked.

"I'm here with my girlfriend," Lincoln told her. He lied smoothly. He was good at that. I'd noticed that Lincoln did a good job thinking on his feet. That was something most people struggled with. Even I had a hard time coming up with lies on the spot, but for Lincoln, it seemed like it was second nature.

"Your girlfriend?" Tameka asked, looking at me. She raised an eyebrow. Then her head swung back to Lincoln. "Really?"

"Really."

"Well, don't leave us hanging. Introductions?" Susan glared at us.

"Oh, yeah, Susan, this is my boyfriend. His name is Lincoln."

Susan stared at Lincoln.

"I wasn't aware that you had a boyfriend."

"She does, and it's me." Lincoln held a hand out to Susan, who was still sitting in the booth. "Nice to meet you."

"Huh."

"How do you and Tameka know each other?" I asked.

"Lincoln is my cousin," Tameka told me carefully. I could tell by the way Lincoln's shoulder tensed that this wasn't the best news. Was he worried that Tameka was going to rat him out? If they were related, she probably knew about his side hustle, right?

At the very least, she had to know his real profession, which meant that if we were going to pretend to be dating, he might have to share his real job information.

Yikes.

I looked over at him, trying to get a read. Were we still on? Was this a go? Or did Tameka's presence change everything?

I was relieved when he didn't start running for the door. Instead, Lincoln gestured for me to sit down in the booth. I slid in first and then he did.

"Cousins," he agreed. "Tammy and I go way back."

"Why are you calling her Tammy?" Susan glared. "That's not her name."

"It's a nickname, Susan. Chill," Tameka said.

"Can I call you Tammy?" I asked. I liked it. It was a cute name, really.

"Absolutely not," Tameka laughed. "Nice try, though."

A moment later, a waitress stopped by our table with our waters and to take our orders. Once she was gone, I looked toward Susan.

"Where's Mom?"

"She couldn't make it."

"What do you mean she couldn't make it?" Mom had really wanted to meet up. At least, as far as I could tell, she'd wanted to. In fact, Mom was really the main reason we'd arranged this entire lunch. Susan was someone Lincoln definitely could have waited to meet.

"I don't really know which part of that you don't understand," Susan said. She sipped her water while staring at me. Her eyes never left mine. She set the glass back down on the table. Still staring at me, she repeated, "she couldn't make it."

I sighed. Okay. Awesome.

So, my mother wasn't here. This meant that Susan was *definitely* going to text her that I had someone with me, and Mom was going to freak out that I hadn't told her. I was mentally trying to figure out how to do damage control when Lincoln spoke up, breaking the silence.

"So, Susan, congratulations on the wedding."

"Thanks. How do you know my sister? No offense, but she hasn't mentioned you."

"Personally, I'm hurt," he said calmly. "Not telling your engaged sister about your boyfriend is a huge social faux pas."

"Right?" Susan grinned. It was the first time I'd seen her smile in a very long time. Okay, so she liked snark. She liked the fact that he was getting mouthy. Personally, I wasn't sure how I felt about that.

"Hey, I was going to tell her," I protested.

"When? At your own wedding?" Susan crossed her arms over her chest. She thought she'd won some sort of invisible fight. She hadn't. There was no fight because Lincoln wasn't really my boyfriend. As much as I really, really wanted him to be. I tried not to start daydreaming about anything like that, either.

This was a business arrangement.

Period.

After Susan's wedding stuff was over, I'd start making excuses as to why Lincoln wasn't coming to events, and I'd phase him out of my life. It would be a slow, easy process. Nobody would be the wiser because hopefully I'd actually get off my ass and start dating someone for real.

Luckily, I was saved from having to make a snarky remark because Lincoln slung his arm around my shoulder and tugged me closer to himself. It was such a soft, gentle touch. It also made me realize that my boyfriends in the past hadn't shown me this kind of physical affection.

Wasn't that weird?

Most of them had been more than happy to fuck, but less than happy to be intimate or gentle with me when we were out. Now that Lincoln was touching me like this, it made me feel...well, it made me feel safe, actually. It made me feel like the world was mine for the taking.

"She was just waiting for the right moment," Lincoln told my sister.

Susan frowned at him before looking at me. She was staring, trying to get me to give something away. That was how Susan worked. If she could get me to reveal information about the situation, she'd be able to use it against me. Well, that wasn't going to work. Not this time.

"How long have you been dating?"

"Not too terribly long," Lincoln gave her a vague, yet strangely true answer. "Feels like forever, though."

Tameka was watching him carefully. She looked from me to Lincoln and back again.

"So, Linc, what have you been up to?" Tameka asked him. A risky question. If he said anything remotely real, it would reveal information about himself to me and Susan that he might not be ready to share. If he lied, Tameka might call him out. Yikes.

"Oh, you know," he smiled, reaching for his glass. "The usual."

"Still spending a lot of time playing in the woods?" Tameka asked carefully. She seemed to be looking at me when she said it.

Strange. It was a question for Lincoln, right? Was she saying that he liked to camp? Maybe he was the outdoorsy type, and I didn't even know it. I'd been under the impression that he was more of an indoor gamer than an outdoor camper, but hey, this was all really new.

Lincoln didn't seem to appreciate her question, though. His eyes narrowed for just a moment, but he quickly played off any irritation he may have felt.

"You know I love being outside," he shrugged. He reached for his drink and sipped, obviously needing something new to focus on. Tameka's question had bothered him, but I didn't really get why. She had just been asking about his hobbies, right? Was there more to the question than that? There had to be. Why else would he have gotten *so* bothered?

"What about you, Ivy? Do you like being...outside?" Tameka asked me slowly. In all of the time I'd known her, she'd never asked me anything like this. In fact, I'd never found it weird or difficult to talk to Tameka. If anything, it had been comfortable. The two of us had bonded easily over the fact that my sister was totally crazy.

"Tameka, you're being weird," I said. I wished I'd ordered an alcoholic beverage. I needed something to take the edge off of this conversation.

"What do you mean?"

"You've known me a long time," I pointed out. She'd known me a long time and had never mentioned a hot-as-hell cousin who was secretly interested in the great outdoors. She'd never mentioned anything about this. Somehow, I kind of felt like she'd done me dirty even though that wasn't true. I didn't play matchmaker with my relatives, either.

What if Lincoln and I had met a different way, though?

What if I'd taken things further at the coffee shop we'd originally met at?

If we'd connected there – *really* connected – then maybe I could have had a real chance at dating someone like him. If I'd just had the guts to ask him out, I wouldn't have been stressing about the idea of bringing him to the wedding as a pretend boyfriend.

"I've known you a long time," Tameka agreed. "I just don't really remember you spending a lot of time...in the woods."

"There was that one trip Susan and I took," I gestured to my sister. She was staring at her phone, though. She definitely texting my mom about this entire thing, which was weird since Mom hadn't bothered to show up. The fact that Susan was texting irritated me. I usually didn't care if people were on their phones. Really, I didn't. Susan had been the one who had wanted this get-together, though. She and my mother had decided that we all needed to meet for lunch, yet it mostly felt like I was just hanging out with Tameka and Lincoln. Annoying.

"What trip?"

"We went hiking in the mountains," I said.

"That was a day trip. You were gone for *maybe* five hours," she pointed out.

"Whatever."

"How's your mom?" Lincoln asked Tameka directly, changing the subject. He looked at me and smiled. "Our moms are sisters. Haven't seen Tameka's mother in some time, though."

Tameka's face softened a little. Her mom was nice. I'd met her a few times and she'd always fed me cocoa and cookies. It was kind of her specialty.

"She's good," Tameka said. "Busy with her knitting."

"And her baking," I told Lincoln. "Have you had her chocolate chip cookies?"

"They're the best," he laughed. "Seriously, the best."

When he said that, though, all I could think about was the fact that *he* was the best.

He was.

And oh, I didn't want this relationship to end.

When it was over, I was going to lose myself. I could already feel it. I was growing attached in ways I shouldn't. If I wasn't very, very careful, then I was going to get hurt. I just knew it. It would be me getting hurt, too. It wouldn't be Lincoln. He was strong. Tough. He was used to starting relationships and then ending them, but that wasn't me. It had never been me.

And now...

After last night, I wasn't sure if I could do it.

I wasn't sure if I could actually tell him goodbye and walk away after all of this was over. I just didn't know. I didn't.

10

Lincoln

WE WERE LEAVING THE restaurant and heading into the parking lot when Tameka reached for her pockets. A look of nervousness washed over her face.

"Shit," she said. "I forgot my keys. Lincoln, come help me."

"I'll wait for you outside," I said. I was certain she could find her keys on her own. My cousin's eyes narrowed, though, and she reached for my hand.

"Come help me," she repeated. I knew better this time than to argue. I didn't want Tameka making a big, huge scene. I didn't want her to know that this relationship was fake or that it was starting to feel not-fake to me.

Last night had been so incredible. It had been wonderful. Really. The problem I was facing was that the woman of my dreams happened to be incredibly sweet, smart, wonderful, and sassy. And oh yeah – she was the woman of my dreams.

In the past, when I'd dated people, it had been nice. Comfortable. Relaxing. My relationships had always been just *fine*, but they'd never been like this. They'd never been passionate like they had last night.

And they'd never been this low-pressure.

Now my hobby was colliding with reality as my cousin dragged me back into the restaurant and pulled me into a corner of the lobby.

"Hey," I looked around. We weren't at the booth. "You didn't forget your keys at all, did you?"

"What the hell are you doing?"

"I could ask you the same question, but you'll probably lie about it again."

"What are you doing?" Tameka wasn't in the mood to play games this afternoon, apparently. Sure. Fine.

"I'm on a date, actually, and I was planning on meeting my girlfriend's mom."

"Something seems sus," she frowned. "You didn't mention a new girlfriend to me."

"I haven't seen you in weeks," I reminded my cousin. "And since when do I call you when I get a new girlfriend? I've literally never done that."

"Since it was one of my best friends' sisters," she snapped.

"Susan? Susan is your best friend?"

There was no way. I knew Tameka better than that. There had to be more to the story here because Susan had not only barely talked to me during lunch, but she'd barely talked to anyone. She'd been completely glued to her phone. While she hadn't been overly friendly, she hadn't been specifically rude, either. She'd just been...distracted.

Yeah, that was it. Distracted.

"Susan is a really nice person, Lincoln."

"And hell feels like a warm summer day."

It was too much. I knew I was taking it too far. Still, I didn't like that Susan was the type of person who would put so much pressure on her family members that they would *hire fake dates* for her wedding. Ivy was so distraught at the idea of upsetting her family that she had sought out a fake boyfriend – me – and had hired me to help her put on a performance.

Oh, it was going to be a damn good performance, but it was still all an act.

I hated that she was going through this.

Hated it.

If it was up to me, Ivy's entire family would see her for the person she was: sweet, kind, passionate. She was a kind woman who deserved for people to treat her kindly, too. She didn't deserve to have people hurting her. She didn't deserve to have to feel this kind of pressure or stress.

She did, though.

She felt it.

"That was too far," Tameka said. "Look, I don't know what you're playing at, but I know that you and Ivy aren't seriously dating. Did she just randomly grab you to bring to the wedding?"

"What the hell?" I bristled. "Tameka, what are you talking about?" I had to work to keep myself acting offended and angry and not concerned. My cousin was a shifter, just as I was, and any strange change of scent or emotion would tip her off that I was lying.

Because yeah, I was lying my ass off about this.

"She doesn't know you're a shifter."

"Is that what your weird outdoorsy comments were about?"

"Yes."

"She's just not as outdoorsy as other people," I threw up my hands, exasperated. "Seriously, Tammy? You need to drop this."

I turned and headed for the door. Just as I reached the exit of the restaurant, Tameka grabbed my arm and spun me back around.

"You haven't told her your secret," she told me. "She doesn't know. So you either aren't as close as you're pretending, or you don't trust her."

"Point being?"

"Look," she said, "I've known Ivy a lot longer than you, and I..." She shook her head. "Shit, I can't even believe I'm saying this. Look, I care about Ivy. A lot." I raised an eyebrow, but Tameka shook her head. "Not like that. Not romantically. She's like a kid sister to me."

"Tameka, she's the same age as you."

"That's not true. I'm 32. She's 31."

I rolled my eyes.

"Same thing, love."

"Whatever. Listen. Don't hurt her."

"Don't hurt her? What is this? Some sort of villain origin story? Tameka, I'm not going to hurt her."

Another lie.

Someone was going to get hurt when this was all over. There was no way that Ivy didn't feel what I felt last night when we'd been drunk in her bed together. Feeling her come for me had been the best damn feeling in the world. She'd been so perfect when she'd arched her back and made these soft little mewling sounds during her release. It was so sweet and so damn sexy.

I already knew that I wasn't going to want to let her go. My inner-tiger definitely wasn't going to let her go. The two of us...well, we needed to get it together, didn't we? Because no matter what happened next...

Nothing was going back to the way it was before.

Nothing.

11

Ivy

The bridal shower was my own personal brand of hell.

The community center my sister and her fiancé had rented was located close to my home. Since it was such a nice night, Lincoln and I had chosen to walk the few blocks from my loft to the party. It wasn't far enough that we'd get overtired or sweaty, and it gave us a little bit of time to be alone and just *enjoy* each other. The birds were chirping and the sun was shining, but then we'd walked into the community center, and I'd been struck in the face with utter chaos.

"What is happening?" Lincoln asked. He turned to me. "I thought this was a bridal shower."

"I...I..."

Normally, when I thought of bridal showers, I pictured a nice, quiet lunch where the ladies of a family would get together and shower the bride with gifts. There might be soft music playing, too. What we'd walked into was some sort of weird circus.

My sister hadn't rented a small community room for the party. Instead, she'd rented the largest gymnasium and had actually hired a band to play. There were lots and lots of couples at the party, including my sister's fiancé, Ray. People were dancing, singing, and talking loudly throughout the space. It didn't resemble a bridal shower – it resembled a wedding reception on steroids.

"What is this?" I whispered.

"I don't know. That's why I asked you. Are you sure we're at the right place?" For the first time since I'd met him, Lincoln looked a little bit nervous. Strange. Lincoln never looked nervous. The room was filled with people. Filled. We had arrived right on time, but the room was packed with guests who were dancing, eating, and drinking. There was a buffet along one wall and a huge table piled high with presents.

"I..."

Before I could say another word, Tameka sidled up to me and draped an arm over my shoulder. She grinned, but there was a tightness to her smile.

"Well? What do you think of your sister's creation?"

"It's..."

Hideous.

Horrible.

Gawdy.

It wasn't a bridal shower. It felt more like a reception or even an engagement party, honestly.

"It's not what I expected," I finally said. That was the understatement of the year. Tameka looked at me knowingly and nodded.

"She thought people might be surprised."

Lincoln choked back a giggle. I knew what he was thinking, but neither one of us was going to say anything. This wasn't really about us, after all. It was about my sister. It was about Susan.

"I am definitely surprised," I agreed.

"It's pretty weird, but that's Susan," Tameka shrugged.

"I don't think anyone has ever described Susan as 'weird' in her life," I pointed out. Susan was the epitome of normal and perfect. She was the kind of person people always aspired to be. She was a trendsetter, she was pretty, and she was popular. In fact, it was really easy to see all of the things Ray liked about her. Despite the fact that the two of us weren't exactly friends, nor would we ever be, it was still pretty simple to understand what people saw in her.

The party, however, was really wild.

"The only thing missing is a stripper," Tameka winked. Suddenly, we spotted motion out of the corner of our eye. Susan was jumping up and down in what appeared to be stilettos. How the hell was she doing that? She was waving wildly to us.

"I think she wants us to come over," Lincoln looked surprised.

"Maybe," Tameka looked over at me. She nodded and shrugged, but she didn't seem to feel totally sure that this was what my sister wanted. Strange. Usually, Tameka and Susan were on the same page. Scratch that: they were *always* on the same page. Despite the fact that their personalities were very different, the two of them had been friends for a very, very long time.

Together, the three of us made our way through the crowd of people and walked over to Susan. I tried counting how many people were in the room. There must have been at least 200, which was insane. The space was definitely made for no more than a hundred.

"Susan," I said once we reached her. "What is this?" I gestured to the space. Seriously, what was happening?

"Oh, good, you're here!"

"You already knew that. You called us over," Lincoln pointed out. Susan ignored him and took my hands.

"I'm so happy you could make it. Ray's brother is here."

"His brother?"

I didn't want to talk to his brother. Ray's brother was a dick. I'd met him three times previously at various parties and every single time, he pissed me off. I wasn't sure how one person managed to do that so easily, yet he did. It was like the dude got off on being cruel and unlikable. I wasn't really sure how to tell my sister that, so I said nothing. Instead, I just stood there looking like an idiot.

"Yeah, the one I was telling you about. You know, he's single now."

I stared at my sister. "You weren't telling me about him. That must have been someone else. Also, I've met Randall. Also, I'm not single."

A lie, but she didn't know that.

Susan rolled her eyes. "Randall's awesome. No offense," she looked at Lincoln, "but my sister needs someone who respects her. Someone serious."

"I'm a pretty serious person," Lincoln said without missing a beat. He seemed to know without me even saying anything that I didn't like Randall one bit.

"Well, this is different," Susan shrugged. "There he is now. Randall!" She waved, jumping again. This time, she slipped a little, but Tameka and I both caught one of her elbows and managed to steady her.

"You need better shoes."

"My shoes are fine," Susan snapped, pulling her elbow away from me.

"Whatever." I wasn't about to argue with someone who was being totally unreasonable. I had zero interest in talking to Randall. Literally zero. I also had no interest in pretending to be polite to him. Literally my only goal was to make it through the wedding unscathed. I spotted Randall moving toward us, but I was done playing this game. "Let's go," I grabbed Lincoln's arm and tugged him away.

"What are you doing?" Susan asked.

"We're going to get some drinks." Anything to get away from her. She said something else, but I ignored her and dragged Lincoln away from her and back through the crowd. This time, instead of heading to the doors we'd come in, I brought him to the bar and ordered two shots of whiskey. When the drinks came, I downed them both and ordered two more. When the second round came, I offered one to Lincoln. He stared at the drink and then at me.

"Are you okay?"

"I'm fine."

"Yes, I can tell," he rolled his eyes. Then he reached for my wrist and touched me gently. When he did that, it was like my entire world stopped spinning and I just felt stable. Safe. Secure. He was like an anchor holding me in place. I really never wanted to let him go. "You don't have to be okay all of the time, Ivy."

And just like that, I realized that I didn't want to let him go.

When this was all over, I didn't want to say goodbye.

I didn't want to walk away.

I didn't want any of that.

I just wanted...him.

IT WASN'T UNTIL THE end of the party, after Susan had opened all of her gifts and the guests had started to leave, that my mother approached me and Lincoln. She'd locked eyes with me a few times during the party, but the two of us had never gotten close enough to talk.

Unlike most bridal showers I'd been to in the past, Susan didn't ask me or Tameka to speak or make toasts or anything like that. There were no party games. Instead, Susan ran everything herself with the assistance of her fiancé, Ray, who had, in fact, made it to the party.

"You must be the man my daughter is shacking up with," Mother said, approaching us. She glared, eyeing us. Lincoln placed his hand on the small of my back. He wasn't nervous. He wasn't upset by this interaction.

Somehow, that knowledge calmed me.

"Hello, Mother."

"Ivy, what the hell is this?"

"Lincoln, this is my mom," I told him. "Eleanor."

"It's nice to meet you," he said.

"I wish I could say the same," she snapped. Turning to me, she frowned. "What happened to Randall?"

"Mom, I'm not interested in Randall, nor have I ever been."

"He thought he was going to be your date to the wedding."

"I have no idea why he would have thought that," I told her. "The two of us have barely had three conversations ever. Also, at no point have either one of us mentioned the wedding."

"Well, he's very disappointed," Mother said.

"That's too bad," I nodded. "Mom, Lincoln is a really nice person. He's actually Tameka's cousin." That seemed to interest my mom. She raised an eyebrow.

"The one who's a construction worker or the one who's an attorney?"

"The one who's an attorney," he said.

I tried to hide my shock. He was a lawyer? We'd discussed potential made-up jobs for him, but we'd basically agreed to keep things as vague as possible. He hadn't told me he was a real-life attorney. I wondered if he had to share that now because Tameka knew the two of us were going to the wedding together. It made things a little more complicated, didn't it?

Mother, however, didn't miss the slight dilation of my eyes when he said that.

"You didn't know he was a lawyer? How did you not know that?"

"I knew it," I said, lying in a way I hoped sounded smooth. "In fact, we just had lunch with his boss a few days ago. It was nice."

"You looked shocked when he said he was an attorney just now."

"I'm not sure what to tell you, Mom."

My mother frowned. For the night being such a happy occasion, she sure did seem pissed.

"It's so nice to finally meet you," Lincoln said, changing the subject. "Ivy has told me so much about you."

"Did she tell you that I'm divorced and that I hate weddings?" Mom growled.

"She mentioned that you and your husband separated when she was a kid. That must have been tough," he said. How the hell did his voice sound like smooth silk? He'd done this before. He must have totally perfected his talking-to-the-parents routine because somehow, the way he spoke seemed to please my mother.

"It was very hard," she agreed. "Raising two young women on my own wasn't really what I saw myself doing."

"Well, I think it's very brave of you. You've obviously done a lovely job," he continued schmoozing. He gestured to the room. The band was still playing, and a few guests were still dancing, but most of the room had emptied. I wondered when the band was going to stop. Were they waiting for the last person to filter out? "This whole party has been so lovely."

"You don't think it's too much?" My mother asked, showing the first signs of weakness I'd seen in years. She was nervous, I realized suddenly. Wait. Why was she nervous? Was it because her own marriage had been such a nightmare? Was she worried that Ray and Susan would have a bad time being married, too?

"I don't think it's too much," he said kindly.

"Susan has always been hard on herself," my mother told Lincoln.

Wait, what?

What the hell was she talking about?

And why did my mom suddenly seem so damn comfortable with Lincoln?

"She's the oldest, so there's always been a lot of pressure there, you know. My ex-husband didn't really know how to be a dad."

"Nobody knows how to be a parent," Lincoln shrugged. "That's why it's so hard, right?"

"Pretty much." My mom laughed. She actually laughed. "Anyway, he was always really hard on both of the girls, but I think Susan really took a lot of it to heart."

"Just that she needed to be on top of the world?"

"She always thought she needed to be good at everything," Mom explained. I watched her as she started pouring her heart out to Lincoln. It was the strangest thing. I couldn't quite believe what was happening. Mom wasn't the type of person who shared her feelings.

Ever.

She never ever shared her feelings.

I'd learned more about her experiences as a single mom in the last three minutes than I had my entire life.

How was that possible?

I looked over at Lincoln. He really looked like he was paying attention. He had a way with people, I realized. Maybe that was why he was so good at this. He seemed to understand exactly what people wanted to say and what they wanted to hear. That was why he made such a great fake date.

Maybe that was why he made a good lawyer, too.

A thought invaded my mind – one I didn't one. What if Lincoln wasn't just working his magic on my mom and friends? What if he was working his magic on me, too?

Last night had been incredible. It was one of the best nights of my entire life. I'd never, ever forget it. Ever. There was no chance of that, but...what if it didn't mean anything to him? He said he didn't sleep with clients, but what if he'd been fooling around with me simply as an exception to the rule and not because he liked me?

Shit.

Of course, that was it. Of course, all of this was for show. It was just that every time he looked at me, every time he touched me, I kept getting the feeling that it wasn't just pretend.

And I didn't want it to be pretend.

I wanted it to be real.

I wanted all of it to be real.

Shit.

12

Lincoln

After the party, we drove back to Ivy's place together and then went our separate ways. I wasn't going to see her again until the rehearsal dinner if everything went according to plan. That was the deal, anyway. It was all part of a carefully planned, carefully crafted situation. The whole thing was pretend. Make-believe. Fake.

If that was true, though, then why did I feel so sad?

Why did I feel so terrible?

Why did I feel like no matter what happened next, I was going to get hurt?

I really, really liked her. A lot. My inner-tiger did, too. When I arrived back at my own house, I parked in the driveway and stripped down right there, tossing my clothes onto the front seat of the car. I could get them later.

My house was located just outside of town, and it was a fairly isolated place. There were trees surrounding the house, driveway, and yard. Nobody could see me. It was the ultimate private hideaway, which was great for me.

It would be perfect for any animal shifter.

I started running toward the surrounding forests, shifting as I did. These days, I shifted almost instantly. I leapt into the air and shifted before my paws hit the ground. It was exhilarating and wonderful. It made me feel like I was floating, actually. It made me feel like the whole world was going to bow to me.

There were plenty of times in my life that I felt powerful. When I was in the courtroom, I felt powerful. When I was helping a client, I felt strong and incredible. There were moments in my life it seemed like I was going to dominate the entire world one day.

Then there were moments when I felt quiet.

When I was with Ivy, it was like nothing else mattered. I loved that feeling. Hated it, too. Why did I have to feel so damn good around her? How come when I was with Ivy, it seemed like my life was not really my own? When I was with her, it was like she was a princess I hadn't known I'd wanted. She was an angel who had floated into my life. I felt like she was there to protect me.

To guard me.

To keep me so very safe.

And I wanted to keep her safe, too.

She didn't know what I was, though. She didn't know who I truly was deep inside. There were plenty of things I'd never shared with my girlfriends and that was one of them. I wasn't ready for people to know I could shift. I didn't really want anyone to know, much less someone as sweet as Ivy.

She deserved to have someone better than me, anyway. She deserved to have someone who was a hero.

I was no hero.

I was just...

Well, I was me.

So, I ran. I ran to clear my mind. I ran to forget about everything that was bothering me. I ran because I needed to feel the wind against my face.

I ran because this dating situation was going to kill me if I wasn't careful.

By the time I got back to my house, I was sweaty and tired, but I wasn't so tired that I didn't notice the asshole sitting on my porch. I shifted as I emerged from the woods and walked naked up to the house. Irritation washed over me as I glared at my uninvited visitor.

"What are you doing here, Fletcher?" I growled. I didn't bother trying to hide my body. I hadn't invited him to stop by. I wasn't going to stress about getting dressed for this guy. Not going to happen.

"Hey, I...woah, you are *really* naked."

What the hell was he doing here?

Why did he care if I was naked?

I tried to keep the bite out of my voice, but irritation washed over me. I hadn't invited him. Hadn't been expecting him. I definitely didn't want to talk to him.

"No shit. What are you doing here?"

"I just wanted to talk," he shrugged as though this was the most normal thing in the world.

"You can't just show up at someone's house because you feel like talking," I pointed out.

"Oh yeah, I know," he told me. "I know that."

If he knew it, then why was he here?

A gust of wind blew, making me cold and quite nearly knocking me over. Fletcher shivered and I gestured for him to follow me inside. I knew that I'd be regretting this, but he obviously needed to talk about something – probably something dumb – so I'd allow him to come inside.

As soon as we walked in the door, I lit a couple of vanilla candles and some incense sticks that were right by the front door. I'd been dealing with a lot of different smells over the past few days. Making it through the bridal shower, for example, had been downright difficult. I kind of hated just how hard it had been to get through.

Everyone there had such strong feelings, such strong emotions. It was like no matter what they were feeling, they had to feel it *loudly.*

"Nice place," Fletcher murmured, looking around. I knew that my house was smaller than some of the places he was probably used to. A lot of the business owners in Rawr County had huge, sprawling estates filled with multiple buildings and garages and guest houses. A few people even had stables, which I thought was a little strange. We were almost all shifters, after all. I wasn't sure how I felt about riding a horse when I could just shift and run somewhere myself. I wasn't really one to judge, though.

That was a lie.

I was *definitely* one to judge.

"Thanks." We were standing in the entryway. The living room was to the right of the house with the kitchen to the left. The office was located just behind the kitchen and there was a bedroom behind the living room. At the very back of the first floor, behind the bedroom, was a bathroom and a staircase that led to a second floor. The second floor was where I spent most of my time. Unless I specifically had guests over, I didn't really enjoy hanging out on the first floor alone.

Despite the fact that I'd decorated the place myself, it still didn't feel homey. For some reason, it still didn't feel like it was *mine*.

"What can I do for you, Fletcher?" I asked again.

"You're still naked," he informed me. "Should you put on some pants?"

"Should you just leave?" I countered. "Get to the point, man."

"Okay," he nodded. "I've got a problem."

"With respecting personal boundaries? I noticed."

"No, not with that," he said quickly. Too quickly.

"Then what's the deal?"

"It's...I have a problem with a girl."

I stared at him.

"And you think I can help you with that?" I gestured to my home. "Do I look like I live with a woman? Why would you come to me?"

If I couldn't help myself, there was no way in hell I could help him. It just wouldn't happen. Not that I didn't want to be helpful, but...

Well, I couldn't help him.

"I've heard you're the best," Fletcher said. He crossed his arms over his chest and looked at me. Just looked at me.

"Who the hell told you that?"

"A mutual friend."

"Are you trying to be discreet? Because you gave up that privilege when you showed up unannounced at my house." Shit, I was losing control. I was tired and frustrated. I was worn out trying to deal with my feelings surrounding Ivy. I was crazy about her in so many ways, but the two of us both definitely knew that nothing was going to happen.

Nothing could happen.

I really wanted it to happen.

"Okay, it was Basil." Fletcher shrugged as he stared at me. He'd given in so easily. Talk about a lack of loyalty. Shit. I mean, I knew that I'd told him to share his source, but he'd given it up so fast. Damn.

But also... "Basil told you I'm good with women?" Was he being serious?

He nodded, and I laughed.

"What the hell does that stupid lion know?" I asked. "Look, I'm not trying to be mean. Really, I'm not, but I'm not the person you think I am."

"So, you aren't a fate wedding date for people?"

"Okay, I'm exactly who you think I am," I informed him. "What does that have to do with me being good with women? I'm not."

"You know how to talk to people, though," he reminded me. "Can you help me?"

"With what? Who is it that you like? And seriously, what kind of shifter are you?"

"I'm...not."

"You're not?" He knew about shifters, though. He seemed to know quite a bit about them. Generally, it was easy for me to figure out who was human and who wasn't. My sense of smell could really be completely overwhelming: thus the obsession with incense and candles. I'd been to two big parties lately, and I'd managed to get through those just fine. For some reason, parties weren't as bad for me. When there were so many *different* smells, everything kind of blended together. I had much more of a problem when I was meeting with three or four different people who all had really strong emotions.

Right now, Fletcher was experiencing some damn strong emotions.

"I'm not a shifter."

"But you hang out with them?"

"Yeah. Actually, I was raised in the wolf pack."

It was my turn to be surprised.

"A human child raised by wolves?"

"Pretty much."

"That's why you went to the party the other night."

"Yeah."

"The weird Alpha one."

"Yeah."

"So, you're into someone who is a wolf?" I asked. Suddenly, I was a little curious. I didn't often hang out with wolf shifters, so I didn't really know very much about them. What was it that drove this guy to fall for a wolf? Who was it that had gotten him all worked up?

And could I actually help him?

"I just want to know what you do to make people believe you're in love with someone."

Now *that* was interesting. I raised an eyebrow.

"Are you going to try to put me out of business, wolf-man?"

"What? No! Nothing like that." Fletcher seemed a little nervous: almost fidgety. "I'm not going to try to put you out of business," he said. "It's just that I..."

I waited, but my patience was almost at its limit.

"Look, I just need to know how to act confident."

"What?"

"Look at me." He gestured to himself. To be honest, Fletcher looked decidedly normal. He was of average height, average weight, and his moppy brown hair looked, well, *average*. There really wasn't anything about him that really stood out, but there also wasn't anything about him that looked bad.

"How to act confident?"

He nodded. "The woman I like is all confidence. She's at like, two hundred percent."

"And you want to know how to win her over."

"No," he said. "I want to know how to act like I'm confident enough to win her over."

"Interesting," I said. I gestured for him to head into the living room. "I'm going to go take a shower. I'll be back soon," I warned him. "Don't touch anything."

He nodded and headed into the living room. As promised, I went to shower. As soon as I was alone, thoughts of Ivy invaded my head once more. I wondered what she was doing, what she was wearing, and whether she was thinking of me. A few strokes of my cock and my dick was alive and at full mast: hard for a woman who didn't even know just how into her I was. I didn't come. Fletcher was waiting and it would be weird. Still, I couldn't keep myself from imagining that Ivy was the one who had been waiting for me on the porch.

I would have fucking devoured her.

Coming back from a run and finding her waiting would have been hot as hell. I would have loved it. I would have *loved* the chance to touch her and tease her...to lick her. There were so many delicious things that I wanted to do to Ivy. There were so many ways I wanted to make her fall apart for me.

Instead of focusing on that, instead of daydreaming, though, I pried myself from the shower, dressed, and headed downstairs to find Fletcher sitting on the couch. His legs were crossed and he had a pillow on his lap. He looked wildly comfortable for someone I barely knew.

"Feel better?"

"Yes."

"Do you have any pets?"

"No."

"You should get one," he told me. "A pet could be great. You wouldn't have to feel lonely. You'd always have someone around to entertain you."

"I'm not lonely."

"You could still have someone around to entertain you," he said.

"Fletcher, pay attention. I'm going to make this short and sweet."

"Okay."

"The key to being confident is to actually be confident. You have to remind yourself that you're important and valuable."

He stared at me, watching.

"Nobody is going to give you that sense of inner-self worth the way you want them to. That's sadly just now how the world works."

"I understand."

"But you have to balance being confident with not being a dick," I reminded him. That was the key. A woman, especially the type of woman who wanted to date a shifter, wasn't going to put up with macho bullshit caused by someone overcompensating and trying *too* hard to be the one in charge. Women didn't like it when a guy was a creep or a loser.

They wanted someone who was stable: someone who was strong with a gentle heart.

"Don't be a dick," Fletcher repeated. "Got it."

I stared at him. Shifters were hard to age. It was hard to tell specifically how old a shifter was because we tended to age at a slower rate in general than our human counterparts. Despite being a human, Fletcher himself was hard to place. He couldn't have been much younger than me. He had to be in his late 20s or early 30s.

So why didn't he know all of this stuff already?

Had he not dated very much?

Had he not had a chance to get a lot of experience?

The two of us talked for a few more minutes. Eventually, he stood up and said he was going to leave. It was overall a really strange night.

"Don't show up again without calling," I told him as he walked out of the house. He was dressed, but he hadn't driven a car. I watched as he walked to the end of the porch, pulled out a bicycle I hadn't noticed, climbed on it, and started peddling away. I stared as he disappeared down the driveway and vanished out of sight.

What a strange man.

I turned and headed back into the house. I didn't need any more of this. I just needed...

Shit.

I needed to get in touch with my damn feelings and figure out where I was supposed to go from here. That wasn't going to happen, so I threw myself down on the couch and closed my eyes. Hopefully I'd pass out fast. Sleep was the next best thing, I knew. I'd wake up tomorrow and hopefully I'd have the answers I wanted. If not, well, I could just sleep some more. I wasn't a bear shifter, but maybe I'd find a way to hibernate for winter. I'd come crawling out in the springtime and have all of the answers I'd been looking for.

I could do it.

13

Ivy

A few days before the rehearsal dinner, I called Lincoln to talk about everything that was going to happen. We were supposed to finalize everything about the evening: our plans for driving, what we'd be wearing, and even the topics we'd discuss. I was a little surprised with just how thorough he believed in being. This was so much more carefully planned than any date I'd ever had in the past.

I really should have done this whole "fake boyfriend" thing a long time ago, I realized. Having someone who could schmooze at the right moments, who would communicate well, and who knew exactly what to say to my relatives was going to be amazing.

Too bad none of it was real.

The phone rang and I sat there with my eyes closed. There was a chance I'd elaborated everything that had happened in my mind. I knew that. Maybe the stuff that had happened between us really had just been something people do when they're getting ready to attend a wedding together.

It didn't mean that it *meant* anything.

None of this had to *mean* anything, right?

He answered on the first ring.

"Hello."

His deep, sultry voice washed over me. I bit my lip. *Get it together, Ivy.* I was sitting on the couch with two of my cats. Orion was on my left side and Jupiter was on my right. These two kitties brought me endless joy. Really, they were incredible. The two of them coupled with Mr. Fuzzypants were better than anyone I'd ever met. I couldn't imagine my world without them.

Still, the comfort my cats brought me all but evaporated when I heard Lincoln's voice.

"It's Ivy," I said when he answered.

"I know." There was this deep chuckle on the other end of the line.

Of course, he knew. It seemed like there wasn't anything that surprised Lincoln. Even if he hadn't been expecting my call, and even if he didn't have me listed as a contact, something told me that he would just know. He always seemed to just know.

"I was just calling about Friday," I explained to him. A knot twisted in my stomach as I realized just how close the wedding was. The entire experience was going to be less awful with him there, but it was still a wedding I felt unwelcome at despite being a bridesmaid.

"I'm looking forward to it. Are we still planning for me to drive us both?" Lincoln asked. That was what we'd discussed previously.

"Um, yeah, if that's okay. I mean, if you don't mind."

I knew it was out of his way. The idea we had was that it might look strange if we drove separately to the wedding. People would either think we'd broken up or that we weren't actually dating, so it would be best for him to pick me up and make our grand arrival at the same time.

"I don't mind. I booked a hotel for myself for the weekend, so I'll be close."

While that made more sense than having him drive back and forth between the two towns, it still felt strange. Almost wasteful. Hotels weren't exactly cheap. Even if he was an attorney, the economy was what it was. Every little bit of money saved helped.

"A hotel?"

"Yes, I don't want to have to be driving back and forth between the events," he explained, echoing my thoughts.

It made sense. It was going to be a lot of driving for sure. Still, the cost of all things aside, I didn't like the idea that he'd have to stay in a plain, boring hotel. What if he got lonely? I didn't want Lincoln to get lonely. Yeah, he was being paid for helping me out as my date. This wasn't a free position or anything, but I still felt like I owed it to him to make sure he had as good of a time as possible.

What if he stayed with me?

What if I invited him?

Oh, I knew that we'd once more be blurring the lines between appropriate behavior, but what if I offered anyway? The worst thing that would happen was he'd laugh at me and say no, but the best thing that could happen was him saying yes.

What if he did?

The two of us were electric together. Our last night spent together basically proved that. I knew that he liked the way I looked. He liked touching me and I liked him touching me, too. I liked so many different things about him that it drove me crazy.

"I have plenty of space," I said before I could stop myself. Shit. I shouldn't have said that. The other end of the line was quiet. Silent. Had he even heard me?

"Lincoln?"

A long pause. Then he spoke.

"That's a dangerous offer, Ivy."

It was. I knew it was. I just didn't care. I didn't want him to stay alone and I...

Well, I didn't want to be alone, either. So there. Maybe I wasn't being a nice person at all. Maybe I was being a terrible person. A greedy, selfish person.

I wanted him with me because I liked him.

A lot.

Even though I wasn't supposed to.

"We don't have to do anything naughty," I told him.

A lie.

Obviously, this was a lie.

I wanted to do so many naughty things with him that it made me sick.

He didn't deserve that, did he?

No, he deserved someone sweet. Kind. Someone who would move heaven and hell to be with him: not someone who just didn't want to sleep alone.

"What if I want to do something naughty?" Lincoln asked me quietly.

I hesitated before I said anything. My breath seemed to catch. Had he really just asked me that?

"What?" I asked him. I must have misheard. Yeah. Definitely. I definitely must have misheard what he'd asked.

Lincoln was smart, though, and he wasn't going to let me play games and get away with it. I loved that about him, but I also hated it. He wasn't going to let me off easy when it came to teasing him. If I wanted Lincoln, then I'd have to earn it. I understood that.

"You heard me," he said gently. His voice seemed to have gotten deeper. Sometimes it did that when we were speaking. I wasn't really sure what it was about him...but sometimes his voice just sounded like it was on the verge of being something else. It was like there was some sort of monster lurking deep inside of Lincoln. Maybe it was his inner bad boy coming out to play.

"I heard you."

I couldn't lie to him.

Wouldn't lie.

If he wanted to play, then we'd play.

If he wanted to tease, then we'd tease.

"And what do you think about what I said?" That was the question, wasn't it? The truth was that I thought it was hot as hell. I was getting turned on just thinking about him sitting at home alone. I pictured him with his legs spread on the couch, cock out, stroking it for me.

"I think it was a very naughty thing to say."

"Well, maybe that's the type of person I am. I'm not a good boy, Ivy...I'm not a hero. I'm just me."

"I never said you were a hero," I whispered. I knew there was more to him than met the eye. I knew that he was the type of person who had secrets I'd never understand...secrets I'd never know. I could tell just by looking at him that there was more to this dude than most people could possibly understand.

I also knew that I didn't care.

"Sometimes when you look at me, I get the feeling that you think I'm a much better person than I am."

I thought about this for a second. Was Lincoln right? Was he correct in saying that I didn't really know anything about him about him? Maybe that was the problem. Maybe the problem was this whole thing was happening so fast that I hadn't really given myself a chance to truly get to know him on a deeper level. He'd asked me endless questions because it was all part of the act, but I'd tried very hard not to ask him too many questions. I'd tried not to impose too much because...

Well, because I didn't want to risk upsetting him or crossing some sort of invisible boundary.

"I don't know where the line is," I whispered.

"What do you mean, Ivy?"

"I mean, I don't know what I'm allowed to say to you. I don't know what I'm allowed to do to you or...well, I don't know what I'm allowed to *want* to do to you."

"Are you saying that you want to get to know me better or that you think I know you too well?"

"I don't know...both, maybe? Maybe both." He knew a lot about me, but on a surface level. He knew I liked my job bartending. He knew I was good at what I did. I could mix drinks like nobody's business, which was strange since I tended to be pretty shy and quiet in real life. At work, though, I came alive.

I loved being able to craft my own cocktails and create my own drinks. It was a damn fun job. Perhaps most of all, when I was behind that counter, the room was mine. I was the one in charge. I was the one who got to be in control.

Out here, out in the real world, I was very aware of the fact that I wasn't in charge. My mom had been in charge of me much of my life, and even when I'd moved out, it had been to live with Susan for a short time while I was in college. Once I'd realized that school wasn't for me, I'd gotten my own place, but I hadn't left my hometown. Because of that, I'd fallen into the trap of everyone thinking they knew what was best for me.

They didn't.

None of them knew what was best for me because none of them knew me.

"There are a lot of ways I want to get to know you better, Ivy. Most of them involve us spending time together without our clothing on."

I swallowed hard, licking my lips.

Yeah, I'd thought about that, too. I'd thought about that so much. It was something I wanted: something I craved. And oh, I needed that.

"Does that mean you've been thinking about the other night?" I asked him. I probably shouldn't have asked him, but I couldn't stop thinking about it. I couldn't stop thinking about all of the things that we've done that night that he'd stayed over. Honestly, it had been a really terrible idea for me to text him back when I was drunk, but I didn't really mind. Everything had worked out so well.

"What do you mean, have I been thinking about it? Of course, I've been thinking about it. It's all I can think about. Every time I close my eyes, I think of you. Every time I shower and the water washes over my skin, it reminds me of you touching me...of you sliding your tongue over me."

It had been some damn good kissing: some damn good touching. Even though we hadn't actually ended up sleeping together sexually, we'd gotten to pass out together physically, and that had been sweet as hell, too, in a weirdly romantic sort of way. The fact that we'd fallen asleep in each other's arms felt intimate in a way I couldn't really describe.

I held my breath for a minute. This really wasn't the way I saw the phone call going. I just called because I thought we needed to coordinate our outfits for the reception. I thought we needed to plan out what we were going to do, to wear, and to say.

But now the two of us were talking and I felt like I was going crazy. My entire body felt hot and achy and needy and wonderful. Everything about me just seemed to feel like it was on fire.

"Lincoln, you have to stop talking to me like this. You don't know what you're doing to me." Or maybe he just didn't care.

Did he care that he was getting me so turned on and horny that my panties were soaked?

Did he care that my pussy felt empty, like it was craving his cock?

No, no he didn't care. He didn't care about any of that.

"Maybe you should tell me what I'm doing to you," his voice was sultry. Sexy. It was everything to me. When he talked to me in this deep, steamy voice I wanted to melt against him. I wanted to rub against him like a damn cat. *That* was what I wanted.

I definitely got the feeling he knew that.

Spreading my legs, I started rubbing myself over my panties. I didn't care that it was weird or inappropriate or strange. Totally didn't care. He didn't have to know, anyway, unless I wanted him to.

Could I come while I was on the phone?

Could I be sneaky and have an orgasm without him knowing?

Now *that* could be a lot of fun, I realized.

That could be a pretty damn good time.

"Well, you said this was supposed to be a business relationship," I reminded him. "To be honest, the things I want to do to you when you talk to me like this aren't very professional."

"Tell me." His voice was demanding. I thought I heard the faint sound of a zipper. Was he stroking his cock while we talked? Was he thinking about all of the wonderful things we'd done together? Oh, this could be fun. This could be *so much fun*.

"Well, I want to finish what we started." That was honest. I hadn't been able to stop thinking about him. Even though we hadn't technically slept together, I wanted that. I wanted all of it. I wanted to feel his hands on my body and his cock in my pussy. I wanted him to fuck me until I forgot my own damn name. That was what I wanted.

"What was it that we started?"

Fuck.

He was going to make me say it, wasn't he?

"I think you know," I whispered. "I think you know what we started."

"I want to hear you say it."

There it was again. He was bossy, wasn't he? Demanding. Dominating.

"You know, for a guy who plays video games, I feel like you're being kind of pushy."

"Baby, anyone who plays multiplayer games knows that every good team needs a leader."

"Are you the leader?"

"Tonight I am."

"And where are you leading me?" I bit my lip. Fuck. I needed to calm down like crazy or I was just going to completely lose it.

"Where do you want to go, pretty girl?"

"Everywhere." I wanted to go everywhere with him. Back when I was young, people used to talk about how "far" you would go with someone. After every date it would be like, "How far did you go?" "Did he kiss you?" "Did he get very far?" Now I really understood that because with Lincoln, I didn't want there to be any sort of limitations. Where did I want to go with him? To the fucking stars. That was where I wanted to go.

"I want that, too, baby," he growled.

"I know we made an agreement," I started.

"Fuck the agreement," he snarled. "If I sleep at your place, Ivy, I'm happy to break the agreement."

Happy to break it?

Did that mean it wouldn't be pretend?

It wouldn't be make-believe?

It would be real?

"I feel the exact same way," I whispered. I wanted to break our agreement, too.

"If I sleep at your place," he continued, "you're getting the full boyfriend treatment."

"What does that mean?"

"It means you get anything you want, Ivy."

Anything I want.

Anything.

"What if that means sex?" I whispered slowly. I really, really needed to make sure we were on the same page with this because that was what I wanted. I wanted to melt into him. I wanted to lose myself in him.

"Is that what you want?"

"Maybe," I whispered.

"I like you, Ivy," he admitted, and my heart felt like it was going to explode.

"Does that mean...does that mean you won't be pretending?" I held my breath. For some reason, it seemed like I wasn't able to physically breathe anymore, like I'd forgotten how to, but I didn't care. If I started breathing and it was too loud or my heart started pounding too wildly, it was going to shatter this perfect moment between us.

Was there a chance that he was going to want to date me when this was all over?

That was what I really wanted. It wasn't just because I didn't want to deal with rejection. I didn't. I also didn't want to deal with the idea that the two of us might not be compatible because oh, I felt compatible with Lincoln.

"I'm not pretending now," he breathed. Fuck. He sounded just as turned on as I was. "Tell me what you're wearing," he said. He was taking control of the situation and I didn't care. I didn't mind at all because it was *nice* to be with someone like this. Lincoln knew exactly what he wanted, but unlike my sister, he wasn't taking things to be selfish. He was demanding because he knew this was going to be good for both of us.

I wanted to lean into this moment, to experience everything he had to offer because I had a feeling that when this was over, I was never going to be the same again. Was Lincoln stroking his cock for me? Was I on speakerphone so he could use both of his hands to touch his body?

"What am I wearing?" I asked quietly. Oh, this was such a hard question. Was I supposed to be honest? Or was I supposed to say something I thought he might like? This was a huge dilemma because the last time we did this, I was drunk. I'd taken off all of my clothing and it hadn't been a big deal at all. Now, however, I was wearing a black tank top, grey pajama pants, and green-and-red socks that had little chili peppers on them.

How could I make that sexy?

"Ivy? Are you still there?"

"I'm here," I whispered. It was going to be best to be honest, I finally figured. "I'm wearing a thin black tank. No bra. My nipples are hard." Because I was playing with them. Because his words were getting me so damn horny. "I'm wearing pajama pants. No panties, of course."

"Is your hand down your pants, Ivy? Are you touching that soft pussy for me?"

Yeah. Yeah, I was doing that. More than that, I was soaked. I was so wet from this conversation that my fingers were starting to slip and slide across my skin.

And oh, I was getting close.

"Is it bad that I'm jealous of your cats? They get to be with you tonight. I want to be there with you."

For some reason that made me laugh. He was so sweet. Even at a moment like this where we were fooling around, he was sweet to me.

"You don't have to be jealous," I chuckled. Then I stopped. "Not of them. Not of anyone."

"No?"

"No," I whispered. Swallowing hard, I said boldly, "because when I'm touching myself like this, Lincoln, the only person I'm thinking of is you."

"Take off the tanktop."

A command.

An order.

I wanted to do it for him. Wanted to obey for him.

"Are you sure this is what you want?"

"Are you trying to give me an out?" It was Lincoln's turn to chuckle.

"You know, I'm just...I don't want you to feel pressured."

"To listen to a gorgeous woman touch herself for me? Ivy, I'm not feeling pressured. Take off your shirt."

"Okay," I whispered. I set the phone down and slipped it off. Then I picked up the phone again to keep talking. While I'd done video calls with people I'd dated before, this felt different. More intimate. It felt almost sweet. The fact that we were only using our voices and had to imagine what the other person was doing was hot as hell. I could definitely get used to this kind of treatment.

"Are you playing with those soft, sweet breasts for me?"

"Yes, Lincoln. Are you rubbing your cock for me?" Shit. I wanted him to be. I wanted him to rub that cock until he came. I wanted him to touch himself over and over until he fucking exploded and got cum everywhere. That was what I wanted. I wanted Lincoln to make a damn mess because he couldn't stop thinking of me.

"Of course, baby. I can't stop thinking about you. I had such a good time with you the other night..."

"Even though we didn't sleep together?"

"Ivy, trust me," he purred, "when I finally sink my cock into that tight pussy of yours, it'll be well worth the wait."

Fuck.

Me.

Silly.

"Tell me more," I whispered.

"I'm close to coming, Ivy," he admitted. "I want you to come for me, too. I want you to come thinking about all of the ways I'm going to make love to you this weekend. I want you to think about all of the ways you're going to take my cock: in your pussy, in your mouth."

I closed my eyes. I tried to speak but it seemed impossible.

"Lincoln..."

"Tell me you want it, too."

"I want it. I want it so bad."

"Then show me," he growled. "Be a good girl and come for me. Do it now."

How could I resist such a command?

When I came, I dropped my phone because the orgasm was so intense. It didn't matter. Lincoln's own orgasm was so hot and loud that I heard it anyway. It was like flames were licking at every inch of my body and I just didn't care because it was so damn good. All of this was so fucking good that I was going to go crazy.

Shit.

How was I going to survive this weekend?

Meekly, I dropped to the floor and felt around until I found my phone.

"Lincoln, are you still there?" I whispered. He just chuckled.

"Yeah, baby, I'm still here."

"That was really hot." You know, just in case he didn't know that it was really, really fucking good for me.

"It was hot as hell," he agreed. "Ivy, I can't wait to see you this weekend."

I couldn't wait, either. I just wasn't sure if my heart could handle it. Lincoln was pure seduction. Pure sin.

And I loved every bit of it.

14

Lincoln

The day of the rehearsal dinner arrived. I was busy at the office until closing time, but the rehearsal dinner was also scheduled to begin at 8:00, so I'd still have enough time to make it over to the event. Considering my relationship with Tameka, I was feeling more nervous than usual about the entire wedding weekend. Tricking Ivy's family was one thing. Playing my cousin was another.

My cousin was a smart woman. She was shrewd and calculating. She wasn't going to let me get away with anything if she could help it. At the very least, she'd make sure that I didn't act like this date was fake. She'd be watching me like a hawk – not a tiger – so I had to be careful. Every move would be carefully analyzed and assessed. I understood that those were the rules of the game, so I'd be careful.

The drive flew by, compliments of my latest anime podcast. There were going to be a couple of new shows dropping soon, so I was making mental notes to check them out. Before I knew it, I was at her apartment. I parked my car and paused for just a moment.

Was I ready for this?

Actually ready?

I thought about our phone call. I thought about the way she took my breath away. I closed my eyes and pictured how I'd felt when she'd made me come using only her dirty mouth and her naughty, naughty words.

Oh yes, I was ready. I was definitely, totally ready.

I took the stairs two at a time until I got to her loft. I buzzed to be let in, but nothing happened. She didn't answer or open the door.

Strange.

Maybe she was listening to music and couldn't hear me. Either that or she was watching something sweet to prep for a stressful evening. I'd given her my DVD copy of *Weathering With You*, so maybe she was hyping herself up for the weekend. I was early. It was almost seven, but that would give us enough time to have a drink before we headed over to the church. We could even just sit and make out like a couple of teenagers if we wanted to.

I tried calling her, but the same thing happened: nothing. No answer. No sounds.

Normally, this was where I'd start to realize that I was being ghosted. It didn't happen often, but in this line of work, sometimes it was a real possibility. People got cold feet or their parents found them a better, more suitable date. Sometimes people just decided not to go to the event at all.

With Ivy, though, there was too much of a connection between us for me to believe that she'd simply ghost me for no reason. No, if Ivy wasn't answering the door, then there was a real problem, and I was going to find out what it was.

I pressed all of the buttons on the apartment door, jamming them over and over until someone finally let me in. Then I raced up to her apartment, skipping steps as I did. When I got to her door, I knocked.

No answer.

I scented the air.

Fear.

She was scared and...sad.

Something was wrong.

"Ivy!" I called out. "Ivy, are you okay?"

I knocked on the door again, but still nothing.

A neighbor peeked a head out, obviously disturbed by the noise. I felt a little bad, but not that bad. Maybe he knew where Ivy was.

"Uh, hey, are you bothering Ivy?" It was a younger guy, probably about 20 or 21. The faint scent of weed wafted from his apartment. He looked sheepish as he met my eyes. I didn't care about the weed. I just wanted to find her.

"I'm not bothering her. I'm trying to find her. I'm worried about her."

I knew how it looked. A big stranger breaking into the building to bang on her door? Yeah, they probably thought I was some sort of stalker. I wasn't. I just wanted to make sure that she was okay because this entire situation had warning bells going off in my head.

Ivy wasn't irresponsible. She wasn't the type of person who was going to blow off her sister's rehearsal dinner or our date without warning. She'd never do that. If anything, Ivy was *too* responsible. She was always prompt and usually early, in fact. So what had happened tonight? Where was she?

"Does she even know you, man? 'Cause uh, I think you should leave."

"I'm worried about Ivy, too," a young woman popped her head out of the door, too. She sniffed the air and then looked at me. I knew what that meant. She was a shifter, too. She knew I wasn't here to hurt Ivy because she, too, could smell the girl's emotions hanging in the air. "Something isn't right."

"Have you seen her?" I asked. I didn't bother to introduce myself. Somehow, it felt like we didn't have enough time for that.

"Not since this morning."

"Have you heard anything from her? Any noises from her apartment?"

They both shook their heads.

Shit.

I looked back at her door. I could break it down, but then I'd definitely have to pay to fix it. Still, if she was hurt, it would be totally worth it to be able to save her from whatever had gone wrong. Ivy didn't deserve to suffer alone. No matter what she was going through, I wanted to help her. I wanted to save her. I wanted to make sure that she was going to be safe and sound and happy because...

Well, because she was my mate, and I was crazy about her.

Love wasn't something I'd been trying to find, yet I had. I'd found it in her. It was in that moment I realized that I'd do just about anything to prove my love to her. I'd go to the ends of the Earth if it meant convincing her that I really did care for her.

I was just about to kick open the door when the lady neighbor cleared her throat.

"If I may?" The woman held up a finger. "Why don't you try the knob first?"

"The knob?"

"If she left in a hurry, she might not have locked the door," the guy said.

"That would be very irresponsible."

They both stared at me, blinking.

"It's a safe neighborhood," the woman finally said. "Not a lot of bad things happen around here that would worry someone like Ivy."

I understood what she was saying. The girl was saying that she had taken on the job of protector of the apartment building. No one was going to do anything crazy to anyone here that she wouldn't know about.

Except, apparently, leave the building.

I reached for the knob and turned. To my surprise, the door opened easily. The neighbors were now invested in my search for Ivy and they joined me as I walked into the apartment.

"Ivy? Are you here?" I called out. "Are you okay?"

"Ivy?" The guy was yelling now. "You okay, neighbor? This guy sneaked into the building for you. Can't tell if he's a stalker or not."

"Jake!" The girl hissed.

"Sorry, Gretchen. It's just that...well, you know. Look at him."

I was bigger than Jake by at least a foot. I also looked a lot more cut than the human. Not that there was anything wrong with him. I knew what he was saying, though. I didn't belong in a place like this. I could barely fit through the doorframe to the apartment.

Now that we were inside, the scent of Ivy's anguish was stronger. My stomach twisted and I felt sick. What the hell had happened here?

"Something bad happened," the woman realized. Gretchen sniffed the air. "She was really upset, wasn't she?"

Jake stared at her. "Babe, you said you weren't going to use your shifter scents around strangers because it's not safe."

"He's a shifter, too."

"Oh, cool," Jake nodded. "How can you tell?"

"Questions are for later, Jakey," I said, rolling my eyes.

Just then, Orion came wandering out of the bedroom. He stopped when he saw me and returned back to the bedroom. Okay, message received. Jupiter peeked a head out of the bathroom and then followed Orion's lead and went back where he'd come from.

Okay, so that was two cats accounted for.

Where was Mr. Fuzzypants?

And where was Ivy?

"Her dress for tonight," Gretchen gasped as she reached for the dress. It was crumpled on the floor. Before she even lifted it up, I realized what was wrong. I glanced over at the countertop where Ivy's computer was sitting open. She'd Googled the address of a cat hospital.

"Gretchen. Jake. Something's wrong with Mr. Fuzzypants," I said. "I need to go."

"I'll drive," Gretchen said, pulling a set of keys from her pocket. "I know a shortcut."

"You've been smoking," I pointed out.

"Just Jakey," she said.

"Hey, don't call me Jakey," Jake pouted.

"Jake, go back to the apartment. I'm taking Ivy's boyfriend to the pet hospital and when I get back, I want you naked and ready for me."

Jake blushed but nodded and left, retreating to the apartment. When Gretchen looked back at me, I raised an eyebrow.

"What?" She shrugged. "Every wolf has their kink. He's mine. Let's go."

THE ANIMAL HOSPITAL was located ten minutes away from her apartment. As soon as Gretchen pulled into the parking lot, I was running into the hospital. I didn't even wait for her to shut off the engine. It felt like there was no time. I burst through the doors of the hospital into the silent waiting room. The receptionist, who had been reading a book, looked up at me sharply.

"I'm here for Ivy," I said, rushing to her desk. "Is Ivy here?"

The woman looked at me. I could tell she wasn't sure whether she should let me know if Ivy was actually in the back or not. I knew there were laws about patient confidentiality. There were probably policies in place that would prevent her from sharing anything with me about whether or not Ivy was at the animal hospital. Even though Ivy wasn't the patient here, she still had rights.

Then I knew what to say.

"I'm here for Mr. Fuzzypants," I said.

As soon as his name left my lips, the woman's face fell, and that was the moment I knew.

I was too late.

I was too late for Ivy.

I was too late for her sweet cat.

I had no idea what had happened. Maybe he'd had an accident. Maybe he was just an old cat. All I knew was that Ivy was somewhere here and she was hurting. She needed me. She needed someone to be here for her because whatever had happened was terrible enough that she shouldn't be dealing with it alone.

"I'll bring you to her," the woman said, standing. Gretchen appeared in the doorway but said nothing. "I'll be right with you," the receptionist said.

"I'm here for Ivy," Gretchen told her. The woman nodded and motioned for both of us to come with her. We followed her back down a hallway and to a small room. The woman paused for a moment and then looked at us. She took a deep breath before she spoke. I knew that this job couldn't have been easy for her. Even if these weren't her pets, she probably really loved her patients and cared deeply for them.

"He's already gone," she whispered. "We did everything we could. She's having a really hard time. You can stay as long as you need."

I pushed the door open and crossed the room to Ivy. I grabbed her, pulling her from the chair she was silently crying in, and I pulled her into my arms. I held her tightly as she kept sobbing. In seconds, my shoulder was wet with her tears. I didn't care about anything except the fact that she was safe. She was safe, and I was here for her.

"You came," she whispered.

"Of course, I came."

"Mr. Fuzzypants..." She couldn't say anything else without crying.

"Don't say anything," I told her. "You don't have to say anything."

"I'm here, too," Gretchen said. She positioned herself behind Ivy and wrapped her arms around her from behind so that Ivy was surrounded by people who loved her on all sides.

"I can't believe he's gone," Ivy sobbed.

My heart cracked. If it hadn't already been broken at the fear of something terrible happening, it was completely shattering now. Ivy loved her cats more than anything else. She didn't have a very strong relationship with her family, which meant these kitties...they were *everything* to her.

I held her as her entire world faded. Gretchen and I both held her. Ivy cried, and she cried, and then she cried just a little bit more.

I didn't tell her I was sorry. I didn't tell her it was going to be okay. Those were things that never helped at a time like this.

Instead, I told her I was there for her.

Instead, I said she didn't have to be alone.

And I held her.

15

Ivy

It wasn't supposed to be like this.

Mr. Fuzzypants had been sick for a long time. I'd known it. Dr. Trianca had known it. Hilda, the receptionist, had known it. We'd all known.

I just didn't know that it was going to be today.

I didn't know that tonight was the night I'd have to say goodbye.

I really, really thought I'd have more time with him, but I didn't.

And it felt like I was slowly choking to death.

That was always the problem with saying goodbye, wasn't it? We always wanted more time. We always thought we had more time. Sometimes, though, time was elusive. Every once in a while, time was something that just slipped from us before we could do anything to stop it.

Gretchen and Lincoln had figured out where I was, and they'd shown up. I had no idea how they'd done that. The two of them had worked some sort of magic because they'd just sort of appeared and wrapped me up in their arms and promised that they were there.

They hadn't said they were sorry, and that was what I appreciated most. Sorry wasn't going to bring him back. Sorry wasn't going to fix things.

They also didn't lie to me, plying me with fake promises like, "it's going to be okay," and "everything happens for a reason."

I wasn't going to be okay.

Nothing about this was okay.

There was no reason I should have lost my pet. Not like this. Not today.

So, there was a part of me that realized just how damn lucky I was to be spending time with two people who truly understood that all I needed was them. I just needed to know that they were there. I just needed to know that I wasn't going to have to face all of this alone.

The next hour was a blur. I had to fill out some paperwork. I had to make some choices. Everyone was very patient with me and helped me through everything. Hilda brought me a little card with my cat's pawprints on it.

"You'll want this," she told me gently. I started crying again, but I took the card. She was right. Yeah, I wanted it. I wanted his little pawprints. Maybe I'd frame it, but maybe looking at those little prints every day would be too hard and I'd put it in a scrapbook or something.

When it was all over, Gretchen and Lincoln drove me back to the lofts. The time on the clock read 8:13. We were late for the rehearsal dinner. I hadn't even realized how long I'd been at the vet's office. Shit. Susan was going to completely flip out and lose her mind, wasn't she? There was a part of me that was embarrassed for worrying. I shouldn't have been so upset or anxious about the whole thing. I shouldn't have even worried.

"When did you get to my place?" I asked Lincoln.

"I had to stay a little late at work," he admitted. "I showed up just before seven."

"Thank you...for what you did," I swallowed, nodding. Then I pointed to the clock. "We're supposed to be at the party now," I whispered. Despite knowing that I'd had a hard day, an impossible day, it was difficult to let go of the idea that I needed to be doing more.

"I already texted Tameka," Lincoln told me. "I let her know we were going to be late."

"Susan is going to be pissed."

"You can skip this entirely, you know," Lincoln told me, brushing back a strand of my hair. "You don't have to go."

"He's right," Gretchen nodded. "This was something really traumatic. You need some time."

Time.

She was right. They both were. The three of us were standing outside of my door for what felt like an eternity. It was hard to accept the reality that when I pushed open that door, it was just going to be me, Orion, and Jupiter. No more Mr. Fuzzypants. No more kitty. No more...

I took a deep breath, though. It was now or never. I pushed the door open.

When I walked into the apartment, it was like my entire world was breaking over and over and over. Orion and Jupiter came over to me right away, meowing. They knew something was wrong. They might not have realized what it was, but they knew something wasn't quite right. Maybe the energy in the room was bad. I wasn't sure. Still, I squatted down and started scratching Orion's ear.

I said, "Everything is going to be okay." It was a lie, of course. It was something that wasn't true and everyone in the room knew it wasn't true. While I'd appreciated Gretchen and Lincoln avoiding that phrase with me, I used it with my cats.

I was a little disappointed in myself.

Even though Orion and Jupiter were cats and not people, I had a feeling they could sense that something was different, too. They knew that everything was changing and there was nothing I could do to stop that. I couldn't bring their friend back no matter how much I really, really wanted to.

The truth was that Mr. Fuzzypants had been sick for a long time. I had tried to prepare myself as best I could, but I still felt completely shocked. Every part of my body hurt and I had a feeling that it wasn't going to take much for me to start crying again.

I looked over at my friends. Gretchen had been so kind to come over. She really hadn't had to do that. Still, it meant a lot to me to know that she was there.

Then of course there was Lincoln: my handsome, wonderful date. Lincoln: the man who drove me crazy. Lincoln... Lincoln: the man who didn't love me but whom I was crazy about.

"You can go. You don't have to be here."

They could leave me alone.

I'd be okay.

I wouldn't do anything crazy like get super drunk. I wouldn't start smoking. I would just sit on the couch and cry as I got ready for the rehearsal dinner. That was okay. I would be okay.

Gretchen and Lincoln exchanged looks. There was something silent they weren't saying to me. I knew that they were both worried even without them actually saying it out loud. Finally, Gretchen spoke.

"It's okay. We're both happy to be here with you."

I knew that they meant it, too. These people...these were *my* people. These were people who weren't going to let anything bad happen to me. They weren't going to let me hurt alone.

Lincoln put a hand on my shoulder. He looked in my eyes, and when I looked at him, it was like I knew that everything was going to be all right. Everything was going to be okay...eventually.

Having them with me made me feel safe. It didn't make the pain go away, and it didn't stop my heart from hurting, but it made me feel like everything eventually would just stop spinning. Someday, my head would stop spinning.

"We're both here for you," Lincoln said, "and I think it might be a good idea for you to stay home tonight."

"What? No. No, I can't stay home tonight."

"You really should think about it. It's just the rehearsal dinner," Gretchen added. "Your sister should understand that you've just gone through something traumatic. You need some time to take care of yourself."

"You obviously don't know my sister." It was mean, but it was also true. Gretchen had never had the privilege of meeting Susan, which was probably a good thing. Susan could be very intense, and Gretchen and her boyfriend Jake were both very laid-back people. They were wonderful neighbors and I really appreciated them. I could count on them for just about anything that I needed. They were really, really kind.

"Hey." That was Lincoln speaking. I looked up to see his eyes staring into mine. He was so serious. I liked that about him, but sometimes it also made me really nervous. Lincoln was the kind of guy who looked like he had a secret. Every time we talked I had the feeling that there was something he wasn't telling me but I couldn't figure out what it might be. I didn't think it was something terrible like he was secretly a serial killer, or he had a really weird hobby. Instead I thought it was something personal, something he wasn't ready to share, but maybe he would eventually.

"Gretchen is right," said Lincoln. "I would be happy to call Tameka and let her know we actually can't make it after all. I could even call your sister and let her know that it's not going to happen tonight."

I wasn't so sure that they would understand. Besides, I didn't want to tell Susan about Mr. Fuzzypants. Susan didn't like cats, and even if she did, I didn't think she'd understand the pain of losing one I had loved for so very long.

It would be better, I thought, to play it cool. I would much rather have my sister think I was too arrogant to pay attention to the time and thus show up late than for her to know something so deeply personal about me.

I wasn't ready to talk.

I didn't know if I would ever be ready to talk.

"I appreciate that," I finally said, "but honestly, I don't really want to sit at my home crying all night and if I don't go, that's what I'm going to do. I'm going to sit here being sad, eating ice cream, and probably paying way too much for cheap delivery food."

Lincoln looked at me carefully. His eyes searched mine. He was looking for just the right bit of information. He wanted to know if I meant it, I realized. He wanted to know if I was really okay or if I was completely full of it. Finally, he seemed to find the answers he was looking for. He nodded.

"Okay then. We'll go. Why don't you take a shower? I'll text Tameka that we're on our way."

"Yeah," I nodded. I could do that. I could handle a shower. I wasn't going to look my best as the rehearsal, but that was okay. This part of the night was really for my sister. It wasn't for me, was it? It was for her.

Gretchen reached out and squeezed my hand. She promised me that she was close if I needed anything, which I appreciated. Then she left, and I was alone with Lincoln. I was alone with the hottest wedding date ever, and my thoughts, and my sadness.

I didn't say anything else. I just focused on getting to the bathroom, on getting into the shower, and getting dressed for the evening.

Fifteen minutes later, I had somehow managed to pull my hair into a loose bow bun, dab on the tiniest amount of makeup, and pull on a dress. It wasn't the one I'd been planning to wear. That dress was gone. I hadn't even seen it on the counter when we came back. I thought maybe Gretchen had taken it. If she wanted to clean it for me or even throw it away, I would be perfectly happy with that. I didn't want a memory of the outfit I've been wearing the night my cat died.

I brought out the sweatpants that I had changed into before driving to the vet's office. I threw them into the trash can. Then I looked over at Lincoln who was still waiting so patiently, so kindly. I didn't deserve him. I didn't deserve this tonight.

He was too good for me.

He was too good for this entire situation.

"Are you sure you're ready for this?"

I wasn't.

In zero ways was I ready, but I nodded and pasted on a smile.

"I'm ready," I lied.

16

Lincoln

When we pulled up to the church, I knew right away that things were going to be a mess. The parking lot was packed. We were an hour late, so it was surprising to me that the rehearsal was still happening. The original plan had been to attend the rehearsal and then have a very, very late dinner. However, it was 9 o'clock now and everyone was still at the church instead of the restaurant just down the street.

What was going on?

When we entered the church, we could see why: chaos had erupted. The wedding party was talking, waving their arms around, and yelling at each other. Nobody was standing at the front of the church, though. People were in random places throughout the sanctuary. Okay, that was weird. I stepped over to a guy I didn't recognize. He was probably a groomsman.

"Hey, what happened?"

"Crazy, right?" I was getting surfer guy vibes from this dude. "It's like, one minute the church is normal. The next minute, a pipe bursts everywhere."

"Everywhere?"

"Oh yeah," he nodded. "Pretty gross. You should see the basement. Hell, you should see the bathrooms on this floor."

Ivy sighed. "That's terrible," she murmured.

"Is there going to be permanent damage?" I asked.

"Doubt it," the guy shrugged. "Probably can't hold a wedding here, though."

That was understandable, I thought. After all, who wanted to force their guests to stand in puddles?

I heard a little wail and looked over to find the source of the sound. Susan was crying to the priest in one corner of the room.

Her fiancé was next to her. The two of them seemed distraught, although Susan was the one who seemed truly upset. The poor priest didn't seem to know what he was supposed to do. I felt bad for the poor guy. It wasn't like he could control the plumbing in the building. That wasn't exactly his job, was it?

The guy we'd been talking to slipped back to his friends. Ivy and I lingered by the door and took in everything that was happening. This really wasn't what I'd expected. I'd been to quite a few different weddings, but none of them had been like this. After a moment, Ivy's mother noticed us and made a beeline toward us.

"You're an hour late."

"Yes, I had a bit of a work emergency." I lied easily. Sometimes I was surprised at just how easy it was to lie. Probably, it was something I needed to work on, but that was an issue for another day. I didn't know whether Ivy wanted her mom to know about her cat. Even if she did want to share that information, it was something that would probably be best discussed in private. Sharing such a personal topic here in the church might just upset Ivy even more. Plus, her family seemed a bit intense. I wouldn't put it past Susan to accuse Ivy of trying to steal her thunder or something like that. No, it was best to be discreet at a time like this.

"A work emergency?" Eleanor raised an eyebrow.

"Yes, a work emergency. You know what being an attorney is like."

Eleanor frowned. "How would I know what being an attorney is like? I'm not an attorney."

Ignoring her question and her rude tone, I gestured to the chaos unfolding around us.

"What's going on?"

Eleanor rolled her eyes. "Just some minor drama with the church. A pipe broke tonight, so we can't practice. In fact, pretty much everything here is completely soaked. They're moving us to a church that's just down the road. It should be just as pretty as this one."

"Then why are we still here?"

It was only me and Eleanor speaking. Ivy hadn't said anything, nor did I expect her to. It was easy to scent the anxiety on her. It was radiating from her body. Tameka would notice it soon if she hadn't already. Then again, everyone in the room seemed anxious as hell, so maybe my cousin wouldn't be able to sniff out this particular human when comparing her to all of the others.

I took a deep breath. I hoped that eventually, I'd get better at dealing with scenting so many different feelings at once. My inner-tiger was clawing at me, begging to get loose. I wanted to run. I wanted to go run until I didn't feel sad anymore, until I didn't feel Ivy's pain anymore.

"Why are we still here?" Eleanor repeated my question. "Because Susan is still trying to figure out if there is some way to dry the carpet and repair the drywall before tomorrow."

I wanted to roll my eyes. Susan was wasting time and she was being dramatic. No, the poor priest couldn't do anything about the wet church. Nobody could. Nobody could stop the church from being wet, so it was time to accept that and move on.

"Maybe I can talk to them," I offered. Ivy still looked pretty shaken. I didn't like the idea that she was in so much pain, but I was proud of her. She had come to this event even though she obviously wasn't in a good place. She wanted to be here for her sister, so she had done it anyway. She'd sucked it up. She'd been brave and she was making a gesture of kindness towards her family members. They didn't even know what fresh hell she'd just come from.

"Sure." Eleanor shrugged her shoulders. She gestured to the room around us. "Do what you like."

Being an attorney for many years, I had picked up a couple of different traits and a couple of different skills that came in useful from time to time. One of those skills was figuring out ways to talk to people and helping to frame things so that the other person thought it was their idea. Even though it was already obvious to everyone in the church that the wedding would be moved to the sister church down the road, Susan was still fighting with the priest. I came up to her and introduced myself.

"Susan, hi! I'm so happy I could be here. I'm Lincoln. Do you remember me from the restaurant the other day?" She definitely did. There was no way to not remember me. Even if she didn't know I was a tiger, I knew that I had a memorable presence people couldn't get over or forget. Not me. I was too cool for her.

Susan glared at me before turning back to the priest. She stared at him but spoke to me. "Yes, of course, I remember you."

"Your mother just told me that we're being offered a chance to move to the church down the street. That's really wonderful. Did you know that that's the church where several local celebrities got married a few years ago? I think it was five years ago, wasn't it?" I looked at the priest who followed my lead and nodded.

"Yes, it was Millie Jacobs and Heath Stewart, wasn't it?"

I nodded. The two of them were huge shifter film stars. Most of the general public didn't realize that they were shifters, but I knew. Pretty much everyone who was a shifter knew. It was always exciting when either of the stars were in a new movie because they always tried to slip "shifter stuff" into the film. Sometimes that meant having big animals in the film. Sometimes it meant referencing shifter traditions. It was always fun.

"What?" Susan grinned. She suddenly looked completely thrilled. "I didn't know that!"

"It's true," I nodded, and it was. What I didn't share was that I'd been a wedding date to the ceremony, so I'd gotten to see the entire thing. Despite the fact that it had been two celebrities trying to have a quiet wedding while battling paparazzi, it really had been a lovely ceremony. It was something I certainly would never forget. I hoped the same was true of every wedding, though. A wedding was a special thing. It didn't have to be grand or big or magnificent to be special. Just the idea of a wedding was like something from a fairy tale. It was something lovely.

"Is it true?" Susan asked the priest. Susan's fiancé was still quiet. Apparently, he was used to letting Susan do most of the talking. At least, that was the vibe I was getting from them.

The priest nodded. "Yes, there have been many celebrity weddings at that church. Most people prefer that particular building because it's slightly bigger than this one."

Susan looked smug. "Well then, what are we waiting for? Let's go."

She turned and marched off. I looked at the priest and at Ray, who both stared at me like I was both the craziest and most brilliant man in the world.

AT DINNER I SAT BETWEEN Ivy and Tameka. It was a strange sort of pairing. Susan was on the other side of Tameka because Tameka was the maid of honor. To be honest, I shouldn't have been sitting where I was, but I also felt the need to separate Ivy. She had been through a lot that night. She'd been having a really hard time. Losing someone you loved was never easy and I didn't want her to have to go through that alone. I also didn't want anyone to say anything to her that might hurt. She didn't need the pressure of trying to keep up appearances when she was dying on the inside.

Tameka kept looking at me and Ivy like she wanted to say something. I just knew that if I let her get talking, she'd try to casually let it slip that I was a tiger shifter. I wasn't ready to share that with Ivy. I wasn't sure if I'd *ever* be sharing that with Ivy, actually.

So instead of acquiescing to her request, I did my best to distract Tameka by asking about mutual cousins, Tameka's mom, and other local events that were happening. Tameka didn't like it, but she went along with my little ploy and didn't complain very much.

From what I could tell, Tameka and I were the only shifters at the rehearsal dinner. That was a little strange for Rawr County. Most people who lived here were shifters of some kind, but not everyone lived their life openly as a shifter. Most people were aware that shifters existed and they were okay with it, but there was always the risk of violence from someone who was close-minded or who thought we were "freaks."

I understood perfectly well why some people didn't want to share who they really were. I really got why, for some shifters, the idea of sharing their personal secret was hard. In my daily life, I didn't usually bring up my shifter status unless it had something to do with me helping clients. If I had a client who *only* wanted to talk to an attorney that was also a shifter, then sure, I'd share who I was: *what* I was.

"You didn't tell her yet, did you?" Tameka asked when Ivy got up to go to the restroom.

"Not yet." It wasn't any of Tameka's business, but I was waiting for the right moment. I really did want to date Ivy, but I knew that I needed to be honest with her. If I couldn't tell her, then the two of us couldn't be together.

It was easy. It was *supposed* to be easy, anyway. How hard could being honest really be?

"Hey, Ivy, by the way, I can shapeshift into a tiger!"

"Hey, Ivy, I've got something really cool to tell you – I'm not human!"

"Hey, so, Ivy, I was thinking...I just wanted you to know that I was a tiger."

The more I thought about it, and the more I *overthought* about it, the harder it seemed to get. For some reason, me opening up to Ivy felt really, really difficult. It was important, though. All of this was important.

I couldn't be with someone who didn't know the truth about me yet sharing the truth was also really impossible.

What if she laughed?

"You need to," Tameka said. "You aren't being fair to her."

"Thanks a lot," I told her, "but you don't tell people you're a shifter, either."

"That's different. I'm not dating Susan. I'm just in her wedding."

"It's not really different," I told her, and I believed that, but I also thought about what she said for quite some time. When the dinner ended and Ivy and I were driving back to her home, I made the decision that I would tell her that night.

I had to.

Maybe it would be best to wait until after the wedding, but I couldn't keep it from her anymore she'd been through so much and she deserved to know the truth. At the very least, maybe me offering her a little bit of honesty would help her to decide how she really felt about me.

Or maybe I was being wrong.

Shit.

I did *not* want to screw this up. I liked her far too much.

When we got inside the apartment, I could see the moment that Ivy started thinking about Mr. Fuzzypants again. Her shoulders slumped, and she instantly descended into sadness.

"Ivy."

I knew a way to make her feel better.

I knew a way to distract her from the pain.

"It's going to be okay."

These were words I wasn't supposed to say: words you were never supposed to promise someone. Unless you knew a way to actually keep someone safe and unless you could actually make these things happen, then...

"I promise," I told her. I reached for her shoulders and spun her around, so she was facing me. Then I tilted her chin up, forcing her to look at me. Those pretty eyes held so much loss, so much sadness. I wanted to kiss that pain away.

"What are you talking about?"

"I'm going to be here for you."

"Lincoln, you can't make these promises..."

Her voice trailed off, but I took a step forward so our toes were touching. I tugged her close, so our fronts were flush against each other. She looked up at me and I cupped her face. Stroking her cheek, I felt the soft curve of her jaw. She really was perfect, wasn't she?

And I'd been so damn lucky to get all of this time to spend with her. It really had been luck. She was a sweet, wonderful woman who was funny, smart, and kind. It wasn't every day that you met someone like Ivy. She needed to be protected at all costs.

"I'm going to protect you, Ivy."

"Lincoln, that's very kind." She licked her lips. Arousal flooded my nostrils. Good. She wasn't thinking about her pain any longer. She wasn't thinking about how she felt sad or lonely or lost. Now she was thinking about something else.

Me.

Sex wasn't something that should be used as a weapon, but it *was* something that could be used as a means of distraction.

It would be hard to stay sad with my cock buried inside of her.

"Lincoln, that's very kind of you," she started slowly. She closed her eyes. She was trying to talk herself out of whatever I was going to suggest, but I was too fast for her. I kissed her then, seizing the moment. I wasn't going to let her feel sad any longer.

She pulled away and looked at me.

"You don't have to do this," she whispered. "When this is over, we can go our separate ways. We can walk away, Lincoln. I know this isn't real."

"You sound like you're trying to convince yourself, little human."

"Human?"

Shit. Okay, bad choice of words. Right now, I needed to focus on making her feel good. I needed to make her comfortable. She was important to me, and I needed to share that with her.

"Do you prefer *princess*?"

"Maybe."

"Darling?"

"Lincoln..."

"I can keep going, Ivy. I know lots of pet names, and you're worthy of all of them."

"I know that this isn't real," she whispered once more.

My heart sank a little bit more. It wasn't real to her. I understood that. It was real to me, though. All of this...it was real. There wasn't a single thing about this that didn't feel real.

In fact, I wondered why I'd been fighting it for so long.

I needed to tell her.

Like, now.

I needed to tell her that I was crazy about her. Honestly, I also needed to tell her that I was a shifter because if I didn't, I was going to regret not sharing this part of myself with her. If I didn't, there was going to be a part of me that always wondered what we could have had, what could have been. What if I'd been brave enough? What if I had just slowed down to talk to the woman I was getting ready to make love to?

"Ivy," I said, taking a breath. "We should talk."

"I don't want to talk. Not right now."

"What do you want, Ivy?"

What did she need?

Maybe Ivy was the kind of person who needed to cry through the pain. Maybe she was like me, and she needed to go running or jogging. As a tiger shifter, running helped me more than almost anything else in the world. Right now, though, what I wanted was to make her feel safe and protected.

Maybe she needed something else.

Something more.

Was it something I could give her?

"Kiss me again," she whispered.

"What?"

"Kiss me."

I wasn't sure if I'd heard her correctly. Surely, I had. Surely, that *was* what she'd said. Kiss her. She'd wanted me to kiss her.

She'd also said that this wasn't real, and I wanted it to be. I knew that falling for Ivy was a bad idea. Falling for a woman who was human, who didn't know my secret, was wrong. This whole thing was wrong. The entire purpose of hiring a fake date was so that she wouldn't have to fall in love with anyone, right?

Still, I could stop myself. "Are you sure that's what you want?"

"I just...I need you to help me forget," she whispered. "I need you to take the pain away, Lincoln. Can you do that?"

I nodded, swallowing hard. "Yeah," I whispered. "Yeah, I can do that." I could take the pain away. I'd take it away for her.

And so, I kissed her.

Grabbing her, I tugged her close to me. I kissed her deeply, running my tongue over hers. I kissed her until everything else faded from my mind.

I kissed her until we were the only two people in my mind who existed.

And then I kissed her more.

And more.

And more.

17

Ivy

We made our way to the bedroom, where I closed the door. Flipping on the lights, I looked up at him, searching his eyes. Everything about Lincoln seemed like it was on fire. His body was hot. His eyes were blazing. Still, I wanted him, craving him with a passion I'd never really known.

"Take off your clothes." He was wearing too much. We both were. I wasn't going to take things slow tonight. Didn't want to. I needed more. We both did.

"Are you sure?" Lincoln looked slightly concerned. While I appreciated his dedication to making sure I was giving consent, my headspace was fine. I wanted this. I wanted all of it.

"Stop asking me if I'm sure. I'm sure," I told him.

I was, too.

This was what I wanted. What I needed.

This was the only way I was going to feel even slightly okay. What I'd gone through had been terrible. It was one of the worst things I could have possibly experienced, I knew, and I needed him to help me.

I wasn't sure that using sex as a form of self-medication was a good idea, but tonight it was just what I needed.

Was I using him?

Yes.

Absolutely.

But there was more to it than that.

My feelings about Lincoln were complicated. Complex. I liked him a lot and I had a feeling that he liked me, too, but there were moments when I couldn't quite figure out what he was thinking.

I grabbed at his clothing, tugging it off. He did the same to me. A moment later, we were naked on the bed, entwined in one another. It was...perfect. He hovered over me and leaned down, kissing my neck. He swiped his tongue over my skin, tasting me like an ice cream cone on a warm summer day.

Oh, I didn't think I'd ever get tired of this.

Of him.

I tugged him toward me, kissing him softly on the mouth.

"You're so perfect," I told him. I believed it, too. With all of my heart, he was perfect for me. I didn't want anyone else. It was only him.

He stroked my face softly as he looked at me.

"You really are beautiful."

"I could say the same about you."

"Tell me what you want."

"Orgasms."

"Lots of them. Good idea," he nodded.

"How will you give them to me?" I asked. I was more than ready to take my share of whatever he could offer me. If he wanted to thrust his cock into me and fuck me until I came, I was okay with that. If he wanted to use his fingers to play with my soft pussy until I exploded for him, that was okay, too. To my surprise, though, he wanted neither of those things. Instead, he just chuckled and grabbed me. Then he flipped us over. Now I was on top of him, and he was lying on his back.

"On my mouth," he told me.

"What?"

"Scoot up, princess."

He grabbed my ass and tugged, pulling me up his body. As soon as I realized what he was trying to do, I tried to resist.

"No! I'll smash you."

"Then it'll be a good way to die," he laughed. "I don't care, Ivy. Sit on my damn mouth."

I resisted only a little, but a second later when I was hovering above him, I could feel his breath against me. All of the excuses floating around in my head that held me from really letting go started to fade away.

You're too heavy.

He won't like it.

He'll hate this.

You're too big for this.

"Ivy, just let go," he said, and he dug his fingers into my hips and pulled me close to his face.

And just like that, I let go.

I let go of everything I'd been feeling - all of the pain, all of the anxiety, all of the frustration. I let go of my embarrassment and my nervousness. I let go of the way I'd allowed myself to feel for so long. I let go of my emotions and my past.

I let go of everything and I just *felt*.

A second later I was riding his face, letting myself really experience everything that he was offering. He moved his tongue like a fucking pro and when I came, it was safe to call it the best orgasm I'd had in my life.

"That's it, princess," he whispered as I climbed off him when I finished. "You are so fucking sexy."

"That was..."

Words couldn't label what that was.

Hot.

Sexy.

Passionate.

Dirty as hell.

He smiled and reached for me, tugging me to his face. He kissed me, and I could taste myself on his lips. Oh, it was forbidden and hot as hell and *dirty*, but I didn't care. All I knew was that I wanted him inside of me, like, now.

"Please."

It was a whisper.

A plea.

Yes, I was begging.

I needed his dick.

Luckily for me, Lincoln seemed more than happy to oblige. He started to pull me closer, and I reached for his cock. I started stroking it, jerking him, and he groaned. Lincoln tossed his head back.

"Baby, if you keep that up, I'm going to come before I ever get inside of you."

"No, I want you to come inside of me," I let go of him. Lincoln only laughed.

"You don't have to stop."

"Please fuck me."

He looked at me carefully, cocking his head. Then he licked his lips.

"You're so polite. Has anyone ever told you that?"

"A few people," I admitted. I tended to be overpolite when I wanted something. It was a problem. I wasn't trying to manipulate people, but I always felt like it was important to be nice when someone was going to do me a favor. Getting Lincoln's cock inside of me felt like a pretty big favor.

"Climb on," he murmured. "Nothing's stopping you, Ivy. Come take what you want."

Nobody had ever given me an offer like that, and I honestly didn't really know what to do. I did want him. I did want his cock. I wanted his body.

I wanted more than that, though.

I wanted his heart.

His future.

I wanted him to be as crazy about me as I was about him because Lincoln was so kind, and so thoughtful, and he was so desperately wild that I didn't think he was the type of person who would ever get married.

But I did what he said, and I took what I wanted.

I straddled his waist and his cock nudged at my entrance.

"Good girl," Lincoln said approvingly. "Just like that." He played with my breasts as I hovered there, slowly sinking down onto him. He groaned once I'd taken all of him.

"That feels really fucking good," I admitted. I felt full. Too full. Still, I started moving slowly and Lincoln smiled up at me. He was enjoying this just as much as I was. The two of us made a good pair, I thought. We were in sync, and this experience was hot as hell.

I already knew that tonight on its own wouldn't be enough.

I wanted more.

I needed more.

I was going to be craving Lincoln for a long damn time.

I had a feeling that fucking Lincoln was something that could quickly turn into an addiction if I wasn't careful, and I needed that. I needed the feeling he was offering me. He fisted my hair, tugging my face close to his for a kiss. And oh, when he kissed me like this, it was like nothing else mattered in the entire world.

"Rub your clit for me," he told me as I rode him.

And I did.

In that moment, I would do anything he wanted. I'd touch myself. I'd play with myself. I'd tease my body until I felt like everything was on fire and iced over at the same time. Touching myself, I rubbed as I rode his cock. He thrust up into me over and over until...

We both came at the same time.

Together.

It was like magic.

It was like magic I hadn't expected: magic I didn't want to end.

That was the problem, though. I knew that it was going to. I knew that eventually, the magic would have to fade, and everything would fall apart, but right now, I didn't want to think about that.

I collapsed on the bed beside him, draping my body over his. In a minute we'd both leave the bed so we could get cleaned up, but in this moment, right now, I just wanted to hold him. I just wanted to pretend that everything was going to be okay.

I just wanted to pretend that life was normal and ordinary and...

And fine.

18

Lincoln

The wedding was in an hour.

We'd overslept, spending the entire night fucking over and over. Every part of my body hurt: aching with pleasure. I shook her shoulder when I realized what had happened. Shit. This was my fault. I should have paid better attention. I should have...

Well, I should have taken better care of her.

Instead of making sure she was well-rested and awake for the wedding, I'd let myself get carried away. I'd lost myself in our lovemaking, ensuring that the two of us spent our evening kissing, touching, and memorizing every inch of each other.

"Ivy," I whispered. "Ivy, we have to go."

Somehow, the two of us managed to get up, shower, and get into our wedding-day clothes. There were cups of coffees and quickly devoured bagels in there, too. We rushed to the church and arrived with ten minutes to spare. Tameka ran outside the second she saw my car pulling up into the parking lot.

She snarled as I stepped out of the vehicle. "Where the hell have you been, tiger?"

My eyes narrowed.

"We're late, but we aren't over-the-top late."

She didn't have to call me *tiger*. Not in front of the woman I loved. She didn't have to hint that I wasn't a human. She didn't have to do a lot of things.

"You could have called," she snapped. "Susan is freaking out that her bridesmaid isn't here."

"Somehow, I doubt that's true," Ivy said sadly. She shook her head as she climbed out of the car, too. She placed her hands on the top of the vehicle. "Tameka, I appreciate your kindness, but we both know that Susan won't bat an eye if I don't show up."

Tameka's jaw dropped. Okay, so maybe she didn't realize just how strained the relationship between the two of them actually was.

"That's not...Ivy, that's not cool."

"I know it's not cool. Nothing about this is cool."

"Let's just get you inside," I said. I felt the need to play interference, at least for a little bit. If I could just get her *inside*, if I could make sure that she was seated at the wedding ceremony, then I had a feeling that everything else would work itself out.

Oh, it would still be messy. Nothing about this was clean and tidy.

As Ivy walked up the steps to the church, Tameka grabbed my arm.

"You didn't tell her, but you slept with her." She sniffed the air. Nosy, wasn't she? What was she checking for? Signs that I'd been balls-deep in the woman I loved? I had. I'd done that.

"I did," I admitted. "And I haven't told her, but I will."

"When?" Tameka snapped. I glanced behind her. Ivy was out of earshot. Luckily, she couldn't have possibly heard what the two of us were saying.

"Soon," I lied. "I'll tell her soon."

Only, after last night, I wasn't sure that telling her today was the best choice. What we'd shared had been wonderful. Magical. Perfect.

Maybe I didn't have to tell her just yet.

Maybe we could just keep doing what we were doing...

Maybe I didn't need to be honest after all.

THE WEDDING STARTED.

The new church was just as beautiful as I remembered. Decorated with fresh flowers – roses, of course – the pews that lined the aisle of the church were filled with excited guests. Loved ones who had traveled from near and far to see the bride and groom take their vows were grinning. They were laughing and chatting excitedly as the first keys of the wedding march began to play.

Almost instantly, people quieted. Everyone turned to watch as the wedding party proceeded down the aisle. All of the usual players were present: the bridesmaids, the flower girls, and the bride.

Only, I didn't care about any of that.

Any of them.

The only one I cared about was her.

I cared about sweet, wonderful Ivy.

I cared about the woman who loved cats.

I cared about the woman who would do anything to make sure her sister had a good wedding.

I loved her.

My eyes were locked firmly on Ivy the entire wedding. I wasn't really sure what vows the bride and groom took and I had no idea what kind of speech the priest gave. All I knew was that Ivy was the one. She was the person I wanted to be with.

Yeah, Tameka was right, I realized. My inner-tiger seemed to growl at me as I realized that I couldn't wait much longer. More importantly, there was no *need* to wait much longer. What I needed really was to be open with her. Truthful.

If I could tell her, then there was a chance that she'd understand, right?

There was a very real possibility that she would understand what I was talking about and what I was going through.

If that happened, then she could...

What?

What was I expecting?

I hated the fact that I was faltering. Suddenly, something that had seemed so very obvious and safe to me before seemed difficult and challenging. It was just a little bit of honesty, I told myself. Just a little bit of honesty and I'd be able to start moving forward.

I wanted her.

I wanted to be able to tell her the truth, I...

"Hey."

She was standing beside me. When did that happen? The wedding ceremony was over, I realized. I was one of the last people still sitting in a pew. I hadn't even noticed everyone filing out.

"You look beautiful," I told Ivy. She did, too. The dress brought out her eyes: making them look even brighter than they had before.

"That's nice of you," she smiled.

"I'm not trying to be nice."

"That's even better," she laughed. "Listen, they want to take some pictures. Want to come with me?"

Yeah, I did. I wanted to come with her so I could protect her. Guard her. She deserved to be taken care of and protected from everything that could possibly hurt her. There was nothing in the world that was going to hurt her on my watch.

She reached for me, tugging me to my feet. Then she wrapped her arms around me tightly and rested her cheek against my chest. For a moment, I forgot where I was. I forgot that this wasn't real. I forgot that we were only doing this to save face for her sister's celebration.

I forgot.

That was the problem with falling in love with a human.

Sometimes they made you believe in happy endings.

Sometimes they made you think that true love was real.

19

Ivy

Something felt off about the wedding, but I couldn't really put my finger on it. I felt like it had something to do with Lincoln, but again, I couldn't *really* be sure. He kept acting strangely, and I wasn't sure if it was because he was still feeling protective of me after everything that happened yesterday, or if it was something else.

Was he frustrated that we had slept together?

Judging by the amount of times he'd gotten off during the night – which felt impossible – I didn't think that was it. I wasn't sure, though.

Lincoln stayed by my side throughout the family pictures and then we went to the reception together. He was silent during the drive – strangely silent. At one point, I looked over to make sure that he was actually still in the car because he was *so* quiet.

"What is it?" Lincoln's voice was tight. Tense.

"Nothing." I still couldn't figure out what was bothering him.

"Something's wrong. Are you nervous about the reception? I'll stay with you the whole time. It'll be completely okay, Ivy."

"It's not that..."

I really couldn't put my finger on it. It was just that there was something going on with Lincoln. Yeah, this thing between us was a business arrangement. No, he wasn't required to share his feelings with me. He didn't have to tell me that he was a lawyer. He hadn't, either, not at first. He didn't have to tell me what his dating history was. It was none of my business.

There was something he wanted to tell me, though.

I felt like an idiot for not being able to figure it out.

"I feel like you're keeping something from me," I finally blurted out. Oh, I hated how insecure and jealous I sounded. I definitely gave myself "crazy girlfriend" vibes in that moment.

"Keeping something?"

His tone was even. Level.

"Yeah," I whispered. Then, I took a deep breath. "Are you?"

"I'm not keeping anything from you, Ivy. I'm just trying to make sure that the reception goes well for you. That's what you want, right? That's why you hired me."

Yeah.

There it was again.

The hiring thing.

There was a part of me that wished I'd never done it. If I'd never taken the risk and jumped into paying for a date, none of this would have happened. I wouldn't have started to fall for him. I wouldn't have started to feel like he was going to make my heart crazy.

None of it.

I had, though.

I had fallen for him hard and fast and wonderfully, and now...

Lincoln pulled into a parking spot at the hotel where the reception was being held. It was the biggest hotel in town and also the most beautiful. Huge pillows stretched up into the sky. They really were the loveliest thing you could imagine. Somehow, though, I couldn't enjoy the architecture of the building because I was too caught up in him.

"Lincoln, I think I'm falling in love with you." I blurted out the words before I could stop myself. As I spoke, I silently wished I could take it all back. It was the wrong time to share such a special secret. I understood that. Still, I couldn't deny how I felt anymore.

The car was stopped. He was in a parking spot. His fingers tightened on the wheel, though, and he turned to look at me.

His eyes seemed darker than they usually were...almost black. He was staring at me like this was the worst news anyone had ever delivered.

Shit.

Okay, so the feeling wasn't mutual.

That was okay. I could live with that.

"I'm sorry," I said right away. "Please just forget that I said anything."

"I need to tell you something," he said.

Just then, however, my sister started knocking on the car window. I turned toward her. The car was already off, so the window wouldn't roll down. Lincoln turned the key so I could roll the window down. I was grateful because I didn't want to get out of the car just yet to face my crazy-ass sister.

"What's going on? Everything okay?"

"Where the hell did you meet this guy?" Susan snapped at me. "How much do you really know about him?"

I heard a voice yelling. Turning, I saw Tameka running across the parking lot toward us.

"Susan, don't do this!"

My sister sneered as she looked at me, though.

"I just overheard a very interesting conversation between Tameka and your boyfriend's aunt. Did you know that he's a shifter?" She grinned, as though this was the best news she'd heard all day. Tameka was still running. Her phone was in her hand. She must have been talking to her mom on the phone when Susan overheard what they were saying.

Now, as I looked up at my sister, a malicious smile spread across her face. She was happy about this. She was *pleased* with the fact that she'd learned something about my boyfriend that I didn't know. She liked that feeling of power - of being able to hold something over me.

"Shifter," she repeated.

"What?" I whispered. I knew what the word meant. Everyone knew. Shifters weren't like us. They weren't like humans. They were different. Cooler, if I was being honest. Someone who was a shifter could change from being a human to being something else. It was like the ultimate life goal, in my opinion.

How cool would it be to be having a bad day and just be able to change into something else?

How nice would it be to get home after a long day dealing with work drama and just be able to change your entire body into an animal?

Sounded pretty good to me, actually. Sounded *really* good.

"A shifter," Susan said again, as though I hadn't heard her the first two times. Shit. She sounded like a broken record. Worse than that: she looked smug. Happy.

"Listen," Lincoln said, reaching for my arm. He placed his hand on my wrist, and I knew what he was going to say. He was going to explain what happened. He was going to tell me that it was true.

Flashes of our time together permeated my mind.

He'd known my emotions.

Flash.

He'd figured out something was wrong with my cat.

Flash.

He'd been keeping something from me.

Flash.

Only, being a shifter hadn't played a role in the way he'd treated me. The fact that he was a shifter had nothing to do with the fact that he'd been the one to basically save me. He'd been there for me through thick and thin in ways my sister certainly never had.

In fact, if it wasn't for Susan, I wouldn't have felt the need to hire a fake date, anyway. Susan was the one who was the troublemaker here – not Lincoln. Lincoln and I weren't officially dating. We'd slept together, yes, but that was just one thing. It was only minutes ago that I'd confessed that I was falling for him, and he was trying to tell me something when Susan showed up.

If I had to guess, he was trying to tell me that he was a shifter of some kind.

As if that mattered.

I wasn't so shallow that I cared. The guy I dated – the guy I *loved* – didn't have to be a human in order to be worthy of love.

Was I going to let my sister ruin this for me?

"Susan, what are you doing?" I asked.

Her smile faltered for just a fraction of a second.

"What do you mean? I thought....I thought you deserved to know," she said.

I reached for the handle of the door and gestured for her to step back so I could get out of the car. I wasn't going to have this discussion sitting down while she stood over me. She'd been standing over me my entire life, I realized suddenly.

Was I really going to let her stomp on this?

Susan stepped back. She was holding the folds of her dress in her hands. It was lovely, and it was a dress she'd only found because Lincoln had suggested the shop that first day when I'd met him in the café.

"Look, Susan, I don't think this is any of your business."

Lincoln said nothing. Tameka looked shocked. She was standing just behind Susan now, but the phone was still in her hand.

"What do you mean? You didn't know."

"Of course, I knew, Susan. He's my boyfriend! Do you really think we wouldn't have had this discussion?"

I heard Lincoln getting out of the car, but I didn't turn around. I wasn't ready to face him just yet. I'd defend him to the end, though. He was the one who had been with me all night. He was the one who had comforted me after I lost my cat. It was him. All him.

And I *loved* him.

I was crazy about him.

It was all very fast and it was all very passionate, but I knew what I felt, and what I felt was that he was incredible. I didn't deserve him. I didn't deserve who he was or what he was offering. I knew that.

I wasn't good enough for him, but I didn't care.

All I wanted was him.

"Well, I..."

"Susan, listen, you need to get inside."

She stared at me and started to sputter. I wasn't going to get into a fight with her on her wedding day. Was she a total bitch? Yes. Did I need to learn to set better boundaries with her and my mother? Also yes. Was I going to make her wedding day about me and my relationship with them? No. No, I wasn't.

"Susan," I reached for my sister's hand. "I appreciate your concern." I didn't. "It's your wedding day, though, and your guests are waiting. You need to get to them."

She looked at me once more, searching my eyes. She wanted me to be tricking her. She wanted proof that I was tricking her. She wouldn't find it. I was going to stay by his side and I was going to defend him until the very end. I would do just about anything for this guy.

"Are you sure?" She looked past me. "What is he?"

"He's the man I love, Susan. You don't need to know anything else right now. We'll talk more later, okay?"

Somehow, she nodded. Tameka reached for her and pulled her back toward the hotel. Tameka looked at me, obviously confused. Yeah, she didn't think he was going to tell me.

As soon as the two of them were out of sight, Lincoln was beside me.

"I wanted to tell you," he said.

I turned to him, reached for him, and cupped his face.

Then I kissed him.

Nothing else mattered.

None of it mattered.

It didn't matter because I didn't care. I didn't care that he was a shifter. I didn't care that he hadn't told me. All I wanted was him.

"Thank you for being there for me," I told him.

"You aren't mad?"

"Actions speak louder than words, Lincoln. Out of everyone, you're the person who came to be with me. You're the person who helped me through Mr. Fuzzypants' death."

I knew there were going to be a lot of hard days in the coming weeks. I knew there were going to be moments when I completely broke down, when I totally lost it. I also knew that he was going to be there for me. If I actually wanted to heal, I'd need to talk about my feelings, and he was going to help me. I got that.

I also knew that the very least I could offer Lincoln was understanding and kindness. After everything he'd done for me, it would have been pretty crazy for me not to offer the same.

"I don't usually tell people I'm a shifter."

"I understand," I nodded. "It's probably not super safe to share that, I'm guessing." The world was a scary place. Even though there were shifters pretty much everywhere now, there was still danger. There were bad people in the world, and there were people who would hurt others.

He had to be careful.

He had to protect himself.

"I don't tell people," he continued, "unless I care very deeply for them."

I looked up at him.

"Lincoln, what are you saying?" Was he saying that he liked me? Loved me, even? Was this his way of saying that he wanted to give "us" a try?

I liked Lincoln a lot. I was crazy about him. I'd allowed myself to feel things for him and I'd allowed myself to fall for him hard and fast and wonderfully.

Now...

Well, I didn't want to get my hopes up if he wasn't taking this in the direction that I thought he was taking it.

"I love you, Ivy."

And he kissed me again.

My heart soared. My body ached with need as he pulled me flush against himself. Love. He loved me. He'd said it, and I felt the same way. I mumbled the words, but I wasn't sure if he heard me. I loved him, too. I was crazy about him.

I was crazy about all of this.

"Are you sure?" I whispered, pulling back.

"Surer than I've ever been," he smiled.

And I knew in that moment that no matter what came next, the two of us were going to figure this out together. Could a shifter and a human date? Maybe. Could we make it work? Definitely. It would be hard work, but it would be worth it. I knew it.

Lincoln and I had something special. The two of us had secrets we'd kept from each other, but now we had something else going for us. We had a bright, wonderful future that we were going to share with one another.

And with Lincoln by my side, the future was going to be wonderful indeed.

Together, he took my hand and led me into the hotel. We were going to celebrate my sister's wedding and then later, when we were all alone, we were going to celebrate us. We were going to celebrate our love. Our passion. Our hopes.

Lincoln was everything I'd ever wanted and everything I hadn't known I'd needed.

I was the luckiest damn girl on the planet.

As we reached the doors of the hotel, I looked over at him.

"Wait a second. You didn't tell me what kind of shifter you are," he said.

Lincoln just laughed. "Haven't you figured it out, love? I'm a tiger. I'm a big cat."

"A cat," I nodded. I could live with that.

Epilogue

Daphne

"The Alpha wants to see you."

Six words that should have made me happy, but they didn't. Instead, I felt a sense of dread wash over me as I made my way down the narrow hallway to his office. The Alpha didn't believe in comfort. He didn't believe in making people feel at ease. Nope. When he called you, you came to him, and he wasn't going to do a single thing to make the experience less terrifying.

As I walked, I wondered whether this was all a huge mistake. Maybe trying to take his place after he retired was a bad idea. A lady Alpha? Perhaps our pack wasn't ready for that. I wanted to believe that we were. I wanted to believe that our pack was progressive enough to be ready to have a woman leading, but there was no way to be sure.

My phone buzzed as I walked to the Alpha's office. Glancing over my shoulder, I made sure that nobody else was around me. The wolf who had told me the Alpha wanted me was gone now. It was just me. I was alone. I swiped to see that Fletcher had texted me.

"You've got this," he said.

I smiled and nodded even though he couldn't see me. So, he'd heard about the meeting and he knew something big was happening. Good for him. Fletcher always seemed to know what was going on. It was something that I loved about him. If anyone could make facing the Alpha seem less scary, it was Fletcher.

When I reached the door, I took a deep breath. This was it. He was either going to tell me that I was next in line to be the pack leader or he was going to tell me to pack my things and leave. The Alpha was dramatic, and there would be no in-between.

I raised my hand and knocked.

And then I waited.

———◦◦◦———

The story continues in The Wolf's Pretend Mate!

Author

Sophie Stern writes vampires, cowboys, werewolves, dragons, and fairy tales. Her books feature deliciously wonderful characters and deliciously naughty adventures. If you enjoyed *The Tiger's Fake Date*, you may like one of her other romances, such as *Dark Favors* or *The Feisty Librarian*.

Of course, you'll also want to check out another story that takes place in Rawr County: The Dragon's Christmas Treasure.

Please make sure you subscribe to Sophie's mailing list *here*[1].

You can also follow her on Facebook[2] for frequent updates.

Thank you so much for reading.

---

1. *http://eepurl.com/bh8v_j*

2. http://www.facebook.com/sexysophiestern/

Books

Other books by Sophie Stern
HONEYPOT DARLINGS
HONEYPOT BABIES
DRAGON ISLE
THE FABLESTONE CLAN
THE FEISTY DRAGONS
DRAGON ENCHANTED
DON'T DATE DEMONS
POLAR BEARS OF THE AIR FORCE
DARK FAVORS
SAVORED
Sophie's books are available wherever eBooks are sold.

If you enjoyed this story, check out these other books by Sophie Stern!

CONQUERED (The Hidden Planet)

ABDUCTED.

Taken.

Locked away.

Fiona doesn't know true fear until she is whisked away from her loving family and doting boyfriend. When she finds herself on an alien ship with only a gHankt beast for company, her fear turns to anger when she realizes her loved ones have betrayed her.

Quinn doesn't know what to do with the squirrely little human aboard his ship. Yeah, he bought her, but only to save her from a worse fate. She has no idea what could have happened to her if he hadn't found her. She has no idea what could have happened on Dreagle. But now she's on his ship and somehow, she's wormed her way into his heart. Can he ever let her go?

CONQUERED is available wherever eBooks are sold.

ALIEN BEAST

He's a war hero.

She's a virgin.

He's broken.

She's perfect.

When he finds her in the midst of an alien war, Luke takes Willow for himself. He can't help himself. He's never taken a prisoner alive before, but Willow is different. He needs her. He wants her. Most of all, he craves her.

Willow is a human who has the worst luck in the world. When the tour ship she's on malfunctions and crash-lands on the wrong planet, she's thrust into the middle of a war: one she has no desire to be in.

Then everything changes.

She's captured by an alien beast unlike anything she's ever seen before.

And the worst part is that after awhile, she's not so sure she wants him to let her go.

ALIEN BEAST is available wherever eBooks are sold.

Don't miss out!

Visit the website below and you can sign up to receive emails whenever Sophie Stern publishes a new book. There's no charge and no obligation.

https://books2read.com/r/B-A-XOYC-ZXYEC

BOOKS 2 READ

Connecting independent readers to independent writers.

Did you love *Shifters of Rawr County: Books 1-3*? Then you should read *Dragon Beast: A Beauty and the Beast Retelling*[3] by Sophie Stern!

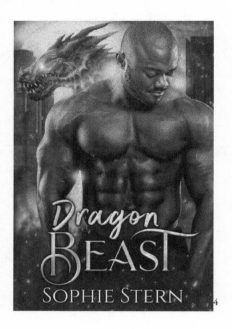
[4]

My sister has been taken by a monster. She's been captured, locked away by the man we all fear more than death itself. She's been abducted, and he won't free her. She belongs to the monster now. She belongs to the dragon.I can't let this happen.I have to offer myself to the beast in her place.I have to offer him everything I am so that he'll let her go free.When the dragon beast accepts my offer, however, I realize suddenly that while my body might be able to handle this trade, my heart cannot.Dragon Beast is a steamy Beauty and the Beast retelling by Sophie Stern, author of ALIEN BEAST and THE FABLESTONE CLAN.

---

3. https://books2read.com/u/bojj9v

4. https://books2read.com/u/bojj9v

Also by Sophie Stern

Alien Chaos
Destroyed
Guarded
Saved
Christmas on Chaos
Alien Chaos: A Sci-Fi Alien Romance Bundle

Aliens of Malum
Deceived: An Alien Brides Romance
Betrayed: An Alien Brides Romance
Fallen: An Alien Brides Romance
Captured: An Alien Brides Romance
Regret
Crazed
For Keeps
Rotten: An Alien Brides Romance

Anchored
Starboard
Battleship

All Aboard
Abandon Ship
Below Deck
Crossing the Line
Anchored: Books 1-3
Anchored: Books 4-6

Ashton Sweets
Christmas Sugar Rush
Valentine's Sugar Rush
St. Patty's Sugar Rush
Halloween Sugar Rush

Bullies of Crescent Academy
You Suck
Troublemaker
Jaded

Club Kitten Dancers
Move
Pose
Climb

Dragon Enchanted
Hidden Mage
Hidden Captive

Hidden Curse

Fate High School
You Wish: A High School Reverse Harem Romance
Freak: A Reverse Harem High School Romance
Get Lost: A Reverse Harem Romance

Good Boys and Millionaires
Good Boys and Millionaires 1
Good Boys and Millionaires 2

Grimalkin Needs Brides
Ekpen (Intergalactic Dating Agency)
Torao (Intergalactic Dating Agency)
Leo (Intergalactic Dating Agency)

Honeypot Babies
The Polar Bear's Baby
The Jaguar's Baby
The Tiger's Baby

Honeypot Darlings
The Bear's Virgin Darling
The Bear's Virgin Mate
The Bear's Virgin Bride

Office Gentlemen
Ben From Accounting

Polar Bears of the Air Force
Staff Sergeant Polar Bear
Master Sergeant Polar Bear
Airman Polar Bear
Senior Airman Polar Bear

Return to Dragon Isle
Dragons Are Forever
Dragon Crushed: An Enemies-to-Lovers Paranormal Romance
Dragon's Hex
Dragon's Gain
Dragon's Rush

Rose Valley Vampires
Vampire Librarian

Shifters at Law
Wolf Case
Bearly Legal
Tiger Clause
Sergeant Bear

Dragon Law

Shifters of Rawr County
The Polar Bear's Fake Mate
The Lion's Fake Wife
The Tiger's Fake Date
The Wolf's Pretend Mate
The Tiger's Pretend Husband
The Dragon's Fake Fiancée
The Red Panda's Fake Mate

Stormy Mountain Bears
The Lumberjack's Baby Bear
The Writer's Baby Bear
The Mountain Man's Baby Bears

Sweet Nightmares
Sweet Nightmares: The Vampire's Melody
Sweet Nightmares 2: The Sound of Roses

Team Shifter
Bears VS Wolves
No Fox Given

The Fablestone Clan

Dragon's Oath
Dragon's Breath
Dragon's Darling
Dragon's Whisper
Dragon's Magic

The Feisty Dragons
Untamed Dragon
Naughty Dragon
Monster Dragon

The Hidden Planet
Vanquished
Outlaw
Conquered

The Wolfe City Pack
The Wolf's Darling
The Wolf's Mate
The Wolf's Bride

Standalone
Saucy Devil
Billionaire on Top
Jurassic Submissive
The Editor

Alien Beast
Snow White and the Wolves
Kissing the Billionaire
Wild
Alien Dragon
The Royal Her
Be My Tiger
Alien Monster
The Luck of the Wolves
Honeypot Babies Omnibus Edition
Honeypot Darlings: Omnibus Edition
The Swan's Mate
The Feisty Librarian
Polar Bears of the Air Force
Wild Goose Chase
Star Princess
The Virgin and the Lumberjacks
Resting Bear Face
By Hook or by Wolf
I Dare You, King
Shifters at Law
Pretty Little Fairies
Seized by the Dragon
The Fablestone Clan: A Paranormal Dragon-Shifter Romance
Collection
Star Kissed
Big Bad Academy
Club Kitten Omnibus
Stormy Mountain Bears: The Complete Collection
Bitten by the Vampires
Beautiful Villain
Dark Favors
Savored

Vampire Kiss

Chaotic Wild: A Vampire Romance

Bitten

Heartless

The Dragon's Christmas Treasure

Out of the Woods

Bullies of Crescent Academy

Craving You: A Contemporary Romance Collection

Chasing Whiskey

The Hidden Planet Trilogy

The Bratty Dom

Tokyo Wolf

The Single Dad Who Stole My Heart

Free For Him

The Feline Gaze

Fate High School

Dragon Beast: A Beauty and the Beast Retelling

Boulder Bear

Megan Slays Vampires

Vampire Professor

Once Upon a Shift

The Feisty Dragons

The Vampire Who Saved Christmas

Dragon Enchanted (Books 1-3)

Grimalkin Needs Brides (Intergalactic Dating Agency): Books 1-3

Nerd Alert

Red: Into the Dark

Alien Darlings

Shifters of Rawr County: Books 4-7

Shifters of Rawr County: Books 1-3